GILBO & CO.

THEODORE ROOSEVELT

Photogravure from a Photograph by Thatcher, of Albany

THE LIBRARY OF ORATORY

Ancient and Modern

with CRITICAL STUDIES *of the* WORLD'S GREAT ORATORS *by* EMINENT ESSAYISTS ᚖᚖ

CHAUNCEY M. DEPEW, LL.D.

United States Senator from the State of New York

EDITOR-IN-CHIEF

NATHAN HASKELL DOLE

CAROLINE TICKNOR   THOMAS CHARLES QUINN

ASSOCIATE EDITORS

𝕰dition de 𝕷uxe

IN FIFTEEN VOLUMES

VOLUME XIV.

ILLUSTRATED

PUBLISHED BY

E. R. DU MONT

NEW YORK   CHICAGO

TABLE OF CONTENTS

VOLUME XIV

(v)

LIST OF ILLUSTRATIONS

VOLUME XIV

(viii)

SIR JOHN THOMPSON

SIR JOHN S. THOMPSON

IR JOHN SPARROW THOMPSON, a distinguished Canadian statesman and jurist, the fourth Premier of the Dominion, was born at Halifax, Nova Scotia, Nov. 10, 1844, and died at Windsor Castle, Dec. 12, 1894. Early in his legal career he was the recognized leader of the Bar of that Province. He became a member of the Provincial government and for a short time was Premier. In 1882, he was appointed a judge, but in 1885 resigned to enter the Federal government, at Ottawa, in which he was appointed Minister of Justice. Upon the retirement of Sir John Abbott, in 1892, he became Premier of Canada and held the position until his sudden and lamented death at Windsor, England, at the early age of fifty. The circumstances of his death were exceedingly dramatic. During the autumn of 1894 he visited England to settle some details of the Bering Sea question, and to be sworn a member of the Imperial Privy Council. For this latter function he was summoned to Windsor Castle to take the oath of office before the Queen on the 12th of December (1894), and while there he was stricken with syncope of the heart and died instantly. His remains were conveyed by a warship to Halifax. Sir John Thompson was one of the best parliamentary debaters of his time. His speeches are remarkable for beauty and finish, for the clearness and vigor of his utterances, and for the cogency of the arguments advanced.

ON THE DEATH OF HON ALEX. MACKENZIE, M. P., PREMIER OF CANADA

DELIVERED IN THE HOUSE OF COMMONS, OTTAWA, APRIL 19, 1892

MR. SPEAKER,—I think that the first duty which the House owes to its own history and to the country, on reassembling after the vacation, is to notice the great loss which the House has sustained, and which Canada has sustained, by the death of the honorable member for East York. If it devolved upon me to-day—if it devolved upon anybody, indeed—to state the great public services, the estimable character and the worth of the late honorable member for East York, I would greatly prefer that that duty should have fallen to some of those among whom he served in public life when he was at his prime, because, when it was my good fortune and my honor to enter this Parliament the honorable gentleman had ceased to take that active part in public affairs in which for many years he occupied so commanding a position and did himself so much honor and the country such useful, zealous services.

Fortunately, however, for me, Mr. Speaker, the history of the country supplies what is deficient in myself in this regard. The achievements of the late honorable gentleman, his zeal in the public service, the great position which he attained, not only officially in this country in connection with its public affairs, but in the estimation of the people of Canada, are all part of the records of this country now. I can only say, on behalf of gentlemen who are co-operating with me in this Parliament, that I am expressing their sentiments when I state that the services which I have mentioned and the qualities which I have referred to evoked from us the greatest esteem—those of us who were in the House when he was active in political struggles, and those of us who had not then entered on our duties here—and that we feel as deeply as I am sure honorable gentlemen on the other side of the House must feel that a great tribute of respect is due to the memory of the gentleman who devoted his great abilities, great zeal, and great talents disinterestedly to the service of Canada. We feel, therefore, that it is incumbent upon the House, out of respect, not only, as I have said, for its own history, but out of respect for the public feeling in Canada, that, instead of transacting the business which is on the order-paper to-day, we should ask an adjournment, and that the adjournment should take place until Thursday next in order that as many members of the House as feel able to do so may be present at the funeral obsequies which I understand are to take place in Toronto to-morrow.

With these observations, Mr. Speaker, which I am sure but very feebly express the sentiments of the House, but which are very cordially given, not only on my part but upon the part of those of whom I am the humble spokesman, I beg to move that when this House adjourns this day it do stand adjourned until Thursday next, in consequence of the lamented death of the Honorable Alexander Mackenzie, late member of the Queen's Privy Council of Canada, and out of respect to his memory.

A QUESTION OF SIMPLE JUSTICE

[Extracts from a speech delivered in the Canadian House of Commons, March 27, 1889, on a motion asking for the disallowance of the "Jesuits' Estate Act." [1]]

NOW, let me call the attention of the House to a brief statement with regard to the position of these estates, not for the purpose of showing that this society in the Province of Quebec, whatever its character and merits may have been, had a legal title to the property, but for the purpose of showing that this is not a question which we can decide, but is one which must and ought to have been left to that authority which the constitution makes, not only competent to deal with such questions, but omnipotent in

---

[1] The Legislature of the Province of Quebec passed an act in 1888 granting $400,000 in full and final settlement of the long-standing dispute between the Jesuits, the clergy of the Roman Catholic Church, and the Province of Quebec, arising out of claims for compensation for property confiscated at the expulsion of the Jesuits from Canada, which property had escheated to the Crown and had become the property of the Province. During the following session of the Federal Parliament, Colonel O'Brien, supported by the late D'Alton McCarthy, Q.C., and eleven other members, brought up the question in the House, moving for an address, asking the Governor-General to exercise the federal veto and disallow the act of the Quebec legislature. The motion was resisted by the government, whose principal defence was made by Sir John Thompson, the Minister of Justice.

dealing with them, subject only to control in so far as the rights of the whole Dominion or the policy of the Empire may be involved.

Now, sir, the House will remember that, long before the cession of Canada to the Crown of Great Britain, the Jesuits had labored in the wilderness, and in the schools of Canada, and in the churches of Canada, and that as a reward for their missionary zeal, for their talent as teachers, and for their services to this, one of the great colonies of France, that Order had been erected into an incorporated body under the most solemn acts which the King of France could pass under his hand, had been endowed with these estates by the King of France and by private donors, who wished to place in their hands the means by which the work of Christianity and civilization among the savages could be carried on, and by which the work of education among the youth of the Province of Quebec could be carried.

These were the terms on which they held their lands when the battle was fought on the Plains of Abraham, and the conqueror took possession of Canada under terms which are in the first place set forth in the capitulation of the city of Quebec, and afterward in the capitulation of the city of Montreal, and under terms which are plainly defined by the law of nations, recognized by every civilized country in the world.

What are these terms? By the law of nations, recognized, as I have said, in every civilized country in the world, the conquering power took possession of all the rights, privileges, and property of the conquered monarch in the country, but he took no more. He took the sovereignty of the country, he took the king's fortifications in the country, he took the king's stores of arms and ammunition in the country, he took the king's lands in the country, he took the king's treasures in the country, but he had no right by the law of nations to lay his hand on the property, movable or immovable, of the humblest subject in the country.

If he had despoiled private property it would have been an outrage which would have disgraced the British arms, and he would have committed an act, let me tell the House, which, irrespective of the law of nations, the conquering general stated in the terms of capitulation begun at Quebec, repeated at Montreal, he would not do. It has been said in the debate that, by the terms of capitulation the Jesuits of the Province of Quebec, and all their property, were placed at the mercy of the conqueror. I do not so read the terms of capitulation. Let me see article 34 of the terms of capitulation of Montreal:

"All the communities [and at that time the Jesuits were in community in the Province of Quebec] and all the priests shall preserve their movables, the property and revenues of the seignories and other estates which they possess in the colony, of what nature soever they be, and the same estates shall be preserved in their privileges, rights, honors, and exemptions."

That was the request made, and the answer given to that request was unequivocal—" Granted." And yet we are told that these estates, which came within the exact words of that provision as to the seignories and property, movable and immovable, of the priests and religious Orders in the Province of Quebec, were reserved to the king's mercy.

It is true that the preceding section 33 was refused until the king's pleasure should be known, and in that there was a distinct reference to the Jesuits, but that article referred, not to the property only of the Jesuits, but asked, in addition to the provisions as to their property in section 34, that they should have all their constitutions and privileges; that their monasteries should not be entered by troops; that safeguards should be given to them from military intrusion; and that they should preserve their rights to nominate to certain curacies and missions as theretofore. Those privileges, vague and undefined by the terms of the article, were met by the words, " Reserved until the king's pleasure be known," although the response to the article, dealing with the properties of these people, was the unequivocal one—" Granted."

The conquering arms of England were used against the soldiers of France, but not against individuals, either religious or secular, either in France or in Canada. Now, we go a step further, and we read the treaty of peace. The war had gone on, and the treaty was not made until 1763, and let me read to the House a passage from the treaty, because the terms of capitulation are liable to be qualified by the final and definitive treaty at the close of the war. . . .

In the year 1800 the last Jesuit died, and I think that by the law of England, applicable, perhaps at that time to this property in Canada, on the death of the last surviving member of the corporation the property escheated to the Crown, and the Crown could have taken possession of it as escheated lands.

Steps were taken to assert this right on the part of the Crown; but the question had been complicated in the meantime by the fact that the Pope had suppressed the Company of Jesus nearly all over the world. By the terms of that suppression and by the terms of the civil law, which, it is contended, still prevailed in the Province of Quebec, the properties, instead of reverting to the Crown, passed to the ordinaries of the dioceses in which they were situated.

I do not mean to say that that is so: I present that to the House as one of the questions which has been raised, and which tends to make this case anything but a plain one. I will do more, I will admit the honorable member for Simcoe's [D'Alton McCarthy, Q.C.] contention that the common law had in the meantime been introduced, that the civil law had been superseded, and that by the terms of the common law these estates had become escheated to the Crown.

One of the questions, however, which has been constantly agitated ever since in the Province of Quebec is this, that if you are to subject this property to the rigor of the common law you at least ought to give the benefit of that principle of the common law which declares that whenever property of any kind has been escheated to the Crown some consideration should be shown to the persons who are morally entitled to it, and regard should be had to the use to which it was intended to be applied.

By this rule of practice the escheat does not wholly result as an emolument to the Crown or as an augmentation of the revenue, but a liberal proportion is appropriated to the intention of the donors or to those who morally may be considered entitled to it. If that consideration were to prevail to any extent, the clergy, and it may be the Jesuits, on the reinstatement of the Order, would have some kind of moral right to compensation respecting these estates.

But let me call the attention of the House to this fact, which I think has been kept out of view, and which certainly the honorable member for Victoria [Mr. Barron] who addressed the House last night, overlooked in his argument, that the very brief by which these properties were taken possession of on the part of the Crown, when they were eventually seized, does not allege the right of escheat, but

declares the right by which the Crown intended to claim the
properties to be the right of conquest,—a right which, as I
have said, is repudiated by the law of nations, was repudiated
by the Crown officers of Great Britain at the time, and which,
after all that has been said in this debate, has not had one
word said in favor of it. That was the only title by which
Great Britain claimed she had a right to these estates. . . .

I contend that the legislature had supreme authority to
decide, and had a perfect right to decide, without veto or
controlling authority at Ottawa, even though we thought they
had decided erroneously.

Now, sir, having asked the House to bear in mind the
situation in which these properties stood in the Province of
Quebec, the way in which an attempted sale was met by
protest which completely frustrated the sale, let me call the
attention of the House to another state of facts as regards
the various claimants upon this property. There were the
bishops of the Province who said:

"As a result of the suppression of the Society of Jesus in
this Province we were vested with all the estates as the
Ordinaries of the various dioceses in which these properties
were situated."

Nay, more, they said:

" We have inherited their moral claim too, because, when
the means were stricken from their hands of carrying on the
missionary work and the work of education, we took it up,
and, by the sacrifice of our people's labors and treasures, we
built up institutions of education all over this country."

The Society of Jesus had in the meantime been reinstated
and reorganized in the Province, and upon this point let me
call the attention of the House to the argument of my honorable friend from Simcoe [Mr. McCarthy] which was that by

the decree of suppression in France the Order became extinct
in Canada. He cited to prove that the decision of the Parliament of Paris, which merely decided that the Jesuits in
France were liable for the debts of the Jesuits in Paraguay,
because the properties of the two sets of men were held in
solidarity. That decision has not the remotest effect upon
the status of the Jesuits in Canada, who, themselves, were a
body corporate under the most solemn instrument which the
King of France could give them to indicate his will in that
regard. I have mentioned that the bishops claimed that they
represented the moral right, which, as I have said, the legislature thought was worthy of compensation, and the Jesuits
claimed it likewise.

Look at this as a business matter. Look at this matter
simply as relating to a piece of land in the city of Quebec,
and tell me how, under these circumstances, the title was
ever to be cleared of this dispute. Obviously not by com-
pensating first one party and then the other, because under
those circumstances the legislature would have had to pay
twice the value of the claim. It could be settled only by
getting the two parties to arbitrate, and to leave it to some
person to settle their mutual dispute, or by saying: " You
must conform to the decision of some person who has authority over you both."

Let me argue this question throughout, if we can, without
feeling that we belong to different religious persuasions, without feeling that the religious question is mixed up with it at
all; and therefore let us leave out for the moment any name
which might excite the prejudices of some portions of the
community. The bishop of Quebec and the other contesting
parties who struggled for compensation for this moral claim
were all members of the same Church, and by their mem-

bership recognized supreme authority in the head of that Church to settle their disputes, even though the settlement should be against their will.

The head of their Church had that authority, not by any provision of the law of Quebec, mind, not by any provision recognized by English law, mind, but by the consent of the parties who were free to belong to that Church and free to leave it, and, while they did belong to it, were subject to a spiritual superior. He had that power by their choice; he had the right to say to one or to the other, no matter how small or how great the proportion might be that was divided between them: "You must submit; it is a fair settlement between you, and I, as your supreme arbiter, bind you by my decision."

The government of Quebec, therefore, having made up its mind to recognize the moral claim, if for no other purpose, for the purposes of public policy, found that they could not arrive at a solution of the question without some person to act between the claimants and to bind them both. It was only by a method like that, that they could reach a solution, paying once, and once only, the value of this moral claim.

Now, that being so, let me see what was done in pursuance of that method of settlement. The head of that Church so possessed with power to preclude the Jesuits from making any further claim, so possessed with power to preclude the bishops from making any further claim, authorized, in 1884, —and this is an important fact, as the House will see when I proceed a little with the argument,—authorized the archbishop of Quebec to act as his attorney in the negotiations for the settlement. . . .

I go further and say that, within the limits of its authority and subject only to the power of disallowance a Provincial legislature is as absolute as is the Imperial Parliament itself. The Imperial Parliament is not restricted as to the subjects over which it can legislate, the Provincial legislatures are restricted in regard to the subjects on which they can legislate, but in legislating upon these subjects a Provincial legislature has all the rights which it is possible for the Imperial Parliament to confer. I say more: I say that a Provincial legislature, legislating upon subjects which are given to it by the British North America Act, has the power to repeal an Imperial statute prior to the British North America Act affecting those subjects. It has been urged upon the House these two days that we had no power, and that the Act of 28 & 29 Victoria—called the Colonial Enactments Act—provided that no statute of a colony should have force as against an Imperial statute.

But after the statute of 28 & 29 Victoria the British North America Act was passed, and it gives us, as I have said, a division of powers between the two bodies; but it gives the two bodies, in legislating in their respective spheres, all the powers that the Imperial legislature possessed. . . .

We will all cherish the principle that there should be no Church control over the State in any part of this country, but my honorable friend proposes something worse than that control. He proposes that we shall step into the domain of a Provincial legislature, and shall say that no Provincial legislature shall have the power to vote any money to any institution if it partakes of a religious character. It may profess any other kind of principle. It may profess any objectionable principle, and it is lawful to endow it; but if it professes the Christian character, it is, forsooth, unconstitutional to allow such an Act to go into operation.

I listened to the remarks which the honorable member for

Simcoe [Mr. McCarthy] addressed to the House on the third branch of his argument, as to the objectionable teachings of this Society, with some surprise, though I do not intend to-night to challenge his ample liberty to differ from me as to correctness and propriety of those observations. I hope that in this discussion he and those who will vote with him will not prove themselves any less friends of religious liberty than they have professed to be in the past, but I assume—I think I have a right to assume—that, when the case of the gentlemen who are opposed to the allowance of this Act is placed in the hands of an honorable member who is so able and so skilled in argument as he, we are not to be condemned for not asking his Excellency to disallow this Act, unless the reasons which he urged with such great force this afternoon are reasons which I could use in addressing his Excellency on this subject. Surely I have a right to assume that the honorable gentleman has put forward the best case he could, and I am not to be condemned unless I could avail myself of his reasons in asking his Excellency to disallow the Act. If I could picture myself going to his Excellency and asking for the disallowance of this Act for the reasons which the honorable gentleman [Mr. McCarthy] presented in the latter part of his address, I would imagine myself just fit to be expelled from his Excellency's presence as quickly as possible.

What would be the reason which I would urge? I am not finding fault now with the strictures that the honorable gentleman made in regard to the Society, but, forsooth, I am to go to his Excellency and ask him to disallow this Act because, in the year 1874, a quarterly review published an article denouncing the Jesuit Society and its teachings. Am I not right in taking the argument and the evidence which he produces to-day as the argument and the evidence which I should produce to his Excellency?

If I were to go to his Excellency and say that the quarterly review, published in 1874, denounced in language as strong as could be the tenets and teachings of these people, his Excellency might ask me a number of perplexing questions, one of which was levelled at the honorable member from North Simcoe this afternoon without much profit to him. Let me suppose that his Excellency asked me: "Mr. Minister of Justice, who is the author?" My answer would have to be—surely I cannot do better than take the answer of the honorable member from Simcoe—my answer would have to be: "I really do not know who is the author; but, your Excellency, I am sure that nothing would be published in the review which could not stand criticism."

I am afraid that his Excellency might not be satisfied with that answer, and that he might put me another more puzzling question: "Mr. Minister of Justice, are you aware that these able and eloquent but anonymous publications in that review have been refuted time and again until the slanders have been worn threadbare?" I would ask my honorable friend from Simcoe what I should answer to that questions? . . .

If I were to advise his Excellency to disallow the Act on the ground of the expulsion of the Huguenots, the Revocation of the Edict of Nantes, the Franco-German war, the expulsion from France in 1818, the expulsion from other countries, I am afraid his Excellency might tell me that all the statements of fact were disputed, and that he might read me a lesson in ancient and modern history of which one of the deductions could be that, in some of these countries, to say that the court was opposed to the Jesuits, or to say that the court was opposed to the Protestant reformers, was no discredit to either the Protestant reformers or to the Jesuits.

I do not think, sir, that I need dwell on that branch of the subject any longer. I think that whenever we touch these delicate and difficult questions which are in any way connected with the sentiments of religion, or of race, or of education, there are two principles which it is absolutely necessary to maintain, for the sake of the living together of the different members of this Confederation, for the sake of the good will and kindly charity of all our people toward each other, and for the sake of the prospects of making a nation, as we can only do by living in harmony and ignoring those differences which used to be considered fundamental. These two principles surely must prevail, that as regards theological questions the State must have nothing to do with them, and that as regards the control which the federal power can exercise over a Provincial legislature in matters touching the freedom of its people, the religion of its people, the appropriations of its people, or the sentiments of its people, no section of this country, whether it be the great Province of Quebec or the humblest and smallest Province of this country, can be governed on the fashion of three hundred years ago.

DEAN STUBBS

ERY REV. CHARLES WILLIAM STUBBS, an eminent English clergyman and author, Dean of Ely, was born at Liverpool, Sept. 3, 1845, and received his education at the Royal Institution School in that town and at Sidney Sussex College, Cambridge, where he graduated with high honors. In 1868, he became senior curate of St. Mary's, Sheffield, and from there he was transferred to Granboro', Buckinghamshire, where he was vicar for thirteen years. From 1884 till 1888 he was vicar of Stokenham, South Devon, and from 1888 to 1894 rector of Wavertree, Liverpool. In the latter year he was appointed Dean of Ely. From 1881 till 1895 he was select preacher at Cambridge, and in 1883, and again in 1898–99 he filled a similar post at Oxford. He served for two years as president of the Liverpool Royal Institution. Among his publications are: "Village Politics," addresses and sermons on the labor question (1878); "Christ and Democracy" (1883); "The Conscience, and Other Poems" (1884); "God's Englishmen," sermons on the prophets and kings of England (1887); "Charles Kingsley and the Christian Socialist Movement" (1898); "Christ and Economics" (1893); "Christus Imperator" (1894); "A Creed for Christian Socialists" (1896); "Pro Patria" (1901). In 1900, he visited the United States, preaching at Harvard University and elsewhere. To visitors from this country to the English Cathedrals, he is perhaps best known by his "Historical Memorials of Ely Cathedral," and by his "Handbook to Ely Cathedral."

INTERNATIONAL PEACE

"A YOUNG MAN'S VISION"

[A sermon preached at The Hague in connection with the Peace Congress, Whit-Sunday, 1899.]

"And it shall come to pass afterward that I will pour out my spirit upon all flesh, and your sons and your daughters shall prophesy, and your old men shall dream dreams, and your young men shall see visions."— Joel ii, 28.

THESE words of the prophet Joel had their fullest accomplishment, as you all know, in that new revelation of God to the world symbolized in the rushing wind and the fiery tongues of Pentecost, which we to-day are commemorating on this Whit-Sunday, on this great Church festival of the Holy Ghost. But the prophetic words have also had a special fulfilment—have been fulfilled from epoch to epoch in the history of the Church of God.

In the ancient Church they found an immediate realization. For almost within the generation in which Joel lived we see the simultaneous rise of prophets of all degrees of cultivation and from every station in life. Amos, the sheep-master of Tekoa, the gatherer of figs, the prophet of simple style and rustic imagery; Zechariah, the cultured priest and gentle, courtly seer; Micah, the wild village anchorite, pouring out his terrible warnings on the drunkenness, the folly, the oppression of his country, and yet telling also of a reign of universal peace when men shall " beat their swords into ploughshares, and their spears into pruning-hooks "; and, greatest of all, Isaiah, the statesman-prophet of Israel, of great and faithful vision, " very bold," as St. Paul says of him, in extending and enlarging the boundaries of the Church, looking beyond the dark and stormy present to the onward destiny of the human race, when God " shall be found of them that seek him not, and made manifest unto them that ask not of him."

These are but a few. There are many prophets of that period whose very names are lost. Some, no doubt, were wild enthusiasts only, whose ravings did perhaps as much harm as good. Some were hypocrites, who " affected the black prophetic dress without any portion of the prophetic spirit." But all were characteristic of one of those great revivals of religion, one of those spiritual flood-tides in the history of humanity, which have, alas! their baser as well as their nobler aspect.

But Joel did more than utter a special prediction for his own time. He declared one of those great principles which, as I have said, are fulfilled over and over again, and play so large a part in human history.

The principle is this: that ever and anon, in a nation's or a Church's history, after some great national calamity, after some long-continued ecclesiastical torpor, there comes a sudden and mighty out-flood of the Spirit, stirring a nation or a people to its depths, vivifying an almost dead Church, rousing dull spirits into energetic life, exalting common men and women above their ordinary selves.

On every side at such periods in the world's history there arise prophets and heroes, warriors and preachers, holy and devoted souls.

Five centuries after Joel, when Israel was a conquered and tributary people, its kings no more, its national and church life crushed down, there came such a flood-tide of the Holy Spirit of God, which is the spirit of holy valor, and patriotism, and national righteousness.

You may read the whole grand story in the Book of Maccabees. It was a time when the tameness and commonness went out of life for all men. New hopes and aims, new daring and strength seemed to pass into every heart. Men and women, in their daily task, lived not only for that, but for their country and their God. Old men dreamed dreams, and young men saw visions, and upon the servants and the handmaids was poured out the new spirit of faithfulness and truth.

Two centuries later the principle was at work again on a vaster scale. The old world was waiting for a new birth. Old religions, old philosophies, old political systems, all seemed to have reached a stage of decrepitude. The power of imperial Rome, the traditional wisdom of Greece, the narrow national cult of the Hebrew,—all seemed to be worn out.

The last element of good seemed to have gone, for hope was dead. The world seemed to have reached—

> " That last drear mood
>   Of envious sloth and proud decrepitude:
>   No faith, no ark, no king, no priest, no God,
>   While round the freezing founts of life in snarling ring
>   Crouched on the bare worn sod,
>   Babbling about the unreturning spring,
>   And whining for dead gods that cannot save,
>   The toothless systems shiver to their grave."

But when the hour was darkest there came the new birth, the founding of the Christian Church, the preaching of the Apostles, the fervor of the Martyrs, the wonders of the first Christian age. St. Peter saw the fulfilment of the prophet Joel's words in their fullest sense on the first Whit-Sunday. The chill and gloom of the Crucifixion Day had passed. The little Church of the first Believers had awakened to a sense of its mighty mission, and every member of it felt the glow of inspiration in his earnest heart.

And ever since that time, nearly two thousand years ago now, men have been living under what is called a new dispensation, a new order of things. Ever since that time when the last great crowning revelation of God was made to man there has been in the world a society of men who looked out upon life in a new way.

They looked out upon this matter-of-fact world of ours, and somehow they came to see that it was not only what it appeared to be from outside; they came to see that life, human life, had not only to do with outward things; that they, as men, had not only to obey certain laws of conduct and living, under penalty of punishment from the governor, or the king, or the emperor, whose subjects they were; but they came to see that they were members also of a great invisible kingdom, ruled over by a Lord whose throne was not upon earth, governed by laws whose sanction rested not in outward things, in penalty or punishment, but lay in a divine compulsion which they felt in their own hearts, in their own inmost spirit, in a conscience, they called it, not a mere outward authority saying to them at every turn. " Thou shalt," and " Thou shalt not," but an inner voice of the soul ever whispering " I ought," and " I ought not."

And this new way of regarding life these men came to think was the most important thing in all the world. They gave up everything, they left their secular callings, their business in life, to go abroad everywhere telling people of this new, wonderful way of regarding things. They could not help it. A mysterious divine compulsion was laid upon them. It burned in their hearts as a divine energy, it touched their tongues with a divine fire.

If we could have asked them what it all meant, they would have said, " It is the baptism of the Holy Ghost and of fire,— it is that enthusiasm, that influence, that energy, which our ascended King promised he would send down upon us, his own Spirit, the Paraclete, the Comforter, the Spirit of Truth who should guide us into all truth."

And, full of this divine compulsion, and because of it, they were able to touch the hearts of other men; they got them to see life as they saw it, to obey the invisible King, as they obeyed him, from love and loyalty of heart; they drew men into their brotherhood, into this society of the Holy Ghost, this spiritual kingdom, this Church of the new believers, of the men who thought about life in a new way.

And now nearly two thousand years, as I said, have passed away, and to-day that little society of earnest believers in that far-distant land has become a mighty corporation, having branches in all parts of the world, with a long history behind

it, a record of heroes, and saints and martyrs, and doctors and
teachers, the holiest and the noblest of our race, and with a
long future before it of beneficence and salvation for the
world.

And in that long history, over and over again as the ages
went on, the words of the prophet Joel have been fulfilled.
For although, alas! it is true that over and over again also
the vision has faded and the prophecy has disappointed; that
at times even the Church itself has only seemed to be
Christian to its own shame and to its Master's dishonor—
"Christiana ad contumeliam Christi"; that the new heavens
and the new earth have never yet fully come; still, still,
thank God, there has been progress—who can deny it?—
progress by periodic movements, flood-tides of the Spirit of
God, on which the ark of humanity and civilization and social
order, the ark of the Church, has ridden nearer and nearer
to the haven where it would be.

> " For while the tired waves, vainly breaking,
>   Seem here no painful inch to gain,
>   Far back, through creeks and inlets making,
>   Comes silent, flooding in, the main.
>   And not by eastern windows only,
>   When daylight comes, comes in the light,
>   In front, the sun climbs slow, how slowly!
>   But westward, look, the land is bright."

For " when Christ ascended up on high, he led captivity
captive and gave gifts unto men ": for the individual the
gift of true life, for society the gift of prophecy and vision
and of dreams. " I will pour out of my spirit upon all flesh;
and your sons and your daughters shall prophesy, and your
young men shall see visions, and your old men shall dream
dreams."

The gift of Prophecy: the power to recognize new truth
from God and to speak it forth, to interpret it to mankind in
words of fire or deeds of light.

The gift of Vision: the strong, clear grasp of master-ideas, the keen, living sense which a young and generous mind feels for great principles struggling perhaps for life in some mean age of scrambling and selfishness and greed; setting the heart strong and resolute to uphold the cause of righteousness and peace and joy in the Holy Ghost through the coming years.

And the gift of Dreams: no longer the fantastic vision of minds half-dazed with new light, but the conviction of the old man's dearly bought experience, that what perhaps he may be unworthy to see or bring to pass shall yet surely come, shall yet be a common thing full of blessing for the world, and while his own hopes depart of seeing it, yet suffers not his heart to harden, but passes solemnly in spirit into another age, and sees God surely bringing life to its perfect end at last.

It would be impossible, of course, in a single sermon to characterize fully any one of those great epochal movements in the history of Christian civilization which has made modern Christendom what it is to-day. And even if I ask you to think only of one aspect of that civilization,—the origin and growth of sentiments of international morality and law,—a subject which must be in all our minds at this time, in this place, on this historic soil,—it is impossible to do more now than place a cursory finger from point to point on that marvellously diversified chart which shows the onward progress of humanity toward higher and nobler and more Christlike conceptions of statecraft and government.

It has been said that when Charles the Great knelt by the high altar of St. Peter's, at Rome, and received from the hand of Pope Leo III the crown of the Cæsars, and the shout of the people rang out through the church,—"*Karolo*

Augusto, a Deo coronato, magno et pacifico imperatori, vita et victoria."[1]—modern history began.

Certainly with him began a new vision of power in Europe, new in reality, new in its relations to society. For the first time since the fall of the Roman Empire in the West a great king had arisen among the new nations to rule with strength and glory, a founder of social order, a restorer of religion, a patron of education, a statesman, a legislator, an emperor, as the popular acclaim had entitled him, truly " great and peace-giving," because his aim was not only to conquer and overthrow and selfishly to enjoy, but to labor long and resolutely, and with deliberate purpose, to bring order out of chaos, government out of confusion, for the benefit of man and the good of the peoples.

It is true that his romantic reign of nearly fifty years was but an episode of political order and statesmanship in a wild and tumultuous age, but the work of Charles—a genius pre-eminently creative—was not lost in the anarchy which followed, for he had laid the foundations upon which, for many generations, men continued to build.

His policy and deeds were gradually wreathed round with a gorgeous mist of legend and romance, but at least he left behind a memory and a tradition of a settled government and of a noble and extensive scheme of polity, an ideal of imperial duty and obligation, to which his successors in a later age could look back with a devout admiration. For so wisdom is justified of all her children, and God fulfils himself in many ways.

And again, in that later time of turbulence and political confusion, through all the disasters of private war and public

---

[1] " To Charles Augustus, crowned of God, the great and peace-giving Emperor, life and victory."

feud which characterized the peoples of Europe from the
tenth to the thirteenth centuries, who shall say that the old
prophecy of Joel, the newer promises of Pentecost, had no
fulfilment? Into " that wilderness of the peoples " the
Church of Christ had gone forth, and had proved herself
" not only a herald of spiritual blessings and of glorious hopes
in another life, but a tamer of cruel natures, the civilizer of
the rude, the cultivator of the waste places, the educator, the
guide, and the protector " of the weak and oppressed. When
little else could be done, was it nothing, do you think, that
the Church organized " the Truce of God "?

" From Thursday evening among all Christians "—so ran
the words of an ordinance of the Council of Limoges in 1031
—" friends or enemies, neighbors or distant, peace must
reign till Monday at sunrise: and during these four days and
four nights there ought to exist a complete security, so that
every one can go about his own affairs in safety from all fear
of his enemies, and under protection of this truce and this
peace. Let those who observe this peace be absolved by the
Father, All-powerful, by Jesus Christ his Son, and by the
Holy Ghost. Let those who have promised truce and have
voluntarily broken it be excommunicated by God."

There are many sad chapters, it is true, in the history of
Christendom, humiliating to the disciple of Christ, but surely
that chapter in the " Gesta Christi " of the Middle Ages is
at least a touching one, which, although it tells, first, of
desolated towns, depopulated villages, wasted fields, plun-
dered peasants, widows and orphans weeping under the curse
of war, yet goes on to speak of that " Crusade of Peace "
preached by the Church for two centuries and more, made
the subject of conciliar and synodical and episcopal enact-
ment, quieting, if only for a time, the waves of strife, in-

spiring men with a new spirit of good will and concord and
brotherhood, under which, it might be for months, or weeks
only, or days, the bloody sword was suffered to rest in its
sheath, the homes of the poor to go unplundered, and the
unwonted " Peace of God " to fall upon a land drenched with
tears and blood.

It was not, however, until the fifteenth century was passed,
and the various communities of Europe, each retaining characteristics of its original source, but each also taking to itself,
with the assertion of individual freedom, new characteristics,
had finally separated by definite national signs into free and
liberal States, that the foundation was laid of the modern
system of International Policy.

The adoption of standing armies, although they may seem
to have created new dangers for our modern industrialism, it
must never be forgotten, disarmed war of half its terror. But
the need of some recognized code of law to regulate the intercourse of the new nations became pressing. In 1625 the
groundwork of such a code was laid by Grotius, Advocate-
General of the Treasury of Holland and Pensionary of Rot-
terdam, in his treatise, " De Jure Belli et Pacis," a work
which has been said by jurists to have contributed more than
any other uninspired book to the commonwealth of nations.

And indeed, in memory of the Pentecostal promise, ought
we to speak of the book as uninspired ?

It is true that such a code as that of Grotius could not have
arisen in any country where the jurisprudence of ancient
Rome had not been the fountain of all legal ideas and the
groundwork of all positive codes, nor could it have been
written by any man who was not a learned student of that
ancient system.

But Hugo Grotius was not only a student of Roman jurisprudence; he was something higher and better. He had been a great Christian poet before he became a great Christian publicist. I venture, therefore, to say that it was because in his youth he had seen poetic visions of the ideal truths of Christianity that in his old age he dreamed wise dreams of the true relations which should bind together the nations of Christendom, and saw clearly how necessary to the maintenance of the social State is the recognition of the sphere of spiritual as well as of temporal government. Certainly his immortal work is permeated, every line of it, in every chapter and in every section, with the Christian spirit. In the first words of his preface he touches the keynote of all Christian progress through comradeship and association when he says:

"The Sacred History doth not a little provoke us to mutual love, by teaching that we are all of us born of the same first parents."

And in the last chapter of his book he strikes once again the true chord of Christian fellowship as he recalls to the memory the parting benediction of the great Master in the memorable words with which he closes:

"A safe and honored peace is not too dearly bought if it may be had by foregoing as well the offending as the charges and damages of war, especially to us Christians, to whom our great Lord and Master hath bequeathed peace as his last legacy. . . . God, who alone can do it, instil these things into the hearts of those who manage the affairs of Christendom!"

Once more, and lastly, for I must hurry to a conclusion, can we doubt that in our own age the Pentecostal prophecy has been and is being fulfilled? Have we no young men nowadays who see visions, no old men who dream dreams, which it will be good for the world to see realized, even in part, of that divine order in which "God shall fulfil himself," not only "in many ways," but in the one way of perfectness—

> " When shall all men's good
> Be each man's rule, and universal peace
> Lie like a shaft of light across the land,
> And like a lane of beams athwart the sea,
> Through all the circle of the golden year? "

English churchmen, at any rate, cannot certainly at this time forget the example of one great English statesman whose body, just a year ago at Whitsuntide, they were burying in Westminster Abbey "with a nation's lamentation," whose splendid political achievements have left an indelible mark on English statesmanship and on English citizenship, whose voice, in the plenitude of his power and strength, had ever been raised, not only for what he thought the good of his own countrymen, but for the deliverance of the oppressed and downtrodden peoples in any part of Christendom, and whose example of Christian fortitude and patience at the last taught lessons to the English people concerning the reality of religion and the power of prayer in daily life, more potent for the inspiration and ennoblement of national life than all the splendid achievement of the strenuous years that lay behind.

And when we recall these things we cannot forget that it was also to Mr. Gladstone that we owe the Geneva Arbitration of 1872, an event by which two great nations, at a time of great bitterness of popular feeling, and when one side felt itself deeply injured, under circumstances which in all past history would have been thought to justify a declaration of war, deliberately controlled their passion of resentment and determined to submit their differences to impartial arbitration, a decision which in its issue has not only largely contributed to the happy brotherly relationship of England and America to-day, but has also thus enabled the modern world to take probably the greatest step forward in history toward the application of right reason and Christian wisdom to the settlement of international disputes.

Nor can we forget many another occasion in which that great Englishman seemed to be taking a prophet's stand, looking forth on the nations, reading the secret causes which make them living or dying, and then, " looking beyond the results of the moment," in the sure conviction of his long and dearly bought experience, dreamed the old man's dreams, among others—can we doubt it ?—of the golden year of International Peace, " satisfied "—I quote his own words— " that though to-day may not see it and to-morrow may not see it, yet the fruits of patience and perseverance will be reaped in the long future of the nation's existence, when the reckoning cannot fail."

And, my friends, if, happily synchronizing with the holy memories of Whitsuntide, the commemoration this week by English churchmen of their great statesman's death-day a year ago takes us back in thought to an old man's prophetic dream, certainly the great event of this week in this place, to be held by history—God grant it—as a perpetual memory of blessing to all civilized peoples, speaks in unmistakable tones of a young man's vision.

Can there be any Christian in this place to-day who, recalling the ancient Pentecostal prophecy and promise of which I have spoken to you, would wish to think that these last words of the young Tsar's rescript are anything but an aspiration and a prayer, sincerely responsive to the leading, piously pleading for the guidance, of God's holy Spirit of Wisdom, Peace, and Love?

" This Conference shall be, by the help of God, a happy presage for the century which is about to open. It would converge in one powerful focus the efforts of all the States which are sincerely seeking to make the great conception of Universal Peace triumph over the elements of trouble and discord. It would at the same time cement their agreement by a corporate consecration of the principles of equity and right on which rest the security of States and the welfare of peoples."

What is it that blocks the way—do we ask?—to this land of Utopia, to the present earthly realization of the young man's vision, the old man's dream?

I can only answer that the mountains of difficulty which some tell us stand in the way are moral difficulties for the most part, faults of character and will, failure of moral courage and purpose,—in a word, want of faith.

And yet, if we be Christians, we cannot, we must not, lose heart. The mountains of difficulty may be there. We cannot deny it. They do block the way to the promised land. But we walk by faith, not by sight. It was a saying of the great Napoleon, looking out from France on the neighboring country of Spain, " There are no more Pyrenees!" The power of the human will, the vaulting ambition of one man, was—so he thought—sufficient to remove this greatest of natural boundaries.

My friends, do we forget the promise of Him who said that by faith we too should remove mountains?

Mountains of difficulty, mountains of misunderstanding, mountains of prejudice, will only vanish before the courage which despises difficulty, before the insight which sees into the heart of stone, before the love which compels confidence.

Ah, yes! the true Christian faith is like that fabled sword of which one reads in the " Song of Roland," by which that renowned Paladin cleft a way for his army through those same Pyrenees mountains to the open land beyond. Such a breach of Roland, doubt it not, will one day be made through the mountain walls of national jealousy and national pride and national prejudice, and open out a way to the land of International Peace.

May God, of his great mercy, send into the hearts of each member of this Peace Congress his great gift of vision! Let us pray for them—and what words could we better use than those in which for so many generations the Church of Christ has yearly sung her Advent antiphon of preparation for the Christmas message of Peace on earth, good will to men—

"*O Sapientia! quæ ex ore Altissimi prodiisti, attingens a fine atque ad finem; fortiter suaviterque disponens omnia: veni ad docendum eos viam Prudentiæ!*"

CHARLES S. PARNELL

HARLES STEWART PARNELL, M. P., great Irish statesman and leader of the Parnellite party in British politics, was born at Avondale, County Wicklow, Ireland, June 28, 1846, and died at Brighton, Sussex, Oct. 6, 1891. His father was a country gentleman of good estate, belonging to an old and well-known Protestant family. Through his mother, C. S. Parnell was a grandson of Commodore Stewart of the United States Navy. He was educated at Magdalene College, Cambridge, and in 1875, entered Parliament as a supporter of the Home Rule movement, which was at that time directed by Mr. Isaac Butt. Mr. Parnell soon became convinced that Mr. Butt's method of furthering the agitation was futile, and that Englishmen would never listen to Irish claims until they should be compelled to do so by the stoppage of the whole machinery of legislation through parliamentary obstruction. He consequently offered this obstruction, and with such effect as presently to compel Englishmen as well as Irishmen to admit that he had discovered an almost irresistible instrument of constitutional propaganda. In 1879, he was chosen President of the Irish Land League, and under the Coercion Act of 1881–82 he was temporarily imprisoned. Thereafter he so thoroughly had his countrymen with him that at the general election of December, 1885, he succeeded in returning to the House of Commons a compact band of 86 Home Rulers, and thus acquired the balance of power in that body, where the Liberals and the Conservatives were nearly equal in respect of numbers. The outcome of this *impasse* was an alliance between Mr. Parnell and Mr. Gladstone and the latter's introduction of the first Home Rule Bill, which, however, was defeated by the secession of the Unionist-Liberals. Some years later, Mr. Parnell was deposed from the leadership of the Irish Nationalist Party by a majority of his followers, owing to his implication in the O'Shea divorce case as co-respondent. He was shattered in body as well as in spirit by the blow, and died in his forty-sixth year. Had Parnell lived and remained the head of an undivided Nationalist party, the second Home Rule Bill, notwithstanding the opposition which it encountered in the House of Lords, would probably have become law. He is known in English and Irish affairs as the originator of the system of "boycotting." After its great leader's death, Parnellism continued to be a force in British politics, but it was a waning force, and suffered by division in its ranks—the majority of the anti-Parnellists or Irish Nationalists choosing Justin McCarthy as their leader, while the minority were led by John Redmond. Before this, Parnell's career had been bound up with the history of the Home Rule movement, a movement which, despite the fact that Mr. Parnell was a Protestant, the Irish priesthood had encouraged and sustained until the church opposed him at the polls as a violator of the marriage sacrament arising out of the O'Shea divorce case. From the London "Times" accusations that he and the Nationalists were responsible for the outbreak of organized outrage, such as the Phœnix Park murders and other assassinations, Mr. Parnell personally was able to free himself and to bring and recover heavy damages from that journal. This the Parliamentary committee, charged with investigating the case, emphatically proved, though Mr. Parnell's party were declared to have been guilty of incitements to intimidation, out of which had grown crimes which they had failed to denounce. See the "Parnell Movement," by T. P. O'Connor.

(30)

CHARLES STEWART PARNELL

AGAINST NON-RESIDENT LANDLORDS

FROM THE SPEECH DELIVERED IN ST. LOUIS, MARCH 4, 1880

MR. PRESIDENT AND LADIES AND GENTLE-
MEN:—I thank you for this magnificent meeting
—a splendid token of your sympathy and appreciation for the cause of suffering Ireland. It is a remarkable fact that while America, throughout the length and
breadth of her country, does her very utmost to show her
sympathy and send her practical help to our people; while
there is scarcely any hand ave America's between the
starvation of large masses of the western peasantry, England alone of almost all the civilized nations does scarcely
anything, although close beside Ireland, to help the terrible suffering and famine which now oppress that country.
I speak a fact when I say that if it had not been for the
help which has gone from America during the last two
months among these, our people would have perished ere
now of starvation.

We are asked: "Why do you not recommend emigration to America?" and we are told that the lands of Ireland are too crowded. The lands of Ireland are not too
crowded; they are less thickly populated than those of
any civilized country in the world; they are far less
thickly populated—the rich lands of Ireland—than any
of your Western States. It is only on the barren hillsides
of Connemara and along the west Atlantic coast that we
have too thick a population, and it is only on the unfertile
lands that our people are allowed to live. They are not allowed to occupy and till the rich lands; these rich lands are

retained as preserves for landlords, and as vast grazing tracts for cattle. And although emigration might be a temporary alleviation of the trouble in Ireland, it would be a cowardly step on our part; it would be running away from our difficulties in Ireland, and it would be an acknowledgement of the complete conquest of Ireland by England, an acknowledgment which, please God! Ireland shall never make.

No! we will stand by our country, and whether we are exterminated by famine to-day, or decimated by English bayonets to-morrow, the people of Ireland are determined to uphold the God-given right of Ireland—to take her place among the nations of the world. Our tenantry are engaged in a struggle of life and death with the Irish landlords. It is no use to attempt to conceal the issues which have been made there. The landlords say that there is not room for both tenants and landlords, and that the people must go and the people have said that landlords must go. But it may—it may, and it undoubtedly will happen in this struggle that some of our gallant tenantry will be driven from their homes and evicted. In that case we will use some of the money with which you are intrusting us in this country for the purpose of finding happier homes in this far western land for those of our expatriated people, and it will place us in a position of great power, and give our people renewed confidence in their struggle, if they are assured that any of them who are evicted in their attempts to stand by their rights will get one hundred and fifty good acres of land in Minnesota, Illinois, or some of your fine Western States.

Now the cable announces to us to-day that the government is about to attempt to renew the famous Irish Coercion acts which expired this year. Let me explain to you

what these Coercion acts are. Under them the Lord Lieutenant of Ireland is entitled at any time to proclaim in any
Irish county, forbidding any inhabitant of that county to
go outside of his door after dark, and subjecting him to a
long term of imprisonment with hard labor if he is found
outside his door after dark. No man is permitted to carry
a gun, or to handle arms in his house; and the farmers of
Ireland are not even permitted to shoot at the birds when
they eat the seed corn on their freshly sowed land. Under
these acts it is also possible for the Lord Lieutenant of Ireland to have any man arrested and consigned to prison without charge, and without bringing him to trial; to keep him
in prison as long as he pleases; and circumstances have been
known where the government has arrested prisoners under
these Coercion acts, and has kept them in solitary confinement for two years and not allowed them to see a single
relative or to communicate with a friend during all that
period, and has finally forgotten the existence of the helpless prisoners. And this is the infamous code which England is now seeking to re-enact. I tell you, when I read
this despatch, strongly impressed as I am with the magnitude and vast importance of the work in which we are engaged in this country, that I felt strongly tempted to hurry
back to Westminster in order to show this English Government whether it shall dare, in this year 1880, to renew this
odious code with as much facility as it has done in former
years. We shall then be able to put to a test the newly-
forged gagging rules that they have invented for the purpose of depriving the Irish members of freedom of speech.
And I wish to express my belief, my firm conviction, that
if the Irish members do their duty that it will be impossible
that this infamous statute can be re-enacted; and if it again

finds its place upon the statute book, I say that the day upon which the royal assent is given to that Coercion Act will sound the knell of the political future of the Irish people. . . .

And now, I thank you in conclusion for the magnificent service that you are doing for the cause of Ireland. Keep up this work; help to destroy the Irish land system which hangs like a millstone around the necks of our people, and when we have killed the Irish land system we shall have done much to kill English misgovernment in Ireland.

We cannot give up the right of Ireland to be a nation, and although we may devote all our energies to remove the deadly upas tree of Irish landlordism, yet still you will trust us and believe that above and before all we recognize and are determined to work for the right of Ireland to regain her lost nationhood. We believe that Ireland is eminently fitted to take her place among the nations of the world. A people who can boast of such a history as ours; who can boast of martyrs like Robert Emmet, whose memory we celebrate to-day; who have had such leaders as Lord Edward Fitzgerald and Wolfe Tone; whose literature has been enriched by a Davis—I say that such a people has shown that although we may be kept down for a time, we cannot long continue deprived of our rights. And I, for one, feel just as convinced that Ireland will be a nation some day or other, as I feel convinced that in a year or two the last vestiges of landlordism will have disappeared from the face of our country.

ON THE COERCION BILL

[In the former part of this speech, delivered in the House of Commons,
April 18, 1887, Mr. Parnell denounced as a forgery the letter purporting to
have been written by him, as giving countenance to the Phœnix Park murders, and published in facsimile in "The Times" of this date.]

SIR,—The right honorable gentleman [Mr. A. J. Balfour]
refrained from answering the speech which I delivered
on the first reading of this Bill, and the Government
refused to allow the adjournment of the debate, in order that
some other member of the Government should have an opportunity of answering it the next day; and now, upon the second
reading of this Bill, he goes back to the speech, and he attempts an answer to it, at a time of the night when he knows
perfectly well that no reply can be made to him; and, with
characteristic unfairness—an unfairness which I suppose we
may expect to be continued in the future—he has refused to
me the ten or twelve minutes that I should have craved to
refer to a villainous and barefaced forgery which appeared
in the "Times" of this morning, obviously for the purpose
of influencing the Division, and for no other purpose.

I got up when the right honorable gentleman the member
for Midlothian [Mr. Gladstone] sat down.   I had not intended
to have made a speech at all upon the second stage of this Bill.
I should not have said more than a very few words in reference to this forgery; but I think I was entitled to have had
from the right honorable gentleman an opportunity of ex-
posing this deliberate attempt to blacken my character at
some time when there would have been some chance of what
I stated reaching the outside world.

I say there is no such chance now. I cannot suppose the right honorable gentleman, in refusing me the ten minutes which I crave, had not in his eye the design of practically preventing my denial of this unblushing calumny having that effect upon public opinion which it would otherwise have had if it had been spoken at a reasonable hour of the night.

It appears that, in addition to the passage of this Coercion Act, the dice are to be loaded—that your great organs of public opinion in this country are to be permitted to pay miserable creatures for the purpose of producing these calumnies. Who will be safe in such circumstances and under such conditions? I do not envy the right honorable gentleman the Chief Secretary for Ireland, this first commencement of suppression of defence—this first commencement of calumny and of forgery which has been made by his supporters.

We have heard of the misdeeds of Mr. Ford, the editor of the "Irish World," but Mr. Ford never did anything half so bad as this.

[Mr. A. J. Balfour.—I do not wish to interrupt the honorable member; but as he makes these accusations, I should like to explain that I intervened between the honorable gentleman and the House simply because I understood that it had been arranged that I should follow the right honorable member for Midlothian, and that the honorable member would follow me. No hint reached me that he was going to confine himself to an explanation of, or deal at all with, the accusation in the " Times " to which he has referred. No hint of that kind reached me, and I conceive that the honorable member might have risen, had he wished, at any time earlier in the evening.]

I was asked officially, at an early hour in the evening, whether I would speak after the right honorable member for Midlothian, and I replied that I would, and that I only

intended to say a few words in reference to this calumny.
I think I ought to have been given the opportunity which
I desired.

Now, sir, when I first heard of this precious concoction—I
heard of it before I saw it, because I do not take in or even
read the " Times " usually—when I heard that a letter of this
description, bearing my signature, had been published in the
" Times," I supposed that some autograph of mine had fallen
into the hands of some person for whom it had not been intended, and that it had been made use of in this way.

I supposed that some blank sheet containing my signature,
such as many members who are asked for their signature
frequently send—I supposed that such a blank sheet had
fallen into hands for which it had not been intended, and that
it had been misused in this fashion, or that something of
that kind had happened.

But when I saw what purported to be my signature, I saw
plainly that it was an audacious and unblushing fabrication.
Why, sir, many members of this House have seen my signature, and if they will compare it with what purports to be
my signature in the " Times " of this morning, they will see
that there are only two letters in the whole name which bear
any resemblance to letters in my own signature as I write it.

I cannot understand how the conductors of a responsible,
and what used to be a respectable, journal, could have been
so hoodwinked, so hoaxed, so bamboozled, and that is the
most charitable interpretation which I can place on it, as to
publish such a production as that as my signature.

My writing—its whole character—is entirely different.   I
unfortunately write a very cramped hand; my letters huddle
into each other, and I write with very great difficulty and
slowness.   It is, in fact, a labor and a toil to me to write

anything at all. But the signature in question is written by
a ready penman, who has evidently covered as many leagues
of letter-paper in his life as I have yards.

Of course, this is not the time, as I have said, to enter into
full details and minutiæ as to comparisons of handwriting;
but if the House could see my signature, and the forged, the
fabricated signature, they would see that, except as regards
two letters, the whole signature bears no resemblance to
mine.

The same remark applies to the letter. The letter does
not purport to be in my handwriting. We are not informed
who has written it. It is not alleged even that it was written
by anybody who was ever associated with me. The name of
this anonymous letter-writer is not mentioned. I do not
know who he can be. The writing is strange to me. I think
I should insult myself if I said—I think, however, that I perhaps ought to say it, in order that my denial may be full and
complete—that I certainly never heard of the letter.

I never directed such a letter to be written. I never saw
such a letter before I saw it in the " Times " this morning.
The subject-matter of the letter is preposterous on the surface.
The phraseology of it is absurd—as absurd as any phraseology that could be attributed to me could possibly be. In
every part of it, it bears absolute and irrefutable evidence of
want of genuineness and want of authenticity.

Politics are come to a pretty pass in this country when a
leader of a party of eighty-six members has to stand up, at
ten minutes past one, in the House of Commons, in order to
defend himself from an anonymous fabrication, such as that
which is contained in the " Times " of this morning. I have
always held, with regard to the late Mr. Forster, that his treatment of his political prisoners was a humane treatment, and

a fair treatment; and I think for that reason alone, if for no other, he should have been shielded from such an attempt as was made on his life by the Invincible Association.

I never had the slightest notion in the world that the life of the late Mr. Forster was in danger, or that any conspiracy was on foot against him, or any other official in Ireland or elsewhere. I had no more notion than an unborn child that there was such a conspiracy as that of the Invincibles in existence, and no one was more surprised, more thunderstruck, and more astonished than I was when that bolt from the blue fell upon us in the Phœnix Park murders.

I know not in what direction to look for this calamity. It is no exaggeration to say that if I had been in the park that day I would gladly have stood between Lord Frederick Cavendish and the daggers of the assassins, and, for the matter of that, between their daggers and Mr. Burke too.

Now, sir, I leave this subject. I have suffered more than any other man from that terrible deed in the Phœnix Park, and the Irish nation has suffered more than any other nation through it.

I go for a moment to the noble Marquis the member for Rossendale [the Marquis of Hartington]. The noble Marquis made a rather curious complaint of me. He said that, having denied point-blank a charge that had been made by him against me and the National League during the general election last year, he was rather surprised that I did not again refer to the matter in the House of Commons.

Well, I was rather surprised that the noble Marquis made a charge which he advanced without a particle of truth. He advanced that charge again to-night without a particle of proof, and I deny that charge, as I denied it before, in point-blank terms.

I said it was absolutely untrue to say that the Irish National League or the Parliamentary Party had ever had any communication whatever, direct or indirect, with a Fenian organization in America or this country. I further said that I did not know who the leaders of the Fenian organization in this country or America were.

I say that still. But the noble Marquis says he knows who they are, at least he tells us that Mr. Alexander Sullivan—I believe that was the name mentioned—was president of the Clan-na-Gael, or Fenian organization. When I asked him how he obtained his knowledge, he said that he obtained it from information he received as a member of her Majesty's Government.

That may be. But I am not in possession of the information with regard to the Clan-na-Gael which is possessed by the members of the present, or of the late Government. The Clan-na-Gael is a secret organization; it is an oath-bound organization; it gives no information with regard to its members to persons who are not members. I presume that the Government, if they obtained their information with regard to Alexander Sullivan, obtained it through their secret agents in America, through means which are not open to me in any capacity as a private person or a public politician.

It is no answer to me to say that because the noble Marquis, a member of the late Government, with all the information obtainable by the wealth and resource of that Government at his disposal, believes Alexander Sullivan was a member and the leader of the Clan-na-Gael, or any secret organization in America.

I have never had any dealings with him, or anyone else, either in Ireland or America, in respect to the doings or proceedings of any secret society whatsoever.

All my doings on, and sayings and doings in Irish public life have been open and above board, and they have stood the test of the searching investigation of the three years' administration of the Crimes Act by Lord Spencer, who has left it on record that neither any of my colleagues nor myself were in any way connected with the commission of, or approving of the commission of, any crime. Here are Lord Spencer's words spoken at Newcastle on the 21st of April 1886:

" Foremost among the many objections are these: It is said that you are going to hand over the government of Ireland to men who have encouraged—nay, some I have heard say even have directed—outrage and crime in Ireland. That is a very grave accusation. Now, I have been in a position in my official capacity to see and know nearly all the evidence that has been given in Ireland in regard to the murder and conspiracies to murder that took place in 1881 and 1882, and I can say, without doubt or hesitation, that I have neither heard nor seen any evidence of complicity with those crimes against any of the Irish representatives.

" It is right that I should clearly and distinctly express my condemnation of many of the methods by which they carried on their agitation. They often used language and arguments that were as unjustifiable as they were unfounded. They sometimes, perhaps from financial grounds, were silent when words would have been golden, when words might have had a great influence on the state of the country. They might even have employed men for their own legitimate purposes who had been employed in illegal acts by others; this I must say, but, on the other hand, I believe those men to have an affection for, and a real interest in, the welfare of their country. Their ability has been shown and acknowledged in the House of Commons by all parties. I believe that, with full responsibility upon them, they will show that the only true way of obtaining the happiness and contentment of Ireland, is for the Government to maintain law and order, and defend the rights and privileges of every class and of every man in the country."

I cordially re-echo those words. I believe that that expresses the only real way of maintaining law and order in
any country—that you must obtain from the majority of the
people of the country sympathy toward the law, without
which the maintenance of the law is impossible; that you
must show the majority of the community that the law is not
only made, but that it is also administered for their benefit,
and fairly and justly to all classes.

In this way, and in this way only, can you ever obtain respect and sympathy for law and order in Ireland, or anywhere
else. The present Bill may put down crime, or it may increase crime. If it puts it down, it will not put it down by
instilling in the minds of the people a sympathy for law and
order. Crime will die out only as the effect of sullen submission. You will be no farther, after you have been administering your Crimes Act, in the direction of the real
maintenance of law and order than you were at the beginning; nay, not nearly so far.

You are crushing by this iron Coercion Bill those beneficial
symptoms in Ireland which a Government of wise statesmen
and wise administrators would cherish and foster. You are
preventing that budding of friendship between the two countries which this generation would never have witnessed in
Ireland had it not been for the great exertions of the right
honorable member for Midlothian.

Who could have predicted, who would have ventured to
predict, that the heat, the passion, the political antipathies
engendered by the working of the Protection Act of 1881
and the Crimes Act of 1882 would have all disappeared in
three or four short months, and that you would have had the
English and the Irish people regarding each other as they did
during that happy, that blessed period, and all this to be put

an end to by the mad, the fatuous conduct of the present Government.

You are going to plunge everything back into the seething cauldron of disaffection. You cannot see what the results of all this may be. We can only point to the experience of what has happened in past times. We anticipate nothing beneficial from this Bill, either to your country or to ours; and we should not be honest men if we did not warn you, with all the little force at our command, of the terrible dangers that may be before you.

I trust before this Bill goes into Committee, or at all events, before it leaves Committee, the great English people will make their voices heard, and impress upon their representatives that they must not go on any further with this coercive legislation.

If this House and its majority have not sense enough to see this, the great heart of this country will see it, for I believe it is a great and generous heart, that can sympathize even when a question is concerned in reference to which there have been so many political antipathies. I am convinced, by what I have seen of the great meetings which have been held over the length and breadth of England and Scotland, that the heart of your nation has been reached—that it has been touched, and though our opponents may be in a majority to-day, that the real force of public opinion is not at their back.

A Bill which is supported by men, many of whom are looking over their shoulders and behind them, like the soldiers of an army which a panic is beginning to reach, to see which is their readiest mode of retreat, is not likely to get through the difficult times before it emerges from Committee. The result will be modifications of the provisions of the most

drastic of the Coercion Acts ever introduced against Ireland
since 1833.

Do not talk to me of comparing the suspension of the
Habeas Corpus Act with the present Bill.   We have suffered
from both.   We have suffered from some of the provisions of
the present Bill, as well as from the Habeas Corpus
Suspension Act, and we are able to compare the one with the
other; and I tell you that the provisions of the Habeas Corpus
Suspension Act empowered you to arrest and detain in prison
those whom you suspected; but it guaranteed them humane
treatment, which did much to soften the asperities that otherwise would have been bred between the two nations by that
Act.   Your prisoners under the Habeas Corpus Act were not
starved and tortured as they will be under this.   Your
political prisoners were not put upon a plank bed, and fed on
sixteen ounces of bread and water per day, and compelled to
pick oakum, and perform hard labor, as they will be under
this Bill.

The Bill will be the means by which you will be enabled
to subject your political prisoners to treatment in your jails
which you reserve in England for the worst of criminals, and
it is idle to talk about comparison between the suspension of
the Habeas Corpus Act, under which your prisoners were
humanely and properly treated—although imprisonment is
hard to bear under the best circumstances; but in the position
in which this Bill will place them, your political prisoners
will be deliberately starved with hunger and clammed with
cold in your jails.   I trust in God, sir, that this nation and
this House may be saved from the degradation and the peril
that the mistake of passing this Bill puts them in.

MICHAEL DAVITT

ICHAEL DAVITT, Irish nationalist, politician, and journalist, one of the founders of the Irish Land League, was born of peasant parents at Straid, County Mayo, Ireland, March 25, 1846. His father, being evicted in 1851, removed to Lancashire, where the son worked in a cotton factory until he was eleven, and then, after a few years' schooling, became a printer. Joining the Irish movement in 1865, he was tried at London in 1870 for "treason-felony" and sentenced to fifteen years' penal servitude, but after seven and a half years' confinement in Dartmoor prison he was released on a ticket of leave. With Parnell and others he founded the Irish Land League, in 1879, and was arrested the same year for seditious utterances, but was soon released. In 1881, he was again arrested on a similar charge, and was sent to Portland prison for fifteen months, and in 1883 was once more arrested and imprisoned for three months. While detained in Portland prison he was elected to Parliament, but was disqualified by vote of the House of Commons, and when reëlected in 1892 was unseated. The same year, however, he entered unopposed for Cork, but resigned in 1893, owing to bankruptcy proceedings against him. In 1895, he was returned to Parliament for East Kerry and South Mayo, retaining his seat until 1899. Mr. Davitt has paid several lecturing visits to this country. He has published "Leaves from a Prison Diary" (1884), "Defence of the Land League" (1891), and "Life and Progress in Australia" (1898).

IN DEFENCE OF THE LAND LEAGUE

FROM SPEECH DELIVERED BEFORE THE SPECIAL COMMISSION, OCTOBER, 1889

I AM only too sensible of the fact that I have trespassed upon the patience and forbearance of the court to an extent which, possibly, would not be permitted to a lawyer. I am thankful, therefore, for such latitude, as well as for the unfailing fairness and courtesy of your lordships toward me, personally, from the very commencement of this inquiry.

I know too well I have spoken hot words and resorted to hard phrases in arguments, which may have been out of place in the calm region of a court like this. But that was because

I felt that the character of the charges I have tried to meet and to answer was such as merited the strongest possible language of condemnation. I came here to address this court contrary to the advice of Mr. Parnell, who was the central figure and chief object of the " Times's " malignant allegations.

I have therefore spoken only for myself. I felt that it was my duty to come here, no matter who should advise me to the contrary. I may be wrong in my opinion, but I thought and believed that if one with my record of suffering, physical and otherwise, at the hands of Irish landlordism and Castle rule; of the conflict of a lifetime with the law as it has been administered in Ireland, and of the punishment which that conflict has entailed: I felt and believed, if I came before this tribunal and pleaded, in my own way, the cause of the Celtic peasantry of Ireland, that perhaps the story which I have told and the case which I have submitted might possibly, in part or in whole, arrest the attention of the people of Great Britain when they come to study your lordships' labors and report.

And I thought and hoped that in the defence which I have made there might possibly be found some help in the task of finally solving this Anglo-Irish struggle. Should my hope be realized, should I have contributed but in the least possible degree to point to a just and feasible solution of a problem which would bring peace and some chance of prosperity to Ireland, I shall be happy in the recollection of the task which I am now bringing to a close.

I can only say that I represent the working classes of my country here as I did in the Land League movement, and I know they feel, as I do, that, no matter how bitter past memories have rankled in our hearts, no matter how much we have suffered in the past in person or in our country's cause, no matter how fiercely some of us have fought against and denounced the injustice of alien misgovernment; I know that, before a feeling of kindness and of good will on the part of the people of England, Scotland, and Wales, and in a belief in their awakening sense of justice toward our country, all distrust and opposition and bitter recollections will die out of the Irish heart, and the Anglo-Irish strife will terminate forever when landlordism and Castle rule are dethroned by Great Britain's verdict for reason and for right.

My lords, I now bring my observations to a close. Whatever legal points are to occupy your lordships' study and care in this long and arduous investigation, it will appear to the public, who will study the report or the decision of this tribunal, that two institutions stood indicted before it.

One has had a life of centuries, the other an existence of but a few brief years. They are charged, respectively, by the accused and the accusers, with the responsibility for the agrarian crimes of the period covered by this inquiry.

One is Irish Landlordism, the other is the Irish Land League. The "Times" alleges that the younger institution is the culprit. The Land League, through me, its founder, repels the accusation, and counter-charges landlordism with being the instigation and the cause, not alone of the agrarian violence and crimes from 1879 to 1887, but of all which are on record, from the times spoken of by Spenser and Davis in the days of Elizabeth, down to the date of this Commission.

To prove this real and hoary-headed culprit guilty, I have not employed or purchased the venal talent of a forger, or offered the tempting price of liberty for incriminatory evidence to unhappy convicts in penal cells. Neither have

I brought convicted assassins or professional perjurers, like the Delaneys and Le Carons, before your lordships. I have not sought assistance such as this with which to sustain my case. Nor have I been aided by the Colemans, Buckleys, and Igos as confederates, or had to scour the purlieus of American cities for men who would sell evidence that might repair the case which Richard Pigott's confession destroyed, and which his self-inflicted death has sealed with tragic emphasis.

I did not go to such sources or resort to such means for testimony against Irish landlordism. I relied not upon the swearing of spies or informers, but upon disinterested facts, left as legacies to Truth by men who are held in reverence by England for services rendered to their country, to justice, to humanity.

I have reproduced the words which these men have placed on record against crime-begetting Irish landlordism. Among those quoted as authorities, but not of them, one with them in their verdicts, though not to be classed otherwise with honored names, I have placed the "Times" newspaper, which is the Land League's accuser: I have made it speak its own condemnation and compelled it historically to exculpate the League. The face of what the first editorial ever written in the "Times" likened to the pagan deity, Janus,—the face which circumstances have sometimes forced to look toward Truth by power akin to that which compels matter to look toward the sun,—I have made to confront and shame, by contrast, the other face of fraud and falsehood, which, like an evil genius, has led England to regard with hate and distrust every effort of the Irish people for right and justice.

I have made the "Times" of 1847 and of 1880 give the lie direct to the "Times" of this Commission, and have caused it to become my strongest historic accuser of the evil system which it now condemns by its very advocacy.

To this testimony I have added the sworn evidence of the persons whom it charges with the deeds of its client; the evidence of the living actors in the Land League movement, and of others who represent every class into which Ireland's population is divided—bishops, priests, members of Parliament, municipal representatives, journalists, merchants, traders, farmers, laborers, mechanics, who one and all say with the " Times's " Red Book of 1880 that eviction and threats of eviction are the chief source of all agrarian crime in Ireland.

But there is another and a higher interest involved in the drama of this Commission now rapidly drawing to a close; an interest far surpassing in importance, and the possible consequences of your lordships' judgment, anything else comprised in this investigation. It stands between the " Times " and landlordism, on the one hand; the persons here charged and the Land League, on the other. In bygone ages, historians, with some prophetic instinct, called it " The Isle of Destiny."

And Destiny seems to have reserved it for a career of trial, of suffering, and of sorrow. That same Destiny has linked this country close to England. Politically it has remained there for seven hundred years or more. During that period few people ever placed upon this earth have experienced more injustice or more criminal neglect at the hands of their rulers than we have.

This even English history will not and dare not deny. This land so tried and treated has nevertheless struggled, generation after generation, now with one means, now with another, to widen the sphere of its contracted religious, social, and political liberties—liberties so contracted by the deliberate policy of its English governing power; and ever and always were these struggles made against the prejudice and might, and often the cruelties, of this same power, backed by the support or the indifference of the British nation.

But, despite all this, the cause so fought and upheld has ever and always succeeded, sooner or later, in vindicating its underlying principles of truth and justice, and in winning from the power which failed to crush them an after-justification of their righteous demands.

A people so persevering in its fight for the most priceless and most cherished of human and civil rights, so opposed, but so invariably vindicated, might surely, in these days of progress and of enlightenment excite in the breasts of Englishmen other feelings than those of jealously, hate, revenge, and fear. To many, thank God, it has appealed successfully, at last, to what is good and what is best in English nature. It has spoken to the spirit of Liberty, and has turned the love of justice in the popular mind toward Ireland, and has asked the British people, in the interests of peace, to put force and mistrust away with every other abandoned weapon of Ireland's past misrule, and to place in their stead the soothing and healing remedies of confidence and friendship, based upon reason and equality.

The verdict of this court, the story that will be told in the report of this Commission, may or may not carry the appeal which Ireland's struggles and misfortunes have addressed to the conscience and fairness of the English nation much farther than it has already travelled in the British mind.

But one thing, at least, the history of this Commission will have to tell to future generations. It will narrate how this progress of conciliation between ruled and rulers was sought to be arrested; how a people asking for justice were answered by ferocious animosity; how men who had suffered imprisonment, degradation, and calumny in their country's service were foully attacked by the weapons of moral assassination, and how every dastard means known in the records of political warfare was purchased and employed to cripple or destroy the elected representative of the Irish nation.

This story will picture this once-powerful organ of English public opinion earning again the title of " literary assassin " which Richard Cobden gave it near thirty years ago. It will stand again in this light when its writers are seen plotting with Houston, planning with Pigott, and bargaining with Delaney how best to reawaken in the English mind the old hate and jealousy and fear of a people who were to be depicted in its columns in the most odious and repulsive character that forgers' or libellers' mercenary talent could delineate in " Parnellism and Crime."

This story will exhibit these men sitting in the editorial rooms of Printing House Square, with professions of loyalty on their lips and poison in their pens; with " honesty " loudly proclaimed in articles which salaried Falsehood had written; with simulated regard for truth, making " Shame ashamed " of their concocted fabrications.

And these men, with the salaries of the rich in their pockets and the smiles of London society as their reward, carrying on a deliberately planned system of infamous allegation against political opponents who were but striving to redeem the sad fortunes of their country, in efforts to bring to an end a strife of centuries' duration between neighboring nations and peoples.

Between the "Times" on the one hand, and the accused on the other, your lordships are, however, first to judge. It is, if I may say so without presumption, as serious and momentous a duty as judges of England were ever called upon to perform. The traditions of your lordships' exalted position, elevated as that position is above the play of political passion of the influence of fear or favor, will call, and will not, I am sure, call in vain, for the exercise of all those great qualities of trained ability, of calmness, of discernment, of judgment, and of courage which are the proud boast of the judicial bench of this land.

Whether or not the test of a cold, indiscriminating law will alone decide an issue in which political passion has played so great a part, and where party feeling has been a moving principle in acts and words; whether the heated language of platform oratory, or the sometimes crude attempts at political reform, are to be weighed in the balance of legal scales,—scales never fashioned, at least in England, to measure the bounds of political action; or whether the test is to lie with a discriminating judicial amalgam of law in its highest attributes and of calm reason applied to the men and motives and means of the Land League, as the accused, and to the "Times," its charges and allegations, as the accuser, I am, as a layman, unable to forecast.

But, be the test what it may, if it be only based upon truth and guided by the simple monitor of common sense; I say on my own behalf and on that of the Land League and of the peasantry of Ireland, hopefully, confidently, fearlessly, "Let justice be done though the heavens fall."

THE CRIMES OF IRISH LANDLORDISM

[A monster demonstration in favor of the Land League movement, which sought to reform the Irish land laws, was held at Straide, County Mayo, February 1, 1880. Mr. Davitt was among the speakers, and a peculiar interest was attached to the meeting from the fact that the platform from which he spoke was erected over the very ruins of the old homestead from which he, with his father and mother, had been evicted many years before. Mr. Davitt delivered the following speech:]

WHILE every nerve must be strained to stave off, if possible, the horrible fate which befel our famine-slaughtered kindred in 1847 and 1848, the attention of our people must not for a moment be withdrawn from the primary cause of these periodical calamities, nor their exertions be relaxed in this great social struggle for the overthrow of the odious system responsible for them.   Portions of the English press had recently declared that the charity of Englishmen would be more spontaneous and generous if this agitation did not stand in the way.   Well, Ireland's answer to this should be that she asks no English alms, and that she scorns charity which is offered her in lieu of the justice which is her right and her demand.   Let landlordism be removed from our country, and labor be allowed the wealth which it creates instead of being given to legalized idlers, and no more famine will darken our land or hold Ireland up to the gaze of the civilized world as a nation of paupers.   England deprives us annually of some seven millions of money for Imperial taxation, and she allows an infamous land system to rob our country of fifteen or twenty millions more each year to support some nine or twelve thousand lazy landlords, and then, when famine extends its destroying wings over the land, and the dread spectre of death stands sentinel at our thresholds, an appeal to English charity—a begging-box outside the London Mansion House—is paraded before the world, and expected to atone for every wrong inflicted upon Ireland by a heartless and hated government, and to blot out the records of the most monstrous land code that ever cursed a country or robbed humanity of its birthright. The press of England may bring whatever charges its prejudices can prompt against this land movement, the Duchess of Marlborough may hurl her gracious wrath at the heads of " heartless agitators," but neither the venomed scurrility of government organs nor the jealous tirades of politico-prompted charity can rob the much-abused land movement of the credit attached to the following acts. The cry of distress and national danger was first raised by the agitators, and all subsequent action, government, viceregal, landlord, and Mansion House, to alleviate that distress, was precipitated by the action of the " heartless agitators." The destroying hand of rackrenting and eviction was stricken down for the moment by the influence of the agitation, and the farmers of Ireland were spared some two or three millions with which to meet the distress now looming on their families and country, while the rooftrees of thousands of homesteads were protected from the crowbar brigade; and the civilized world has been appealed to against the existence of a land monopoly which is responsible for a pauperized country, a starved and discontented population, and every social evil now afflicting a patient and industrious people, until a consensus of home and foreign opinion has been evoked in favor of a lasting and efficacious remedy. With these services rendered to Ireland, with a resolve to do the utmost possible to save our people from the danger immediately threatening them, the " heartless agitators " will not relax a single effort or swerve one iota from their original purposes,—to haul down the ensign of land monopoly and plant the banner of the " land for the people " upon the dismantled battlements of Irish landlordism. Against what have we declared this unceasing

strife, and whence the justification for the attitude we are
calling upon the people to assume? The resolution so eloquently proposed by my friend Mr. Brennan declares that the
present land code had its origin in conquest and national spoliation, and has ever since been the curse of our people and
the scourge of Ireland. Does not the scene of domestic devastation now spread before this vast meeting bear testimony
of the crimes with which landlordism stands charged before
God and man to-day? Can a more eloquent denunciation of
an accursed land code be found than what is witnessed here
in this depopulated district? In the memory of many now
listening to my words that peaceful little stream which
meanders by the outskirts of this multitude sang back the
merry voices of happy children and wended its way through
a once populous and prosperous village. Now, however, the
merry sounds are gone, the busy hum of hamlet life is hushed
in sad desolation, for the hands of the home destroyers have
been here and performed their hellish work, leaving Straide
but a name to mark the place where happy homesteads once
stood, and whence an inoffensive people were driven to the
four corners of the earth by the ruthless decrees of Irish
landlordism. How often in a strange land has my boyhood's
ear drunk in the tale of outrage and wrong and infamy per-
petrated here in the name of English laws and in the interest of territorial greed. In listening to the accounts
of famine and sorrow, of deaths from landlordism, of coffin-
less graves, of scenes—

> On highway's side, where oft were seen
> The wild dog and the vulture keen
> Tug for the limbs and gnaw the face
> Of some starved child of our Irish race,

what wonder that such laws should become hateful, and, when
felt by personal experience of their tyranny and injustice,

that a life of irreconcilable enmity to them should follow, and
that standing here on the spot where I first drew breath, in
sight of a levelled home, with memories of privation and tor-
tures crowding upon my mind, I should swear to devote the
remainder of that life to the destruction of what has blasted
my early years, pursued me with its vengeance through manhood, and leaves my family in exile to-day far from that Ireland which is itself wronged, robbed, and humiliated through
the agency of the same accursed system? It is no little con-
solation to know, however, that we are here to-day doing battle against a doomed monopoly, and that the power which has
so long domineered over Ireland and its people is brought to
its knees at last and on the point of being crushed forever. It
is humiliating to the last degree that a few thousand land-
sharks should have so long and so successfully trod upon the
necks of millions of Irishmen and defrauded them of the
fruits of their land, while at the same time robbing, insult-
ing, and dragooning our country with an inhumanity unsurpassed by the titled plunderers of the middle ages. An average landlord may be likened to a social vulture hovering over
the heads of the people and swooping down upon the earnings and the food which that industry produces whenever
his appetite or his avarice prompts him. The tenantry in
the past have stood by like a flock of frightened sheep, timid
and terrified, unable to prevent this human bird of prey from
devouring their own and their children's substance. While
rackrents were paid the farmer and his family must live in
semi-starvation, in wretched hovels, amid squalor and priva-
tions, barbed by the thought that the money earned by labor
and sweat from day to day was being spent by his own and
his children's deadly enemy in another land in voluptuous
ease and sensual gratification. If the rackrent was not paid

and this blackmail levied upon labor in the shape of rent
was not forthcoming, to be squandered by one who never
earned a penny of it, out upon the roadside the earners would
be cast, to take their choice of death by exposure, workhouse
degradation, or banishment from home and Ireland forever.
Is it possible that our fathers could have tolerated such a
giant wrong, submitted to so monstrous an infamy, and bequeathed to us an acceptance of it as an inevitable decree
of God, to be borne in meek submission, or to plod on in
sluggish servitude from sire to son, from age to age, proud
of our trampled nature? Such, however, is not our resolve.
We accept no such blasphemous excuse for the abrogation
of our manhood, nor will we allow a horde of vampires to
fatten upon our soil, to degrade us by their assumption of
superiority, and keep our country before the world as the
property and the preserve of the deadliest enemies to her
social and political welfare. We demand the right to live
like civilized men in our land; we demand the right to enjoy
life here, and we are resolved to labor unitedly and unceas-
ingly for the privilege to do so. We ask these demands
upon the God-given right to mankind to hold in proportion
to their wants and deserts the land which was created for
their sustenance. The principles upon which this land movement rests are founded upon obvious and natural justice,
and if in advocating them we outstep the barriers of political
conventionalities we are justified by the monstrous wrongs
which are upheld by a system that justice and reason alike
condemn, and which civilization has stamped out in every
other country. In demanding the land for the people we
are but claiming the right which is ours in virtue of our creation and the decrees of our Creator. Land was created for
man's sustenance, and declared to be the property of the

human family, to be worked by labor and made productive
in food for the children of men.   To hold that, because robbery and fraud have succeeded in gaining possession of the
soil of Ireland, landlordism was in the Divine intention and
has a right to the land of the country, is a libel on God's
immutable ordinances and a doctrine opposed alike to reason
and common sense.   Landlordism has worked the deadliest
wrong to our country and our race.   Its gifts to Ireland are
famines, discontent, bloodshed, national impoverishment, and
national degradation.   It robs our country of £20,000,000
annually and disposes of our people as so much vermin.   It
bars our social progress and deprives us of those advantages
which are enjoyed by those who have freed themselves from
landlordism.   Remove the land monopoly, and famine will be
exorcised from Ireland.   Strike down this giant fraud upon
a people, and peace and plenty will take the place of disturbance and starvation.   Give labor its claim upon the
wealth it creates, remove the restrictions which this feudal
code places upon the proper cultivation of the soil of Ireland,
and the charity of other lands will no more be appealed to
on our behalf, or our national pride be humiliated by our
being exhibited in the eyes of the world as a nation of
paupers.   Organize, then, for so glorious a consummation.
Vow that you will never cease striking until land monopoly
is crushed forever in Ireland.   Forward with the glorious
watchword of "The land for the people."   The cause of
Ireland to-day is that of humanity and labor throughout the
world, and the sympathy of all civilized people is with us in
the struggle.   Stand together, then, in this contest for the
soil of your fatherland, and victory will soon crown your
efforts with success.   Remember, with courage and with
pride, that seven hundred years of wrong failed to crush the
soul of Ireland.

LORD ROSEBERY

LORD ROSEBERY

RCHIBALD PHILIP PRIMROSE, P.C., K.G., LL.D., fifth Earl of Rosebery, a distinguished English Liberal statesman, was born at London, May 7, 1847, and was educated at Eton and Christ Church College, Oxford University. He succeeded to the title in 1868 by the death of his grandfather, before he reached his majority, and his first appearance in Parliament was in the House of Lords. His first speech was made in 1871, when he was selected by Mr. Gladstone to second ·he address in reply to the Queen's speech from the throne. During the next few years he took part occasionally in the debates, always speaking with animation, and with eloquence and force. A Liberal in politics, and a warm admirer of the late Mr. Gladstone, he sat in the latter's cabinet in 1881–83 as under-secretary of home affairs. During the brief Liberal rule of 1885 he was lord privy seal and first commissioner of public works, and in 1886 he was appointed secretary of foreign affairs. While holding this position he conducted the foreign policy on the general lines followed in the preceding Conservative government and endeavored to keep it removed as far as possible from the influence of party strife. He was one of the most ardent supporters in the House of Lords of Gladstone's first Home Rule Bill. In 1888, he became a member of the London county council, and in the last Gladstone administration was again minister of foreign affairs. On the retirement of Mr. Gladstone, in March, 1894, Lord Rosebery succeeded him as Prime Minister, holding office until the return of the Conservative party to power in 1895. Lord Rosebery is a man of wide sympathies, and has manifested much interest in ameliorating the condition of the laboring classes. He was lord rector of Aberdeen University, 1878–81, and of Edinburgh University, 1882–83. He has published a "Life of Pitt"(1891); "Speeches, 1874–96" (1896); "Appreciations and Addresses" (1889); and an interesting study of "Napoleon." Unlike most of the Liberal party, with which he is not always politically in accord, he is a pronounced Imperialist.

THE TRUE LEVERAGE OF EMPIRE

DELIVERED AT THE SOCIAL SCIENCE CONGRESS, GLASGOW,
SEPTEMBER 30, 1874

IF, in addressing this great meeting, I were to speak out of the fulness of my heart, I should tell of nothing but my own misgivings. But it is too much the practice on these occasions to take up time selfishly in apologies. You asked me kindly and generously to come here to-night. I thought it a clear duty to obey your summons and reciprocate your sympathy. But none the less sensible am I of my own deficiencies and of my need of your further large indulgence; none the less do I feel as if I were only placed in this prominent position to serve as a foil to the ripe wisdom of so many in this Congress.

It is impossible for any one at my age to pretend to instruct—few can have adequate knowledge; none sufficient experience. I can offer, then, no fresh contribution to your stock of information. I can only, as it were, set in motion my small share of electric current of sympathy and interest, which is surely not the least valuable of the features of this Congress. But I would before all express my pride and my joy at making this first visit to Glasgow under the auspices of your association. There are probably few places to which an Englishman can point with more pride than to Glasgow; none perhaps which a Scotchman can regard with so much.

I suppose that there are in this city 500,000 inhabitants; that the rental amounts to £2,500,000; that the shipbuilding of the Clyde is supreme in the world. How long has it taken to produce this immense result? What is the origin of this great population? Whence dates this easy predominance in shipping, this vast collection of material wealth?

Two centuries ago Glasgow was officially described as " a neat burghe town, consisting of foure streets." At that time she possessed twelve vessels carrying 957 tons. In the year 1718, little more than a century and a half ago, the first Scottish ship that ever crossed the Atlantic—a vessel of sixty tons—was launched in the Clyde, which has since witnessed the building of the Cunard line of steamers. And as for her rental of £2,500,000, it has been computed that the

rental of the whole of Scotland did not a century ago exceed
£1,000,000 sterling.

We could not, indeed, have chosen a more suggestive scene
for our Congress, or one where social science should be more
dear. For here we have a great material result rapidly produced by the exertions of a vast laboring population; and no
one surely, in considering the labors of this Congress and its
functions, can avoid seeing that the most vital and perpetual
question before it is the well-being of our working classes; a
vital question, because on the apt solution of it depends the
commercial supremacy, the political solidarity, nay, the very
existence of our empire. To my mind a body like ours has
no more direct or important duties than the attempt to raise
the condition of the nation by means which Parliament is
unable or disdains to apply.

Here we have an illimitable field of operations. Parliament can give a workman a vote; it cannot give him a comfortable home. Nor can it sift and exhibit the many con-
trivances which may be placed before him for bettering himself or increasing his capacities and enlarging his enjoyments.

All this lies within our province, and it is work incalculably more important than the great mass of our parliamentary legislation. In this century we are surrounded by a great
aggregation of humanity, seething, laboring, begrimed humanity; children of toil who have made Glasgow what she
is and can alone raise and maintain her; not mere machines
of production, but vehicles of intelligence, mixed in nationality and various in opinion.

You cannot appeal to them by common feelings or uniform
interests. They are there, a dark and mighty power, like the
Cyclopean inmates of Ætna. I must honestly avow my conviction—though to those who see how many there are who

profess to represent and understand the working classes it may seem rash, while to others it may seem a truism—that this vast laboring population of ours has not made itself, its wants, its creeds, and its interests sufficiently intelligible to many of us. How indeed, if it be otherwise, is it that the problems connected with their condition have advanced so little toward solution? How is it, otherwise, that each political party claims with equal certainty and on every point to possess the sympathy and confidence of the workingman? How else is it that, when the working class makes its voice heard on any question, it comes upon us like thunder in a clear sky? I avow myself no exception to the rule, but for that very reason, perhaps, I can conceive no subjects more interesting than those which relate to the welfare of our laboring population.

Perhaps, then, you will allow me to disregard the ordinary precedent upon these occasions. The opening address of this Congress has commonly surveyed the present position of those questions with which your Society is accustomed to deal, or which it watches with interest. But speaking, as I do, in the presence of many who, in the various sections, will discuss such subjects with ripe authority of knowledge and experience, I should feel it presumptuous in me to poise a light sentence or hazard a shallow conjecture where my hearers can for themselves sound the very depth and perhaps approximate solution.

I will, then, if you please, attempt to-night to take stock in some degree of the various means by which it is sought to raise the condition of the working classes; a group of subjects some of which appear under different divisions in your programme, but which are ultimately—I had almost said solemnly—connected together; and I would do so rather

as a sign of humble interest in them than with the slightest
pretension of having anything original to advance.

The moment is as suitable as the place for the discussion
of these vital and national questions. In times such as these,
of high wage, of general peace, of immunity from furious
political discord, the well-being of the laboring classes often
appears secured and does not always attract the attention of
statesmen. It is, however, precisely then that it is possible
to take measures which, without exciting jealousy on one
hand and suspicion on the other, may secure that well-being
in less prosperous times. It is then that even the Greeks
may innocently bring gifts.

But should there come a European war such as we
weathered successfully at the beginning of the century, but
which left us surrounded for the most part with battered
wrecks and with stranded hulls, we might possibly find our
teeming population, confined within so small an ark, a perilous and disheartening agency.

Moreover, while our numbers increase in a greater proportion daily, it would seem that for a few years our principal
outlet for emigration may be partially blocked up. It appears more than probable that for some time, owing to late
commercial disasters, and it may be because corn-growing in
the West has been somewhat overdone, the United States
will not find employment for that million and a quarter of
emigrants, more or less, that we are accustomed annually to
send to her. This is the most important problem which can
occupy statesmen; and at the same time the most difficult
for a statesman to face. For Parliament can seldom see its
way to interference. Nor is it, indeed, desirable that it
should do so.

Legislatures and governments have at various times, by

direct laws, attempted to benefit the working classes; but the most obvious instances of this—the National Workshops of 1848, and the decrees of the Parisian Commune in 1871— have been conspicuous failures.

It is well, then, that in this present time, so peaceful and blessed for us, we can here discuss, however slowly and imperfectly, the pregnant topics which our programmes suggest. And there is so much to be done; our civilization is so little removed from barbarism! At this moment there is a daily column in the newspapers devoted to recording brutal outrages, where human beings have behaved like wild beasts. Every policeman in London is assaulted on an average about once in two years. Within the memory of living men, the workmen at the salt-pans of Joppa, only a mile or two from Edinburgh, were serfs—*adscripti glebæ*—and sold along with the land on which they dwelt. Neither they nor their children could remove from the spot or alter their calling. The late Lord Provost of Edinburgh, who bears the honored name of Chambers, records his having talked to such men.

What a hell, too, was that described to Lord Ashley's Commission of 1842. In the mines were women and children employed as beasts; dragging trucks on all fours, pursuing in fetid tunnels the degraded tasks which no animal could be found to undertake. We know that equal horrors existed in the brickfields two or three years ago, where there were 30,000 children employed, looking like moving masses of the clay they bore, whose ages averaged from three and one-half years to seventeen; and when an average case was thus described:

" I had a child weighed very recently, and though he was somewhat over eight years old he weighed but 52½ pounds, and was employed carrying 43 pounds of clay on his head an average distance of 15 miles daily, and worked 73 hours a week.   This is only an average case of what many poor children are doing in England at the present time ; and we need not wonder at their stunted and haggard appearance when we take into account the tender age at which they are sent to their Egyptian tasks."

Then again:

"All goodness and purity seems to become stamped out of these people; and were I to relate [says a witness who has worked himself in the brickfields] what could be related, the whole country would become sickened and horrified."

It would not indeed be difficult, and it would be painfully instructive, to draw out a dismal catalogue of facts to prove how little the splendor of our civilization differs from the worst horrors of barbarism.

And yet, after all, we can only come to the hackneyed conclusion that the sole remedy for this state of things is education, a humanizing education.   It is not a particularly brilliant or original thing to say, but severe truth is seldom brilliant and original.   There is a noble passage in De Tocqueville, known probably to all and too long to quote here, which points out that knowledge is the arm of democracy; that every intellectual discovery, every development of science, is a new source of strength to the people; that thought and eloquence and imagination, the divine gifts which know no limit of class, even when bestowed on the enemies of the popular cause, yet serve it by exalting the natural grandeur of man; and that literature is the vast armory, open to all indeed, but where the poor, who have hardly any other, may always find their weapons.   These, I say, are features of education which all recognize, though some may profess to dread them.

But there is a general expediency besides.   Take the case
of machinery.   The winter nights of 1830 were bright with
blazing rick-yards.   No farmer in the southern counties felt
his stacks safe.   There was a time of terror in England, and
of retribution.

"In Kent," says Miss Martineau, "there were gibbets
erected in Penenden Heath, and bodies swung there in the
December winds, bodies of boys about eighteen or nineteen
years old, but looking much younger; brothers who had said
to each other on arriving at the gallows, 'That looks an
awful thing!'"

Again, take the Luddite riots of 1812 and 1816, where
cunning and furious mobs nearly stamped out lace manufacture at Nottingham.   The broken frames and the burning
ricks were ignorant protests against machinery.   Well, intelligence has marched a little, and what is the case now?
What do the associated masters—no unduly partial authority
—affirm?   The accuracy of this statement is manifest from
the fact that the operatives are now the earnest advocates for
improvements in machinery; whereas twenty years ago it was
no uncommon thing for them to strike at the factory where
they were introduced.   Here, it seems to me, we can put our
finger on definite and tangible progress, due solely to increased intelligence.

Take another case which shows the need of it.   Wages
were probably never so high in England as in 1873.   Nine
years before, an increasing spirit duty paid £9,692,515 to the
Excise.   In the last financial year the Excise receipts from
spirits amounted to £14,639,562.

I am not one of those who are appalled, certainly not surprised, by this expenditure.   But see how it strengthens the
argument.   A man who has but natural instincts to guide

him comes into a fortune, and at once procures himself an increased quantity of what has been in smaller doses an enjoyment and a solace. Has he been educated to find his amusement elsewhere? If one of us should succeed to a large fortune to-morrow, we certainly should not spend our inheritance in drink; but the difference, I venture to say, is solely one of culture.

Well, my contention is that in an educated country, among a nation educated not in Shakespeare and the musical glasses, but so instructed as to be able to find amusement outside the skittle-alley and the public-house, a great increase in wages would not have been followed by so enormous an increase in the consumption of spirits; and an enormous consumption of spirits means an enormous amount of crime and pauperism. . . .

I now come to a large division of the subject where we may thankfully remember that much has been effected during the last session of Parliament.

We have considered some of the means, at any rate, of ameliorating, morally and physically, the great mass of the nation; and as we have discussed how, by education, we can ensure the progressive march of intellect among rising and future generations, so it will not be out of place if I dwell here for a moment on another question which relates to the physical preservation and improvement of our race.

We all know to a certain extent the history of factory legislation, how the sacred tradition of the great work was handed down by the first Sir Robert Peel, whose claims to national gratitude have been so beautifully obscured by the greater claims of his illustrious son: to Oastler and Vadler, and Hobhouse and Ashley, and Mundella. In the last session of Parliament the main principles of Mr. Mundella's

Factory Bill, embodied in a government measure, passed through both Houses, so that the hours of labor for women and children are now limited to fifty-six and a half in a week.

But although much has been effected, it may be regarded as serious that so keen and independent a thinker as Mr. Fawcett should have offered determined resistance to the bill. But his argument was founded on the assumption that those whom the bill is taking care of are well able to take care of themselves, which is at least a doubtful proposition; and that legislative interference, to be logical, should be complete, and should extend even to women employed in domestic service.

But no one would deny that if great injury to women were to be apprehended as an effect of domestic service,—that if, for example, every master was a Legree and every mistress a Brownrigg,—the legislature would have to interfere for the protection of maids. Nothing of the sort is, however, pretended.

Now we have evidence, and very complete evidence, that injury is done to women, and not merely to women but to their descendants, by their undue employment in factories. Parliament must in consequence determine what limitation must be placed on factory labor, not merely for the protection of weak women now, but in its own imperial interests for the preservation of health in the children of these women— the future citizens of the country.

Nor is it certain that Mr. Fawcett's other assumption, that the classes affected are well able to take care of themselves, is in any degree correct. It is certain that women, from love of approbation, as well as from those feelings of unselfishness which do honor to them as wives, are only too easily led to work beyond their powers. . . .

The conditions of life in this country are rapidly reversing themselves. Wealth is doubling itself and increasing the population; greater care in management and subtlety in mechanical appliances are diminishing, and must further diminish, the proportion of persons employed, especially in agriculture. Here is the problem: daily a greater population, daily in all probability less work, which means less subsistence.

We are shut up by a sea with our surging myriads,—a source of strength if guided and controlled; if not, an immeasurable volcanic power. Many of them must go forth to people the world. Our race has colonized and colonizes, has influenced and influences; and in future ages seems likely further to colonize and influence a great part of the habitable globe.

So great has been our field of influence that we can only view it with awe. It has been, and is, a great destiny for this country to sway so mightily the destinies of the universe. But the great privilege involves a sacred trust. We must look to it that the fertile race we send forth to the waste places of the earth is a race physically, morally, and intellectually equal to its high duties.

At present we will not compel our children to be educated, however rudely; at present, in one of our cities nearly a quarter of the infants born die before they are one year old. In one of your sections you propose to discuss, " What are the best means of drawing together the interests of the United Kingdom, India, and the Colonies?" I submit that the primary means are to send forth colonists who may be worthy the country they leave and the destiny they seek.

The different agencies I have noticed to-night all tend to this: Whether we keep them in England or they pass from

us, we must look to the nurture of this race of kings. We
annually distribute through the world a population nearly as
large as that of Birmingham. In the last two years more
emigrants have left our shores than there are inhabitants in
Glasgow and Dundee put together. After all, whatever our
commerce or political influence may be, this is the most gigantic enterprise in which this or any other nation can be
engaged; and the responsibility for its success, not merely
for the present, but for countless future generations, lies
with us.

Will this great stream pass from us a turbid flood, composed of emigrants like some we now send forth, who shake
the dust from their feet and swear undying enmity to us; or
shall it be a broad and beneficent river of life, fertilizing as
the Nile, beloved as the Ganges, sacred as the Jordan, separated from us indeed by the ocean, but, like that fabled fountain, Arethusa, which, passing under the sea from Greece
into Sicily, retained its original source in Arcadia?

We do not know what our fate may be. We have no
right, perhaps, to hope that we may be an exception to the
rule by which nations have their period of growth, and of
grandeur, and of decay. It may be that all we most esteem
may fade away like the glories of Babylon. But if we have
done our duty well, even though our history should pass
away, and our country become—

> ——" an island salt and bare,
> The haunt of seals, and orcs, and seamews' clang,"

—she may be remembered, not ungratefully, as the mother
of great commonwealths and peaceful empires that shall perpetuate the best qualities of the race.

I have only mentioned one of the topics with which a
Social Science Congress is called upon to deal; yet how vast

this single subject appears! Indeed, it is difficult to see any limit to the possible usefulness of a meeting like the present.

We live in remarkable times—times of social development so ominous that we may be approaching a period of social revolution. What a change from that old world whence this fertile brood of nations sprang! On the one side, a dark surging mass of barbarians; on the other, the inevitable, stern immobility of the Roman Empire.

Now the whole universe seems undergoing the volcanic influence of social theory. Everywhere there is breaking out some strange manifestation. The grotesque congregation of the Shakers, the agricultural socialism of Harris, the polygamous socialism of Mormon, the lewd quackery of Free Love, the mad, blank misery of Nihilism, the tragic frenzy of the Parisian Commune, are portents no observer can neglect.

Some try to solve the problem by abolishing property; some by a new religion. Most of these experiments thrive in America, which alone has room for such diversities of opinion and practice. It is too much the practice to treat these various organizations as a mixture of knavery and folly. Two, indeed, of these phases of humanity will receive more attention from the historian of the future than they attract from their contemporaries,—I mean the Commune of Paris, and the Church of the Latter-Day Saints. That eccentric church is a socialism founded on a polygamous religion and ruled by a supreme pontiff. But it would be a mistake, I think, to suppose that polygamy is an essential part of Mormonism. The traveller in Utah will be struck most, not by the plurality of wives, but by the prevailing industry and apparent external brotherhood. These are the outward features of an extraordinary community.

That it should largely increase; that it should have converted a desert into a garden; that it should, in the last few
years, have attracted to it thousands of the working classes
(not by polygamy, for that is expensive, and almost all the
emigrants are poor), will seem, to a future age, a strange sign
of our times.

Again, whatever may be thought of the Commune of Paris,
which issued quaintly ingenuous decrees, and which ended in
blood and iron, it will always remain one of the sinister facts
of our age.   Like the Ninevite king, it perished in a blazing
pyre of what was fairest in its habitation; and the world lost
so much in those flames that it cannot now pass judgment
with complete impartiality.

But as a gigantic outbreak of class hostility, as a desperate
attempt to found a new society in the very temple of the old,
it has hardly, perhaps, received sufficient attention.   Far be
it from me to attempt to palliate the horrors of that disastrous
conflict.   They are, however, only terrible accessories.   But
the ominous fact of that sudden social revolution is a portent
that cannot be blotted from the history of humanity.   While
human beings remain human beings, and while efforts like
these are made for complete social reorganization, a Social
Science Congress has even more scope than a Parliament. . . .

Never was a league of the friends of humanity more
needed than now.   Never was there, on all sides, so much of
energy and skill given to the preparation of those efforts by
which civilization is retarded and mankind made miserable.
The armies of the four great military Powers, when on a
war footing, engross three and a quarter millions of men in
the prime and flower of life.   Three and a quarter millions
of men in four countries with their swords ready to the grind-

stone form a portentous, silent fact which we cannot ignore
in the halls where we discuss the efficacy of arbitration in
settling disputes between nations.

In Spain we see a war of dynasty; in America a conflict
of color. The night is dark and troubled; we can but labor
steadfastly, hoping for the dawn, united by the sympathy of
the living and animated by the example of the dead.

THE LORDS' VETO

DELIVERED IN ST. GEORGE'S HALL, BRADFORD, ENGLAND, OCTOBER 27, 1894

I PROPOSE to speak about the House of Lords to-night.
But if I do not do so with all the passion, and with all
the fervour, and with all the power of invective which
orators in a less responsible situation might be able to indulge in—to your unbounded delight and their own—you
must put it down not so much to my want of zeal in the
cause as to the fact that I should be wanting in my duty as
a Minister if I approach the greatest constitutional question
that has arisen in England for two centuries or more without a solemn sense of the responsibility of my words. Now,
gentlemen, this question of the House of Lords is not a new
question. It is over a hundred years since Mr. Pitt declared
that it was the part of the Constitution which would first
give way. It is just under a hundred years since Mr. Burke
said:—"Fuerunt. There is an end of that part of the Constitution." But for ninety-nine years the House of Lords has
continued to exist, and, if you will pardon me one word of
egotism, I will say all through my political life it is the question to which I have attached the most importance. On two
occasions I have brought it before the notice of the House

of Lords themselves, and on neither occasion have I spared or minced my language. And some five years ago, when at a great Liberal conference in Scotland, they spread out their plan of operations, and the number of objects with which they proposed to deal, I told them that their programme was a foolish programme, for it omitted the one question which took the first place in the realization of all their pro-. jects, and that was a drastic dealing with the House of Lords. Well when I have said these things, all my sagacious friends have said, "Why do you tilt at this windmill? Why don't you take up practical subjects? That question will settle itself." But that question will not settle itself. It cannot settle itself, and, if you do not take care, it will wreck many Liberal measures and many Liberal Governments before you have done with it. I will tell you why. When Liberal Governments come back to the country to give an account of their stewardship, they do so too often with many promises unfulfilled against their will owing to the action of the House of Lords. But the country does not nicely scrutinize the reason for that emptiness. They blame the Liberal Ministry and the Liberal majority.

Well, now, gentlemen, is this the moment at which to deal with the House of Lords? I think it is. And I think I could show you on the testimony of our opponents, that no more fitting time could be found. I know well the ad-vantage that the Lords have in representing an English ma-jority against Irish Home Rule. I know that, linked to that majority, they occupy a stronger position in many ways than they have for some years past. Nor will I on this oc-casion exaggerate the importance of the Leeds Conference, great as it was; but I will say this, that if it is a time of calm-ness and apathy in regard to the House of Lords, as our opponents say, that is precisely the reason for dealing with it now; because great constitutional questions should not be dealt with at moments of passion and revolution. They should be dealt with by the calm and unbiased reason of the people of the country. Well, what has been the course of history on this question? There have been paroxysms of passion against the House of Lords, followed by intervals of reaction or calm. When the nation has been thwarted on some great question in which it took an interest, and it has flamed into a fury, the House of Lords has given way. The nation then has relapsed, and has given the House of Lords a new lease of life; and these periods of passion and reaction have been so sudden that they have not given any time, perhaps so favourable as the present, for showing to our opponents an earnest intention of dealing with this question. And what is more unfortunate, perhaps, about these sudden paroxysms against the House of Lords is this, that in England your passions against the House of Lords are selfish passions, you are stirred into a rage when the House of Lords defeats some bill that affects England and is dear to England, but you will not flame up when the House of Lords deals in the same way with Scotland, or Ireland, or Wales. In that way I might make an allusion—taking a metaphor from Roman history—to the powers exercised by the Praetorian Guards. You might say that by giving way to the English Praetorians the House of Lords buys the right to deal as it chooses with the more distant provinces of the Empire. And the misfortune of that is this—that it produces a feeling of neglect and of differential treatment as between England, on the one hand, and Scotland, Ireland, and Wales, on the other, which in itself is a great danger to, and dissolvent of your Empire. Well, then, gentlemen, I

contend that this is a favourable moment. This is, on the
Tory hypothesis, not a moment of passion. It is not a moment of reaction. If the Tories say this is a moment of
calmness and apathy with regard to the House of Lords, we
reply that is then a reason for dealing with the House of
Lords as a constitutional subject. But if, on the other
hand, there is, as we believe it to be, a feeling of deep, subdued but persistent resentment against the House of Lords,
it is equally a moment for dealing with it.

But, gentlemen, I shall be asked the question that Lord
Melbourne asked about every great political problem, "Why
not leave it alone?" After all, it may be said we have got
on with it for many centuries. We have prospered in spite
of it. There are worse things than it, such as our climate—
and if we can bear with our climate, is it worth while working ourselves up in a rage against the House of Lords?
Well, that might have been very well if things had remained
as they were. But while the House of Lords has remained
as it was, the circumstances have changed all round it. If
you pull down a street and rebuild it all with the exception
of one house, you will probably find in the course of a year
that the house will be condemned as a dangerous structure.
On three separate occasions you have in the last sixty years,
popularised the House of Commons. In 1832 you passed
the first great Reform Bill. The House of Lords resisted
it to the point of death. Had it resisted a little more, you
would have had no question of the House of Lords to deal
with now. Well, that changed the balance of the constitution, because not merely did it make the House of Commons
in itself infinitely more powerful and infinitely more representative, but it diminished the influence of the House of
Lords, which up to that time, through the medium of the

rotten boroughs, had directly controlled the majority of the House of Commons. Therefore the Reform Bill of 1832 was a nail, and a deep nail, in—I won't say the coffin—but in the future arrangements of the House of Lords. In 1867 you had another great democratic Reform Bill, which, I may note in passing, the House of Lords allowed to become law at once, because it was introduced by a Tory Government. And in 1884 you had another Reform Bill, which completed the measure of 1867 to a certain extent, which, as it was introduced by a Liberal Government, was fiercely resisted by the House of Lords, which opposition produced another great outburst of popular feeling, but which again ended by strengthening enormously the power of the House of Commons itself. And in 1886 another event took place, which still further weakened the House of Lords. For one peculiarity of the situation is this, that all these three strengthenings of the popular element in the House of Commons have been accompanied, strangely enough, by a diminution of the strength of the popular element in the House of Lords. Even up to the time of the last Reform Bill of 1884 there was some sort of balance between the two parties in the House of Lords. I even recollect, I believe, once in my life being in a majority in the House of Lords— but that could not have been on any vital question. But in 1886 the House of Lords changed its character for good or for evil. In 1886 the proposal of the Irish Home Rule Bill alienated the great remaining mass of the Whig or Liberal Peers, and from that time to this the House of Lords has represented no balance of parties whatever, but an over- whelming mass of Tories and so-called Liberal Unionists, with a handful of Liberals thrown in.

And so, gentlemen, we come to the present state of things.

What is that state of things? It is on the one side a House elected on almost the most popular possible basis, representing with freedom and directness the wishes of an aspiring and educated people, and on the other side a House almost entirely composed of hereditary Peers—and of hereditary Peers opposed to popular aspirations. That House so composed claims a right to control and to veto in all respects, except finance, the proposals of the House of Commons. See how it stands according to figures. The House of Commons consists of 670 members, of whom 350 or thereabouts support the Government—the Government of the day. The House of Lords consists of some 570 members, of whom about 30 support the Government of the day. Nor can there be any possible change in these conditions. No Liberal Government, however liberal or however little liberal it may be, can ever hope to possess much more than 5 per cent. of the whole House of Lords in its support, and any Tory Government would be disgraced if it possessed much less than the remaining 95 per cent. And you must remember that this House, which contains 5 per cent. of Liberals and 95 per cent. of another party, which I will not now define, rules Scotland, which sympathizes with the 5 per cent.; rules Wales, which sympathises with the 5 per cent.; rules Ireland, which sympathises with the 5 per cent.; and rules England, which, except on the question of Home Rule ,does, I believe, in fact and in general practice sympathise with the 5 per cent. also. Now, gentlemen, suppose at the next election you were to send back only 100 Liberals to the House of Commons. There would be 30 Liberal Peers. Suppose you were to send 200 Liberals back to the House of Commons. There would be 30 Liberal Peers. Suppose you were to send back 300 Liberals to the House of Commons. There

would be 30 Liberal Peers. Suppose you were to send 500
Liberals back to the House of Commons. There would be
30 Liberal Peers. Suppose you sent 600 Liberals back—(A
Voice: "We'll do that.")—I am sure the gentleman would
do it if he could, but still then, even if he succeeded, there
would be only 30 Liberal Peers. Gentlemen, what a mockery is this!

We boast of our free institutions. We swell as we walk
abroad and see other countries—we make broad the phylac-
teries of freedom on our foreheads. We thank God that we
are not as other less favoured men; and all the time we endure the mockery of this freedom. You are bound hand and
foot. You may vote and vote until you are black in the
face. It will not change the face of matters at all. The
House of Lords still will control at its will the measures of
your representatives. You will have to go hat in hand to
the House of Lords, and ask them to pass your measures in
however mutilated a shape. It has practically come to this.
We know the House of Lords is a party body of one com-
plexion. We cannot any longer introduce the bills we think
fit unless we want to waste the time of the House of Commons in an absolutely bootless and fruitless process, or else
we can only introduce bills which we may think will have
some possible chance of passing the Tory party in the House
of Lords. Now, of course, you may think that it is some
pique, and blighted and mortified ambition at not leading a
majority in the House of Lords that induces me to take so
gloomy a view of that body. But I think I could show you
by a very simple illustration that it is a grave constitutional
question, which does not depend merely on the party to
which you belong. Suppose we were to reverse the case, and
suppose the House of Lords were to consist permanently of

520 Liberals and some 30 or 40 Conservatives. Don't you think, then, that the Conservatives would find that there was a great constitutional question involved? How long do you think the Conservative party would stand up for the House of Lords as an essential part of the Constitution if it found out that it only carried its measures through Parliament on the sufferance of a permanent Liberal majority against them?

I confess quite freely that I am a Second Chamber man in principle. I am all for a Second Chamber. I am not for the uncontrolled government of a single Chamber any more than I am for the uncontrolled government of a single man. the temptation of absolute power is too great for any man or any body of men, and I believe—though I am speaking from recollection—that so keen and ardent a Radical as John Stuart Mill held that opinion, too. I am also strongly, of opinion that all experience points to having a Second Chamber of some sort. That, however, does not imply an admiration for the House of Lords. The American constitution-makers, who made the constitution under the inspiration of their fresh breath of freedom and independence, created a much stronger Second Chamber than we shall ever see in this country, and what is more, the feeling of the country on the whole coincides with my principle in that respect. There may be differences of opinion on that point, and I am aware there are; but I am bound to tell you what is my conviction. I should not be worthy of your confidence if I did not. But I am bound to say that if I am asked to choose between no Second Chamber at all and a Second Chamber constituted as the House of Lords is—I will not make my choice before this assembly—but I will say that there is ground for hesitation with regard to my principle. The fact is that to my mind it is an absolute danger, an invitation to revolution, that there should be an assembly of this kind in this position; and therefore it is as a lover of the Constitution as well as a lover of freedom that I implore you to take this question into your immediate consideration. If I hesitate between no Second Chamber and the House of Lords—between my dislike for a single Chamber and the doubt as to whether the House of Lords is better than none—it is for this reason, that, in my judgment, the House of Lords is not a Second Chamber at all. I will not say it is a Tory caucus, because that might be considered an offensive expression, and, moreover, a caucus is a temporary body. But I will say this, that it is a permanent party organisation, controlled for party purposes and by party managers.

I remember Lord Salisbury's defence of the House of Lords in 1888. It was a very ingenious defence, and tickled my fancy immensely; for, admitting that the House of Lords were not always wise or experienced, he said there seemed to him to be a considerable advantage in having a House composed of persons not particularly versed in political affairs, who brought a fresh, and innocent, and unbiased judgment to the consideration of the topics presented to their notice. And I confess I think that there is something rather attractive in that idea. But you must remember, gentlemen, these innocent political sheep require a shepherd, and Lord Salisbury is that shepherd; and when he commends them for this very process of innocence and readiness to accept conviction, we know whose conviction it is that they are ready to accept. And when they are so led, and when they are so guided, it very little matters to those who wish for Liberal measures to pass whether they are as innocent and

unbiased as Lord Salisbury represents, or whether they are
a collection of political hacks.

To show how little of a Second Chamber is the House of
Lords, I will recall to you Lord Salisbury's speeches before
the election of 1892, in which, if I am not mistaken, he appealed more than once to the almost certainty of the House
of Lords reversing any verdict that might be returned by the
people in favour of Home Rule. Well that could not be said
of any unbiased or proper Second Chamber, and I think we
may say, without dispute, that on that occasion the Tory
leader recognised that he had the House of Lords in his
pocket. I will give you another testimony of the same kind.
You all know Mr. Chamberlain. There was a time when
Mr. Chamberlain was a strong Liberal, and in those days
there were no words too corrosive, too bitter, and too con-
temptuous for him to address to the Second Chamber. But
the other day, having become closely allied—to put it no
further—with another political party, he described the
House of Lords as an institution that might no doubt be re-
formed, but certainly as one on which he places considerable value. Surely that illustrates clearly enough the party
aspect and quality of the House of Lords. Of course, the
Senate of the United States, which is, perhaps, the first
Second Chamber in the world, is also guided by political feeling, but is guided first by one party and then by another. It
is constantly refreshed by contact with election; but the
House of Lords is stereotyped—fixed—and as I have already
pointed out to you, no change whatever in the opinion of the
country can affect its composition. Even if there is a change
in the House of Lords, it is all in one direction.

Now and then a Liberal peer leaves us with a great flourish of trumpets, and the daily papers of the Unionist per-

suasion, and the weekly papers of the same kind, devote articles of so much agonising interest to this important defection that you would think another Cardinal Newman had left the English Church. Indeed, the other day one of these left us, and issued the usual encyclical giving his motives for leaving and his advice. His encyclical, in the words of my friend the chairman, urbi et orbi, advised the world in general; and his advice to the Government was that, as he could not follow them, they had better retire into obscurity. Why, surely that is a strange piece of advice—because he cannot follow us to invite us to join him.

Now, then, gentlemen, I say this—I will not go further into the different attributes of the House of Lords—you know them well enough, and I cannot go into them at great length to-night—I say that this is a great national question, and a great national danger. If the other party, which professes to have a monopoly of statesmanship had had any statesmanship at all, they would have settled it long ago by bringing the House of Lords into some sort of relation to the feelings of the people. But they have preferred to keep it, like a sort of Tory Old Guard, to bring up when the necessities of the case required. But an Old Guard is a dangerous weapon, because when you have brought up your last reserve all goes with it. Napoleon had an Old Guard, and he brought it up at Waterloo, and when the Old Guard was done with, not merely the battle was done with, but Napoleon and all concerned with him. But we are told the Peers never definitely resist the will of the people. I want to know how the wishes of the people can be better expressd than through the representatives of the people. Who gave the Peers the right or the instinct to decide as to what are, or are not, the wishes of the people when these wishes are ex-

pressed through their elected representatives? I suppose
that this contention implies that the Peers give their assent
to any reform which is passed, as the Reform Bill of 1832
was passed, under the threat of an immediate revolution—
when Birmingham was arming, and Glasgow was arming,
and Bristol was in flames. Are we always to wait for demon-
strations of popular feeling of that kind? To assert this,
gentlemen, is to go far. It is laying down the proposition
that Liberal legislation is always to be carried by the menace
of revolution. Tory legislation is to descend like the blessed
rain from heaven. Ours is only to come in wind, and rain,
and snow, and vapour. Theirs is to be the fertilising over-
flow of the Nile. Ours is to come as a tornado or a hurri-
cane. Theirs is to be the benign effect, ours the catastrophe
and convulsion of Nature. So the result must be that if we
are never to be allowed to carry any measure without threat
of thunder and lightning, or evoking the fell spirits of the
storm to convince the Lords that the nation is in earnest,
then our legislation will always be troublous and unpeaceful,
and the only way to get legislation quietly passed is to con-
fide it to the Tory and Unionist party. I only allude to this
to show what the real danger is of the House of Lords from
a constitutional point of view. It invites unrest; it invites
agitation; and in certain cases the cup may boil over; and it
might invite revolution. And I repeat this is a great national question, and it is a great national danger. It is a
great question, not merely from its enormous importance,
but from the difficulty of dealing with it.

Now, the difficulty of dealing with it is this—first, that
there is a great constitutional issue involved; and secondly,
that the method of dealing with that constitutional issue is
extremely complex and difficult. As to the issue, it is tre-

mendous. If I knew any stronger word by which I could describe it, I would use that stronger word. It is the greatest issue that has been put to this country since your fathers resisted the tyranny of Charles I. and of James II. You had a great measure passed in 1832, but that was a much less measure than this, because you were only enlarging constituencies already existing. But now you have to deal with a question of the revision of the entire constitution. You have to deal with two out of the three estates of the realm. You have to deal with a council which has survived many centuries and many storms, and which has existed up till now partly from the disinclination of the English people to constitutional change, and partly also owing perhaps to the personal popularity and ability of some of its members. You will have against you all those causes which see in the House of Lords their strongest bulwark and their last rampart. All those who are opposed to any form of Irish Home Rule will be amongst the most stalwart defenders of the House of Lords. All those who think that churches are benefited by establishment will be found to have their citadel in the House of Lords. Those who are supporters of the liquor interest will be found behind the fortifications of the House of Lords. In fact, some of the princes of that interest will be found seated on its benches.

But I take another question. There is a question which interests everybody here. It is a question of registration. We have great difficulties to contend with in regard to registration, and we have great difficulties to contend with in regard to labour representation. Well, I believe if you could put the expenses of elections upon the public funds, local or imperial, and if you could have a second ballot, so as to control the application of that expenditure, you would have

largely got rid of the allegation of undue or unworthy representation, which is at the bottom of our labour difficulty.
But what chance have you got of inducing the House of
Lords to pass a measure like that? And, therefore, I say
that it is those who wish for that reform who will find, in
the crusade against the House of Lords, their principal enemies in its defenders. Why, gentlemen, do I recapitulate all
this? It is to impress upon you that you are entering upon
a great campaign; that if your give the seal of your consent
to an entrance upon that campaign, it will not be an affair
of rose water. You must be prepared to take off your waist-
coats—not merely your coats. You must be prepared to
gird up your loins; and if you once put your hands to the
plough, you must take a solemn resolution that you will not
look back. Now, to some great issues like this—to some
grievances—there is an obvious remedy.

The misfortune of this grievance and this issue is that the
remedy is not obvious within the limits of the constitution.
You can only deal with the House of Lords, with the powers
of the House of Lords, by a bill passed through both Houses.
Anything but that is, constitutionally speaking, a revolution—is overriding one of the Chambers of Parliament
against its own will, without legislation passed by its own
consent. Well, apply that principle—which is a principle
which unfortunately no one can controvert—apply that principle to the remedies offered for the constitution of the
House of Lords. In the first place, no such bill as a bill
for the abolition of the House of Lords, or the limitation of
the veto of the House of Lords, which are the two remedies
suggested, would ever pass the House of Lords. Unless you
overawe the House of Lords, or make it perfectly clear that
the country is determined that its requirements shall take

effect, no such bill can ever be made to pass the House of
Lords. Well, of course, you may get the House of Lords to
surrender, as you get a fortress to surrender—by making it
clear that it is encompassed and besieged without hope of
deliverance. But that itself is not an easy task with the garrison that, as I have described, is sure to defend it. We now
come to a question which seems a much simpler one, that of
the abolition of the veto of the House of Lords. Now, abolition of the veto is greeted with great applause, and I should
not be disposed to withhold my applause, but that, unfortunately, as a direct plan the abolition of the veto by a bill
is a subject of the same difficulties as a bill for the abolition.
You cannot get the House of Lords to pass a bill for the
abolition of their veto, because they would say there was
no use then in there being a House of Lords at all. But
there is this further difficulty.

What do you mean by the Veto? Do you mean that the
House of Lords is to be obliged under certain circumstances
to pass the second reading and the third reading of a bill
sent up by the House of Commons? Do you allow it, in
fact, any power of revision in Committee? If you allow it
any power of dealing with a bill of the House of Commons
in Committee, your abolition of the veto would be absolutely fruitless. The House of Lords could give a bill a
second reading. It could knock the bottom out of a bill in
Committee; and it could send it back for third reading, saying, "We have not exercised our veto. Here is your bill."
Look at the Employers' Liability Bill. The House of Lords
read it a second and a third time. It introduced however
one apparently small amendment in Committee, and yet
when the bill came back from the House of Lords it stank in
the nostrils of the House of Commons. Well, then I sup-

pose the abolition of the veto means the abolition of revision
in Committee; because the one without the other would be
fruitless and useless. But if you abolish the veto, and abolish the power of dealing in Committee—if you abolish the
power of dealing with a bill on the second or third reading,
or in Committee—what is the use of the House of Lords
at all? You would simply keep it as a high court of justice,
or a sort of State prison for a number of able and eminent
men. It is, moreover, perfectly clear that the House of
Lords would infinitely prefer total abolition to an abolition
of the veto such as I have described, because by abolition
they would be able to enter the House of Commons, and
many of them would be rather formidable candidates. By
abolition of the veto you would simply keep them in a state
of suspended animation, if, indeed, you could call it a state
of animation at all; and in order to induce them to put
themselves into this unpleasant condition of suspended existence, you would have to use means as violent as you
would have to employ in order to procure their abolition.

Well, gentlemen, after this discussion—of course, brief
and imperfect, but still not wholly inadequate—of the
methods of pure abolition and the abolition of veto, you
come to find yourselves face to face once more with the
salient facts of the situation, which is, that you can only
deal with the House of Lords by bill or by revolution. There
is no third way at all. That seems to be a discouraging
result to arrive at. But I would not have you lose heart
so quickly. It will not come to a revolution in the case of
the House of Lords. There are means of making the will
of the country felt without any violence or unconstitutional
methods such as I have described. In this country, whatever the difficulty may be, the good sense of the constituent

body is such that we usually arrive at an agreement without
any of the cataclysms that rend other countries. But I do
wish you to realise precisely in your minds what is the constitutional aspect of the case—firstly, in order that you may
realise the enormous difficulty of the task that you are ready
to approach; and secondly, for another reason that I will
proceed to set forth. Gentlemen, it would be foolish for
me to disguise the fact that some of our candid friends have
been somewhat disappointed with the tardiness of the Government in taking action against the House of Lords. They
have said, "Why, there was a conference at Leeds. It
passed resolutions for the abolition of the veto. We sent
them up to London, and we expected that the veto of the
House of Lords would be ended in about a fortnight. Bless
me, there is something wrong here." We seem to hear
from the different organs of disappointed opinion, "The
Government must be lukewarm. There must be something
wrong." Well, gentlemen, I know that the Government
are responsible for everything—responsible for cholera, for
the crops, for the weather, and for anything else that happens to go wrong. But I think you will admit that, in this
particular case, it was not one in which we could move, under
all the circumstances of the case, in any violent hurry.

I think also that those political philosophers seemed to
imagine that some of the Government, from being Peers,
were rather too much attached to the House of which they
were members. Now, I am attached to individuals of the
House of Lords, as I am attached to individuals in the House
of Commons; but I confess that I should be either below or
above human nature if I were attached to the House of
Lords as a body. If you think it an agreeable thing for the
head of a Government which has a majority in the House

of Commons to sit on a bench in the other House with half-a-dozen empty benches behind him and nothing else—(A voice, "Fill them up.") I see the gentleman has aspirations toward the peerage himself. But I should want to know more about him before I took any step in that direction, because peers are apt to change their opinions when once they get their peerage. Well, gentlemen, if you think that is an agreeable position, you may be able to believe that I am attached to the House of Lords. If you think it is an agreeable position, with a House of Commons majority behind your back, to come as a suppliant to the House of Lords for every bill you want passed, then you may believe that I am attached to the House of Lords. If you think it is agreeable to hear the sounds of conflict in the only place that really possesses political power, and to be shut up in a sort of gilded dungeon with your bitterest political enemies, you may believe that I am attached to the House of Lords. Gentlemen, I confess that I feel no ground in my conscience for any such impeachment, and if you still have any lurking distrust of my wish to deal with the House of Lords in a drastic manner, I will at once remind you— I will at once forbid any wrong or indecent inference from the proverb I am going to parody—that it may not sometimes be a bad thing to set a peer to catch a peer.

Well, gentlemen, I fully acknowledge the responsibility that lay upon the Government. It was because that responsibility was so grave that we have been silent. I fully acknowledge the importance to be attached to the Leeds conference. I acknowledge the sincerity and earnestness with which its proceedings were conducted. But one swallow does not make a summer, and one conference in itself does not make the overwhelming mass of public opinion

which alone will enable you to deal effectively with the
House of Lords. At any rate, it was not sufficient to justify
action in the last days of the last session. I would ask you
to remember two vital questions in connection with the present attitude of the Government to the House of Lords. In
the first place, at the last general election, you gave the
Government no mandate to deal with the House of Lords;
and in the second place, even if you had, you did not give
the Government a sufficient majority to deal with it. Therefore, gentlemen, in my opinion, we should not merely have
been guilty of levity and want of forethought—we should
have been culpable and criminal if, without a mandate and
without sufficient majority, we had risked all the measures
—and there were many of them, on the acknowledgement
of Mr. Chamberlain himself—in which you and I set store,
in order to cast them into a seething whirlpool of constitutional agitation. As leaders of the Liberal Party, we should,
in my opinion, have merited, if we had followed any such
course, not your applause and confidence, but your severest
censure and severest condemnation. No, gentlemen, if you
are going to proceed and to enter upon this great campaign,
you must walk boldly but must walk warily. You will have
to work with perseverance. You must not expect the most
prompt and immediate results. You will not carry the
House of Lords by storm or by rush. You will rather have
to imitate that great captain, the Duke of Wellington, at
Torres Vedras, who carefully entrenched his position before
he made his effective and fatal attack. I confess, therefore,
that I feel "my withers unwrung" by any censure as to our
tardiness.

I know well that before we deal with this, the greatest of
constitutional questions, if we wish to deal with it success-

fully, we must bring into play the greatest constitutional force we possess. What is that greatest constitutional force? In the first place it is the House of Commons. No lesser force than the House of Commons can confront the House of Lords. No lesser force than the House of Commons is competent to insist upon the position and privileges of the House of Commons. No lesser body than the House of Commons is able to lay down, in clear and unmistakable terms, that shifting in the balance of the Constitution, which has been produced by the great Reform Bills of 1832, 1867, and 1884. Well, it is quite clear that our first step, if we propose to deal with the House of Lords—and we do propose to deal with the House of Lords—is to bring the House of Commons into play.

And how are we to bring the House of Commons into action? The House of Commons, in my opinion, after a long consideration of this most difficult of subjects, can only proceed in the first place—as it has always proceeded in its contests with the House of Lords—by resolution. In regard to the powers of the House of Lords over finance, they were restricted once, twice, and thrice by resolutions of the House of Commons. As regard the powers of the House of Lords to interfere in elections to the House of Commons, those have been equally restricted by resolutions of the House of Commons. But the great resolution which I suppose we should have in our minds, in framing a resolution which will assert the privileges of the House of Commons as against the irresponsible control of the House of Lords, the resolution of 1678—as I think it is—which asserts the free and uncontrolled right of the House of Commons to represent the people in matters of finance—and I suppose—of course I do not pledge myself at this moment to the exact form of the resolution—but I take it that that resolution would declare in clear and unmistakable terms what I have once before said, in a phrase which I have often heard since, that the House of Commons, in the partnership with the House of Lords, is unmistakably the predominant partner.

I hear you say—"But the House of Commons has passed such resolutions before." That no doubt is true; I think indeed that there was some little resolution of that kind passed this year. But there will be one vital and essential and pervading difference between such a resolution as I suggest and any resolution that has been passed before. This resolution will be passed at the instance and on the responsibility of the Government itself. It will be the duty of the Government to move the House of Commons to pass such a resolution; and I cannot doubt, in the temper of the House of Commons, that it will do so. It will be the duty of the Government to move the House of Commons to pass such a resolution, and if it be passed, remember this—that never before in the history of Parliament has such a resolution at the instance of the responsible Government been passed in the House of Commons against the House of Lords. What will that represent? It will represent the joint demand of the Executive Government of the day and of the House of Commons for a revision of the Constitution; and in that way the question will enter in itself on a new phase. The resolution will stand forever upon the journals of the House. No Government, however bold or cynical it may be, that may eventually succeed ourselves will be bold enough or cynical enough to propose its reversion. Not all the perfumes of Araby itself will wash that resolution out of the books of the House of Commons. Even if the verdict of the country should go against us on that resolution, I believe no leader of the House of Commons would be daring enough to propose its reversal.

But the verdict of the country will not be against us. I feel as sure of the country as I do of the House of Commons. Neither the House of Commons nor the country would stultify themselves by sending up a majority to reverse any such resolution as that; and therefore I may consider that if such a resolution be passed, it will stand, perhaps not as a law of the Medes and Persians, but as substantially as the resolution of 1678, to which I have alluded. The resolution in itself would be a new charter, or, as the Americans would say, a new constitutional amendment; and this would be the first act of a great drama of which, perhaps, we may have to see a third, fourth, and a fifth, as well as a second act. But, gentlemen, you may ask—"Will this be enough? The House of Lords may snap their fingers at your resolution. They may say, 'We have had resolutions of this kind before, and we do not care a fig for your resolutions.'" Well, I admit that, in my judgment, it will probably not be enough. Powerful as the House of Commons is, for such a purpose as this it must have a power greater than itself. That power can only be given, that strength can only be conferred, that inspiration which I have been derided for demanding can only be afforded by the people of Great Britain and Ireland. Nothing else will suffice for us. To that august tribunal we will appeal. We will ask it to give us strength and authority—a majority and a mandate—to deal with that question, and to go back with power to deal in your name with the question of constitutional revision.

The Government then will put this force in motion at the proper time. It will ask the House of Commons to pass

such a resolution as I have indicated; and at the proper
time it will endeavour to appeal to the country on such a
resolution. Why do I say at the proper time? Why don't
I say, "Do it at once?" Why don't I call Parliament together, and at once put a resolution before them, and at
once ask the Queen to grant the Ministry a dissolution upon
that resolution? Well, I think the members of the House
of Commons would answer the question without the slightest
difficulty. In the first place, the course of this Parliament
is not entirely run. We hope to pass some useful, if not
much useful, legislation before we end this Parliament. In
the second place, it would be rather hard to punish the House
of Commons for the faults of the House of Lords. This,
then, gentlemen, is the second act. The first act is the resolution. The second act is an appeal to the country to support that resolution. Beyond that I cannot go to-night.
For the will of the people is the final and supreme court of
appeal. It will be for the nation to decide between the
House of Lords and its own responsible representatives.
And therefore what we are, what we shall be, practically
asking you is this—for a popular reference, such as in other
countries is called the referendum—for a direct popular reference as to whether you desire a revision of the Constitution in this sense, or whether you do not.

We think, then, that the time has come, or has nearly
come, for a free popular reference, to ask the people of
Great Britain and Ireland to settle this question of the Constitution of this country once for all—not in reference
merely to tradition, but in reference also to accomplished
facts. And then will come your part. The Government
will have done its part, and it will then be your turn. If
you have come to the conviction that the House of Lords

understands your wishes better than do your own representatives, you will give effect by your verdict to that impression. You will annihilate your own representation and
abide contentedly by the unbiased, patriarchal mellow wisdom of the House of Lords. You will thank them for having done you the favour of having been born. It will be
unnecessary any further to go through the musty and super-
fluous process of popular election; for you will have beside
you a self-constituted body that will save you any trouble
of the kind.

But if, gentlemen, you take a different view—if for years
you have been champing and chafing under the bit of the
House of Lords—if for years you have been wondering at
this strange survival of an almost apparently antediluvian
period—if for years you have been instructing your representatives to do all that in them lies to maintain your rights
against their interference—why, then, you will give your
verdict in accordance with the facts, and you will make
ready for the fight. You will remember, as I have told you
before, that in this great contest there are behind you, to
inspire you, all the great reforms, all the great aspirations,
and all the great measures on which you have set your
hearts. Before you are encamped all the forces of prejudice and privilege. Before you frown the sullen ramparts,
behind which are concealed the enemies you long to fight,
and so long have fought. And I would ask you, if you are
prepared to go into this fight, to fight it as your old Puritan
forefathers fought—fight with their stubborn, persistent,
indomitable will—fight as those old Ironsides fought in
Yorkshire, never knowing when they were beaten—and determined not to be beaten. Fight, as they would have said
themselves, not with the arm of the flesh, but with the arm

of the spirit. Fight by educating your fellow men—not as to the object, for in that you are clear already, but as to the proper means of obtaining that object. And if you believe that we of the Government are in earnest in this matter, and capable of dealing in this matter, you will give us your support. We fling down the gauntlet. It is for you to back us up.

Vol. 14—7

SENATOR THURSTON

OHN MELLEN THURSTON, American politician and publicist, was born at Montpelier, Vt., Aug. 21, 1847, and removed with his parents to Madison, Wis., in 1854. His education was obtained at the public schools and at Wayland College, Wis., while he supported himself by farm work and other manual labor. After studying law he was admitted to the Bar in 1869, and in the same year took up his residence at Omaha, Neb. In 1872, he was elected to the Omaha city council, and in 1874 became city attorney. He was a member of the Nebraska legislature in 1875, and president of the Republican League of the United States, 1888–91. In 1877, he was appointed assistant attorney of the Union Pacific Railway Company, and in 1888 became general solicitor of the entire Union Pacific system, a position which he retained until 1895, when he was elected to the United States Senate.

CUBA MUST BE FREE

DELIVERED IN THE UNITED STATES SENATE, MARCH 24, 1898

M R. PRESIDENT,—I am here by command of silent lips to speak once and for all upon the Cuban situation. I trust that no one has expected anything sensational from me. God forbid that the bitterness of a personal loss should induce me to color in the slightest degree the statement that I feel it my duty to make. I shall endeavor to be honest, conservative, and just. I have no purpose to stir the public passion to any action not necessary and imperative to meet the duties and necessities of American responsibility, Christian humanity, and national honor. I would shirk this task if I could, but I dare not. I cannot satisfy my conscience except by speaking, and speaking now.

Some three weeks since, three Senators and two Representatives in Congress accepted the invitation of a great metropolitan newspaper to make a trip to Cuba and personally investigate and report upon the situation there.   Our invitation was from a newspaper whose political teachings I have never failed to antagonize and denounce, and whose journalism I have considered decidedly sensational.   But let me say, for the credit of the proprietor of the paper in question, that I believe the invitation exended to us was inspired by his patriotic desire to have the actual condition of affairs in Cuba brought to the attention of the American people in such a way that the facts would no longer remain in controversy or dispute.

We were not asked to become the representatives of the paper; no conditions or restrictions were imposed upon us; we were left free to conduct the investigation in our own way, make our own plans, pursue our own methods, take our own time, and decide for ourselves upon the best manner of laying the results of our labors before the American people. For myself I went to Cuba firmly believing that the condition of affairs there had been greatly exaggerated by the press, and my own efforts were directed in the first instance to the attempted exposure of these supposed exaggerations.

Mr. President, there has undoubtedly been much sensationalism in the journalism of the time, but as to the condition of affairs in Cuba there has been no exaggeration, because exaggeration has been impossible.   I have read the careful statement of the junior senator from Vermont [Mr. Proctor], and I find that he has anticipated me in almost every detail. From my own personal knowledge of the situation, I adopt every word of his concise, conservative, specific presentation as my own; nay, more, I am convinced that he has, in a measure, understated the facts.   I absolutely agree with him in the following conclusions:

After three years of warfare and the use of 225,000

Spanish troops, Spain has lost control of every foot of Cuba not surrounded by an actual intrenchment and protected by a fortified picket line.

She holds possession with her armies of the fortified seaboard towns, not because the insurgents could not capture many of them, but because they are under the virtual protection of Spanish warships, with which the revolutionists cannot cope.

The revolutionists are in absolute and almost peaceful possession of nearly one half of the island, including the eastern provinces of Santiago de Cuba and Puerto Principe. In those provinces they have an established form of government, levy and collect taxes, maintain armies, and generally levy a tax or tribute upon the principal plantations in the other provinces, and, as is commonly believed, upon the entire railway system of the island.

In the four so-called Spanish provinces there is neither cultivation nor railway operation except under strong Spanish military protection or by consent of the revolutionists in consideration of tribute paid.

Under the inhuman policy of Weyler not less than 400,000 self-supporting, simple, peaceable, defenceless country people were driven from their homes in the agricultural portions of the Spanish provinces to the cities and imprisoned upon the barren waste outside the residence portions of these cities and within the lines of intrenchment established a little way beyond. Their humble homes were burned, their fields laid waste, their implements of husbandry destroyed, their live stock and food supplies for the most part confiscated. Most of these people were old men, women, and children. They were thus placed in hopeless imprisonment, without shelter or food. There was no work for them in the cities to which they were driven. They were left there with nothing to depend upon except the scanty charity of the inhabitants of the cities and with slow starvation their inevitable fate.

It is conceded upon the best ascertainable authority, and those who have had access to the public records do not hesitate to state, that upward of 210,000 of these people have already perished, all from starvation or from diseases incident to starvation.

The government of Spain has never contributed one dollar to house, shelter, feed, or provide medical attention for these its own citizens. Such a spectacle exceeds the scenes of the Inferno as painted by Dante.

There has been no amelioration of the situation except through the charity of the people of the United States. There has been no diminution in the death rate among these reconcentrados except as the death supply is constantly diminished. There can be no relief and no hope except through the continued charity of the American people until peace shall be fully restored in the island and until a humane government shall return these people to their homes and provide for them anew the means with which to begin again the cultivation of the soil.

Spain cannot put an end to the existing condition. She cannot conquer the insurgents. She cannot re-establish her sovereignty over any considerable portion of the interior of the island. The revolutionists, while able to maintain themselves, cannot drive the Spanish army from the fortified sea-coast towns.

The situation, then, is not war as we understand it, but a chaos of devastation and depopulation of undefined duration, whose end no man can see.

I will cite but a few facts that came under my personal

observation, all tending to fully substantiate the absolute
truth of the foregoing propositions.   I could detail incidents
by the hour and by the day, but the senator from Vermont
has absolutely covered the case.   I have no desire to deal
in horrors.   If I had my way, I would shield the American
public even from the photographic reproductions of the awful
scenes that I viewed in all their original ghastliness.

Spain has sent to Cuba more than 225,000 soldiers to subdue the island, whose entire male population capable of bearing arms did not exceed at the beginning that number.
These soldiers were mostly boys, conscripts from the Spanish
hills.   They are well armed, but otherwise seem to be absolutely unprovided for.   They have been without tents and
practically without any of the necessary supplies and equipment for service in the field.   They have been put in bar-
racks, in warehouses, and old buildings in the cities where all
sanitary surroundings have been of the worst possible character.   They have seen but little discipline, and I could not
ascertain that such a thing as a drill had taken place in the
island.

There are less than 60,000 now available for duty.   The
balance are dead or sick in hospitals, or have been sent back
to Spain as incapacitated for further service.   It is currently
stated that there are now 37,000 sick in hospital.   I do not
believe that the entire Spanish army in Cuba could stand an
engagement in the open field against 20,000 well-disciplined
American soldiers.

As an instance of the discipline among them I cite the
fact that I bought the machete of a Spanish soldier on duty
at the wharf in Matanzas, on his offer, for $3 in Spanish
silver.   He also seemed desirious of selling me his only remaining arm, a revolver.

The Spanish soldiers have not been paid for some months, and in my judgment they, of all the people on the earth, will most gladly welcome any result which would permit them to return to their homes in Spain.

The pictures in the American newspapers of the starving reconcentrados are true. They can all be duplicated by the thousands. I never saw, and please God I may never again see, so deplorable a sight as the reconcentrados in the suburbs of Matanzas. I can never forget to my dying day the hope-less anguish in their despairing eyes. Huddled about their little bark huts, they raised no voice of appeal to us for alms as we went among them.

There was almost no begging by the reconcentrados them-selves. The streets of the cities are full of beggars of all ages and all conditions, but they are almost wholly of the residents of the cities and largely of the professional-beggar class. The reconcentrados—men, women, and children—stand silent, famishing with hunger. Their only appeal comes from their sad eyes, through which one looks as through an open window into their agonizing souls.

The present autonomist governor of Matanzas (who speaks excellent English) was inaugurated in November last. His records disclose that at the city of Matanzas there were 1,200 deaths in November, 1,200 in December, 700 in January, and 500 in February—3,600 in four months, and those four months under the administration of a governor whom I be-lieve to be a truly humane man. He stated to me that on the day of his inauguration, which I think was the 12th of last November, to his personal knowledge fifteen persons died in the public square in front of the executive mansion. Think of it, oh, my countrymen! Fifteen human beings dying from starvation in the public square, in the shade of the palm-trees, and amid the beautiful flowers, in sight of the open windows of the executive mansion!

The governor of Matanzas told us that for the most part the people of the city of Matanzas had done all they could for the reconcentrados; and after studying the situation over I believe his statement is true. He said the condition of affairs in the island had destroyed the trade, the commerce, and the business of the city; that most of the people who had the means assisted the reconcentrados with food just as long as they could, but he said to us that there were thousands of the people living in fine houses on marble floors who were in deep need themselves and who did not know from one day to the other where their food supply was coming from.

The ability of the people of Matanzas to aid is practically exhausted. The governor told us that he had expended all of his salary and all that he could possibly afford of his private means in relief work. He is willing that the reconcentrados shall repass the picket line and go back to seek work in the interior of the island. He expresses his willingness to give them passes for that purpose, but they are no longer physically able to take advantage of that offer. They have no homes to return to; their fields have grown up to weeds; they have no oxen, no implements of husbandry with which to begin anew the cultivation of the soil. Their only hope is to remain where they are, to live as long as they can on an insufficient charity, and then die. What is true at Matanzas is true at all the other cities where these reconcentrados have been gathered.

The government of Spain has not and will not appropriate one dollar to save these people. They are now being attended and nursed and administered to by the charity of the United States. Think of the spectacle! We are feeding these citizens of Spain; we are nursing their sick; we are saving such as can be saved, and yet there are those who still say it is right for us to send food, but we must keep hands off. I say that the time has come when muskets ought to go with the food.

We asked the governor if he knew of any relief for these people except through the charity of the United States. He did not.

We then asked him, " Can you see any end to this condition of affairs? " He could not.

We asked him, " When do you think the time will come that these people can be placed in a position of self-support? "

He replied to us, with deep feeling, " Only the good God or the great government of the United States can answer that question."

I hope and believe that the good God by the great government of the United States will answer that question.

I shall refer to these horrible things no further. They are there. God pity me; I have seen them; they will remain in my mind forever—and this is almost the twentieth century. Christ died nineteen hundred years ago, and Spain is a Christian nation. She has set up more crosses in more lands, beneath more skies, and under them has butchered more people than all the other nations of the earth combined.

Europe may tolerate her existence as long as the people of the Old World wish. God grant that before another Christmas morning the last vestige of Spanish tyranny and oppression will have vanished from the Western Hemisphere.

Mr. President, the distinguished senator from Vermont has seen all these things; he knows all these things; he has described all these things; but after describing them he says he has nothing to propose, no remedy to suggest. I have. I

am only an humble unit in the great government of the
United States, but I should feel myself a traitor did I remain
silent now.

I counselled silence and moderation from this floor when
the passion of the nation seemed at white heat over the destruction of the " Maine; " but it seems to me the time for
action has now come. Not action in the " Maine " case! I
hope and trust that this government will take action on the
Cuban situation entirely outside of the " Maine " case.
When the " Maine " report is received, if it be found that
our ship and sailors were blown up by some outside explosive,
we will have ample reparation without quibble or delay; and
if the explosion can be traced to Spanish official sources there
will be such swift and terrible punishment adjudged as will
remain a warning to the world forever.

What shall the United States do, Mr. President?

I am a Republican, and I turn to the last platform of my
party and I read:

" From the hour of achieving their own independence the
people of the United States have regarded with sympathy the
struggles of other American people to free themselves from
European domination. We watch with deep and abiding
interest the heroic battle of the Cuban patriots against cruelty
and oppression, and our best hopes go out for the full success
of their determined contest for liberty.

" The government of Spain having lost control of Cuba
and being unable to protect the property or lives of resident
American citizens, or to comply with its treaty obligations,
we believe that the government of the United States should
actively use its influence and good offices to restore peace and
give independence to the island."

Mr. President, when that declaration was read before the
St. Louis convention, over which I had the distinguished
honor to preside, it was greeted with a mighty shout which

seemed to lift the very roof of that great convention hall, and it was adopted as a part of the platform of the Republican party by unanimous vote. On the 29th day of June, 1896, William McKinley, standing upon his vine-clad porch at Canton, Ohio, in accepting the nomination then officially tendered him, said:

" The platform adopted by the Republican national convention has received my careful consideration and has my unqualified approval. It is a matter of gratification to me, as I am sure it must be to you and Republicans everywhere and to all our people, that the expressions of its declaration of principles are so direct, clear, and emphatic. They are too plain and positive to leave any chance for doubt or question as to their purport and meaning."

That platform of the Republican party, that indorsement by its nominee for President, was ratified by more than seven million American voters. That platform has marked my path of duty from the hour of its adoption up to the present time.

It is an honored boast of the Republican party that it always keeps its promises and that its platform declarations are always carried out by its administrations. I have no reason to doubt, I have every reason to believe, that the present Chief Magistrate of the United States still stands upon the platform of the Republican party. I have no reason to doubt, I have every reason to believe, that he will make its fulfilment a part of the glorious history of the world.

Mr. President, that platform was adopted almost two years ago. Has there been any such change in the Cuban situation as to relieve the Republican party from its obligations? None whatever. There has been no change except such as to strengthen the force of our platform assertion that Spain has lost control of the island. Twice within the last two years I

have voted for a resolution according the rights of belligerents
to the Cuban revolutionists.

I believed at those times, I still believe, that such a recognition on our part would have enabled the Cuban patriots to
have achieved independence for themselves; that it would
have given them such a standing in the money markets of the
world, such rights on the sea, such flag on the land, that ere
this the independence of Cuba would have been secured, and
that without cost or loss of blood or treasure to the people of
the United States.   But that time has passed; it is too late
to talk about resolutions according belligerent rights; and
mere resolutions recognizing the independence of the Cuban
republic would avail but little.   Our platform demands that
the United States shall actively use its influence for the independence of the island.

I am not here to criticize the present administration.   I
yield to no man living in my respect, my admiration for, and
my confidence in the judgment, the wisdom, the patriotism,
the Americanism of William McKinley.   When he entered
upon his administration he faced a difficult situation.   It was
his duty to proceed with care and caution.   At the first
available opportunity he addressed a note to Spain, in which
he gave that government notice, as set forth in his message
to the Congress of the United States, that the United States—

—" could be required to wait only a reasonable time for the
mother country to establish its authority and restore peace
and order within the borders of the island; that we could not
contemplate an indefinite period for the accomplishment of
this result."

The President further advised us:

" This government has never in any way abrogated its
sovereign prerogative of reserving to itself the determina-

tion of its policy and course according to its own high sense of right and in consonance with the dearest interests and convictions of our own people should the prolongation of the strife so demand."

This was the proper, the statesmanlike beginning of the performance of the promise of the Republican platform. It was in accordance with the diplomatic usages and customs of civilized nations. In the meantime the whole situation apparently changed. In Spain the liberal ministry of Sagasta succeeded that of Canovas; the cruel and inhuman Weyler was recalled, and succeeded by the humane Blanco, who, under the Sagasta ministry, has unquestionably made every effort to bring about peace in the island of Cuba under the promise of autonomy—a decided advance beyond any proposition ever before made for the participation of the Cubans in their own domestic affairs.

It was the plain duty of the President of the United States to give to the liberal ministry of Spain a reasonable time in which to test its proposed autonomy. That time has been given. Autonomy is conceded the wide world over to be a conspicuous failure. The situation in Cuba has only changed for the worse. Sagasta is powerless; Blanco is powerless to put an end to the conflict, to rehabilitate the island, or to relieve the suffering, starvation, and distress.

The time for action has, then, come. No greater reason for it can exist to-morrow than exists to-day. Every hour's delay only adds another chapter to the awful story of misery and death. Only one Power can intervene—the United States of America. Ours is the one great nation of the New World, the mother of American republics. She holds a position of trust and responsibility toward the peoples and the affairs of the whole Western Hemisphere.

It was her glorious example which inspired the patriots of
Cuba to raise the flag of liberty in her eternal hills. We cannot refuse to accept this responsibility which the God of the
universe has placed upon us as the one great power in the
New World. We must act! What shall our action be?
Some say the acknowledgment of the belligerency of the
revolutionists. As I have already shown, the hour and the
opportunity for that have passed away.

Others say, Let us by resolution or official proclamation
recognize the independence of the Cubans. It is too late
even for such recognition to be of great avail. Others say,
Annexation to the United States. God forbid! I would
oppose annexation with my latest breath. The people of
Cuba are not our people; they cannot assimilate with us;
and beyond all that I am utterly and unalterably opposed to
any departure from the declared policy of the fathers which
would start this Republic for the first time upon a career of
conquest and dominion utterly at variance with the avowed
purposes and manifest destiny of popular government.

Let the world understand that the United States does not
propose to annex Cuba, that it is not seeking a foot of Cuban
soil or a dollar of Spanish treasure. Others say, Let us intervene for the pacification the island, giving to its people
the greatest measure of autonomy consistent with the continued sovereignty of Spain. Such a result is no longer possible. It is enough to say that it would be resisted by all
classes of the Cuban population, and its attempt would simply
transfer the putting down of the revolution and the subjugation of the Cuban patriots to the armies of the United States.

There is also said to be a syndicate organization in this
country, representing the holders of Spanish bonds, who are
urging that the intervention of the United States shall be for

the purchase of the island or for the guaranteeing of the Spanish debt incurred in the attempted subjugation of the Cuban revolutionists. Mr. President, it is idle to think for a single moment of such a plan. The American people will never consent to the payment of one dollar, to the guaranteeing of one bond, as the price paid to Spain for her relinquishment of the island she has so wantonly outraged and devastated.

Mr. President, there is only one action possible, if any is taken; that is, intervention for the independence of the island; intervention that means the landing of an American army on Cuban soil, the deploying of an American fleet off Havana; intervention which says to Spain, Leave the island, withdraw your soldiers, leave the Cubans, these brothers of ours in the New World, to form and carry on government for themselves. Such intervention on our part would not of itself be war. It would undoubtedly lead to war. But if war came it would come by act of Spain in resistance of the liberty and the independence of the Cuban people.

Some say these Cubans are incapable of self-government; that they cannot be trusted to set up a republic. Will they ever become better qualified under Spanish rule than they are to-day? Sometime or other the dominion of kings must cease on the Western continent.

The senator from Vermont has done full justice to the native population of Cuba. He has studied them, and he knows that of all the people on the island they are the best qualified and fitted for government. Certainly any government by the Cuban people would be better than the tyranny of Spain.

Mr. President, there was a time when " jingoism " was abroad in the land; when sensationalism prevailed, and when

there was a distinct effort to inflame the passions and prejudices of the American people and precipitate a war with
Spain. That time has passed away. "Jingoism" is long
since dead. The American people have waited and waited
and waited in patience; yea, in patience and confidence—confidence in the belief that decisive action would be taken in
due season and in a proper way. To-day all over this land
the appeal comes up to us; it reaches us from every section
and from every class. That appeal is now for action.

In an interview of yesterday, the senior senator from
Maine [Mr. Hale] is reported as saying: "Events have
crowded on too rapidly, and the President has been carried
off his feet."

I know of no warrant for such an assertion, but I do know
this, that unless Congress acts promptly, meeting this grave
crisis as it should be met, we will be swept away, and we
ought to be swept away, by the tidal wave of American indignation.

The President has not been carried off his feet.

The administration has been doing its whole duty. With
rare foresight and statesmanship it has hastened to make
every possible preparation for any emergency. If it be true
that the report in the "Maine" case has been delayed, it has
been delayed in order that we might be prepared at all points
for defensive and offensive action. There are some who say,
but they are mostly those who have procrastinated from the
beginning up to the present time, "Let Congress hold
its peace, adjourn, go home, and leave the President to
act."

I for one believe that the Congress of the United States is
an equal and co-ordinate branch of the federal government,
representing the combined judgment and wisdom of the

many. It can more safely be depended on than the individual judgment and wisdom of any one man. I am a Senator of the United States, and I will never consent to abdicate my right to participate in the determination as to what is the solemn duty of this great Republic in this momentous and fateful hour. We are not in session to hamper or cripple the President; we are here to advise and assist him. Congress can alone declare war; Congress can alone levy taxes; and to this Congress the united people of this broad land, from sea to sea, from lake to gulf, look to voice their wishes and execute their will.

Mr. President, against the intervention of the United States in this holy cause there is but one voice of dissent; that voice is the voice of the money-changers. They fear war! Not because of any Christian or ennobling sentiment against war and in favor of peace, but because they fear that a declaration of war, or the intervention which might result in war, would have a depressing effect upon the stock market.

Mr. President, I do not read my duty from the ticker; I do not accept my lessons in patriotism from Wall Street. I deprecate war. I hope and pray for the speedy coming of the time when the sword of the soldier will no longer leap from its scabbard to settle disputes between civilized nations. But, it is evident, looking at the cold facts, that a war with Spain would not permanently depreciate the value of a single American stock or bond.

War with Spain would increase the business and the earnings of every American railroad, it would increase the output of every American factory, it would stimulate every branch of industry and domestic commerce, it would greatly increase the demand for American labor, and in the end every certificate that represented a share in an American business enterprise would be worth more money than it is to-day. But in the meantime the spectre of war would stride through the stock exchanges, and many of the gamblers around the board would find their ill-gotten gains passing to the other side of the table.

Let them go ; what one man loses at the gambling-table his fellow gambler wins. It is no concern of yours, it is no concern of mine, whether the " bulls " or the " bears " have the best of these stock-deals. They do not represent American sentiment ; they do not represent American patriotism. Let them take their chances as they can. Their weal or woe is of but little importance to the liberty-loving people of the United States. They will not do the fighting ; their blood will not flow ; they will keep on dealing in options on human life. Let the men whose loyalty is to the dollar stand aside while the men whose loyalty is to the flag come to the front.

There are some who lift their voices in the land and in the open light of day insist that the Republican party will not act, for they say it sold out to the capitalists and the money-changers at the last national election.

It is not so. God forbid ! The 7,000,000 freemen who voted for the Republican party and for William McKinley did not mortgage the honor of this nation for a campaign fund, and if the time ever comes when the Republican party hesitates in its course of duty because of any undue anxiety for the welfare of the accumulated wealth of the nation, then let the Republican party be swept from the face of the earth and be succeeded by some other party, by whatever name it may be called, which will represent the patriotism, the honesty, the loyalty, and the devotion that the Republican party exhibited under Abraham Lincoln in 1861.

Mr. President, there are those who say that the affairs of

Cuba are not the affairs of the United Sates, who insist that we can stand idly by and see that island devastated and depopulated, its business interests destroyed, its commercial intercourse with us cut off, its people starved, degraded, and enslaved. It may be the naked legal right of the United States to stand thus idly by.

I have the legal right to pass along the street and see a helpless dog stamped into the earth under the heels of a ruffian. I can pass by and say that is not my dog. I can sit in my comfortable parlor with my loved ones gathered about me, and through my plate-glass window see a fiend outraging a helpless woman near by, and I can legally say this is no affair of mine—it is not happening on my premises; and I can turn away and take my little ones in my arms, and, with the memory of their sainted mother in my heart, look up to the motto on the wall and read, " God bless our home."

But if I do I am a coward and a cur unfit to live, and, God knows, unfit to die. And yet I cannot protect the dog or save the woman without the exercise of force.

We cannot intervene and save Cuba without the exercise of force, and force means war; war means blood. The lowly Nazarene on the shores of Galilee preached the divine doctrine of love, " Peace on earth, good will toward men." Not peace on earth at the expense of liberty and humanity. Not good will toward men who despoil, enslave, degrade, and starve to death their fellow men. I believe in the doctrine of Christ. I believe in the doctrine of peace ; but, Mr. President, men must have liberty before there can come abiding peace.

Intervention means force. Force means war. War means blood. But it will be God's force. When has a battle for humanity and liberty ever been won except by force?

What barricade of wrong, injustice, and oppression has ever been carried except by force?

Force compelled the signature of unwilling royalty to the great Magna Charter; force put life into the Declaration of Independence and made effective the Emancipation Proclamation; force beat with naked hands upon the iron gateway of the Bastile and made reprisal in one awful hour for centuries of kingly crime; force waved the flag of revolution over Bunker Hill and marked the snows of Valley Forge with blood-stained feet; force held the broken line at Shiloh, climbed the flame-swept hill at Chattanooga, and stormed the clouds on Lookout Heights; force marched with Sherman to the sea, rode with Sheridan in the valley of the Shenandoah, and gave Grant victory at Appomattox; force saved the Union, kept the stars in the flag, made " niggers " men. The time for God's force has come again. Let the impassioned lips of American patriots once more take up the song:

> " In the beauty of the lilies Christ was born across the sea,
> With a glory in his bosom that transfigured you and me,
> As he died to make men holy, let us die to make men free,
> For God is marching on."

Others may hesitate, others may procrastinate, others may plead for further diplomatic negotiation, which means delay, but for me, I am ready to act now, and for my action I am ready to answer to my conscience, my country, and my God.

Mr. President, in the cable that moored me to life and hope the strongest strands are broken. I have but little left to offer at the altar of Freedom's sacrifice, but all I have I am glad to give. I am ready to serve my country as best I can in the Senate or in the field. My dearest wish, my most earnest prayer to God is this, that when death comes to end all, I may meet it calmly and fearlessly as did my beloved, in the cause of humanity, under the American flag.

GEORGE E. FOSTER

IGHT HON. GEORGE EULAS FOSTER, P.C., D.C.L., a Canadian statesman and orator of the Liberal-Conservative party, was born in Carleton Co., New Brunswick, Sept. 3, 1847. After receiving a common-school education and studying privately, he entered the University of New Brunswick, whence he graduated at the head of his class, and in 1871 was appointed professor of classics and history in his Alma Mater. He resigned in 1879 and devoted himself to lecturing on temperance and prohibition. In 1882, he was elected to the Canadian House of Commons and immediately made his mark as a parliamentary speaker. In 1885, he was appointed Minister of Marine and Fisheries and took charge of the Canadian interests in the Joint Commission that sat at Washington in 1888. He then succeeded Sir Charles Tupper as Minister of Finance, a position which he held through four Conservative administrations until July, 1896. He was returned to the eighth Dominion Parliament as a member for York, N. B. Mr. Foster advocated the building of the Canadian Pacific Railway and favored the idea of an imperial federation of the British dominions, in which each country, while free to manage its own domestic affairs, should be leagued with all the others in a community of trade and defence under the British flag. At the unveiling of the Macdonald monument at Montreal in June, 1895, he delivered an impressive oration.

DEFENCE AND PROTECTION

[Extract from a speech delivered in the Canadian House of Commons, January 16, 1896, during the debate on the Address in reply to the Speech from the Throne delivered by his Excellency in opening the session of Parliament.]

MY honorable friend also drew attention to the section in the Address which refers to the arming and the strengthening of the militia and defences of Canada. He spoke words none too hearty, he spoke none too approvingly of the militia of this country, and he voiced what is the general sentiment of this House and the country, that its militia deserves well at its hands, and it is the duty of the country to put the best and the newest arms in the hands of the militia, and see that they are well taken care of and equipped in this respect.

(117)

But he had to qualify that by saying that he could perceive in it the flavor of a "jingo" policy.

Well, sir, I leave it to the honorable gentleman and all reasonable men to say if, taking up that paragraph in reply to the Speech, they can see anything in it which savors of defiance or in the least approaches to a jingo policy. It is a modest and straightforward expression, meaning exactly what he says and nothing more, and my honorable friend, I think, will agree that it does not in the least show a tendency in the direction suggested.

No person in Canada who loves his country and desires its peace and prosperity can, in the present juncture of circumstances, whatever may be said at other times, think of breathing a spirit of defiance and jingoism. This would be furthest removed possible from the sensible and well-developed sentiment of Canada, which, while it honors love of country, feels the evidence of strength in its arms, and cherishes in its heart the full purpose to defend that country and stand by it whenever it is threatened, yet, relying on its own calmness, force, and strength, does not ask for declamation and does not flaunt itself in defiance.

But he would read the signs of the times not aright in these somewhat troublesome days, when the great mother Empire stands splendidly isolated in Europe, with interests stretching over the wide world, with a commerce the greatest any nation of the world has ever possessed and vulnerable on every quarter of the sea, who did not feel as Britain feels to-day, and is showing it, that the country's weal, the country's progress, the country's stability, all of the country's pride and glory must base itself upon the strong arms and willing, loyal hearts of the citizenship of that Empire from one end of it to the other.

It is the right and duty of Britain herself and of every dependency that belongs to her to be ready, aye, ready as well as steady in its sentiments of loyalty and devotion for the Empire as a whole. It is in that spirit, and not in any spirit that asks for war or trouble, that that modest reference was placed in the Queen's Speech. And in pursuance of that it is the determination of this government to put the militia and the defences of this country, so far as can possibly be done by Canada, into a state which is adequate to the feelings, the interests, and the security of this country in itself, and as a portion of the Empire.

Now, sir, my honorable friend [Mr. Laurier] has referred to the development of foreign markets. I would not speak of that for a single moment except that he introduced a specious fallacy which is often thrown at the Liberal-Conservative party.

It is this: You tell me that the farmer of Great Britain is seeking for protection, that to-day the weight of competition is being felt by the English farmer who, when raising his wheat one hundred miles from London, is at a disadvantage in competition with the man who raises his wheat three thousand miles away under other and freer conditions; and that therefore the British farmer is looking for protection to aid him in the unequal competition. But, says my honorable friend, if the British farmer gets the protection that he needs, it is a death-blow to you as a protectionist in Canada.

That I think, sir, is not a view that takes in the whole of the situation. We shall have time to discuss that by and by, but there is just one great question to-day which is pressing itself to the front, which is becoming every day more and more considered by the best statesmen of Great Britain and

the colonies, and that is as to whether, these forces and outside circumstances conjoining together, the time is not approaching when it shall not become a question simply as to
whether Great Britain shall give protection to her farmers,
but when the greater problem will appear for solution as
to whether the needs of the Empire cannot be best met within
the Empire itself; as to whether the Empire's markets cannot be supplied by the Empire's producers, and practical independence of foreign countries in food-supplies be secured,
so that in time of trial and war the Empire's producers may
be rid of that great danger of the present time, in this, that
the Empire itself shall be sufficient to feed and to produce
for the needs of the Empire.

FOODS FOR THE HOMELAND

CLOSING ARGUMENT AND PERORATION OF SPEECH DELIVERED IN
THE CANADIAN HOUSE OF COMMONS, JANUARY 31, 1896

IS there any reason why we should change our line of
reasonable protection in order to adopt any of those
facile political faiths which have been confessed from
time to time by honorable gentlemen opposite? Is there any
reason for change to be found in the general circumstances
of the world to-day? If in 1878 the people of this country
thought that a reasonable protection was necessary to give
them the vantage-ground in competing with the world and
building up and establishing industrial life in this country,
is it any less necessary to-day? Is the competition less keen
to-day than it was in 1878? Are the tariff lines of the
various countries of the world lower to-day than in 1878?

Is the tendency of the commercial countries of the world changed in the direction of freer trade and lower duties?

No, sir, they have changed and are changing in the direction of greater stringency and more prohibitive tariffs and circumstances. If they have changed from 1878 to this time, they are stronger to-day in the direction of making Canada keep, for the sake of her trade and business interests, to the line of reasonable protection, instead of taking the line of free trade or partial free trade.

Why, to-day, after the Democratic administration had lowered the duties to a small extent, but so far away from free trade that they enjoy a tariff with an average of 42 per cent on dutiable articles for home consumption in that country, when they had given Canada some little better footing in their market by lowering to some extent duties on agricultural products, what to-day has happened? A Republican majority in the House of Representatives has sent to the Senate a bill which proposes to raise the rate of taxation on all those articles, and to raise them so as to be prohibitive as regards the introduction of the products of Canada into the United States. Is that a reason why we should change our line of policy? If in 1878 there was a reason for the adoption of this policy, in 1895 there is greater reason that this policy should be continued and we should hold to it in Canada.

But there is a line which I think it is possible, and I believe it is right, that the statesmanship of this country as well as of Great Britain and other colonies of the Empire should consider and ponder carefully and well, and that is whether it is not possible for statesmanship in the colonies and Great Britain to bring about between the colonies as among them-

selves, and between the colonies and Great Britain, concurrent action which will be conducive to the commercial interests of both, and which will result in greater power and
strength.   I read an article but a little time ago in the " Nineteenth Century Review," in which the general question which
is agitating many thoughtful minds at the present day was
raised and discussed, as to whether the Empire would be able
to feed itself in the event of war against Great Britain which
would cut off her supplies from hostile nations.

Feed itself!   Why, sir, if statesmanship is not able practically to solve that question, statesmanship must find it impossible to solve any of the great questions which from time
to time present themselves for consideration.   The Empire
able to feed itself!   Yes.   This article showed that 100,000,-
000 bushels of wheat were necessary to England other than
what the colonies afforded her at the present time, in order
to feed the people of the Empire there.

One hundred million bushels of wheat!   Why, 50,000
Canadian farmers with 100 acres each in wheat, and raising
twenty bushels to the acre, would produce the 100,000,000
of bushels of wheat needed by Great Britain.   And what is
50,000 farmers cultivating 5,000,000 of acres, compared with
the English farmers wanting employment and the numbers
of millions of acres of good wheat land in Manitoba and the
Northwest Territories, which has not yet been scratched by
the plow ?

Meats to the value of $140,000,000 would need to be sup-
plied by the colonies to make up for Great Britain's deficiency
supplied now from foreign countries.   Well, cattle and horses
and pigs in illimitable quantity could be raised in this country.   As to butter and cheese : 50,000 farmers owning each
50 cows, amounting to 2,500,000 in numbers, would supply

butter and cheese going far to meet the demands of Great Britain for such supplies. And, with the vast lands of the Northwest, that is not an estimate which cannot be reached if adequate means were taken to bring it about.

So, sir, I might go on to amplify this. The sugar which is necessary for the consumption of Great Britain could be supplied by the West Indies, and by the East Indies, with the cultivation of the cane lands which are now going out of use, and which by its diminution is impoverishing the planters and the laborers of the West Indies. That industry might again have its period of flourishing and its reward of remunerative production were concurrent action taken in Britain and the islands.

So all the way through. It is a problem which requires only time and good statesmanship to solve. And, as I said before, it is for Canada, for Australia, for the other colonies of Great Britain, and for Great Britain herself, to ponder seriously and carefully; to consider whether or not an arrangement cannot become to which will make the Empire and its dependencies sufficient within themselves to feed the Empire, and by doing that add to the volume of business and to a mutually remunerative production. And, sir, the statesmanship which could formulate some such policy of mutually beneficial trade would achieve an end infinitely higher and more wide-reaching. It would evolve from the dark foreground of the not-distant future a national life of singular strength and beauty, in which Canadian Britain, and Australasian Britain, the Britain of Asia and Africa and of the Isles of the Sea, would group themselves in grand imperial unity; the old enriching the new, and the new imparting fresh strength to the old,—through whose world-wide realm the blood of a common commerce should mingle with the blood of a common patriotism, whose power would compel peace, and whose millions of happy people would march in the van of the fullest freedom and the highest civilization.

PRUDENT COMPROMISE

[Peroration of speech on the Manitoba Remedial Separate School Bill, delivered in the Canadian House of Commons, March 13, 1896.]

AFTER six years, sir, we stand here under circumstances such as I have detailed. What is it, then, for this Parliament to do? On the one hand, there is a well-founded repugnance to interfere, and do what, even though clearly within our right to do, the province can do more easily and far better than ourselves. There is along with that a number of subordinate reasons arising, either from considerations of principle or of personal concern, or of party interests that tend to induce some to vote against this bill and against remedial legislation.

On the other hand, what is there? There is the genius and spirit of the constitutional compacts of this country. There is the splendid lesson of toleration and of compromise which has been read to you in that constitution, and which has been evidenced in its harmonious workings for nearly thirty years. There is the cry of the minority, small in the area of those who directly suffer, but large, let me tell you, in the area of those who sympathize with it in this country from one end to the other. There are the minorities in other provinces demanding of you where they shall stand and how they shall be treated if in future years their time of trial comes, and they will have to appeal to this same high court of Parliament and invoke this same jurisdiction.

There is the Parliament, sir, invested, knowingly, definitely, positively invested by the fathers of confederation in the constitution with the jurisdiction to maintain these rights and to restore them if they are taken away. This Parliament is appealed to. It is watched by Canada, it is watched by the world. On grounds of courage, on grounds of justice, on grounds of good faith, make you answer to those who appeal, make you answer to Canada, which is watching you, and to the world, which will judge of your actions. History, sir, is making itself in these eventful days. Shall the chapter be a record of nobleness and adequacy, or a record of weakness and inefficiency? Shall we stamp ourselves as petty and provincial, or shall we be recorded to future ages as magnanimous and imperial? Let us plant our feet in the firm paths of constitutional compact and agreement of good faith, and of honest, fair dealing. Let us take and pass on that gleaming touch of prudent compromise under whose kindly light the fathers of confederation marched safely through in times far more troublous and far less advanced than ours into an era of harmony and continued peace.

Let us do justice to a weak and patient minority, and thus settle forever the question of the sufficiency of the guarantees of confederation. Let us follow with cheerful emulation the shining example of our great mother country, whose foundations were laid on the solid granite of good faith, and whose world-wide and wondrous superstructure has been joined together with the cement of a strong and generous toleration.

Let us prove ourselves now, in the thirtieth year of our existence as in the stress of our natal days, a people fit for Empire, and worthy to rank among the best and greatest of nations.

JOHN M. ALLEN

OHN M. ALLEN, LL.B., American congressman, was born in Tishomingo County, Miss., July 8, 1847. He received a common-school education up to the time of his enlistment as a private in the Confederate army, in which he served throughout the war. At the close of the war he attended the law school at Cumberland University, Lebanon, Tenn.; graduated in law in 1870 at the University of Mississippi, and began the practice of his profession at Tupelo Miss. In 1870, he was elected district attorney for the first judicial district of that State, from which office he retired after a service of four years. Since 1885, Mr. Allen has represented his State in Congress, having been elected to the forty-ninth Congress and to the five subsequent Congresses. He was also unanimously reëlected to the fifty-sixth Congress. Mr. Allen is a Democrat, and is known in Congress and throughout the South for the humor of his speeches.

TUPELO SPEECH

DELIVERED IN THE HOUSE OF REPRESENTATIVES, FEBRUARY 20, 1901

MR. CHAIRMAN, I do not deem it necessary to take up twenty minutes time of this committee to pass this amendment, but as this fish hatchery is to be established at Tupelo, and I find among some people in the country—even some newspaper men, who are supposed to impart information to others, and some gentlemen who have been elected to Congress, and who tell me that they have not only been to school but gone through college—so much ignorance about Tupelo that I think I ought—in justice to them, not to Tupelo—to enlighten them some on this subject.

If I were willing to avail myself of all the traditions and many well authenticated but not absolutely accurate histor-

(126)

ical suspicions, I might invest this subject with much more historical and romantic interest. But I propose to confine my remarks to well-authenticated facts, ignoring such traditions, believed by many of our people to be true, as that when Christopher Columbus had his interview with Ferdinand and Isabella of Spain, that in his efforts to persuade them to back him in his expedition that led to the discovery of America, he assured them that an all-wise Creator, creating a world like this, was bound to have made somewhere near its center such a place as Tupelo.

The first authentic account we have of the section of country that will one day be included in the corporate limits of Tupelo is that the great Indian chief, Chicksa, from whom that great and warlike tribe, the Chickasaw Indians, took its name, was west of the great Mississippi River and that he, with his followers, followed a pole guided and supported by invisible hands across the Mississippi River to the vicinity of Tupelo. There, we are informed, the pole stopped, stood upright, planted in the ground, and there the Chickasaw Indians made their home. No people, Mr. Chairman, were ever directed by a wise Providence to a fairer land. 'Twas in the rolling woodland just north of one of the most beautiful prairies on which the eye of man or beast ever rested. The country abounded with all sorts of game; the streams were full of fishes, and on this continent there was no more enticing place for this poetic race of the forest. Here the Chickasaws grew to be, as they are to this time, one of the greatest and most powerful of the Indian tribes.

In 1513 the knightly Ponce de Leon landed upon the coast of Florida, and perverted history has it that he started out to look for the fountain of youth and limitless gold fields, when in truth and in fact he really started to look for Tu-

pelo. You are all familiar with the disaster that overtook
his expedition. Later, in 1540, the great and adventurous
discoverer, Hernando de Soto, landed his expedition on the
coast of Florida, and finally succeeded in reaching and dis-
covering, for the first time by a white man, Tupelo.

Here he stopped in the midst of the Chickasaws until
attacked by them and driven west to what is now the city of
Memphis, where he discovered the great Mississippi River.

The Chickasaws were then left in peaceable possession, so
far as the white man was concerned, of this beautiful section for nearly two hundred years, when, in 1736, Bienville,
with his expedition, came up from Florida, and D'Arta-
guiett from the Illinois attempted to meet and take from
the Chickasaws what is now Tupelo. D'Artaguiette got
there before Bienville, and was defeated by the Chickasaws.
He and almost all of his expedition perished at their hands.
Bienville arrived later, was also defeated and driven back
with great loss to his expedition; and now, in laying out and
grading avenues and boulevards for Tupelo, the bones, spurs,
weapons, epaulets, etc., of the slain of these ill-fated expe-
ditions are plowed up.

This is something of the early history of the place about
which we find so much ignorance. My colleague, General
Catchings, told me not many days ago that some newspaper
man had asked him if there really was such a place as Tupelo.

I do not assert that all of these historical events to which
I have referred took place immediately in the town of
Tupelo, but they were in that vicinity and were on territory
that we expect to have incorporated into the city some day.
To come down to a later period, those of you who know anything of the history of your country will remember the contentions and contest that lasted for many years between the

French, English, and Spanish governments for the ownership of the Mississippi territory. I am informed by those
familiar with the real designs of those great nations at that
time that the real motive of all of them was the ownership
of Tupelo.

Finally, the United States, appreciating the importance
of the position, took advantage of their dissensions and acquired Tupelo.

About the year 1848 it became a matter of great concern
to the Great Northwest to secure a market for their products, so they gave aid and encouragement to the building
of the northern end of what is now the Mobile and Ohio
Railroad. The city of Mobile, on the Gulf, recognizing also
the great advantages of direct connection with Tupelo,
helped along this enterprise, and the road was built from
Mobile to Tupelo.

Everything went on very well until about 1861, when the
South concluded to secede from the Union. I am reliably
informed that when Horace Greeley and others sought Mr.
Lincoln and asked him to "let the wayward sisters depart
in peace," he shook his head and said, "No; this secession
takes from the United States Tupelo, and we will not submit to it." And it was to rescue to the Union this town that
brought on the war.

The armies of the Union were first directed against the
capital of the Confederacy at Richmond, Va., but some ob-
structions were thrown in the way of that army at Bull Run,
and they were persuaded to return to Washington. Another
great army was then marshaled under the command of General Grant, who landed at Pittsburg Landing, on the Ten-
nessee River, and began his operations against Tupelo.

General Albert Sidney Johnston and myself met General

Grant's army at Shiloh, and for most of the first day we had
a real good time with them, and but for General Johnston
being killed and me being scattered on the evening of that
day there is no knowing what might have happened or how
the history of this country might have been changed.

Suffice it to say, I retired on Corinth, and when we were
there, sorely pressed, President Davis ordered General
Beauregard to fall back to Tupelo, and there make a great
and desperate stand for the life of the Confederacy. And
it seems that Generals Grant and Halleck were so much
impressed with the dogged determination of the Confederate
Army to defend Tupelo to the death of the last man that
they turned away in other directions. Later, General
Sturgis started from Memphis with a well-equipped army,
with a view of capturing Tupelo, and breaking the backbone
of the Confederacy. But on the road down there, when
he had gotten within a few miles of Tupelo, General Forrest,
that great cavalry commander, appreciating what the loss
of Tupelo would mean to the Confederacy, met Sturgis at
Brices Crossroads, took from him all of his artillery and
wagons, sent him back to Memphis without an organized
company and with the remnant of his army, in about one-
fourth of the time that had been consumed by forced
marches in going down.

But Mr. Lincoln seemed never to have lost sight of the
importance of Tupelo to the Union, and he marshaled another army under that able commander, General A. J.
Smith, and started them to capture Tupelo. General
Stephen D. Lee and General Forrest, with their commands,
were sent to intercept him, but in maneuvering for positions
General Smith got between Forrest and Lee and Tupelo and
succeeded in capturing the town; and in an effort to dislodge

him from there the desperate and bloody battle of Harris-
burg, which is in the suburbs of Tupelo, was fought, in
which nobody had any decided advantage, but General Smith
evacuated the town and went back to Memphis. But the
very fact that Tupelo had fallen seems to have broken the
spirit of the Confederacy, and we never did much good after
that.

You will find, Mr. Chairman, in the Congressional Library
a book the title of which is "Tupelo." It was written by a
Northern Presbyterian preacher and school-teacher who
happened to be down in that section when the war began.
I remember him very well. This book treats of his trials
and tribulations about Tupelo, where he was arrested, imprisoned, and would have been shot but for his timely escape
from prison; and, as I remember the substance, as he puts
it, of his offense was a suspicion that he entertained secret
doubts as to the divine origin and right of African slavery.

After the close of the war, when we had returned to our
peaceful avocations, one of our brightest and most far-
sighted young men, having in mind the great future as well
as the great past of this town, settled in Tupelo, and afterwards became a member of this body and is not about ter-
minating a great career of sixteen years here. What this
nation and this House owes to Tupelo for this contribution
I leave for others to say. My modesty forbids my speaking
of it. Some fifteen years ago Kansas City and Memphis,
appreciating the fact that if they ever hoped to do any good
as cities they must have direct connection with Tupelo, built
a railroad from Kansas City, through Memphis, to Tupelo.
Birmingham, realizing that with all of its marvelous resources they could never be developed and properly distrib-
uted without direct railroad connection with Tupelo, saw to
it that the road was built from Birmingham to Tupelo.

Mr. Chairman, during the discussion on the river and harbor bill in this House recently, I heard so many statistics as to the tonnage of the various cities that were seeking appropriations in that bill that it stimulated me to inquire into the tonnage at Tupelo, and I find that during last year there were about 4,000,000 tons of freight passed through Tupelo. It was only the other day that you saw in great headlines in all of our newspapers that the Southern Railroad had purchased the Mobile and Ohio Railroad, running from St. Louis to Mobile, through Tupelo.

The president of the Southern road was in Washington a few days later, and I met him for the first time, and in a conversation I had with him I gathered the reason for this purchase. It was that the Southern system had already about 7,000 miles of railroad, which had cost them hundreds of millions of dollars; they found this great system, after all this expenditure, practically useless to them, because they had no direct connection or terminal facilities at Tupelo. They therefore spent many millions more for 900 miles of railroad that would take them into Tupelo and give them good terminal facilities there.

Many of you gentlemen have never been to Tupelo. I hope none of you entertain any idea of dying without going there. I should hate to have it said of any member of this Congress—for all of whom I have such a kindly feeling— that they did not aspire to visit Tupelo before they died. I extend you all an invitation to come, and promise you a royal welcome. Come and go with me on College Hill some evening and see one of our Tupelo sunsets.

Come and see one of our Southern, silvery, Tupelo moons! I think it is the only place in the South where we have the same beautiful moons we had before the war. I

have often been asked about the size of Tupelo. I confess
I have not been able to get the exact figures from the last
census. The tabulating machines do not seem to have been
able to work it out yet; but I can say, Mr. Chairman, that
by sufficiently extending the corporate limits of our town
we can accommodate a population larger than the city of
London. The truth is that our lands about Tupelo have
been so valuable for agricultural purposes that we have not
yielded them up for building a city as rapidly as we should
have done.

I can say, Mr. Chairman, that while there are larger
places than Tupelo, I do not think there is any other place
just exactly like it. Tupelo is very near, if not exactly, in
the center of the world. The horizon seems about the same
distance in every direction. The sun, when doing business
on regular schedule, comes right over the town, and sometimes gives us a hot time in the old town. It is a great
place for the investment of capital, where it will be welcomed and protected. Come early, gentlemen, and avoid
the rush!

This, Mr. Chairman, is a proposition to establish there a
fish hatchery. We have the ideal place for a fish hatchery.
Why, sir, fish will travel over land for miles to get into the
water we have at Tupelo. Thousands and millions of unborn fish are clamoring to this Congress to-day for an opportunity to be hatched at the Tupelo hatchery.

Now, Mr. Chairman, I only wish to say in conclusion that
if there is a member here who wishes to have his name connected by future generations with that of Judas Iscariot and
Benedict Arnold, if he wishes to have himself and his posterity pointed at with scorn, if he desires to be despised by
men and shunned by women, let him vote against this amendment and he will secure all this infamous notoriety.

ARTHUR J. BALFOUR

IGHT HON. ARTHUR JAMES BALFOUR, P. C., M. P., D. C. L., a distinguished
English statesman and author, first lord of the treasury in Lord Salisbury's
cabinet, and leader of the House of Commons, was born in Scotland, July 25,
1848, and was educated at Eton and Trinity College, Cambridge. He entered Parliament in 1874 as member for Hertford, which he represented till 1885, since
which time he has sat for East Manchester. He was private secretary to his uncle, Lord
Salisbury, 1878–80, and for a short period acted with a few Conservatives led by Lord
Randolph Churchill, and known as the "Fourth Party." He was created a privy
councillor in 1885, appointed secretary for Scotland, 1886–87, and chief secretary for
Ireland, 1887–91, his Irish policy being not altogether to the liking of some of the
Conservatives. He was first lord of the treasury, 1891–92, and again in 1895. He
became Conservative leader of the House in 1891 and in the following year delivered
many speeches against the Home Rule Bill. Mr. Balfour was lord rector of St. Andrew's University in 1880, and of Glasgow University in 1890. His writings comprise
"A Defence of Philosophic Doubt" (1879); "Essays and Addresses" (1893); "The
Foundations of Belief," a work which has attracted general attention (1895). He is a
scholar, a metaphysician, and a brilliant debater.

THE PLEASURES OF READING

DELIVERED AT ST. ANDREW'S UNIVERSITY, DECEMBER 10, 1887

TRŪLY it is a subject for astonishment that, instead of
expanding to the utmost the employment of this
pleasure-giving faculty, so many persons should set
themselves to work to limit its exercise by all kinds of arbi-
trary regulations.

Some persons, for example, tell us that the acquisition of
knowledge is all very well, but that it must be useful knowledge,—meaning usually thereby that it must enable a man
to get on in a profession, pass an examination, shine in conversation, or obtain a reputation for learning. But even
if they mean something higher than this—even if they mean
that knowledge, to be worth anything, must subserve ulti-

(134)

mately, if not immediately, the material or spiritual interests of mankind,—the doctrine is one which should be energetically repudiated.

I admit, of course, at once, that discoveries the most apparently remote from human concerns have often proved themselves of the utmost commercial or manufacturing value. But they require no such justification for their existence, nor were they striven for with any such object.

Navigation is not the final cause of astronomy, nor telegraphy of electro-dynamics, nor dye-works of chemistry. And if it be true that the desire of knowledge for the sake of knowledge was the animating motives of the great men who first wrested her secrets from nature, why should it not also be enough for us, to whom it is not given to discover, but only to learn as best we may what has been discovered by others?

Another maxim, more plausible but equally pernicious, is that superficial knowledge is worse than no knowledge at all. That " a little knowledge is a dangerous thing " is a saying which has now got currency as a proverb stamped in the mint of Pope's versification,—of Pope who, with the most imperfect knowledge of Greek, translated Homer; with the most imperfect knowledge of the Elizabethan drama, edited Shakespeare; and with the most imperfect knowledge of philosophy, wrote the " Essay on Man."

But what is this " little knowledge " which is supposed to be so dangerous? What is it " little " in relation to? If in relation to what there is to know, then all human knowledge is little. If in relation to what actually is known by somebody, then we must condemn as " dangerous " the knowledge which Archimedes possessed of mechanics, or Copernicus of astronomy; for a shilling primer and a few

weeks' study will enable any student to outstrip in mere information some of the greatest teachers of the past.

No doubt that little knowledge which thinks itself to be
great many possibly be a dangerous, as it certainly is a most
ridiculous, thing. We have all suffered under that eminently absurd individual who, on the strength of one or two
volumes, imperfectly apprehended by himself and long dis-
credited in the estimation of every one else, is prepared to
supply you on the shortest notice with a dogmatic solution
of every problem suggested by this " unintelligible world; "
or the political variety of the same pernicious genus whose
statecraft consists in the ready application to the most complex question of national interest of some high-sounding
commonplace which has done weary duty on a thousand platforms, and which even in its palmiest days was never fit for
anything better than a peroration.

But in our dislike of the individual do not let us mistake
the diagnosis of his disease. He suffers not from ignorance,
but from stupidity. Give him learning, and you make him,
not wise, but only more pretentious in his folly.

I say, then, that so far from a little knowledge being undesirable a little knowledge is all that on most subjects any
of us can hope to attain, and that as a source, not of worldly
profit, but of personal pleasure, it may be of incalculable
value to its possessor.

But it will naturally be asked, " How are we to select from
among the infinite number of things which may be known
those which it is best worth while for us to know? " We are
constantly being told to concern ourselves with learning what
is important, and not to waste our energies upon what is
insignificant.

But what are the marks by which we shall recognize the

important, and how is it to be distinguished from the insignificant? A precise and complete answer to this question which
shall be true for all men cannot be given. I am considering
knowledge, recollect, as it ministers to enjoyment, and from
this point of view each unit of information is obviously of
importance in proportion as it increases the general sum
of enjoyment which we obtain from knowledge. This, of
course, makes it impossible to lay down precise rules which
shall be an equally sure guide to all sorts and conditions
of men; for in this, as in other matters, tastes must differ,
and against real difference of taste there is no appeal.

There is, however, one caution which it may be worth your
while to keep in view,—Do not be persuaded into applying
any general proposition on this subject with a foolish impartiality to every kind of knowledge. There are those who
tell you that it is the broad generalities and the far-reaching
principles which govern the world, which are alone worthy
of your attention.

A fact which is not an illustration of a law, in the opinion
of these persons, appears to lose all its value. Incidents
which do not fit into some great generalization, events which
are merely picturesque, details which are merely curious—
they dismiss as unworthy the interest of a reasoning being.

Now, even in science, this doctrine in its extreme form
does not hold good. The most scientific of men have taken
profound interest in the investigation of facts from the determination of which they do not anticipate any material
addition to our knowledge of the laws which regulate the
universe. In these matters I need hardly say that I speak
wholly without authority. But I have always been under
the impression that an investigation which has cost hundreds
of thousands of pounds; which has stirred on three occasions

the whole scientific community throughout the civilized world; on which has been expended the utmost skill in the construction of instruments and their application to purposes of research (I refer to the attempts made to determine the distance of the sun by observations of the transit of Venus), would, even if they had been brought to a successful issue, have furnished mankind with the knowledge of no new astronomical principle.

The laws which govern the motions of the solar system, the proportions which the various elements in that system bear to one another, have long been known. The distance of the sun itself is known within limits of error, relatively speaking, not very considerable. Were the measuring-rod we apply to the heavens, based on an estimate of the sun's distance from the earth, which was wrong by (say) three per cent, it would not, to the lay mind, seem to affect very materially our view either of the distribution of the heavenly bodies or of their motions. And yet this information, this piece of celestial gossip, would seem to be that which was chiefly expected from the successful prosecution of an investigation in which whole nations have interested themselves.

But though no one can, I think, pretend that science does not concern itself, and properly concern itself, with facts which are not in themselves, to all appearance, illustrations of law, it is undoubtedly true that for those who desire to extract the greatest pleasure from science, a knowledge, however elementary, of the leading principles of investigation and the larger laws of nature, is the acquisition most to be desired. To him who is not a specialist, a comprehension of the broad outlines of the universe as it presents itself to the scientific imagination, is the thing most worth striving to attain.

But when we turn from science to what is rather vaguely called history, the same principles of study do not, I think, altogether apply, and mainly for this reason,—that while the recognition of the reign of law is the chief amongst the pleasures imparted by science, our inevitable ignorance makes it the least among the pleasures imparted by history.

It is no doubt true that we are surrounded by advisers who tell us that all study of the past is barren except in so far as it enables us to determine the laws by which the evolution of human societies is governed. How far such an investigation has been up to the present time fruitful in results I will not inquire. That it will ever enable us to trace with accuracy the course which states and nations are destined to pursue in the future, or to account in detail for their history in the past, I do not indeed believe.

We are borne along like travellers on some unexplored stream. We may know enough of the general configuration of the globe to be sure that we are making our way towards the ocean. We may know enough by experience or theory of the laws regulating the flow of liquids, to conjecture how the river will behave under the varying influences to which it may be subject. More than this we cannot know. It will depend largely upon causes which, in relation to any laws which we are ever likely to discover, may properly be called accidental, whether we are destined sluggishly to drift among fever-stricken swamps, to hurry down perilous rapids, or to glide gently through fair scenes of peaceful cultivation.

But leaving on one side ambitious sociological speculations, and even those more modest but hitherto more successful investigations into the causes which have in particular cases been principally operative in producing great political changes, there are still two modes in which we can derive what I may call " spectacular " enjoyment from the study of history.

There is first the pleasure which arises from the contemplation of some great historic drama, or some broad and well-marked phase of social development. The story of the rise, greatness, and decay of a nation is like some vast epic which contains as subsidiary episodes the varied stories of the rise, greatness, and decay of creeds, of parties and of statesmen. The imagination is moved by the slow unrolling of this great picture of human mutability, as it is moved by the contrasted permanence of the abiding stars. The ceaseless conflict, the strange echoes of long-forgotten controversies, the confusion of purpose, the successes which lay deep the seeds of future evils, the failures that ultimately divert the otherwise inevitable danger, the heroism which struggles to the last for a cause foredoomed to defeat, the wickedness which sides with right, and the wisdom which huzzas at the triumph of folly— fate, meanwhile, through all this turmoil and perplexity, working silently toward the predestined end,—all these form together a subject the contemplation of which need surely never weary.

But there is yet another and very different species of enjoyment to be derived from the records of the past, which require a somewhat different method of study in order that it may be fully tasted. Instead of contemplating, as it were, from a distance, the larger aspects of the human drama, we may elect to move in familiar fellowship amid the scenes and actors of special periods.

We may add to the interest we derive from the contemplation of contemporary politics, a similar interest derived from a not less minute and probably more accurate knowledge of some comparatively brief passage in the political history of the past. We may extend the social circle in which we move—a circle perhaps narrowed and restricted through circumstances beyond our control—by making intimate acquaintances, perhaps even close friends, among a society long departed, but which, when we have once learnt the trick of it, it rests with us to revive.

It is this kind of historical reading which is usually branded as frivolous and useless, and persons who indulge in it often delude themselves into thinking that the real motive of their investigation into bygone scenes and ancient scandals is philosophic interest in an important historical episode, whereas in truth it is not the philosophy which glorifies the details, but the details which make tolerable the philosophy.

Consider, for example, the case of the French Revolution. The period from the taking of the Bastille to the fall of Robespierre is of about the same length as very commonly intervenes between two of our general elections. On these comparatively few months libraries have been written. The incidents of every week are matters of familiar knowledge. The character and the biography of every actor in the drama has been made the subject of minute study; and by common admission, there is no more fascinating page in the history of the world.

But the interest is not what is commonly called philosophic, it is personal. Because the Revolution is the dominant fact in modern history, therefore people suppose that the doings of this or that provincial lawyer, tossed into temporary eminence and eternal infamy by some freak of the revolutionary wave, or the atrocities committed by this or that mob, half-drunk with blood, rhetoric and alcohol, are of transcendent importance.

In truth their interest is great, but their importance is small. What we are concerned to know as students of the philosophy of history is, not the character of each turn and eddy in the great social cataract, but the manner in which the currents of the upper stream drew surely in toward the final plunge, and slowly collected themselves after the catastrophe, again to pursue, at a different level, their renewed and comparatively tranquil course.

Now, if so much of the interest of the French Revolution depends upon our minute knowledge of each passing incident, how much more necessary is such knowledge when we are dealing with the quiet nooks and corners of history—when we are seeking an introduction, let us say, into the literary society of Johnson or the fashionable society of Walpole! Society, dead or alive, can have no charm without intimacy, and no intimacy without interest in trifles which I fear Mr. Harrison would describe as "merely curious."

If we would feel at our ease in any company, if we wish to find humor in its jokes and point in its repartees, we must know something of the beliefs and the prejudices of its various members—their loves and their hates, their hopes and their fears, their maladies, their marriages, and their flirtations. If these things are beneath our notice, we shall not be the less qualified to serve our queen and country, but need make no attempt to extract pleasure out of one of the most delightful departments of literature.

That there is such a thing as trifling information, I do not of course question; but the frame of mind in which the reader is constantly weighing the exact importance to the universe at large of each circumstance which the author presents to his notice, is not one conducive to the true enjoyment of a picture whose effect depends upon a multitude of slight and seem-

ingly insignificant touches, which impress the mind often
without remaining in the memory.

The best method of guarding against the danger of reading
what is useless is to read only what is interesting,—a truth
which will seem a paradox to a whole class of readers, fitting
objects of our commiseration, who may be often recognized
by their habit of asking some adviser for a list of books, and
then marking out a scheme of study in the course of which
all these are to be conscientiously perused.

These unfortunate persons apparently read a book principally with the object of getting to the end of it. They
reach the word " *Finis* " with the same sensation of triumph
as an Indian feels who strings a fresh scalp to his girdle.
They are not happy unless they mark by some definite performance each step in the weary path of self-improvement.
To begin a volume and not to finish it would be to deprive
themselves of this satisfaction; it would be to lose all the reward of their earlier self-denial by a lapse from virtue at the
end.   The skip, according to their literary code, is a form
of cheating: it is a mode of obtaining credit for erudition on
false pretences; a plan by which the advantages of learning
are surreptitiously obtained by those who have not won them
by honest toil. But all this is quite wrong. In matters
literary, works have no saving efficacy. He has only half
learned the art of reading who has not added to it the even
more refined accomplishments of skipping and of skimming;
and the first step has hardly been taken in the direction of
making literature a pleasure, until interest in the subject, and
not a desire to spare (so to speak) the author's feelings, or
to accomplish an appointed task, is the prevailing motive of
the reader.

LORD R. CHURCHILL

ANDOLPH HENRY SPENCER CHURCHILL, a noted English politician, son of the sixth Duke of Marlborough, was born at Blenheim Palace, Woodstock, Feb. 15, 1849, and died at London, Jan. 24, 1895. He was educated at Merton College, Oxford, and entered the House of Commons as member for Woodstock in 1874. After 1880 he was conspicuous for his attacks upon the Liberal party and was the leader of the so-called "Fourth Party." He was Secretary of State for India in 1885, and Chancellor of the Exchequer and leader of the House during Lord Salisbury's second administration in 1886. He resigned in December of that year and was then returned to the House as member for South Paddington, and again in 1892. He travelled in South Africa in 1891 on account of failing health, and on his return to England was again active in Parliament as a leader of the Opposition and in making platform speeches about the country. He is remembered in the United States as having married a daughter of Leonard Jerome, their son being the well-known English novelist and war correspondent, Winston Spencer Churchill. His death occurred in his forty-sixth year. He was one of the most prominent Tory politicians of his time, and a versatile and audacious speaker, but his political course was erratic and intractible. He was the author of "Men, Mines, and Animals in South Africa" (1892) and a collection of "Speeches."

ON THE EGYPTIAN CRISIS

A SPEECH DELIVERED IN PRINCE'S HALL, PICCADILLY, FEBRUARY 16, 1884

[The fall of Sinkat and the massacre of its garrison excited indignation in all Conservative minds. When the announcement was made in the House of Lords (Feb. 12, 1884), Lord Salisbury moved a vote of censure on the government, describing its policy pursued in Egypt as "vacillating and inconsistent," and also as "an act of blood-guiltiness." A similar vote was moved in the House of Commons by Sir Stafford Northcote. Indignation meetings were held everywhere, and the Liberal government seemed tottering to its fall.]

M Y LORDS AND GENTLEMEN,—I rise for the purpose of moving the first resolution, and in order that we may consider that resolution with advantage I would beg all these gentlemen here who do not altogether concur with the views which we are going to expound, to listen to the discussion with equanimity, and, if possible, to reply to the arguments we may urge.

(144)

It would conduce more to the dignity of a London meeting, it will conduce more to the maintenance of the high character of the citizens of this great metropolis, if any gentleman who have counter-opinions to urge to those of the majority of the meeting will come to the platform and address us. We have, gentlemen, to-day to set an example to the country: let us first set an example of order. The resolution which I have to propose is in these terms:

" That in the opinion of this meeting, her Majesty's government are solely responsible for the anarchy which prevails in Egypt, and the bloodshed which has occurred, and which is imminent in the Soudan, and that the vacillitating and pusillanimous policy of the Ministers deserve the severest censure of the country."

We are gathered together this afternoon for a serious purpose; no other, indeed, than to pronounce, after due deliberation, the strongest and most resolute condemnation of Mr. Gladstone's Egyptian policy, and our detestation and abhorrence of the bloodshed and misery of which he has been the immediate and direct cause. I say Mr. Gladstone's Egyptian policy, because I utterly decline to recognize as responsible agents either his ministerial colleagues or his parliamentary supporters.

Those parties have so wallowed in a stifling morass of the most degraded and servile worship of the Prime Minister that they have sunk below the level of slaves; they have become mere puppets, the objects of derision and contempt; they have lost all claim to the title of Englishmen, and I think they have lost all claim to the title of rational human beings.

To give you an instance of the abject imbecility which has struck down the Liberal party, I would mention what occurred in the House of Commons on Thursday night. Mr.

Forster, in that great speech which he made that evening—a speech in which he promised one vote to the government in the House of Commons, and alienated a hundred thousand votes from the government in the country—Mr. Forster, I say, expressed the opinion that the government ought to have rescued the garrison of Sinkat.

" How ? " cried out some importunate Liberals. " How ? " was the plaintive cry they raised.

" How ? " shouted Mr. Forster, turning upon them, so that they wished themselves a hundred leagues under the sea, " How ? why, by doing a fortnight earlier what they are doing now, sending British soldiers to the garrison's rescue."

There is a good instance of the hopeless and incurable mental alienation to which the once free and independent Liberal party have been reduced by Mr. Gladstone! It was indeed a melancholy spectacle.

I said that our purpose this afternoon was a serious one, and it is so. It is a serious thing for Englishmen to meet together in open day for the purpose of doing all they can to destroy a government. But we are not alone. Thousands of your countrymen have already met, and thousands more will meet, animated by the same feelings as yourselves, and, like yourselves, resolved to exhaust their energies in a supreme effort to avert further disgrace from our names, future defeat from our army, and ultimate ruin from our country, by dashing from his pride of place the evil and moonstruck minister who has brought England into grievous peril.

Perilous, I say, is our condition, for it is perilous for a country to shed human blood in vain; it is perilous for a country to assume responsibilities which it is too cowardly to discharge; it is perilous for a country to permit its foreign interests to be in such a condition that any morning we may awake to hear Europe demanding reparation and even vengeance.

Once again, for the fourth time in four years, do the ministry, whose programme was peace, and whose component parts were Quakers, call upon you to give them authority to wage a bloody war.

Of their former wars the results have been either infamous or futile—infamy in the south of Africa; futility in the north of Africa. Will you, I ask, with these memories still fresh in your minds, permit these false guides again to direct your course?

There can be but one answer. If war is again to be urged; if British blood and British treasure are again to be poured forth; if the regeneration of Egypt and the East is once more to be taken in hand, then other heads must do the work and other policies must be pursued.

A Parliament which has long ceased to represent England must be dissolved, and a ministry, for a parallel to which you must go back to the days of Shaftesbury or Lord North, must be placed on its trial by the people.

We have to provide for the safety of the hero Gordon; for the safety of the 4,000 British soldiers sent to Suakim; for the safety of the garrisons of the Soudan, 30,000 souls in all, whose one and only hope is now reposed in you. Above all, we have to provide for the safety of our position in the Delta of the Nile.

Shall labors such as these, interests so tremendous and so vital, be committed to the hands of Mr. Gladstone and his colleagues, men who have on their souls the blood of the massacre of Maiwand, the blood of the massacre of Laing's Nek, the blood of Sir George Colley, the blood of Lord Frederick Cavendish and Mr. Burke, and many other true and loyal subjects of the Crown in Ireland, the blood of Hicks Pasha and his 10,000 soldiers, the blood of the army of General Baker, the blood of Tewfik Bey and his 500 heroes?

For four years this ministry has literally waded in blood; their hands are literally dripping and reeking with blood. From massacre to massacre they march, and their course is ineffaceably stamped upon the history of the world by an overflowing stream of blood. How many more of England's heroes—how many more of England's best and bravest, are to be sacrificed to the Moloch of Midlothian?

This, too, is shocking and horrible—the heartless indifference and callousness of the Liberal party to narratives of slaughter and unutterable woe. Fifteen times did Mr. Gladstone on Tuesday night, in his reply to the grave and measured accusations of Sir Stafford Northcote,—fifteen times, I say, did he excite the laughter of his Liberal supporters with a frivolity which was too hideous to contemplate.

Talk of Bulgarian atrocities! Add them together, and even multiply them if you will, and you will not exceed the total of the atrocities and the infamies which have distinguished with an awful reputation the most blood-stained and withal the most cowardly government which England has ever seen.

Well, we are met together this afternoon, as loyal subjects of the Queen and as lovers of our country, for this purpose, and this purpose only,—to put a stop to further wicked and wanton bloodshed. We know that great empires must sometimes fight great battles, and that empires which fear to fight battles will soon cease to be empires; but we are resolved that the battles which we have to fight shall be fought for definite objects and for noble ends, and that poltroons and traitors, in the garb of ministers of the Crown, shall sacrifice no longer, for worthless and degraded aims, the life-blood of our country. The supporters of the present government exclaim that the Tory party, although prodigal of censure, is deficient in a policy of its own; and with many taunts they call upon us to disclose the direction in which our efforts would be turned in the event of a change in the councils of the Crown.

The demand cannot be considered unfair, and the reply is not so difficult as some people seem to think. We recognize to the very uttermost the immense responsibilities which this country has incurred toward Egypt, and toward the interests of Europe there, and to the discharge of these responsibilities we would be prepared to apply all the resources, if need be, of the Empire of the Queen; and till those responsibilities are satisfied we would neither stop nor stay.

The history of the Tory party in the past is, I fearlessly assent, an ample guarantee that the recognition of a responsibility and the full discharge of a responsibility are inseparable and consequential. I cannot claim to have the smallest share in the councils of the leaders of the Tory party, whoever they may be—and therefore, as far as they are concerned, I speak without authority.

But having studied with some care the history of our party in the past, possessing an unbounded faith in its future, and being not altogether ignorant of the state of public opinion, I will venture to say this much—that the policy of the Tory party, should it be placed in power, will be the policy of calling things by their right names. The occupation of Egypt by the British forces will be called a Protectorate of Egypt by the British Empire, having for its object the establishment, in process of time, of a government at Cairo which shall be consonant with the legitimate and laudable aspirations of the Egyptian people; which shall be able to protect itself alike from internal tumult and from foreign intrigue; which, while it shall develop the undoubted resources of Egypt, shall faithfully discharge the equitable liabilities of its people; and which, as far as human governments can do, shall give promise of prosperity and happiness in the land of the Nile.

We are now in Egypt by the sufferance of Europe, but we must endeavor to be in Egypt by the mandate of Europe. Our Protectorate, to be effective, and authoritative, and secure, should be acquiesced in by a European Congress in which Turkey shall be adequately represented and the rights and powers of the Sultan loyally secured. Our Protectorate, if it is to be crowned with success, must not shrink from dealing comprehensively and boldly with the financial indebtedness of Egypt, even though such dealing should involve some pecuniary liability on ourselves.

The work, if you undertake it, will be a work of time,— perhaps a long time. It will be a work of difficulty, and perhaps a work of danger; but it would also be a work of duty and a work of honor; and from work of that kind Britain has never yet recoiled. It is a work which, if courageously persisted in, will bind more closely to us than heretofore the sympathies of the Mohammedan races, and will establish on deeper foundations our dominions in the East. Our aims are honor, peace, and freedom, and we should not shrink from prosecuting those aims, if need be, by force of arms. Conscious of their magnanimity, we would go boldly forward, knowing well that the results of our policy would surely be to undo the heavy burdens and to let the oppressed go free.

AUGUSTINE BIRRELL

UGUSTINE BIRRELL, K. C., M. P., LL. D., a brilliant English essayist, critic, and chancery lawyer, was born near Liverpool, Jan. 19, 1850. The son of the Rev. Charles Birrell, a Baptist clergyman, he received his education at Trinity Hall, Cambridge, where he graduated in 1872, was called to the Bar in 1875, and fourteen years later was elected Liberal member of Parliament for West Fifeshire. In 1896, he was appointed Quain professor of law at University College, London. Among his best-known publications are "Obiter Dicta" (1884 and 1887); "Life of Charlotte Brontë" (1885); "Res Judicatæ" (1892); "Men, Women, and Books" (1894); besides his professional "Lectures on the Duties and Liabilities of Trustees" (1896). He is also editor of an edition of Boswell's "Life of Johnson."

EDMUND BURKE

A LECTURE DELIVERED BEFORE THE EDINBURGH PHILOSOPHICAL SOCIETY

MR. JOHN MORLEY, who among other things has written two admirable books about Edmund Burke, is to be found in the Preface to the second of them apologizing for having introduced into the body of the work extracts from his former volume — conduct which he seeks to justify by quoting from the Greek (always a desirable thing to do when in a difficulty), to prove that, though you may say what you have to say well once, you cannot so say it twice.

A difficulty somewhat of the same kind cannot fail to be felt by every one who takes upon himself to write on Burke; for, however innocent a man's own past life may be of any public references to the subject, the very many good things other men have said about it must seriously interfere with true liberty of treatment.

Hardly any man, and certainly no politician, has been so

bepraised as Burke, whose very name, suggesting, as it does, splendor of diction, has tempted those who would praise him to do so in a highly decorated style, and it would have been easy work to have brought together a sufficient number of animated passages from the works of well-known writers all dedicated to the greater glory of Edmund Burke, and then to have tagged on half-a-dozen specimens of his own resplendent rhetoric, and so to have come to an apparently natural and long desired conclusion without exciting any more than the usual post-lectorial grumble.

This course, however, not recommending itself, some other method had to be discovered. Happily, it is out of the question within present limits to give any proper summary of Burke's public life. This great man was not, like some modern politicians, a specialist, confining his activities within the prospectus of an association; nor was he, like some others, a thing of shreds and patches, busily employed to-day picking up the facts with which he will overwhelm his opponents on the morrow; but was one ever ready to engage with all comers on all subjects from out the stores of his accumulated knowledge.

Even were we to confine ourselves to those questions only which engaged Burke's most powerful attention, enlisted his most active sympathy, elicited his most bewitching rhetoric, we should still find ourselves called upon to grapple with problems as vast and varied as Economic Reform, the Status of our Colonies, our Empire in India, our Relations with Ireland both in respect to her trade and her prevalent religion; and then, blurring the picture, as some may think—certainly rendering it titanesque and gloomy—we have the spectacle of Burke in his old age, like another Laocoön, writhing and wrestling with the French Revolution; and it may serve to give us some dim notion of how great a man Burke was, of how affluent a mind, of how potent an imagination, of how resistless an energy, that even when his sole unassisted name is pitted against the outcome of centuries, and we say Burke and the French Revolution, we are not overwhelmed by any sense of obvious absurdity or incongruity.

What I propose to do is merely to consider a little Burke's life prior to his obtaining a seat in Parliament, and then to refer to any circumstances which may help us to account for the fact that this truly extraordinary man, whose intellectual resources beggar the imagination, and who devoted himself to politics with all the forces of his nature, never so much as attained to a seat in the Cabinet,—a feat one has known to be accomplished by persons of no proved intellectual agility. Having done this, I shall then, bearing in mind the aphorism of Lord Beaconsfield, that it is always better to be impudent than servile, essay an analysis of the essential elements of Burke's character.

The first great fact to remember is, that the Edmund Burke we are all agreed in regarding as one of the proudest memories of the House of Commons was an Irishman. When we are in our next fit of political depression about that island, and are about piously to wish, as the poet Spenser tells us men were wishing even in his time, that it were not adjacent, let us do a little national stocktaking, and calculate profits as well as losses.

Burke was not only an Irishman, but a typical one—of the very kind many Englishmen, and even possibly some Scotchmen, make a point of disliking. I do not say he was an aboriginal Irishman, but his ancestors are said to have settled in the county of Galway, under Strongbow, in King Henry the Second's time, when Ireland was first conquered and our troubles began. This, at all events, is a better Irish pedigree than Mr. Parnell's.

Skipping six centuries, we find Burke's father an attorney in Dublin—which somehow sounds a very Irish thing to be —who in 1725 married a Miss Nagle and had fifteen children. The marriage of Burke's parents was of the kind called mixed—a term which doubtless admits of wide application, but when employed technically signifies that the religious faith of the spouses was different; one, the father, being a Protestant, and the lady an adherent to what used to be pleasantly called the " old religion." The severer spirit now dominating Catholic councils has condemned these marriages on the score of their bad theology and their lax morality; but the practical politician, who is not usually much of a theologian—though Lord Melbourne and Mr. Gladstone are distinguished exceptions—and whose moral conscience is apt to be robust (and here I believe there are no exceptions), cannot but regret that so good an opportunity of lubricating religious differences with the sweet oil of the domestic affections should be lost to us in these days of bitterness and dissension.

Burke was brought up in the Protestant faith of his father, and was never in any real danger of deviating from it; but I cannot doubt that his regard for his Catholic fellow subjects, his fierce repudiation of the infamies of the penal code—whose horrors he did something to mitigate—his respect for antiquity, and his historic sense, were all quickened by the fact that a tenderly loved and loving mother belonged through life and in death to an ancient and an outraged faith.

The great majority of Burke's brothers and sisters, like those of Laurence Sterne, were " not made to live ; " and out of the fifteen but three, beside himself, attained maturity.

These were his eldest brother, Garrett, on whose death Edmund succeeded to the patrimonial Irish estate, which he sold; his younger brother, Richard, a highly speculative gentleman, who always lost; and his sister, Juliana, who married a Mr. French, and was, as became her mother's daughter, a rigid Roman Catholic—who, so we read, was accustomed every Christmas Day to invite to the Hall the maimed, the aged, and distressed of her vicinity to a plentiful repast, during which she waited upon them as a servant. A sister like this never did any man any serious harm.

Edmund Burke was born in 1729, in Dublin, and was taught his rudiments in the country—first by a Mr. O'Halloran, and afterwards by a Mr. FitzGerald, village pedagogues both, who at all events succeeded in giving their charge a brogue which death alone could silence.

Burke passed from their hands to an academy at Ballitore, kept by a Quaker, from whence he proceeded to Trinity College, Dublin. He was thus not only Irish born, but Irish bred.

His intellectual habit of mind exhibited itself early. He belonged to the happy family of omnivorous readers, and, in the language of his latest schoolmaster, he went to college with a larger miscellaneous stock of reading than was usual with one of his years; which, being interpreted out of pedagogic into plain English, means that "our good Edmund" was an enormous devourer of poetry and novels, and so he remained to the end of his days.

That he always preferred Fielding to Richardson is satisfactory, since it pairs him off nicely with Dr. Johnson, whose preference was the other way, and so helps to keep an interesting question wide open. His passion for the poetry of Virgil is significant. His early devotion to Edward Young,

the grandiose author of the " Night Thoughts," is not to
be wondered at; though the inspiration of the youthful
Burke, either as poet or critic, may be questioned when we
find him rapturously scribbling in the margin of his copy:

> " Jove claimed the verse old Homer sung,
> But God himself inspired Dr. Young."

But a boy's enthusiasm for a favorite poet is a thing to rejoice
over. The years that bring the philosophic mind will not
bring—they must find—enthusiasm.

In 1750, Burke (being then twenty-one) came for the first
time to London, to do what so many of his lively young
countrymen are still doing—though they are beginning to
make a grievance even of that—eat his dinners at the Middle
Temple, and so qualify himself for the Bar. Certainly that
student was in luck who found himself in the same mess with
Burke; and yet so stupid are men—so prone to rest with
their full weight on the immaterial and slide over the essential—that had that good fortune been ours we should probably have been more taken up with Burke's brogue than with
his brains.

Burke came to London with a cultivated curiosity, and in
no spirit of desperate determination to make his fortune.
That the study of the law interested him cannot be doubted,
for everything interested him, particularly the stage. Like
the sensible Irishman he was, he lost his heart to Peg Wof-
fington on the first opportunity. He was fond of roaming
about the country, during, it is to be hoped, vacation-time
only, and is to be found writing the most cheerful letters to
his friends in Ireland (all of whom are persuaded that he
is going some day to be somebody, though sorely puzzled to
surmise what thing or when, so pleasantly does he take life),
from all sorts of out-of-the-way country places, where he

lodges with quaint old landladies who wonder maternally why he never gets drunk, and generally mistake him for an author until he pays his bill.

When in town he frequented debating societies in Fleet Street and Covent Garden, and made his first speeches; for which purpose he would, unlike some debaters, devote studious hours to getting up the subjects to be discussed. There is good reason to believe that it was in this manner his attention was first directed to India. He was at all times a great talker, and, Dr. Johnson's dictum notwithstanding, a good listener. He was endlessly interested in everything—in the state of the crops, in the last play, in the details of all trades, the rhythm of all poems, the plots of all novels, and indeed in the course of every manufacture. And so for six years he went up and down, to and fro, gathering information, imparting knowledge, and preparing himself, though he knew not for what.

The attorney in Dublin grew anxious, and searched for precedents of a son behaving like his, and rising to eminence. Had his son got the legal mind?—which, according to a keen observer, chiefly displays itself by illustrating the obvious, explaining the evident, and expatiating on the commonplace.

Edmund's powers of illustration, explanation, and expatiation could not indeed be questioned; but then the subjects selected for the exhibition of those powers were very far indeed from being obvious, evident, or commonplace; and the attorney's heart grew heavy within him. The paternal displeasure was signified in the usual manner—the supplies were cut off. Edmund Burke, however, was no ordinary prodigal, and his reply to his father's expostulations took the unexpected and unprecedented shape of a copy of a second and enlarged edition of his treatise on the "Sublime and

Beautiful," which he had published in 1756 at the price of three shillings. Burke's father promptly sent the author a bank-bill for £100,—conduct on his part which, considering he had sent his son to London and maintained him there for six years to study law, was, in my judgment, both sublime and beautiful.

In the same year Burke published another pamphlet—a one-and-sixpenny affair—written ironically, in the style of Lord Bolingbroke, and called " A Vindication of Natural Society; or, a View of the Miseries and Evils Arising to Mankind from Every Species of Civil Society." Irony is a dangerous weapon for a public man to have ever employed, and in after-life Burke had frequently to explain that he was not serious.

On these two pamphlets' airy pinions Burke floated into the harbor of literary fame. No less a man than the great David Hume referred to him, in a letter to the hardly less great Adam Smith, as an Irish gentleman who had written a " very pretty treatise on the Sublime." After these efforts, Burke, as became an established wit, went to Bath to recruit, and there, fitly enough, fell in love. The lady was Miss Jane Mary Nugent, the daughter of a celebrated Bath physician; and it is pleasant to be able to say of the marriage that was shortly solemnized between the young couple, that it was a happy one, and then to go on our way, leaving them—where man and wife ought to be left—alone.

Oddly enough, Burke's wife was also the offspring of a " mixed marriage "—only in her case it was the father who was the Catholic; consequently both Mr. and Mrs. Edmund Burke were of the same way of thinking, but each had a parent of the other way. Although getting married is no part of the curriculum of a law-student, Burke's father seems to have come to the conclusion that after all it was a greater distinction for an attorney in Dublin to have a son living amongst the wits in London, and discoursing familiarly on the " Sublime and Beautiful," than one prosecuting some poor countryman, with a brogue as rich as his own, for stealing a pair of breeches; for we find him generously allowing the young couple £200 a year, which no doubt went some way toward maintaining them. Burke, who was now in his twenty-eighth year, seems to have given up all notion of the law. In 1758 he wrote for Dodsley the first volume of the " Annual Register," a melancholy series which continues to this day. For doing this he got £100.

Burke was by this time a well-known figure in London literary society, and was busy making for himself a huge private reputation. The Christmas Day of 1758 witnessed a singular scene at the dinner-table of David Garrick. Dr. Johnson, then in the full vigor of his mind, and with the all-dreaded weapons of his dialectics kept burnished by daily use, was flatly contradicted by a fellow guest some twenty years his junior, and, what is more, submitted to it without a murmur. One of the diners, Arthur Murphy, was so struck by this occurrence, unique in his long experience of the Doctor, that on returning home he recorded the fact in his journal, but ventured no explanation of it.

It can only be accounted for—so at least I venture to think—by the combined effect of four wholly independent circumstances: First, the day was Christmas Day, a day of peace and good will, and our beloved Doctor was amongst the sincerest, though most argumentative of Christians, and a great observer of days. Second, the house was David Garrick's, and consequently we may be certain that the dinner had been a superlatively good one; and has not Boswell

placed on record Johnson's opinion of a man who professed
to be indifferent about his dinner ? Third, the subject under
discussion was India, about which Johnson knew he knew
next to nothing. And fourth, the offender was Edmund
Burke, whom Johnson loved from the first day he set eyes
upon him to their last sad parting by the waters of death.

In 1761 that shrewd old gossip, Horace Walpole, met
Burke for the first time at dinner, and remarks of him in a
letter to George Montague :—

" I dined at Hamilton's yesterday; there were Garrick,
and young Mr. Burke, who wrote a book in the style of
Lord Bolingbroke, that was much admired. He is a sensible
man, but has not worn off his authorism yet, and thinks there
is nothing so charming as writers, and to be one. He will
know better one of these days."

But great as were Burke's literary powers, and passionate
as was his fondness for letters and for literary society, he
never seems to have felt that the main burden of his life lay
in that direction. He looked to the public service, and this
though he always believed that the pen of a great writer was
a more powerful and glorious weapon than any to be found
in the armory of politics. This faith of his comes out sometimes queerly enough. For example, when Dr. Robertson
in 1777 sent Burke his cheerful " History of America " in
quarto volumes, Burke, in the most perfect good faith, closes
a long letter of thanks thus:

" You will smile when I send you a trifling temporary production made for the occasion of the day, and to perish with
it, in return for your immortal work."

I have no desire, least of all in Edinburgh, to say anything
disrespectful of Principal Robertson; but still, when we re-

member that the temporary production he got in exchange
for his " History of America " was Burke's immortal letter
to the sheriffs of Bristol on the American war, we must, I
think, be forced to admit that, as so often happens when a
Scotchman and an Irishman do business together, the former
got the better of the bargain.

Burke's first public employment was of an humble character, and might well have been passed over in a sentence
had it not terminated in a most delightful quarrel, in which
Burke conducted himself like an Irishman of genius.

Some time in 1759 he became acquainted with William
Gerard Hamilton, commonly called " Single-Speech Hamilton," on account of the celebrity he gained from his first
speech in Parliament, and the steady way in which his ora-
torical reputation went on waning ever after. In 1761 this
gentleman went over to Ireland as Chief Secretary, and
Burke accompanied him as the Secretary's secretary, or, in
the unlicensed speech of Dublin, as Hamilton's jackal.

This arrangement was eminently satisfactory to Hamilton,
who found, as generations of men have found after him,
Burke's brains very useful, and he determined to borrow
them for the period of their joint lives. Animated by this
desire, in itself praiseworthy, he busied himself in procuring
for Burke a pension of £300 a year on the Irish establishment, and then the simple " Single-Speech " thought the
transaction closed. He had bought his poor man of genius,
and paid for him on the nail with other people's money.
Nothing remained but for Burke to draw his pension and devote the rest of his life to maintaining Hamilton's reputation. There is nothing at all unusual in this, and I have no
doubt Burke would have stuck to his bargain had not Hamilton conceived the fatal idea that Burke's brains were ex-

clusively his (Hamilton's). Then the situation became one
of risk and apparent danger.

Burke's imagination began playing round the subject: he
saw himself a slave, blotted out of existence—mere fuel for
Hamilton's flame. In a week he was in a towering
passion. Few men can afford to be angry. It is a
run upon their intellectual resources they cannot meet. But
Burke's treasury could well afford the luxury; and his letters
to Hamilton make delightful reading to those who, like myself, dearly love a dispute when conducted according to the
rules of the game by men of great intellectual wealth.

Hamilton demolished and reduced to stony silence, Burke
sat down again and wrote long letters to all his friends, telling them the whole story from beginning to end. I must be
allowed a quotation from one of these letters, for this really
is not so frivolous a matter as I am afraid I have made it
appear—a quotation of which this much may be said, that
nothing more delightfully Burkean is to be found anywhere:

"My Dear Mason,—I am hardly able to tell you how much
satisfaction I had in your letter. Your approbation of my
conduct makes me believe much the better of you and myself; and I assure you that that approbation came to me very
seasonably. Such proofs of a warm, sincere, and disinterested friendship were not wholly unnecessary to my support
at a time when I experienced such bitter effects of the perfidy
and ingratitude of much longer and much closer connections.
The way in which you take up my affairs binds me to you
in a manner I cannot express; for, to tell you the truth, I
never can (knowing as I do the principles upon which I always endeavor to act) submit to any sort of compromise of
my character; and I shall never, therefore, look upon those
who, after hearing the whole story, do not think me perfectly
in the right, and do not consider Hamilton an infamous
scoundrel, to be in the smallest degree my friends, or even
to be persons for whom I am bound to have the slightest es-

teem, as fair and just estimators of the characters and conduct of men.

" Situated as I am, and feeling as I do, I should be just as well pleased that they totally condemned me, as that they should say there were faults on both sides, or that it was a disputable case, as I hear is (I cannot forbear saying) the affected language of some persons. . . . You cannot avoid remarking, my dear Mason, and I hope not without some indignation, the unparalleled singularity of my situation. Was ever a man before me expected to enter into formal, direct, and undisguised slavery? Did ever man before him confess an attempt to decoy a man into such an alleged contract, not to say anything of the impudence of regularly pleading it? If such an attempt be wicked and unlawful (and I am sure no one ever doubted it), I have only to confess his charge, and to admit myself his dupe, to make him pass, on his own showing, for the most consummate villain that ever lived.

" The only difference between us is, not whether he is not a rogue—for he not only admits but pleads the facts that demonstrate him to be so; but only whether I was such a fool as to sell myself absolutely for a consideration which, so far from being adequate, if any such could be adequate, is not even so much as certain. Not to value myself as a gentleman, a free man, a man of education, and one pretending to literature; is there any situation in life so low, or even so criminal, that can subject a man to the possibility of such an engagement? Would you dare attempt to bind your footman to such terms? Will the law suffer a felon sent to the plantations to bind himself for his life, and to renounce all possibility either of elevation or quiet? And am I to defend myself for not doing what no man is suffered to do, and what it would be criminal in any man to submit to? You will excuse me for this heat."

I not only excuse Burke for his heat, but love him for letting me warm my hands at it after a lapse of a hundred and twenty years.

Burke was more fortunate in his second master, for in 1765, being then thirty-six years of age, he became private

secretary to the new Prime Minister, the Marquis of Rockingham; was by the interest of Lord Verney returned to
Parliament for Wendover, in Bucks; and on January 27,
1766, his voice was first heard in the House of Commons.

The Rockingham Ministry deserves well of the historian,
and on the whole has received its deserts. Lord Rockingham, the Duke of Richmond, Lord John Cavendish, Mr.
Dowdeswell, and the rest of them, were good men and true,
judged by an ordinary standard; and when contrasted with
most of their political competitors, they almost approach the
ranks of saints and angels. However, after a year and
twenty days, his Majesty King George III managed to get
rid of them, and to keep them at bay for fifteen years.

But their first term of office, though short, lasted long
enough to establish a friendship of no ordinary powers of endurance between the chief members of the party and the
Prime Minister's private secretary, who was at first, so ran
the report, supposed to be a wild Irishman, whose real name
was O'Burke, and whose brogue seemed to require the allegation that its owner was a popish emissary.

It is satisfactory to notice how from the very first Burke's
intellectual pre-eminence, character, and aims were clearly
admitted and most cheerfully recognized by his political and
social superiors; and in the long correspondence in which he
engaged with most of them, there is not a trace to be found,
on one side or the other, of anything approaching to either
patronage or servility. Burke advises them, exhorts them,
expostulates with them, condemns their aristocratic languor,
fans their feeble flames, drafts their motions, dictates their
protests, visits their houses, and generally supplies them with
facts, figures, poetry, and romance.

To all this they submit with much humility. The Duke of

Richmond once indeed ventured to hint to Burke, with exceeding delicacy, that he (the Duke) had a small private estate to attend to as well as public affairs; but the validity of the excuse was not admitted. The part Burke played for the next fifteen years with relation to the Rockingham party reminds me of the functions I have observed performed in lazy families by a soberly clad and eminently respectable person who pays them domiciliary visits, and, having admission everywhere, goes about mysteriously from room to room, winding up all the clocks. This is what Burke did for the Rockingham party—he kept it going.

But fortunately for us, Burke was not content with private adjuration, or even public speech. His literary instincts, his dominating desire to persuade everybody that he, Edmund Burke, was absolutely in the right, and every one of his opponents hopelessly wrong, made him turn to the pamphlet as a propaganda, and in his hands—

> " The thing became a trumpet, whence he blew
> Soul-animating strains."

So accustomed are we to regard Burke's pamphlets as specimens of our noblest literature, and to see them printed in comfortable volumes, that we are apt to forget that in their origin they were but the children of the pavement, the publications of the hour.

If, however, you ever visit any old public library, and grope about a little, you are likely enough to find a shelf holding some twenty-five or thirty musty, ugly little books, usually lettered " Burke," and on opening any of them you will come across one of Burke's pamphlets as originally issued, bound up with the replies and counter-pamphlets it occasioned. I have frequently tried, but always in vain, to read these replies, which are pretentious enough—usually

the works of deans, members of Parliament, and other dig-
nitaries of the class Carlyle used compendiously to describe
as " shovel-hatted "—and each of whom was as much entitled to publish pamphlets as Burke himself.

There are some things it is very easy to do, and to write
a pamphlet is one of them; but to write such a pamphlet as
future generations will read with delight is perhaps the most
difficult feat in literature. Milton, Swift, Burke, and Sydney
Smith are, I think, our only great pamphleteers.

I have now rather more than kept my word so far as
Burke's pre-parliamentary life is concerned, and will proceed
to mention some of the circumstances that may serve to account for the fact, that when the Rockingham party came
into power for the second time in 1782, Burke, who was their
life and soul, was only rewarded with a minor office.

First, then, it must be recorded sorrowfully of Burke that
he was always desperately in debt, and in this country no
politician under the rank of a baronet can ever safely be in
debt. Burke's finances are, and always have been, marvels
and mysteries; but one thing must be said of them—that the
malignity of his enemies, both Tory enemies and Radical
enemies, has never succeeded in formulating any charge of
dishonesty against him that has not been at once completely
pulverized, and shown on the facts to be impossible.

Burke's purchase of the estate at Beaconsfield in 1768,
only two years after he entered Parliament, consisting as it
did of a good house and 1,600 acres of land, has puzzled a
great many good men—much more than it ever did Edmund
Burke. But how did he get the money? After an Irish
fashion—by not getting it at all.

Two thirds of the purchase-money remained on mortgage,
and the balance he borrowed; or, as he puts it, " With all I

could collect of my own, and by the aid of my friends, I have established a root in the country." That is how Burke bought Beaconsfield, where he lived till his end came; whither he always hastened when his sensitive mind was tortured by the thought of how badly men governed the world; where he entertained all sorts and conditions of men— Quakers, Brahmins (for whose ancient rites he provided suitable accommodation in a greenhouse), nobles and abbés flying from revolutionary France, poets, painters, and peers; no one of whom ever long remained a stranger to his charm.

Burke flung himself into farming with all the enthusiasm of his nature. His letters to Arthur Young on the subject of carrots still tremble with emotion. You all know Burke's " Thoughts on the Present Discontents." You remember— it is hard to forget—his speech on Conciliation with America, particularly the magnificent passage beginning, " Magnanimity in politics is not seldom the truest wisdom, and a great empire and little minds go ill together."

You have echoed back the words in which, in his letter to the sheriffs of Bristol on the hateful American war, he protests that it was not instantly he could be brought to rejoice when he heard of the slaughter and captivity of long lists of those whose names had been familiar in his ears from his infancy, and you would all join with me in subscribing to a fund which would have for its object the printing and hanging up over every editor's desk in town and country a subsequent passage from the same letter:

" A conscientious man would be cautious how he dealt in blood. He would feel some apprehension at being called to a tremendous account for engaging in so deep a play without any knowledge of the game. It is no excuse for presumptuous ignorance that it is directed by insolent passion. The poorest being that crawls on earth, contending to save itself from injustice and oppression, is an object respectable in the eyes of God and man.

"But I cannot conceive any existence under heaven (which in the depths of its wisdom tolerates all sorts of things) that is more truly odious and disgusting than an impotent, helpless creature, without civil wisdom or military skill, bloated with pride and arrogance, calling for battles which he is not to fight, and contending for a violent dominion which he can never exercise. . . .

"If you and I find our talents not of the great and ruling kind, our conduct at least is conformable to our faculties. No man's life pays the forfeit of our rashness. No desolate widow weeps tears of blood over our ignorance. Scrupulous and sober in a well-grounded distrust of ourselves, we would keep in the port of peace and security; and perhaps in recommending to others something of the same diffidence, we should show ourselves more charitable to their welfare than injurious to their abilities."

You have laughed over Burke's account of how all Lord Talbot's schemes for the reform of the king's household were dashed to pieces because the turnspit of the king's kitchen was a Member of Parliament. You have often pondered over that miraculous passage in his speech on the Nabob of Arcot's debts, describing the devastation of the Carnatic by Hyder Ali—a passage which Mr. John Morley says fills the young orator with the same emotions of enthusiasm, emulation, and despair that (according to the same authority) invariably torment the artist who first gazes on "The Madonna" at Dresden, or the figures of "Night" and "Dawn" at Florence.

All these things you know, else are you mighty self-denying of your pleasures. But it is just possible you may have forgotten the following extract from one of Burke's farming letters to Arthur Young:

" One of the grand points in controversy (a controversy indeed chiefly carried on between practice and speculation) is that of deep plowing. In your last volumes you seem, on the whole, rather against that practice, and have given several reasons for your judgment which deserve to be very well considered. In order to know how we ought to plow, we ought to know what end it is we propose to ourselves in that operation. The first and instrumental end is to divide the soil; the last and ultimate end, so far as regards the plants, is to facilitate the pushing of the blade upward and the shooting of the roots in all the inferior directions.

" There is further proposed a more ready admission of external influences—the rain, the sun, the air, charged with all those heterogeneous contents, some, possibly all, of which are necessary for the nourishment of the plants. By plowing deep you answer these ends in a greater mass of the soil. This would seem in favor of deep plowing as nothing else than accomplishing, in a more perfect manner, those very ends for which you are induced to plow at all.

" But doubts here arise, only to be solved by experiment. First, it is quite certain that it is good for the ear and grain of farinaceous plants that their roots should spread and descend into the ground to the greatest possible distances and depths? Is there not some limit in this? We know that in timber, what makes one part flourish does not equally conduce to the benefit of all; and that which may be beneficial to the wood does not equally contribute to the quantity and goodness of the fruit; and, vice versa, that what increases the fruit largely is often far from serviceable to the tree.

" Secondly, is that looseness to great depths, supposing it is useful to one of the species of plants, equally useful to all?

" Thirdly, though the external influences—the rain, the sun, the air—act undoubtedly a part, and a large part, in vegetation, does it follow that they are equally salutary in any quantities, at any depths? Or that, though it may be useful to diffuse one of these agents as extensively as may be in the earth, that therefore it will be equally useful to render the earth in the same degree pervious to all.

" It is a dangerous way of reasoning in physics, as well as morals, to conclude, because a given proportion of anything is advantageous, that the double will be quite as good, or that it will be good at all. Neither in the one nor the other is it always true that two and two make four."

This is magnificent, but it is not farming, and you will easily believe that Burke's attempts to till the soil were more costly than productive. Farming, if it is to pay, is a pursuit of small economies; and Burke was far too Asiatic, tropical, and splendid to have anything to do with small economies. His expenditure, like his rhetoric, was in the " grand style." He belongs to Charles Lamb's great race, " the men who borrow." But indeed it was not so much that Burke borrowed as that men lent.

Right-feeling men did not wait to be asked. Dr. Brocklesby, that good physician, whose name breathes like a benediction through the pages of the biographies of the best men of his time, who soothed Dr. Johnson's last melancholy hours, and for whose supposed heterodoxy the dying man displayed so tender a solicitude, wrote to Burke, in the strain of a timid suitor proposing for the hand of a proud heiress, to know whether Burke would be so good as to accept £1,000 at once, instead of waiting for the writer's death. Burke felt no hesitation in obliging so old a friend.

Garrick, who, though fond of money, was as generous-hearted a fellow as ever brought down a house, lent Burke £1,000. Sir Joshua Reynolds, who has been reckoned stingy, by his will left Burke £2,000, and forgave him another £2,000 which he had lent him. The Marquis of Rockingham, by his will, directed all Burke's bonds held by him to be cancelled. They amounted to £30,000. Burke's patrimonial estate was sold by him for £4,000; and I have seen it stated that he had received altogether from family sources as much as £20,000.

And yet he was always poor, and was glad at the last to

accept pensions from the Crown in order that he might not leave his wife a beggar. This good lady survived her illustrious husband twelve years, and seemed, as his widow, to have some success in paying his bills, for at her death all remaining demands were found to be discharged.

For receiving this pension Burke was assailed by the Duke of Bedford, a most pleasing act of ducal fatuity, since it enabled the pensioner, not bankrupt of his wit, to write a pamphlet, now of course a cherished classic, and introduce into it a few paragraphs about the House of Russell and the cognate subject of grants from the Crown. But each of Burke's debts and difficulties, which I only mention because all through his life they were cast up against him.

Had Burke been a moralist of the calibre of Charles James Fox, he might have amassed a fortune large enough to keep up half a dozen Beaconsfields, by simply doing what all his predecessors in the office he held, including Fox's own father, the truly infamous first Lord Holland, had done—namely, by retaining for his own use the interest on all balances of the public money from time to time in his hands as Paymaster of the Forces. But Burke carried his passion for good government into actual practice, and, cutting down the emoluments of his office to a salary (a high one, no doubt), effected a saving to the country of some £25,000 a year, every farthing of which might have gone without remark into his own pocket.

Burke had no vices save of style and temper; nor was any of his expenditure a profligate squandering of money. It all went in giving employment or disseminating kindness. He sent the painter Barry to study art in Italy. He saved the poet Crabbe from starvation and despair, and thus secured to the country one who owns the unrivalled distinction of having been the favorite poet of the three greatest intellectual factors of the age (scientific men excepted),—Lord Byron, Sir Walter Scott, and Cardinal Newman.

Yet so distorted are men's views that the odious and anti-social excesses of Fox at the gambling-table are visited with a blame usually wreathed in smiles, whilst the financial irregularities of a noble and pure-minded man are thought fit matter for the fiercest censure or the most lordly contempt.

Next to Burke's debts, some of his companions and intimates did him harm and injured his consequence. His brother Richard, whose brogue we are given to understand was simply appalling, was a good-for-nothing, with a dilapidated reputation. Then there was another Mr. Burke, who was no relation, but none the less was always about, and to whom it was not safe to lend money. Burke's son, too, whose death he mourned so pathetically, seems to have been a failure, and is described by a candid friend as a nauseating person To have a decent following is important in politics.

A third reason must be given: Burke's judgment of men and things was often both wrong and violent. The story of Powell and Bembridge, two knaves in Burke's own office, whose cause he espoused, and whom he insisted on reinstating in the public service after they had been dismissed, and maintaining them there, in spite of all protests, till the one had the grace to cut his throat and the other was sentenced by the Queen's Bench to a term of imprisonment and a heavy fine, is too long to be told, though it makes interesting reading in the twenty-second volume of Howell's " State Trials," where at the end of the report is to be found the following note :—

" The proceedings against Messrs. Powell and Bembridge

occasioned much animated discussion in the House of Commons, in which Mr. Burke warmly supported the accused. The compassion which on these and all other occasions was manifested by Mr. Burke for the sufferings of those public delinquents, the zeal with which he advocated their cause, and the eagerness with which he endeavored to extenuate their criminality, have received severe reprehension, and in particular when contrasted with his subsequent conduct in the prosecution of Mr. Hastings."

The real reason for Burke's belief in Bembridge is, I think, to be found in the evidence Burke gave on his behalf at the trial before Lord Mansfield. Bembridge had rendered Burke invaluable assistance in carrying out his reforms at the Paymaster's Office, and Burke was constitutionally unable to believe that a rogue could be on his side; but, indeed, Burke was too apt to defend bad causes with a scream of passion, and a politician who screams is never likely to occupy a commanding place in the House of Commons.

A last reason for Burke's exclusion from high office is to be found in his aversion to any measure of Parliamentary reform. An ardent reformer like the Duke of Richmond—the then Duke of Richmond—who was in favor of annual Parliaments, universal suffrage, and payment of members, was not likely to wish to associate himself too closely with a politician who wept with emotion at the bare thought of depriving Old Sarum of parliamentary representation.

These reasons account for Burke's exclusion, and jealous as we naturally and properly are of genius being snubbed by mediocrity, my reading at all events does not justify me in blaming any one but the Fates for the circumstance that Burke was never a Secretary of State. And after all, does it matter much what he was? Burke no doubt occasionally felt his exclusion a little hard; but he is the victor who re-

mains in possession of the field; and Burke is now, for us
and for all coming after us, in such possession.

It now only remains for me, drawing upon my stock of as-
surance, to essay the analysis of the essential elements of
Burke's mental character, and I therefore at once proceed to
say that it was Burke's peculiarity and his glory to apply the
imagination of a poet of the first order to the facts and the
business of life.　Arnold says of Sophocles—

" He saw life steadily, and saw it whole."

Substitute for the word " life " the words " organized society," and you get a peep into Burke's mind.

There was a catholicity about his gaze.　He knew how the
whole world lived.　Everything contributed to this; his vast
desultory reading; his education, neither wholly academical
nor entirely professional; his long years of apprenticeship
in the service of knowledge; his wanderings up and down
the country; his vast conversational powers; his enormous
correspondence with all sorts of people; his unfailing interest in all pursuits, trades, manufactures,—all helped to
keep before him, like motes dancing in a sunbeam, the huge
organism of modern society, which requires for its existence
and for its development the maintenance of credit and of
order.

Burke's imagination led him to look out over the whole
land: the legislator devising new laws, the judge expounding
and enforcing old ones, the merchant despatching his goods
and extending his credit, the banker advancing the money of
his customers upon the credit of the merchant, the frugal
man slowly accumulating the store which is to support him
in old age, the ancient institutions of Church and University
with their seemly provisions for sound learning and true re-

ligion, the parson in his pulpit, the poet pondering his rhymes, the farmer eyeing his crops, the painter covering his canvases, the player educating the feelings.

Burke saw all this with the fancy of a poet, and dwelt on it with the eye of a lover. But love is the parent of fear, and none knew better than Burke how thin is the lava layer between the costly fabric of society and the volcanic heats and destroying flames of anarchy. He trembled for the fair frame of all established things, and to his horror saw men, instead of covering the thin surface with the concrete, digging in it for abstractions, and asking fundamental questions about the origin of society, and why one man should be born rich and another poor.

Burke was no prating optimist: it was his very knowledge how much could be said against society that quickened his fears for it. There is no shallower criticism than that which accuses Burke in his later years of apostasy from so-called Liberal opinions. Burke was all his life through a passionate maintainer of the established order of things, and a ferocious hater of abstractions and metaphysical politics.

The same ideas that explode like bombs through his diatribes against the French Revolution are to be found shining with a mild effulgence in the comparative calm of his earlier writings. I have often been struck with a resemblance, which I hope is not wholly fanciful, between the attitude of Burke's mind toward government and that of Cardinal Newman toward religion.

Both these great men belong, by virtue of their imaginations, to the poetic order, and they both are to be found dwelling with amazing eloquence, detail, and wealth of illustration on the varied elements of society. Both seem as they write to have one hand on the pulse of the world, and to be forever alive to the throb of its action; and Burke, as he regarded humanity swarming like bees into and out of their hives of industry, is ever asking himself, How are these men to be saved from anarchy? whilst Newman puts to himself the question, How are these men to be saved from atheism? Both saw the perils of free inquiry divorced from practical affairs.

" Civil freedom," says Burke, " is not, as many have endeavored to persuade you, a thing that lies hid in the depth of abstruse science. It is a blessing and a benefit, not an abstract speculation; and all the just reasoning that can be upon it is of so coarse a texture as perfectly to suit the ordinary capacities of those who are to enjoy and of those who are to defend it."

" Tell men," says Cardinal Newman, " to gain notions of a Creator from his works, and if they were to set about it (which nobody does), they would be jaded and wearied by the labyrinth they were tracing; their minds would be gorged and surfeited by the logical operation. To most men argument makes the point in hand more doubtful and considerably less impressive. After all, man is not a reasoning animal, he is a seeing, feeling, contemplating, acting animal."

Burke is fond of telling us that he is no lawyer, no antiquarian, but a plain, practical man; and the Cardinal, in like manner, is ever insisting that he is no theologian—he leaves everything of that sort to the Schools, whatever they may be, and simply deals with religion on its practical side as a benefit to mankind.

If either of these great men has been guilty of intellectual excesses, those of Burke may be attributed to his dread of anarchy, those of Newman to his dread of atheism. Neither of them was prepared to rest content with a scientific frontier, an imaginary line. So much did they dread their enemy, so alive were they to the terrible strength of some of his positions, that they could not agree to dispense with the protection afforded by the huge mountains of prejudice and the ancient rivers of custom. The sincerity of either man can only be doubted by the bigot and the fool.

But Burke, apart from his fears, had a constitutional love for old things, simply because they were old. Anything mankind had ever worshipped, or venerated, or obeyed, was dear to him. I have already referred to his providing his Brahmins with a greenhouse for the purpose of their rites, which he watched from outside with great interest. One cannot fancy Cardinal Newman peeping through a window to see men worshipping false though ancient gods. Warren Hastings's hind-handed dealings with the temples and time-honored if scandalous customs of the Hindoos filled Burke with horror. So, too, he respected Quakers, Presbyterians, Independents, Baptists, and all those whom he called Constitutional Dissenters.

He has a fine passage somewhere about Rust, for with all his passion for good government he dearly loved a little rust. In this phase of character he reminds one not a little of another great writer—whose death literature has still reason to deplore—George Eliot; who, in her love for old hedgerows and barns and crumbling moss-grown walls, was a writer after Burke's own heart, whose novels he would have sat up all night to devour; for did he not deny with warmth Gibbon's statement that he had read all five volumes of "Evelina " in a day? " The thing is impossible," cried Burke; " they took me three days, doing nothing else." Now, " Evelina " is a good novel, but " Silas Marner " is a better.

Wordsworth has been called the High Priest of Nature.

Burke may be called the High Priest of Order—a lover of settled ways, of justice, peace, and security. His writings are a storehouse of wisdom, not the cheap shrewdness of the mere man of the world, but the noble animating wisdom of one who has the poet's heart as well as the statesman's brain.

Nobody is fit to govern this country who has not drunk deep at the springs of Burke. " Have you read your Burke ?" is at least as sensible a question to put to a parliamentary candidate, as to ask him whether he is a total abstainer or a desperate drunkard. Something there may be about Burke to regret, and more to dispute; but that he loved justice and hated iniquity is certain, as also it is that for the most part he dwelt in the paths of purity, humanity, and good sense. May we be found adhering to them !

HENRY CABOT LODGE

HENRY CABOT LODGE

HENRY CABOT LODGE, Ph. D., LL. D., American Republican senator, historian, and man of letters, was born at Boston, Mass., May 12, 1850. He graduated at Harvard College in 1871, and at the Law School in 1874. In 1875, he received the degree of Ph. D. for his thesis on the "Land Law of the Anglo-Saxons." He was university lecturer on American History at Harvard from 1876 to 1879, and edited the "North American Review" in 1873–76, and the "International Review" in 1879–81. He served two terms in the Massachusetts legislature in 1880–81, and was a delegate to the Republican national conventions of 1880 and 1884. He was for two years chairman of the Republican State Committee, and in 1886 was elected to Congress. He served through the fiftieth, fifty-first, and fifty-second congresses and was reëlected to the fifty-third, but having been called to the United States Senate, Jan. 17, 1893, to succeed Henry L. Dawes, he resigned his seat in the House and in March took his seat in the Senate. During his congressional career Mr. Lodge was a member of several important committees, made several able speeches upon tariff, financial, and election laws, and presented the Force Bill in the fifty-first Congress. His career in the Senate has also been signalized by many able speeches on important measures. He was elected an overseer of Harvard University in 1884, and was awarded the honorary degree of LL. D. by Williams College in 1895. His published works embrace lives of "George Cabot" (1877); "Alexander Hamilton" (1882); "Daniel Webster" (1883); "George Washington" (1889); "A History of Boston" (1891); "Studies in History" (1884); "The Story of the American Revolution" (1889); "Short History of the English Colonies in America" (1881); and "Historical and Political Essays."

ORATION ON DANIEL WEBSTER

DELIVERED AT THE UNVEILING OF HIS STATUE IN WASHINGTON, JANUARY 18, 1900

STATUES and monuments can justify their existence on only two grounds—the nature of the subject they commemorate or as works of art. They ought, of course, to possess both qualifications in the fullest measure. Theoretically, at least, a great art should ever illustrate and should always have a great subject.

But art cannot command at will a fit subject, and it is therefore fortunately true that if the art be great it is its own all-sufficient warrant for existence. That Michael Angelo's unsurpassed figure called "Meditation" should be in theory a portrait statue and bear the name of one of the most worthless of the evil Medicean race is, after all, of slight moment. The immortal art remains to delight and to uplift every one who looks upon it with considerate eyes; and it matters little that all the marvellous figures which the chapel of the Medici enshrines were commanded and carved in order to keep alive the memory of a family steeped in crime and a curse to every people among whom they came.

On the other hand, hard as it often is, we can endure bad art if there be no question that the great man or the shining deed deserves the commemoration of bronze or marble. But when the art is bad and the subject unworthy or ephemeral, then the monument, as was said of Sir John Vanbrugh's palaces, is simply a heavy load to the patient earth and an offence to the eyes of succeeding generations.

In these days the world sins often and grievously in this way, and is much given to the raising of monuments, too frequently upon trifling provocation. Yet the fault lies not in the mere multiplication of monuments. The genius of Greece and of the Renaissance multiplied statues, and very wisely, too, because art then was at once splendid and exuberant. But great sculptors and painters are as few now as they were plentiful in the age of Phidias or of Michael Angelo and Donatello, and we erect statues and monuments with a prodigal hand chiefly because we are very rich, and because mechanical appliances have made easy the molding of metal and the carving of stone.

It behooves us, therefore, not only to choose with care artists who can give us work worthy for posterity to look upon, but also to avoid recklessness in rearing monuments upon slight grounds. At present there seems no disposition to heed these salutary principles. The cities and towns of Europe and of England swarm with modern statues and monuments, as a rule ugly or commonplace, too often glaring and vulgar, and very frequently erected to the memory and the glory of the illustrious obscure and of the parish hero.

We Americans sin less numerously, I think, in these respects than the Old World, but we follow their practice none the less and with many melancholy results. We should break away from the example of Europe and realize that the erection of an enduring monument in a public place is a very serious matter. We should seek out the best artists and should permit no monuments to deeds or to men who do not deserve them and who will not themselves be monumental in history and before the eyes of posterity.

Here in Washington, especially, we should bear this principle in mind, for this is the city of the nation, and it should have no place for local glories or provincial heroes. Yet even here we have been so careless that while we have given space to one or more statues of estimable persons, the fact of whose existence will be known only by their effigies, we have found as yet no place for a statue of Hamilton, the greatest constructive statesman of our history, or of the great soldier whose genius made the campaign of Vicksburg rival that of Ulm.

To-day no such doubts or criticisms need haunt or perplex us. We can thank the artist who has conceived, and most unreservedly can we thank the generous and public-spirited citizen of New Hampshire who has given the statue which we unveil this morning. If anyone among our statesmen has a title to a statue in Washington it is Daniel Webster, for this

is the national capital, and no man was ever more national
in his conceptions and his achievements than he.

Born and bred in New Hampshire, which first elected him
to the House, he long represented Massachusetts, the State
of his adoption, in the Congress of the United States, and
thus two historic Commonwealths cherish his memory. But
much as he loved them both, his public service was given to
the nation, and so given that no man doubts his title to a
statue here in this city. Why is there neither doubt nor question as to Webster's right to this great and lasting honor half
a century after his death?

If we cannot answer this question so plainly that he who
runs may read, then we unveil our own ignorance when we
unveil his statue and leave the act without excuse. I shall
try, briefly, to put the answer to this essential question into
words. We all feel in our hearts and minds the reply that
should be made. It has fallen to me to give expression to
that feeling.

What, then, are the real reasons for the great place which
Webster fills in our history? I do not propose to answer this
question by reviewing the history of his time or by retelling
his biography. Both history and biography contain the
answer, yet neither is the answer. They are indeed much
more, for they carry with them, of necessity, everything concerning the man, his strength and his weakness, his virtues
and his defects, all the criticism, all the differences of opinion
which such a career was sure to arouse and which such an
influence upon his country and upon its thought, upon his
own time and upon the future, was equally sure to generate.

There is a place for all this, but not here to-day. We do
not raise a monument to Webster upon debatable grounds,
and thus make it the silent champion of one side of a dead

controversy. We do not set up his statue because he changed
his early opinions upon the tariff, because he remained in
Tyler's cabinet after that President's quarrel with the Whigs,
or because he made upon the 7th of March a speech about
which men have differed always and probably always will
differ. Still less do we place here his graven image in
memory of his failings or his shortcomings. History, with
her cool hands, will put all these things into her scales and
mete out her measure with calm, unflinching eyes. But this
is history's task, not ours, and we raise this statue on other
grounds.

> " Not ours to gauge the more or less,
> The will's defect, the blood's excess,
> The earthy humors that oppress
>   The radiant mind.
> His greatness, not his littleness,
>   Concerns mankind."

To his greatness, then, we rear this monument. In what
does that greatness, acknowledged by all, unquestioned and
undenied by any one, consist? Is it in the fact that he held
high office? He was a brilliant member of Congress; for
nineteen years a great senator; twice Secretary of State. But
" the peerage solicited him, not he the peerage."

Tenure of office is nothing, no matter how high the place.
A name recorded in the list of holders of high office is little
better than one writ in water if the office-holding be all. We
do not raise this statue to the member of Congress, to the
senator of the United States, or to the Secretary of State,
but to Daniel Webster.

That which concerns us is what he did with these great
places which were given to him; for to him, as to all others,
they were mere opportunities. What did he do with these
large opportunities? Still more, what did he do with the
splendid faculties which nature gave him? In the answer

lies the greatness which lifts him out of the ranks and warrants statues to his memory.

First, then, of those qualities which he inherited from the strong New England stock that gave him birth, and which Nature, the fairy who stands by every cradle, poured out upon him. How generous, how lavish she was to that "infant crying in the night; that infant crying for the light" in the rough frontier village of New Hampshire a hundred and eighteen years ago. She gave him the strong, untainted blood of a vigorous race—the English Puritans—who in the New World had been for five generations fighting the hard battle of existence against the wilderness and the savage.

His father was a high type of this class, a farmer and a frontiersman, a pioneer and Indian fighter, then a soldier of the Revolution. On guard the night of Arnold's treason, Washington in that dark hour declared that Captain Webster was a man who could be trusted; simple words, but an order of merit higher and more precious than any glowing ribbon or shining star. So fathered and so descended, the child was endowed with physical attributes at once rare and inestimable.

When developed into manhood he was of commanding stature and seemed always even larger and taller than he really was. Strong, massive, and handsome, he stood before his fellow men looking upon them with wonderful eyes, if we may judge from all that those who saw him tell us. "Dull anthracite furnaces under overhanging brows, waiting only to be blown," says Carlyle, and those deep-set, glowing eyes pursue us still in all that we read of Webster, just as they seemed to haunt everyone who looked upon them in life.

When in a burst of passion or of solemn eloquence he fixed his eyes upon his hearers, each man in a vast audience felt that the burning glance rested upon him alone and that there was no escape.

Above the eyes were the high, broad brow and the great leonine head; below them the massive jaw and the firm mouth " accurately closed." All was in keeping.

No one could see him and not be impressed. The English navvy with his " There goes a king," Sydney Smith, who compared Webster to " a walking cathedral," and the great Scotchman, harsh in judgment and grudging of praise, who set him down as a " Parliamentary Hercules," all alike felt the subduing force of that personal presence.

Look upon some of the daguerreotypes taken of him in his old age, when the end was near. I think the face is one of the most extraordinary, in its dark power and tragic sadness, of all the heads which any form of human portraiture has preserved. So imposing was he that when he rose to speak, even on the most unimportant occasions, he looked, as Parton says, like " Jupiter in a yellow waistcoat," and even if he uttered nothing but commonplaces, or if he merely sat still, such was his " might and majesty " that all who listened felt that every phrase was charged with deep and solemn meaning, and all who gazed at him were awed and impressed. Add to all this a voice of great compass, with deep organ tones, and we have an assemblage of physical gifts concentrated in this one man which would have sufficed to have made even common abilities seem splendid.

But the abilities were far from common. The intellect within answered to the outward vesture. Very early does it appear when we hear of " Webster's boy " lifted upon a stone wall to read or recite to the teamsters stopping to water their horses near the Webster farm. They were a rough, hardy set, but there was something in the child with the

great dark eyes that held them and made them listen.   And
the father, gallant and quite pathetic soul, with a dumb and
very manifest love of higher things, resolved that this boy
should have all the advantages which had been denied to
himself.

Like the Scottish peasants, who toiled and moiled and
pinched and saved that their boy might go to the university
to cultivate learning on a little oatmeal, so with many silent
sacrifices Ebenezer Webster sent his son to school and college
and gave him every opportunity the little State afforded.
The boy was not slow to make the most of all that was thus
opened to him.   The dormant talents grew and burgeoned
in the congenial soil.   Love of books made him their reader
and master.   Rare powers of memory and of acquisition
showed themselves; a strong imagination led him to the great
makers of verse, and natural taste took him to the masters of
style, both in English and Latin.

When he passed out of college his capacity for work
brought him hardly earned pittances as a school teacher, and
then carried him through the toilsome, early stages of the
law.

As he advanced, the eager delight of acquisition was succeeded, as is ever the case, by the passionate desire for expression, and soon the signs come of the power of analysis,
of the instinct of lucid statement at once so clear and so forcible as to amount to demonstration.   We see before us as we
study those early years the promise of the great master of
words to whom a whole nation was one day to listen.

And with all these gifts, physical and mental, possibly, but
not necessarily, the outcome of them all, we see that Webster
had that indefinable quality which for lack of a better name
we call " charm."   He exercised a fascination upon men and

women alike, upon old and young, upon all who came in contact with him. When as a boy he returned from the country fair, his mother said to him, " Daniel, what did you do with your quarter ? "

" Spent it."

" Ezekiel, what did you do with yours ? "

" Lent it to Daniel."

As with the elder brother then, so it was through life. Webster strode along the pathway of his great career in solemn state, and there were always people about him ready to lend to him and to give to him; not money, merely, but love and loyalty and service, ungrudging and unreasoning, without either question or hope of reward. A wonderful power this, as impalpable as the tints of the rainbow, and yet as certain as the sun which paints the colors on the clouds and makes all mankind look toward them for the bow of hope and promise.

So he went on and up from the college, the schoolhouse, and the country jury, until he stood at the head of the American bar before the supreme court of the nation. On and up he went, from the early, florid orations of youth until he became the first orator of his time, without superior or rival. He frightened and disappointed his father by refusing the safe harbor of a clerk of court, and strode onward and upward until he stood at the head of the Senate and directed from the State Department the foreign policy of his country. Up and on from the farmhouse and the schoolhouse, from the stone wall whence he read to the rude audience of teamsters, to the times when thousands hung upon his words, when he created public opinion and shaped the political thought of his nation.

What a triumphant progress it was, and of it all what now

remains to make men say fifty years after his death that he merits not only a statue but lasting remembrance? Is it to be found in his success as a great advocate and lawyer, the acknowledged head of his profession? There is nothing which demands or calls forth greater intellectual powers or larger mental resources than the highest success at the bar, and yet no reputation is more evanescent. The decisions of judges remain and become part of the law of the land, lasting monuments of the learning and the thought which brought them forth. But the arguments which enlightened courts, which swayed juries, upon which public attention was fixed in admiration, fade almost in the hour, while the brilliant lawyer who uttered them soon becomes a tradition and a memory.

We must look beyond his triumphs at the bar to find the Webster of history. Beyond his work as a lawmaker, also, for, although he had a lion's share in the legislation of his time, it is not as a constructive statesman that he lives for us to-day. In the first rank as a lawmaker and as a lawyer, something very great must remain behind if we can readily and justly set aside such claims as these and say the highest remembrance rests on other grounds.

Yet such is the case, and the first, but the lesser, of these other grounds is his power of speech. Eminent as a legislator, still more distinguished as a lawyer, Webster was supreme as an orator. I had occasion some years ago to make a very careful study of Webster's speeches and orations. I read with them, and in strict comparison, all that was best in Greek, Latin, French, and English oratory, and all that is best and finest—I do not say all that is fine and good—is is to be found in those four languages. Webster stood the comparison without need of deduction or apology. I do not think that I am influenced by national feeling, for my object was to exclude the historical as well as the personal valuation, and to reach a real estimate.

When all was done, it seemed to me that Webster was unequalled. I am sure that he is unsurpassed as an orator. There was no need for him to put pebbles in his mouth to cure stammering, or to rehearse his speeches on the seashore in conflict with the noise of the wave. He had from the hand of nature all the graces of person and presence, of voice and delivery, which the most exacting critic could demand, and these natural gifts were trained, enhanced, and perfected by years of practice in the Senate, the court room, and before the people.

In what he said he always had distinction—rarest of qualities—and he had also the great manner, just as Milton has it in verse. To lucid statement, to that simplicity in discussion which modern times demand for practical questions, to nervous force, he added, at his best, wealth of imagery, richness of diction, humor, and pathos, all combined with the power of soaring on easy wing to the loftiest flights of eloquence. Above all he had that highest quality, the "σπουδαιότην" or high and excellent seriousness which Aristotle sets down as one of the supreme virtues of poetry, and without which neither oratory nor poetry can attain to supremacy.

Charles Fox was the author of the famous aphorism that "no good speech ever read well." This is the declaration in epigrammatic form that the speech which is prepared like an essay and read or recited, which, in other words, is literature before it is oratory, is not thoroughly good, and of the soundness of the doctrine there can be, I think, no doubt. But this proposition is not without its dangers.

Charles Fox lived up to his own principle. He was, in my opinion, the greatest of English orators at the moment of speech, but he is little read and seldom quoted now. What he said has faded from the minds of men despite its enchanting, its enormous effect at the moment.

On the other hand, the speech which is literature before it is spoken is ineffective or only partially effective at the moment, and if it is read afterwards, however much we may enjoy the essay, we never mistake it for the genuine eloquence of the spoken word. Macaulay is an example of this latter class, as Fox is of the former. Macaulay's speeches are essays, eloquent and rhetorical, but still essays, literature, and not speeches. He was listened to with interest and delight, but he was not a great parliamentary debater or speaker.

The highest oratory, therefore, must combine in exact balance the living force and freshness of the spoken word with the literary qualities which alone ensure endurance. The best examples of this perfection are to be found in the world of imagination, in the two speeches of Brutus and Mark Antony in the play of Julius Cæsar. They are speeches and nothing else—one cool, stately, reasonable; the other a passionate, revolutionary appeal, hot from the heart and pouring from the lips with unpremeditated art, and yet they both have the literary quality, absolutely supreme in this instance, because Shakespeare wrote them.

It is not the preparation or even the writing out beforehand, therefore, which makes a speech into an essay, for these things can both be done without detracting from the spontaneity, without dulling the sound of the voice which the wholly great speech must have, even on the printed page. The speech loses when the literary quality becomes predominant, and absolute success as high as it is rare comes only from the nice balance of the two essential ingredients.

You find this balance, this combination, in Demosthenes and Isocrates, although I venture to think that those two great masters lean, if at all, too much to the literary side. In Cicero, although in matter and manner the best judges would rank him below the Greek masters, the combination is quite perfect. One of his most famous speeches, it is said, was never delivered at all, and none the less it is a speech and nothing else, instinct with life and yet with the impalpable literary feeling all through it, the perfect production of a very beautiful and subtle art.

Among English orators Burke undoubtedly comes nearest to the union of the two qualities, and while the words of Fox and Pitt are unread and unquoted, except by students, Burke's gorgeous sentences are recited and repeated by successive generations. Yet there is no doubt that Burke erred on the literary side, and we find the proof of it in the fact that he often spoke to empty benches, and that Goldsmith could say of him:

> " Too deep for his hearers, still went on refining,
> And thought of convincing while they thought of dining."

Burke was a literary man as well as an orator and a statesman. Webster was not a literary man at all. He never wrote books or essays, although, in Dr. Johnson's phrase, he had literature and loved it. He was an orator, pure and simple; his speeches, good, bad, or indifferent, are speeches—never essays or anything but speeches—and yet upon all alike is the literary touch. In all is the fine literary quality, always felt, never seen, ever present, never obtrusive. He had the combination of Shakespeare's Brutus or Antony, of

Demosthenes or Cicero, and when he rose to his greatest heights he reached a place beyond the fear of rivalry.

Would you have a practical proof and exhibition of this fact, turn to any serious and large debate in Congress, and you will find Webster constantly quoted, as he is in every session, quoted twenty times as often as any other public man in our history. He said many profound, many luminous, many suggestive things; he was an authority on many policies and on the interpretation of the constitution. But there have been others of whom all this might be said; there were kings before Agamemnon, but they are rarely quoted, while Webster is quoted constantly.

He had strong competitors in his own day and in his own field, able, acute, and brilliant men. He rose superior to them, I think, in his lifetime, but now that they are all dead Webster is familiar to hundreds to whom his rivals are little more than names. So far as familiarity in the mouths of men goes, it is Eclipse first and the rest nowhere. It is the rare combination of speech and literature; it is the literary quality, the literary savor, which keeps what Webster said fresh, strong, and living. When we open the volumes of his speeches it is not like unrolling the wrappings of an Egyptian mummy, to find within a dried and shrivelled form, a faint perfume alone surviving to faintly recall the vanished days, as when—

"Some queen, long dead, was young."

Rather it is like the opening of Charlemagne's tomb, when his imperial successor started back before the enthroned figure of the great emperor looking out upon him, instinct with life under the red glare of the torches.

Let us apply another and surer test. How many speeches to a jury in a criminal trial possessing neither political nor public interest survive in fresh remembrance seventy years after their delivery? I confess I can think of no jury speeches of any kind which stand this ordeal except, in a limited way, some speeches of Erskine, and those all have the advantage of historical significance, dealing as they do with constitutional and political questions of great moment. But there is one of Webster's speeches to a jury which lives to-day, and no more crucial test could be applied than the accomplishment of such a feat. The White murder case was simply a criminal trial, without a vestige of historical, political, or general public interest. Yet Webster's speech for the prosecution has been read and recited until well-nigh hackneyed. It is in readers and manuals; and is still declaimed by schoolboys. Some of its phrases are familiar quotations and have passed into general speech. Let me recall a single passage:

" He has done the murder. No eye has seen him; no ear has heard him. The secret is his own, and it is safe.

" Ah, gentlemen, that was a dreadful mistake. Such a secret can be safe nowhere. The whole creation of God has neither nook nor corner where the guilty can bestow it and say it is safe. . . . A thousand eyes turn at once to explore every man, everything, every circumstance connected with the time and place; a thousand ears catch every whisper; a thousand excited minds intensely dwell on the scene, shedding all their light, and ready to kindle the slighest circumstance into a blaze of discovery. Meantime the guilty soul cannot keep its own secret. It is false to itself; or, rather, it feels an irresistible impulse of conscience to be true to itself. It labors under its guilty possession, and knows not what to do with it. The human heart was not made for the residence of such an inhabitant. It finds itself preyed on by a torment which it dares not acknowledge to God or man. A vulture is devouring it, and it can ask no sympathy or assistance either from heaven or earth. The secret which the murderer possesses soon comes to possess him, and, like the evil spirits of which we read, it overcomes him, and leads him whithersoever it will.   He feels it beating at his heart, rising to his throat, and demanding disclosure.   He thinks the whole world sees it in his face, reads it in his eyes, and almost hears its workings in the very silence of his thoughts. It has become his master.   It betrays his discretion, it breaks down his courage, it conquers his prudence.   When suspicions from without begin to embarrass him and the net of circumstance to entangle him, the fatal secret struggles with still greater violence to burst forth.   It must be confessed; it will be confessed.   There is no refuge from confession but suicide, and suicide is confession."

Those are words spoken to men, not written for them.   It is a speech and nothing else, and yet we feel all through it the literary value and quality which make it imperishable.

Take another example.   When Webster stood one summer morning on the ramparts of Quebec and heard the sound of drums and saw the English troops on parade, the thought of England's vast world-empire came strongly to his mind. The thought was very natural under the circumstances, not at all remarkable nor in the least original.   Some years later, in a speech in the Senate, he put his thought into words, and this, as everyone knows, is the way he did it:

" A Power which has dotted over the surface of the whole globe with her possessions and military posts, whose morning drumbeat, following the sun and keeping company with the hours, circles the earth with one continuous and unbroken strain of the martial airs of England."

The sentence has followed the drumbeat round the world, and has been repeated in England and in the Antipodes by men who never heard of Webster and probably did not know that this splendid description of the British empire was due to an American. It is not the thought which has carried these words so far through time and space. It is the beauty of the imagery and the magic of the style.

Let me take one more very simple example of the quality which distinguishes Webster's speeches above those of others, which makes his words and serious thoughts live on when others, equally weighty and serious, perhaps, sleep or die. In his first Bunker Hill oration he apostrophized the monument, just as anyone else might have tried to do, and this is what he said:

" Let it rise, let it rise till it meet the sun in his coming; let the earliest light of morning gild it, and parting day linger and play on its summit."

Here the thought is nothing, the style everything. No one can repeat those words and be deaf to their music on insensible to the rhythm and beauty of the prose with the Saxon words relieved just sufficiently by the Latin derivatives.

The ease with which it is done may be due to training, but the ability to do it comes from natural gifts which, as Goethe says, " we value more as we get older because they cannot be stuck on." Possibly to some people it may seem very simple to utter such a sentence as I have quoted. To them I can only repeat what Scott says somewhere about Swift's style, perhaps the purest and strongest we have in the language. " Swift's style," said Scott, " seems so simple that one would think any child might write like him, and yet if we try we find to our despair that it is impossible."

Such, then, were the qualities which in their perfect combination put Webster among the very few who stand forth as the world's greatest orators. In this age of ours when the

tendency is to overpraise commonplace work, to mistake
notoriety for fame, and advertisement for reputation, it is of
inestimable worth to a people to have as one of their own
possessions such a master of speech, such a standard of distinction and of real excellence as we find in Webster. Such
an orator deserves a statue.

But there is yet another ground, deeper and more serious
than this. Webster deserves a statue for what he represented, for the message he delivered, and for that for which
he still stands and will always stand before his countrymen
and in the cold, clear light of history.

He was born just at the end of the war of the Revolution,
when the country was entering upon the period of disintegration and impotence known as that of the Confederation. He
was too young to understand and to feel those bitter years
of struggle and decline which culminated in the adoption of
the constitution. But the first impressions of his boyhood
must have been of the prosperity, strength, and honor which
came from the new instrument of government and from the
better union of the States. His father followed his old chief
in politics as he had in the field, and Webster grew up a
Federalist, a supporter of Washington, Hamilton, and Adams
and of the leaders of their party.

As he came to manhood he saw the first assault upon the
national principle in the Virginia and Kentucky resolutions.
He had entered public life when the second attack came in
the movement which ended with the Hartford Convention,
and with which, New England Federalist as he was, he could
feel no sympathy. Again fifteen years passed and the third
assault was delivered in the Nullification doctrines of South
Carolina.

Webster was then at the zenith of his powers, and he came

forward as the defender of the constitution. In the reply to
Hayne he reached the highest point in parliamentary oratory
and left all rivals far behind. He argued his case with consummate skill, both legally and historically. But he did far
more than this. He was not merely the great orator defend-
ing the constitution, he was the champion of the national
principle. Whether the constitution was at the outset an
experiment or not, whether it was a contract from which each
or all of the signatories could withdraw at will, was secondary.
The great fact was that the constitution had done its work.
It had made a nation. Webster stood forth in the Senate and
before the country as the exponent of that fact and as the defender of the nation's life against the attacks of separatism.
This was his message to his time. This was his true mission.
In that cause he spoke as none had ever spoken before and
with a splendor of eloquence and a force of argument to
which no one else could attain.

It is not to be supposed for an instant that Webster discovered the fact that the constitution had made a nation or
that he first and alone proclaimed a new creed to an unthink-
ing generation. His service was equally great, but widely
different from this. The great mass of the American people
felt dumbly, dimly perhaps, but none the less deeply and
surely, that they had made a nation some day to be a great
nation, and they meant to remain such and not sink into
divided and petty republics.

This profound feeling of the popular heart Webster not
only represented, but put into words. No slight service this,
if rightly considered; no little marvel this capacity to change
thought into speech, to give expression to the feelings and
hopes of a people and crystallize them forever in words fit
for such a use. To this power, indeed, we owe a large part

of the world's greatest literature. The myths and legends of
Greece were of no one man's invention. They were children
of the popular imaginings—vague, varying—floating hither
and thither, like the mists of the mountains. But Homer
touched them, and they started up into a beautiful, immortal
life, to delight and charm untold generations. Æschylus and
Sophocles put them upon the stage, and they became types
of the sorrows of humanity and of the struggle of man with
fate. The Sagas of the far north, confused and diffuse, but
full of poetry and imagination, slumbered until the Minne-
singers wove them into the Niebelungen Lied and again until
a great composer set them before our eyes, so that all men
could see their beauty and pathos and read their deeper mean-
ings. Sir Thomas Mallory rescued the Arthurian legends
from chaos, and in our own day a great poet has turned them
into forms which make their beauty clear to the world. Thus
popular imaginings, dumb for the most part, finding at best
only a rude expression, have been touched by the hand of
genius and live forever.

So in politics Jefferson embodied in the Declaration of Independence the feelings of the American people and sounded
to the world the first note in the great march of Democracy,
which then began. The " Marseillaise," in words and music,
burned with the spirit of the French Revolution and inspired
the armies which swept over Europe.

Thus Webster gave form and expression, at once noble and
moving, to the national sentiment of his people. In what he
said men saw clearly what they themselves thought, but
which they could not express. That sentiment grew and
strengthened with every hour, when men had only to repeat
his words, in order to proclaim the creed in which they believed; and after he was dead Webster was heard again in

the deep roar of the Union guns from Sumter to Appomattox.

His message, delivered as he alone could deliver it, was
potent in inspiring the American people to the terrible sacrifices by which they saved the nation when he slept silent in
his grave at Marshfield. Belief in the Union and the constitution, because they meant national greatness and national
life, was the great dominant conviction of Webster's life. It
was part of his temperament. He loved the outer world, the
vast expanses of sea and sky, all that was large and un-
fettered in nature. So he admired great States and empires
and had little faith in small ones or in the happiness or worth
of a nation which has no history and which fears its fate too
much to put its fortune to the touch when the accepted time
has come.

It was not merely that as a statesman he saw the misery
and degradation which would come from the breaking of the
Union as well as the progressive disintegration which was
sure to follow, but the very thought of it came home to him
with the sharpness of a personal grief which was almost agonizing. When, in the 7th of March speech, he cried out,
" What States are to secede? What is to remain American?
What am I to be?" a political opponent said the tone of the
last question made him shudder as if some dire calamity was
at hand. The greatness of the United States filled his mind.
He had not the length of days accorded to Lord Bathurst,
but the angel of dreams had unrolled to him the future, and
the vision was ever before his eyes.

This passionate love of his country, this dream of her future, inspired his greatest efforts, were even the chief cause
at the end of his life of his readiness to make sacrifices of
principle which would only have helped forward what he

dreaded most, but which he believed would save that for which he cared most deeply. In a period when great forces were at work which in their inevitable conflict threatened the existence of the Union of States, Webster stands out above all others as the champion, as the very embodiment of the national life and the national faith. More than any other man of that time he called forth the sentiment more potent than all reasonings which saved the nation. It was a great work, greatly done, with all the resources of a powerful intellect and with an eloquence rarely heard among men. We may put aside all his other achievements, all his other claims to remembrance, and inscribe alone upon the base of his statue the words uttered in the Senate, " Liberty and Union, now and forever, one and inseparable." That single sentence recalls all the noble speeches which breathed only the greatness of the country and the prophetic vision which looked with undazzled gaze into a still greater future. No other words are wanted for a man who so represented and so expressed the faith and hopes of a nation. His statue needs no other explanation so long as the nation he served and the Union he loved shall last.

SPEECH AT REPUBLICAN CONVENTION

DELIVERED AT PHILADELPHIA, JUNE 20, 1900

ONE of the greatest honors that can fall to any American in public life is to be called to preside over a Republican National Convention. How great that honor is you know, but you cannot realize, nor can I express the gratitude which I feel to you for having conferred it upon me. I can only say to you in the simplest phrase, that I thank you from the bottom of my heart. " Beggar that I am, I am even poor in thanks, and yet I thank you."

We meet again to nominate the next President of the United States. Four years have passed since we nominated the soldier and statesman who is now President, and who is soon to enter upon his second term. Since the Civil War no Presidential term has been so crowded with great events as that which is now drawing to a close. They have been four memorable years.

To Republicans they show a record of promises kept, of work done, of unforeseen questions met and answered. To the Democrats they have been generous in the exhibition of unfulfilled predictions, in the ruin of their hopes of calamity and in futile opposition to the forces of the times, and the aspirations of the American people. I wish I could add that they had been equally instructive to our opponents, but while it is true that the Democrats, like the Bourbons, learn nothing, it is only too evident that the familiar comparison cannot be completed, for they forget a great deal which it would be well for them to remember.

In 1897 we took the Government and the country from the hands of President Cleveland. His party had abandoned him and were joined to their idols, of which he was no longer one. During the last years of his term we had presented to us the melancholy spectacle of a President trying to govern without a party.

The result was that his policies were in ruin, legislation was at a standstill, and public affairs were in a perilous and incoherent condition. Party responsibility had vanished, and with it all possibility of intelligent action, demanded by the country at home and abroad. It was an interesting, but by no means singular, display of Democratic unfitness for the practical work of government. To the political student it was instructive, to the country it was extremely painful, to business disastrous.

We replaced this political chaos with a President in thorough accord with his party, and the machinery of government began again to move smoothly and effectively. Thus we kept at once our promise of better and more efficient administration. In four months after the inauguration of President McKinley we had passed a tariff bill. For ten years the artificial agitation, in behalf of what was humorously called tariff reform, and of what was really free trade, had kept business in a ferment, and had brought a Treasury deficit, paralyzed industries, depression, panic, and, finally, continuous bad times to a degree never before imagined.

Would you know the result of our tariff legislation, look about you. Would you measure its success, recollect that it is no longer an issue, that our opponents, free traders as they are, do not dare to make it an issue, that there is not a State in the Union to-day which could be carried for free trade against protection. Never was a policy more fully justified by its works, never was a promise made by any party more absolutely fulfilled.

Dominant among the issues of four years ago was that of our monetary and financial system. The Republican Party promised to uphold our credit, to protect our currency from revolution, and to maintain the gold standard. We have done so. We have done more. We have been better than our promise.

Failing to secure, after honest effort, any encouragement for international bimetallism, we have passed a law strengthening the gold standard and planting it more firmly than ever in our financial system, improving our banking laws, buttressing our credit, and refunding the public debt at 2 per cent interest, the lowest rate in the world.

It was a great work well done. The only argument the Democrats can advance to-day in their own behalf on the money question is that a Republican Senate, in the event of Democratic success, would not permit the repeal of a Republican law. This is a specious argument when looked at with considerate eyes, and quite worthy of the intellects which produced it. Apply it generally. Upon this theory, because we have defeated the soldiers of Spain and sunk her ships we can with safety dispense with the army and navy which did the work.

Take another example. There has been a fire in a great city; it has been checked and extinguished, therefore let us abolish the fire department and cease to insure our homes. Distrust in our currency, the dread of change, the deadly fear of a debased standard were raging four years ago, and business lay prostrate before them. Republican supremacy and Republican legislation have extinguished the fires of doubt and fear, and business has risen triumphant from the ashes. Therefore abolish your fire department, turn out the Republicans and put in power the incendiaries who lighted the flames and trust to what remains of Republican control to avert fresh disaster.

The proposition is its own refutation. The supremacy of the party that has saved the standard of sound money and guarded it by law is as necessary for its security and for the existence of honest wages and of business confidence now as it was in 1896.

The moment the Republican Party passes from power, and the party of free silver and fiat paper comes in, stable currency and the gold standard, the standard of the civilized world, are in imminent and deadly peril. Sound currency and a steady standard of value are to-day safe only in Republican hands.

But there were still other questions in 1896. We had already thwarted the efforts of the Cleveland Administration to throw the Hawaiian Islands back to their dethroned Queen and to give England a foothold for her cables in the group. We then said that we would settle finally the Hawaiian question. We have done so. The traditional American policy has been carried out. The flag of the Union floats to-day over the crossroads of the Pacific.

We promised to deal with the Cuban question. Again comes the reply, we have done so. The long agony of the island is over. Cuba is free. But this great work brought with it events and issues which no man had foreseen, for which no party creed had provided a policy. The crisis came, bringing war in its train.

The Republican President and the Republican Congress met the new trial in the old spirit. We fought the war with Spain. The result is history known of all men. We have the perspective now of only a short two years, and yet how clear and bright the great facts stand out, like mountain peaks against the sky, while the gathering darkness of a just oblivion is creeping fast over the low grounds, where lie forgotten the trivial and unimportant things, the criticisms and the fault findings which seemed too huge when we still lingered among them.

Here they are, these great facts: A war of a hundred days, with many victories and no defeats, with no prisoners taken from us and no advance stayed, with a triumphant outcome startling in its completeness and in its worldwide meaning. Was ever a war more justly entered upon, more quickly fought, more fully won, more thorough in its results? Cuba is free. Spain has been driven from the Western Hemisphere. Fresh glory has come to our arms and crowned our flag.

It was the work of the American people, but the Republican Party was their instrument. Have we not the right to say that here, too, even as in the days of Abraham Lincoln, we have fought a good fight, we have kept the faith, we have finished the work?

War, however, is ever like the sword of Alexander. It cuts the knots. It is a great solvent and brings many results not to be foreseen. The world forces unchained in war perform in hours the work of years of quiet.

Spain sued for peace. How was that peace to be made? The answer to this great question had to be given by the President of the United States. We were victorious in Cuba, in Porto Rico, in the Philippines. Should we give those islands back to Spain? "Never!" was the President's reply. Would any American wish that he had answered otherwise? Should we hand them over to some other Power? "Never!" was again the answer.

Would our pride and self-respect as a nation have submitted to any other reply? Should we turn the islands, where we had destroyed all existing sovereignty, loose upon the world to be a prey to domestic anarchy and the helpless spoil of some other nation? Again the inevitable negative. Again the President answered as the nation he represented would have had him answer.

He boldly took the islands, took them knowing well the burden and responsibility, took them from a deep sense of duty to ourselves and others, guided by a just foresight as to our future in the East, and with an entire faith in the ability of the American people to grapple with the new task. When future conventions point to the deeds by which the Republican Party has made history, they will proclaim with especial pride that under a Republican Administration the War of 1898 was fought, and that the peace with Spain was the work of William McKinley.

So much for the past. We are proud of it, but we do not expect to live upon it, for the Republican Party is pre-eminently the party of action, and its march is ever forward. We are not so made that we can be content to retreat or to mark time. The traditions of the early days of our party are sacred to us, and are hostages given to the American people that we will not be unworthy of the great leaders who have gone.

The deeds of yesterday are in their turn a pledge and a proof that what we promise we perform, and that the people who put faith in our declarations in 1896 were not deceived, and may place the same trust in us in 1900. But our pathway has never lain among dead issues, nor have we won our victories and made history by delving in political graveyards.

We are the party of to-day, with cheerful yesterdays and confident to-morrows. The living present is ours, the present of prosperity and activity in business, of good wages and quick payments, of labor employed and capital invested, of sunshine in the market place, and the stir of abounding life in the workshop and on the farm. It is with this that we have replaced the depression, the doubts, the low wages, the idle labor, the frightened capital, the dark clouds which overhung industry and agriculture in 1896. This is what we would preserve, so far as sound government and wise legislation can do it. This is what we brought to the country four years ago. This is what we offer now.

Again we promise that the protective system shall be maintained, and that our great industrial interests shall go on their way unshaken by the dire fear of tariff agitation and of changing duties. Again we declare that we will guard the national credit, uphold a sound currency, based upon gold, and keep the wages of the workingman and the enterprise of the man of business free from that most deadly of all evils, a flucutating standard of value.

The deficit which made this great country in a time of profound peace a borrower of money to meet its current expenditures has been replaced by abundant revenue, bringing a surplus, due alike to prosperity and to wise legislation, so ample that we can now safely promise a large reduction of taxation without imperilling our credit or risking a resort to loans.

We are prepared to take steps to revive and build up our merchant marine, and thus put into American pockets the money paid for carrying American freights. Out of the abundant resources which our financial legislation has brought us we will build the Isthmian Canal, and lay the cables which will help to turn the current of eastern trade to the Golden Gate. We are on good terms with all nations, and mean to remain so, while we promise to insure our peace and safety by maintaining the Monroe Doctrine, by ample coast defences, and by building up a navy which no one can challenge with impunity.

The new problems brought by the war we face with confidence in ourselves, and a still deeper confidence in the American people, who will deal justly and rightly with the islands which have come into their charge. The outcry

against our new possessions is as empty as the cant about
" militarism," and " imperialism " is devoid of sense and
meaning.

Regard for a moment those who are loudest in shrieking
that the American people are about to enter upon a career
of oppression, and that the republic is in danger. Have they
been in the past the guardians of freedom? Is safety for
liberty now to be found most surely in the party which was
the defender of domestic slavery?

Is true freedom to be secured by the ascendancy of the
party which beneath our very eyes seeks to establish through
infamous laws the despotic rule of a small and unscrupulous
band of usurpers in Kentucky, who trample there not upon
the rights of the black men only, but of the whites, and which
seeks to extend the same system to North Carolina and
Missouri?

Has it suddenly come to pass that the Democratic Party
which to-day aims whenever it acquires power to continue
in office by crushing out honest elections and popular rule;
has it indeed come to pass, I say, that that party is the chosen
protector of liberty? If it were so the outlook would be
black indeed.

No. The party of Lincoln may best be trusted now, as in the
past, to be true, even as he was true, to the rights of man to
human freedom, whether within the borders of the United
States or in the islands which have come beneath our flag.
The liberators may be trusted to watch over the liberated.
We who freed Cuba will keep the pledge we made to her and
will guide her along the road to independence and stable
government until she is ready to settle her own future by the
free expression of her people's will. We will be faithful to
the trust imposed upon us, and if among those to whom this

great work is confided in Cuba, or elsewhere, wrongdoers shall be found, men not only bad in morals, but dead to their duty as Americans and false to the honor of our name, we will punish these basest of criminals to the extent of the law.

For the islands of Hawaii and Porto Rico the political problem has been solved, and by Republican legislation they have been given self-government, and are peaceful and prosperous under the rule of the United States.

In the Philippines we were met by rebellion, fomented by a self-seeking adventurer and usurper. The duty of the President was to repress that rebellion, to see to it that the authority of the United States, as rightfully and as righteous in Manila as in Philadelphia, was acknowledged and obeyed. That harsh and painful duty President McKinley has performed firmly and justly, eager to resort to gentle measures wherever possible, unyielding when treachery and violence made force necessary. Unlike the opponents of expansion, we do not regard the soldiers of Otis and Lawton and McArthur as " an enemy's camp."

In our eyes they are the soldiers of the United States, they are our army, and we believe in them and will sustain them. Even now the Democrats are planning, if they get control of the House, to cut off appropriations for the army and thus compel the withdrawal of our troops from the Philippines. The result would be to force the retirement of such soldiers as would remain in Manila, and their retreat would be the signal for the massacre and plunder of the great body of the peaceful inhabitants of the islands who have trusted to us to protect and guard them.

Such an event would be an infamy. Is the government, is the House, to be given over to a party capable of such a policy? Shall they not rather be intrusted to the party

which will sustain the army and suppress the brigands and
guerrillas who, under pretence of war, are now adding so
freely to the list of crimes committed in the name of liberty
by usurpers and pretenders, and who, buoyed up by the
Democratic promises, keep up a highwayman warfare in hope
of Democratic success in November? It is for the American
people to decide this question.

Our position is plain. The restoration of peace and order
now so nearly reached in the Philippines shall be completed.
Civil government shall be established, and the people advanced as rapidly as possible along the road to entire freedom
and to self-government under our flag. We will not abandon
our task. We will neither surrender nor retreat. We will
not write failure across this page of our history. We will do
our duty, our full duty, to the people of the Philippines, and
strive by every means to give them freedom, contentment and
prosperity.

We have no belief in the old slaveholders' doctrine that the
constitution of its own force marches into every newly acquired territory, and this doctrine, which we cast out in
1860, we still reject. We do not mean that the Philippines
shall come within our tariff system or become part of our
body politic. We do mean that they shall under our teaching learn to govern themselves and remain under our flag,
with the largest possible measure of home rule. We make
no hypocritical pretence of being interested in the Philippines solely on account of others. While we regard the welfare of those people as a sacred trust, we regard the welfare
of the American people first. We see our duty to ourselves
as well as to others. We believe in trade expansion.

By every legitimate means within the province of government and legislation we mean to stimulate the expansion of

our trade and to open new markets.   Greatest of all markets is China.   Our trade there is growing by leaps and bounds.

Manila, the prize of war, gives us inestimable advantages in developing that trade.   It is the corner-stone of our Eastern policy, and the brilliant diplomacy of John Hay in securing from all nations a guarantee of our treaty rights and of the open door in China rests upon it.

We ask the American people whether they will throw away these new markets and widening opportunities for trade and commerce by putting in power the Democratic Party, who seek under cover of a newly-discovered affection for the rights of man to give up these islands of the East and make Dewey's victory fruitless?

The choice lies between this Democratic policy of retreat and the Republican policy which would hold the islands, give them freedom and prosperity and enlarge those great opportunities for ourselves and our posterity.

The Democratic attitude toward the Philippines rests wholly upon the proposition that the American people have neither the capacity nor the honesty to deal rightly with these islands.   They assume that we shall fail.

They fall down and worship a Chinese half-breed whose name they had never heard three years ago, and they slander and cry down and doubt the honor of American soldiers and sailors, of admirals and generals, and public men who have gone in and out before us during an entire lifetime.

We are true to our own.   We have no distrust of the honor, the humanity, the capacity of the American people. To feel or do otherwise is to doubt ourselves, our government and our civilization.

We take issue with the Democrats who would cast off the Philippines because the American people cannot be trusted with them, and we declare that the American people can be trusted to deal justly, wisely, and generously with these distant islands and will lift them up to a higher prosperity, a broader freedom, and a nobler civilization than they have ever known.   We have not failed elsewhere.   We shall not fail here.

Those are the questions we present to the American people in regard to the Philippines.   Do they want such a humiliating change there as Democratic victory would bring?   Do they want an even more radical change at home?   Suppose the candidate of the Democrats, the Populists, the foes of expansion, the dissatisfied, and the envious should come into power, what kind of an administration would he give us? What would his cabinet be?

Think what an electric spark of confidence would run through every business interest in the country when such a cabinet was announced as we can readily imagine he would make.   More important still, we ask the American people whether they will put in the White House the hero of uncounted platforms, the prodigal spendthrift of words, the champion of free silver, the opponent of expansion, the assailant of the courts; or whether they will retain in the Presidency the Union soldier, the leader of the House of Representatives, the trained statesman who has borne victoriously the heavy burdens of the last four years; the champion of protection and sound money, the fearless supporter of law and order wherever the flag floats?   But there is one question we will put to the American people in this campaign which includes and outweighs all others.

We will say to them: You were in the depths of adversity under the last Democratic Administration; you are on the heights of prosperity to-day.   Will that prosperity continue if you make a change in your President and in the party which administers your government? How long will your good times last if you turn out the Republicans and give political power to those who cry nothing but " Woe! woe!"

The lovers of calamity and foes of prosperity who hold success in business to be a crime and regard thrift as a misdemeanor? If the Democrats should win do you think business would improve? Do you think that prices would remain steady, that wages would rise and employment increase when that result of the election was known? Business confidence rests largely upon sentiment. Do you think that sentiment would be a hopeful one the day after Bryan's election?

Business confidence is a delicate plant. Do you think it would flourish with the Democratic Party? . . .

Do you not know from recent and bitter experience what that arrest of movement, that fear of the future, means? It means the contraction of business, the reduction of employment, the increase of the unemployed, lower wages, hard times, distress, unhappiness.

We do not say that we have panaceas for every ill. We do not claim that any policy we, or any one else, can offer will drive from the world sorrow and suffering and poverty, but we say that so far as government and legislation can secure the prosperity and well being of the American people, our administration and our policies will do it. We point to the adversity of the Cleveland years lying dark behind us. It has been replaced by the prosperity of the McKinley years. Let them make whatever explanation they will, the facts are with us.

It is on these facts that we shall ask for the support of the American people. What we have done is known, and about what we intend to do there is neither secrecy nor deception.

What we promise we will perform. Our old policies are here, alive, successful and full of vigor. Our new policies have been begun, and for them we ask support. While the clouds of impending civil war hung dark over the country in 1861 we took up the great task then laid upon us and never flinched until we had carried it through to victory.

Now, at the dawn of a new century, with new policies and new opportunities opening before us in the bright sunshine of prosperity, we again ask the American people to entrust us with their future. We have profound faith in the people. We do not distrust their capacity of meeting the new responsibilities even as they met the old, and we shall await with confidence, under the leadership of William McKinley, the verdict of November.

HENRY W. GRADY

ENRY WOODFEN GRADY, an American journalist and orator, was born at Athens, Ga., May 24, 1850, and died at Atlanta, Ga., Dec. 23, 1889. He received his education at the State universities of Georgia and Virginia. Engaging in journalism, he was editor successively of the "Courier" and "Commercial" at Rome, Ga., and, after removing to Atlanta, in 1871, was for six years editorially connected with the Atlanta "Herald." In 1880, he became editor and part owner of the Atlanta "Constitution," and was its editor at the time of his death, which was greatly lamented in Georgia, where Mr. Grady was the idol of his State. In the latter part of his career, Grady's remarkable eloquence as an orator won him a national reputation. Among his best-known speeches are his address before the New England Club of New York city, December 21, 1886, a famous prohibition speech at Atlanta in 1887, an address at the Texas State Fair in 1888, and the speech delivered at Boston, Mass., a few days before his death, on "The Future of the Negro." Mr. Grady was an enthusiastic supporter of the prohibition movement, and his speeches on the political situation helped to foster good feeling between North and South. A biography of him has been written by Joel Chandler Harris, while his memory is preserved by a public monument at Atlanta, Ga.

THE NEW SOUTH

SPEECH DELIVERED BEFORE THE NEW ENGLAND CLUB, NEW YORK, DECEMBER 21. 1886

THERE was a South of slavery and secession—that South is dead. There is a South of union and freedom—that South, thank God, is living, breathing, growing every hour.

These words, delivered from the immortal lips of Benjamin H. Hill, at Tammany Hall in 1866, true then and truer now, I shall make my text to-night.

Mr. President and Gentlemen—Let me express to you my appreciation of the kindness by which I am permitted to address you. I make this abrupt acknowledgment advisedly, for I feel that if, when I raise my provincial voice in this ancient and august presence, I could find courage for no more than the opening sentence, it would be well if in that sentence

(215)

I had met in a rough sense my obligation as a guest, and had perished, so to speak, with courtesy on my lips and grace in my heart. Permitted, through your kindness, to catch my second wind, let me say that I appreciate the significance of being the first Southerner to speak at this board, which bears the substance, if it surpasses the semblance, of original New England hospitality, and honors the sentiment that in turn honors you, but in which my personality is lost and the compliment to my people made plain.

I bespeak the utmost stretch of your courtesy to-night. I am not troubled about those from whom I come. You remember the man whose wife sent him to a neighbor with a pitcher of milk, and who, tripping on the top step, fell with such casual interruptions as the landings afforded into the basement, and, while picking himself up, had the pleasure of hearing his wife call out: " John, did you break the pitcher?" " No, I didn't," said John, " but I'll be dinged if I don't."

So, while those who call me from behind may inspire me with energy if not with courage, I ask an indulgent hearing from you. I beg that you will bring your full faith in American fairness and frankness to judgment upon what I shall say. There was an old preacher once who told some boys of the Bible lesson he was going to read in the morning. The boys, finding the place, glued together the connecting pages. The next morning he read at the bottom of one page, " When Noah was one hundred and twenty years old he took unto himself a wife who was "—then turning the page—" 140 cubits long, 40 cubits wide, built of gopher wood, and covered with pitch inside and out." He was naturally puzzled at this. He read it again, verified it, and then said: " My friends, this is the first time I ever met this

in the Bible, but I accept this as an evidence of the assertion
that we are fearfully and wonderfully made." If I could
get you to hold such faith to-night I could proceed cheerfully
to the task I otherwise approach with a sense of consecration.

Pardon me one word, Mr. President, spoken for the sole
purpose of getting into the volumes that go out annually
freighted with the rich eloquence of your speakers, the fact
that the Cavalier as well as the Puritan was on the continent
in its early days, and that he was " up and able to be about."
I have read your books carefully and I find no mention of
that fact, which seems an important one to me for preserv-
ing a sort of historical equilibrium if for nothing else.

Let me remind you that the Virginia Cavalier first challenged France on the continent; that Cavalier John Smith
gave New England its very name, and was so pleased with the
job that he has been handing his own name around ever
since; and that while Myles Standish was cutting off men's
ears for courting a girl without her parents' consent, and
forbade men to kiss their wives on Sunday, the Cavalier was
courting everything in sight, and that the Almighty had
vouchsafed great increase to the Cavalier colonies, the huts
in the wilderness being as full as the nests in the woods.

But having incorporated the Cavalier as a fact in your
charming little books, I shall let him work out his own salvation, as he has always done, with engaging gallantry, and we
will hold no controversy as to his merits. Why should we?
Neither Puritan nor Cavalier long survived as such. The
virtues and good traditions of both happily still live for the
inspiration of their sons and the saving of the old fashion.
But both Puritan and Cavalier were lost in the storm of the
first Revolution, and the American citizen, supplanting both
and stronger than either, took possession of the republic

bought by their common blood and fashioned to wisdom, and charged himself with teaching men government and establishing the voice of the people as the voice of God.

My friends, Dr. Talmage has told you that the typical American has yet to come. Let me tell you that he has already come. Great types, like valuable plants, are slow to flower and fruit. But from the union of these colonies, Puritans and Cavaliers, from the straightening of their purposes and the crossing of their blood, slow perfecting through a century, came he who stands as the first typical American, the first who comprehended within himself all the strength and gentleness, all the majesty and grace of this republic— Abraham Lincoln.

He was the sum of Puritan and Cavalier, for in his ardent nature were fused the virtues of both, and in the depths of his great soul the faults of both were lost. He was greater than Puritan, greater than Cavalier, in that he was American, and that in his honest form were first gathered the vast and thrilling forces of his ideal government—charging it with such tremendous meaning and elevating it above human suffering that martyrdom, though infamously aimed, came as a fitting crown to a life consecrated from the cradle to human liberty. Let us, each cherishing the traditions and honoring his fathers, build with reverend hands to the type of this simple but sublime life, in which all types are honored, and in our common glory as Americans there will be plenty and to spare for your forefathers and for mine.

Dr. Talmage has drawn for you, with a master's hand, the picture of your returning armies. He has told you how, in the pomp and circumstance of war, they came back to you, marching with proud and victorious tread, reading their glory in a nation's eyes! Will you bear with me while I tell

you of another army that sought its home at the close of the
late war—an army that marched home in defeat and not in
victory—in pathos and not in splendor, but in glory that
equalled yours, and to hearts as loving as ever welcomed
heroes home! Let me picture to you the footsore Confederate soldier, as, buttoning up in his faded gray jacket the
parole which was to bear testimony to his children of his
fidelity and faith, he turned his face southward from Appomattox in April, 1865.

Think of him as ragged, half-starved, heavy-hearted, en-
feebled by want and wounds, having fought to exhaustion, he
surrenders his gun, wrings the hands of his comrades in
silence, and lifting his tear-stained and pallid face for the
last time to the graves that dot old Virginia hills, pulls his
gray cap over his brow and begins the slow and painful
journey. What does he find—let me ask you who went to
your homes eager to find, in the welcome you had justly
earned, full payment for four years' sacrifice—what does he
find when, having followed the battle-stained cross against
overwhelming odds, dreading death not half so much as surrender, he reaches the home he left so prosperous and beautiful?

He finds his house in ruins, his farm devastated, his slaves
free, his stock killed, his barns empty, his trade destroyed,
his money worthless, his social system, feudal in its magnificence, swept away; his people without law or legal status,
his comrades slain, and the burdens of others heavy on his
shoulders. Crushed by defeat, his very traditions are gone.
Without money, credit, employment, material, or training,
and, besides all this, confronted with the gravest problem that
ever met human intelligence,—the establishing of a status
for the vast body of his liberated slaves.

What does he do—this hero in gray with a heart of gold? Does he sit down in sullenness and despair? Not for a day. Surely God, who had stripped him of his prosperity, inspired him in his adversity.   As ruin was never before so overwhelming, never was restoration swifter.   The soldier stepped from the trenches into the furrow; horses that had charged Federal guns marched before the plow, and fields that ran red with human blood in April were green with the harvest in June; women reared in luxury cut up their dresses and made breeches for their husbands, and, with a patience and heroism that fit women always as a garment, gave their hands to work.   There was little bitterness in all this. Cheerfulness and frankness prevailed.

" Bill Arp " struck the key-note when he said: " Well, I killed as many of them as they did of me, and now I'm going to work."   Of the soldier returning home after defeat and roasting some corn on the roadside, who made the remark to his comrades: " You may leave the South if you want to, but I'm going to Sandersville, kiss my wife, and raise a crop, and if the Yankees fool with me any more I'll whip 'em again."

I want to say to General Sherman, who is considered an able man in our parts, though some people think he is a kind of careless man about fire, that from the ashes he left us in 1864 we have raised a brave and beautiful city; that somehow or other we have caught the sunshine in the bricks and mortar of our homes, and have builded therein not one ignoble prejudice or memory.

But what is the sum of our work?   We have found out that in the summing up the free negro counts more than he did as a slave.   We have planted the schoolhouse on the hilltop and made it free to white and black.   We have sowed towns and cities in the place of theories, and put business above politics. We have challenged your spinners in Massachusetts and your iron-makers in Pennsylvania. We have learned that the $400,000,000 annually received from our cotton crop will make us rich when the supplies that make it are home-raised. We have reduced the commercial rate of interest from twenty-four to six per cent, and are floating four per cent bonds.

We have learned that one northern immigrant is worth fifty foreigners; and have smoothed the path to southward, wiped out the place where Mason and Dixon's line used to be, and hung out our latch-string to you and yours. We have reached the point that marks perfect harmony in every household, when the husband confesses that the pies which his wife cooks are as good as those his mother used to bake; and we admit that the sun shines as brightly and the moon as softly as it did before the war. We have established thrift in city and country. We have fallen in love with our work. We have restored comfort to homes from which culture and elegance never departed. We have let economy take root and spread among us as rank as the crabgrass which sprung from Sherman's cavalry camps, until we are ready to lay odds on the Georgia Yankee as he manufactures relics of the battlefield in a one-story shanty and squeezes pure olive oil out of his cotton seed, against any Down-Easter that ever swappped wooden nutmegs for flannel sausage in the valleys of Vermont. Above all, we know that we have achieved in these "piping times of peace" a fuller independence for the South than that which our fathers sought to win in the forum by their eloquence or compel in the field by their swords.

It is a rare privilege, sir, to have had part, however

humble, in this work.   Never was nobler duty confided to human hands than the uplifting and upbuilding of the prostrate and bleeding South—misguided, perhaps, but beautiful in her suffering, and honest, brave, and generous always.   In the record of her social, industrial, and political illustration we await with confidence the verdict of the world.

But what of the negro?   Have we solved the problem he presents or progressed in honor and equity toward solution? Let the record speak to the point.   No section shows a more prosperous laboring population than the negroes of the South, none in fuller sympathy with the employing and land-owning class.   He shares our school fund, has the fullest protection of our laws and the friendship of our people.   Self-interest as well as honor demand that he should have this.   Our future, our very existence, depend upon working out this problem in full and exact justice.

We understand that when Lincoln signed the Emancipation Proclamation, your victory was assured, for he then committed you to the cause of human liberty, against which the arms of man cannot prevail—while those of our statesmen who trusted to make slavery the corner-stone of the Confederacy doomed us to defeat as far as they could, committing us to a cause that reason could not defend or the sword maintain in sight of advancing civilization.

Had Mr. Toombs said, which he did not say, " that he would call the roll of his slaves at the foot of Bunker Hill," he would have been foolish, for he might have known that whenever slavery became entangled in war it must perish, and that the chattel in human flesh ended forever in New England when your fathers—not to be blamed for parting with what didn't pay—sold their slaves to our fathers—not to be praised for knowing a paying thing when they saw it.

The relations of the southern people with the negro are close and cordial. We remember with what fidelity for four years he guarded our defenceless women and children, whose husbands and fathers were fighting against his freedom. To his eternal credit be it said that whenever he struck a blow for his own liberty he fought in open battle, and when at last he raised his black and humble hands that the shackles might be struck off, those hands were innocent of wrong against his helpless charges, and worthy to be taken in loving grasp by every man who honors loyalty and devotion.

Ruffians have maltreated him, rascals have misled him, philanthropists established a bank for him, but the South, with the North, protests against injustice to this simple and sincere people. To liberty and enfranchisement is as far as law can carry the negro. The rest must be left to conscience and common sense. It must be left to those among whom his lot is cast, with whom he is indissolubly connected, and whose prosperity depends upon their possessing his intelligent sympathy and confidence. Faith has been kept with him, in spite of calumnious assertions to the contrary by those who assume to speak for us or by frank opponents. Faith will be kept with him in the future, if the South holds her reason and integrity.

But have we kept faith with you? In the fullest sense, yes. When Lee surrendered—I don't say when Johnston surrendered, because I understand he still alludes to the time when he met General Sherman last as the time when he determined to abandon any further prosecution of the struggle—when Lee surrendered, I say, and Johnston quit, the South became, and has since been, loyal to this Union.

We fought hard enough to know that we were whipped, and in perfect frankness accept as final the arbitrament of the sword to which we had appealed. The South found her jewel in the toad's head of defeat. The shackles that had held her in narrow limitations fell forever when the shackles of the negro slave were broken. Under the old régime the negroes were slaves to the South; the South was a slave to the system. The old plantation, with its simple police regulations and feudal habit, was the only type possible under slavery. Thus was gathered in the hands of a splendid and chivalric oligarchy the substance that should have been diffused among the people, as the rich blood, under certain artificial conditions, is gathered at the heart, filling that with affluent rapture, but leaving the body chill and colorless.

The old South rested everything on slavery and agriculture, unconscious that these could neither give nor maintain healthy growth. The new South presents a perfect democracy, the oligarchs leading in the popular movement—a social system compact and closely knitted, less splendid on the surface, but stronger at the core—a hundred farms for every plantation, fifty homes for every palace—and a diversified industry that meets the complex need of this complex age.

The new South is enamored of her new work. Her soul is stirred with the breath of a new life. The light of a grander day is falling fair on her face. She is thrilling with the consciousness of growing power and prosperity. As she stands upright, full statured and equal among the people of the earth, breathing the keen air and looking out upon the expanded horizon, she understands that her emancipation came because through the inscrutable wisdom of God her honest purpose was crossed, and her brave armies were beaten.

This is said in no spirit of time-serving or apology. The South has nothing for which to apologize. She believes that

the late struggle between the States was war and not rebellion; revolution and not conspiracy, and that her convictions
were as honest as yours. I should be unjust to the dauntless
spirit of the South and to my own convictions if I did not
make this plain in this presence. The South has nothing to
take back. In my native town of Athens is a monument that
crowns its central hill—a plain, white shaft. Deep cut into
its shining side is a name dear to me above the names of
men—that of a brave and simple man who died in a brave and
simple faith. Not for all the glories of New England, from
Plymouth Rock all the way, would I exchange the heritage he
left me in his soldier's death. To the foot of that I shall
send my children's children to reverence him who ennobled
their name with his heroic blood. But, sir, speaking from
the shadow of that memory which I honor as I do nothing else
on earth, I say that the cause in which he suffered and for
which he gave his life was adjudged by higher and fuller
wisdom than his or mine, and I am glad that the omniscient
God held the balance of battle in his Almighty hand and that
human slavery was swept forever from American soil, the
American Union was saved from the wreck of war.

This message, Mr. President, comes to you from consecrated ground. Every foot of soil about the city in which I
live is as sacred as a battle-ground of the republic. Every
hill that invests it is hallowed to you by the blood of your
brothers who died for your victory, and doubly hallowed to
us by the blood of those who died hopeless, but undaunted in
defeat—sacred soil to all of us—rich with memories that
make us purer and stronger and better—silent but staunch
witnesses, in its red desolation, of the matchless valor of
American hearts and the deathless glory of American arms—
speaking an eloquent witness in its white peace and prosperity

to the indissoluble union of American States and the imperishable brotherhood of the American people.

Now, what answer has New England to this message? Will she permit the prejudice of war to remain in the hearts of the conquerors when it has died in the hearts of the conquered? Will she transmit this prejudice to the next generation, that in their hearts which never felt the generous ardor of conflict it may perpetuate itself? Will she withhold, save in strained courtesy, the hand which, straight from his soldier's heart, Grant offered to Lee at Appomattox? Will she make the vision of a restored and happy people, which gathered above the couch of your dying captain, filling his heart with grace; touching his lips with praise, and glorifying his path to the grave—will she make this vision on which the last sigh of his expiring soul breathed a benediction, a cheat and delusion? If she does, the South, never abject in asking for comradeship, must accept with dignity its refusal; but if she does not refuse to accept in frankness and sincerity this message of good will and friendship, then will the prophecy of Webster, delivered in this very Society forty years ago amid tremendous applause, become true, be verified in its fullest sense, when he said: " Standing hand to hand and clasping hands, we should remain united as we have been for sixty years, citizens of the same country, members of the same government, united, all united now and united forever." There have been difficulties, contentions, and controversies, but I tell you that in my judgment—

> ——" those opened eyes,
> Which, like the meteors of a troubled heaven,
> All of one nature, of one substance bred,
> Did lately meet in th' intestine shock,
> Shall now, in mutual well-beseeming ranks,
> March all one way."

CHARLES E. LITTLEFIELD

CHARLES E. LITTLEFIELD, an American congressman and lawyer, was born at Lebanon, York Co., Me., June 21, 1851. He was educated in the common schools, and, after pursuing the study of law, was admitted to the Bar in 1876. He entered the lower house of the Maine legislature in 1885, and was Speaker of the House in 1887, and from 1889 to 1893 filled the post of attorney-general of Maine. In 1899, he was elected to the fifty-sixth Congress to fill the vacancy in the House of Representatives caused by the death of Nelson Dingley, the Republican representative.

THE PEARL OF THE ANTILLES, THE EVER-FAITHFUL ISLE

SPEECH DELIVERED IN THE HOUSE OF REPRESENTATIVES, FEB. 23, 1900

MR. CHAIRMAN AND GENTLEMEN OF THE COMMITTEE,—I believe that the pending bill is un-Republican, un-American, unwarranted, unprecedented, and unconstitutional. Inasmuch as I am in the painful position of differing with a large majority of my political brethren, and as I believe this measure is one of vast importance, of far reaching consequence, involving results that perhaps none of us can now anticipate, I feel that I should, perhaps, render the reasons for my position.

I concede, and I gladly concede, the right of leadership to the distinguished men who, by their long experience and great abilities, have the responsibility and the honor of leading the Republicans in this House. The leaders of the Republican party will find me, upon all measures that involve Republican policy, following loyally in their footsteps. When an issue, however, arises that involves, in my judgment, grave questions of right and wrong, great questions of prin-

ciple, I feel, and I have no doubt they feel, that every individual member of the Republican party must be allowed to
think, speak, and act for himself. . . .

The people of Porto Rico had the same pro rata representation in the Spanish Cortes as the citizens of the Empire,
in Spain itself. They had sixteen members in the lower
house, and four members in the upper house. Every citizen
of Porto Rico had the same legal rights as a citizen of Spain.
With reference to tariff conditions, for several years preceding the advent of Miles upon their soil, they had a ten per
cent preferential tariff between themselves and Spain. By
virtue of a budget which had been adopted and accepted, and
by a statute which had been enacted by the Spanish Cortes,
this tariff of ten per cent was to expire on the first of July,
1898, so that on, and after that date, there would have been
perfect free trade between Porto Rico, and the parent State,
Spain.

The suggestions which have been made by the gentleman
who immediately preceded me—the gentleman from Connecticut—in relation to the revenues collected in Porto Rico
are, I submit, somewhat misleading. I shall not undertake
here, because I have not the time according to the plan which
I have marked out for my address, to discuss such matters
in detail. I only call attention to the operation of the tariff
between Porto Rico and Spain. The license fees that were
collected, the taxes that were collected upon incomes, the
internal revenue taxes, should not properly be reckoned as
any part of the taxation by way of a tariff imposed on products going from Porto Rico to Spain, or upon the products of
Spain, going into Porto Rico.

Such a statement is an unfair presentation of the fiscal

condition of this island. The gentleman from Connecticut ingeniously, and confusingly combined them all in his description of fiscal conditions on the island, when nothing but the tariff has any proper place in the consideration of the pending measure. For years, has this island been populated by this white, Caucasian population. It never has had a dollar of public indebtedness. Time, and time again, the island from its own taxation has loaned to Spain money with which to carry on its various wars; and it has loaned to Santo Domingo and Cuba money for their public purposes. When the American flag was raised over this island, it had a surplus of $1,500,000 in its treasury.

The people who inhabit this island are a self-respecting, valorous, and heroic people.

Four times, during the eighteenth century, unaided and alone, the citizens of Porto Rico repelled the atacks of the English navy, once under the command of Drake, and once under the command of Abercrombie, and preserved Porto Rican soil for Porto Rico, against the most powerful of foreign invaders, although it was then a dependency of Spain.

In 1873 there existed upon the island of Porto Rico 39,000 slaves. In 1860 there existed in the Republic 3,000,000 slaves. The Republic freed its slaves at a cost that staggers humanity. It did not free the slaves " until all the wealth piled by the bondsman's two hundred and fifty years of unrequited toil " had been sunk and " until every drop of blood drawn by the lash had been paid by another drawn with the sword."

Porto Rico, in 1873, manumitted its slaves without tumult, without disturbance, without convulsion, without bloodshed, without murder, without outrage, and without revolution. With the consent of the Spanish Cortes, upon motion of a representative of Porto Rico, in one moment 39,000 persons who before that time had been held in human bondage, became freemen.

One day found them slaves; the next day they continued in their employment for the same masters, but working for hire—their own masters. On one day they bent down, bondmen. The next day they stood erect, freemen. This great change was wrought as quietly, and silently, as the dawn precedes the rising of the sun. The little island of Porto Rico paid for those slaves, by its own revenue, from its own prosperity, $7,800,000 in 1873, with a loan that required only fourteen years to pay, and, adding the interest and principal, aggregating the magnificent sum of $12,000,000—paid by whom?

By the people that live to-day in Porto Rico.

For what?

To emancipate 39,000 human bondmen. This nation of " illiterates," this people to whom we now propose to act the part of a " good Samaritan! " That was a deed worthy of the highest triumph of Christian civilization anywhere. The mechanics of Porto Rico, consisting of masons, blacksmiths, leather-workers, and silversmiths, are superior in their various branches to similar mechanics in nearly every part of the civilized world. The carpenters and cabinetmakers do not rank so high.

This is the condition of the island; this is the character of the people for whom the American Congress is about to legislate. They are an intelligent people, not barbarians, not slaves, but a free people, and I submit, as I shall submit later to the Republican party—for I do not stand here to address gentlemen upon the other side of this House—I submit, as I shall submit later to the Republican party, that they are a people who, by their history, by their character, by their intelligence, their endeavor, and inheritance, are entitled to fair treatment at the hands of the Republic, and to the maintenance of its plighted faith.

Thus stood the Pearl of the Antilles, " The Ever Faithful Isle," when, a rich and willing prize, it fell into our hands. I devote a moment to the question of raising revenue in Porto Rico for their own purposes, and then I pass from this branch of the question, to a discussion of the provisions of this bill.

It is estimated that $3,000,000 annually is necessary for the wants of this island, $1,000,000 to be devoted to public administration, $1,000,000 to be devoted to schools, and $1,000,000 to be devoted to public works. This is a large estimate, a liberal and a generous estimate. The amount that was used for schools in Porto Rico last year, and the preceding years, was only $345,000; and no wise and economical administration can properly expend in Porto Rico in the next two or three years three times the sum that is now being used, because it is a practical impossibility, under what they have there as a common-school system, to make such an expenditure economically.

It was conceded by the gentleman from Ohio [Mr. Grosvenor] in his speech yesterday, that $1,500,000 will be raised from the internal revenue tax upon rum. It is also conceded that under ordinary methods of local taxation they will raise about $500,000 besides, taking the island in its present prostrated condition, in all $2,000,000 of the $3,000,000 necessary to be raised.

Just a word as to their condition and situation. This estimate which I have given you of $500,000 is based upon the present condition of Porto Rico. And what is that? As was very handsomely and accurately described by the able chair-

man of the Ways and Means Committee, it is one of utter
and awful devastation and ruin, with the absolute prostration
of every industry in the island of Porto Rico. . . .

The estimate is, that even in that condition, with agriculture paralyzed, the amount which I have stated can be raised.
And I should say here, perhaps, for the information of gentlemen that while this island is fertile, and its soil only needs
to be tickled with a hoe to laugh with a harvest, that its fields
when once allowed to pass out from under cultivation, go
back in less than a year's time into a state of natural wildness,
so that they have to be reclaimed again, before any profit
can be made from them in agriculture. A large portion of
the island is in that condition to-day. Yet, in that condition,
it is conceded that by the ordinary methods of taxation this
amount can be raised. The ordinary method of taxation
there is simply this: It is in the nature of an income tax—
a percentage on the income of the planter of sugar, tobacco,
or coffee, or the man who is engaged in business, professional
or otherwise—a reasonably fair method of taxation.

It is estimated by men capable of judging upon this question that when this island once gets back to its pristine condition (which will, perhaps, require two years' time), with
the improved conditions of agriculture and methods of manufacture, that it is expected will be carried into this island
by American industry, energy, enterprise, and intelligence,
that the tax, upon the same basis, would aggregate from
$5,000,000 to $10,000,000. This island, this Pearl of the
Antilles, is no pauper or mendicant, standing begging at the
doors of the American Congress for alms, or for the work of
a "good Samaritan." All that the island of Porto Rico asks
is to have the American Congress give it a stable government,
an opportunity to take care of itself, and then take off its

hands and let it take care of itself, a thing that it can well do. . . .

We had better listen, and think now, than to listen later. A word here as to the assertion of the President of the United States as to " the plain duty " of the Republican party and of the American Congress. It is as much the duty of the Democrats as the Republicans, because later, when I reach that stage in this discussion, I shall base it upon the broad proposition that, to my mind, appeals to every patriot, and every man who believes in the good faith of the Republic, its honor, and its integrity. Every Democrat who sits on this floor is interested in that proposition as well as my Republican friends, with whom I just now can not act upon this bill.

As to the suggestion of the gentleman from Ohio that there had been a change in conditions I would like any gentlemen here to suggest what change there has been. He suggested—and I want to call your attention to this particularly—he suggested that there had been a change in conditions. The report of General Davis was made September 5, 1899. In the middle of the preceding August that awful tornado, that terrific cyclone, swept over this fateful island and carried these coffee plantations from the mountain sides, an indistinguishable mass of ruin, into the valleys below. That awful ruin had visited the Pearl of the Antilles, before this report was made by General Davis to the President of the United States. No calamity has visited the island since. No calamity is now impending over it, except what may be involved in this measure now pending.

There has been no change in conditions, there has been nothing that can be suggested. When William McKinley— and, by the way, I shall spend no time in this discussion in referring to Andrew Jackson, or Thomas Jefferson, or Tom Benton, or any of that great galaxy of men—for me it is sufficient if William McKinley, the honored President of this Republic, the distinguished representative of the Republican party, who is enthroned in the hearts and affections of all our people, will follow in the footsteps of Washington and Lincoln. A great many things have been done by the other distinguished gentlemen that I would not like to have any Republican President undertake to do, or even think of.

What does President McKinley say? He said when he sent his message to the House—and I have received no communication from the President of the United States since— mark that—he communicated to me through the constitutional channel; I say since then, neither directly nor indirectly, have I received any communication from the President of the United States that would tend to indicate that when he said—not that it was his opinion, not that he thought, nor that he would advise or suggest, but that it was " the plain duty "—stop and listen to that a minute—" the plain duty " of the Republican Congress to give free trade between Porto Rico and the United States, he did not mean it. That is an assertion of fact. It was either true or false.

If conditions have changed, let some gentleman suggest it while I am speaking. If there has been any change of conditions that could be mentioned by any gentleman since the President of the United States said it was our " plain duty," let him assert it now. That statement was either true or false when he made it, and if it was true or false when he made it, it is true or false now. I believe it was absolutely true.

I say to my friends that I am not ready, upon the question of policy even, to cast a vote in this House against what the

President of the United States has truthfully said was my
" plain duty." I stand upon that proposition. I stand by
the President of the United States, and a little later I will
call your attention to some significant reasons why.

What is this bill? I take it in detail. The second provision in it imposes what they call an import duty on the
manufactures and products of the United States " coming
into Porto Rico." The bill imposes a duty on all goods
" coming from Porto Rico " into the United States and on
goods " coming into Porto Rico " from the United States.
" Coming " both ways. I suppose the language of the bill
is so couched, in the futile effort to get rid of a provision
of the constitution which provides that " no tax or duty shall
be laid on articles exported from any State." (Constitution,
Article I, section 9, paragraph 5.) I submitted to two members of the Ways and Means Committee the question, as to
whether they could give me any legal distinction between
these propositions: First, a vessel is loaded with lumber,
say in Portland, and starts for Porto Rico. Under this bill
we will assume the tariff to be one thousand dollars.

Under this bill they collect the duty when she arrives,
and who collects it? The United States government. Into
whose pocket does it go? Into the United States government's. Second, what legal distinction is there between collecting the duty when she clears from Portland for Porto
Rico, before she leaves the State, or collecting it afterwards
in Porto Rico? The same hand collects it either in Portland,
or in San Juan. It goes into the same pocket in either case,
into the same Treasury, and is to be disbursed, under the
provisions of this bill, without any appropriation from the
public Treasury, which the constitution provides. But I do
not suppose the constitution is anything between friends

I suggested that question to the chairman of the Ways and Means Committee, and asked him if the tax was collected in the city of Portland on the products of the United States going into Porto Rico, whether it would not be a tax on " articles exported from any State," and he could not tell me. I asked him what the legal distinction was, when the same duty, on the same cargo, was collected by the same hand, for the same Treasury, in Porto Rico. He could not tell me what the distinction was, or whether there was any. I heard his speech after I had put the question to him; he occupied an hour and a half about other things, and he did not tell me then. I put the same question to another member of the Ways and Means Committee, who gave me no answer. He has not yet made a speech. I suppose when he gets round to it he may answer it. But I have not had the pleasure of hearing that question answered, much as I have desired to have it answered in order to bring me to the support of this branch of the measure, by reason of its harmony with the constitution. I sought from two members of the Ways and Means Committee an answer to this question more than four days ago—yes, last week. It is not answered yet.

What did they do ? I imagine they suggested the question to the distinguished gentleman from New York [Mr. Ray], the chairman of the Judiciary Committee—a man of eminence, ability, and character, a man whose suggestion ought to have weight with this House, and does. How did he answer it ? I did not hear his speech, but I have read a part of it in the " Record." He states that he spent a whole day looking up the lexicographers and dictionaries, for the purpose of finding a definition of " export." I have an idea that the gentleman rather looked for a definition that would help his case; because, being on that committee, I know that if he had whirled round in his revolving chair in that committee room, and reached his hand out to the revolving bookcase, he could have put it upon Bouvier's "Law Dictionary," where he would have found in one minute's time a very good definition. After his exhaustive research he discovered that "export" meant the exporting of goods "to a foreign country;" but Bouvier would have shown him this:

"Export: The act of sending goods and merchandise from one country to another."

Now, in the name of all the gods at once, is it possible that by virtue of a treaty, or by virtue of conquest, we have eliminated Porto Rico from the map of the earth and it is no longer even a "country?"

Let me read another definition. I think the gentleman ought not to have spent so much time on this question. "Much study is a weariness of the flesh." The gentleman referred to the "Standard Dictionary," which is not yet old enough in its present form to have been cited by the courts as an authority.

I understand the gentleman from New York to admit that if "export" as used in the constitution does not mean going into a "foreign country," then the act is unconstitutional as providing for an export duty. I am not going to weary myself very much on this point as it is not the important feature. I am simply suggesting this as one of the inconsistencies of the bill.

I read the definition as given in the "American and English Encyclopedia of Law:"

"To export an article of commerce is to carry such article out of a country or place."

When an article passes from the United States to Porto

Rico does it, or does it not, go out of " a country or place ? "
It seems to me it does; and it seems to me that when it goes
out of the country, then, according to this legal authority—I do not refer to the literary authority quoted by the
gentleman, but according to this legal authority—it becomes
an export, and does not necessarily involve the idea of going
to a " foreign country."

Let us turn to the " Century Dictionary," which has been
quoted quite frequently by the courts. Its definition is:

" Export: That which is exported; a commodity carried
from one place or country to another, for sale; generally in
the plural."

That unfortunate island is, it seems, for some purposes
foreign, and for other purposes domestic, corresponding with
the condition of certain gentlemen in this House some years
ago who undertook to be present and absent at one and the
same time, according as one or another purpose was to be
accomplished. In order to sustain the validity of the tariff
upon goods coming into the United States from Porto Rico,
Porto Rico is held to be a foreign country. In order to
sustain the validity of the tariff upon goods exported from
the United States to Porto Rico, under this discovery of the
chairman of the Judiciary Committee, Porto Rico is a domestic country. I think I understand the argument, but I do not
feel impressed or oppressed with its weight.

The gentleman from New York, who made his speech
under some degree of excitement, said that he would like
to look in the face of any lawyer who would undertake to
dissent from some of the propositions which he laid down.
I do not see the gentleman in his seat, but if he wants to see
me he can look into my face, for I have never turned my
back on any man. That is one of the things I do not do.

One of his propositions, as I understand, is that because the constitution says that under some circumstances a State can lay an export duty, with the consent of Congress, and because Congress has the powers of the general government and the States (which they have discovered in connection with some of these cases which they undertake to discuss), therefore—what?

Under the constitution, Congress can suspend the operation of that clause of the constitution which provides that no export duty shall be imposed on articles sent out of a State; that is, the State could act with the consent of the Congress; but as it has been held in general terms, in discussing a clause of the constitution that has no connection whatever with this, that Congress has the powers of the State as to a possession, it can give its consent, and then act for the State, and when it acts for the State it is supposed to give its own consent, and hence you have the absolute repeal, by the mere operation of logic, of an express prohibition of the constitution. I think this proposition may be fairly designated as metaphysical, and while it is as well founded undoubtedly as many of the propositions upon which the Committee rely, little is hazarded when it is asserted that if the court ever sustain this clause of the bill it will not be upon this attenuated ground.

I have another objection to this branch of the bill. I submit that it is un-Republican. When—and I asked this question of the chairman of the Committee on Ways and Means, and if I misrepresent or misquote him I will thank him to correct me at once—I asked the chairman of the Committee on Ways and Means when in the history of the Republican party, that party ever voted to impose a tariff upon American capital and American labor? Ever before? He did not answer. He did not answer in his speech. Will any man on this floor answer? Where is the warrant in the history, or the platforms, of the Republican party, the party of protection to what? To American labor and American capital, against foreign labor and foreign capital. Where is the warrant in the platforms of the Republican party, or in the history of the Republican party, or in the assertion of any man who undertook to belong to the Republican party, for imposing a tariff upon American labor and American capital?

The necessaries of life—flour, rice, codfish, pork, bacon, corn meal, fresh beef, and mutton—to-day go into Porto Rico free. Bags for sugar, shooks, rough lumber, agricultural implements, machinery, trees, shrubs, seeds, and school furniture are all free under an Executive order. They have been going in free since October 21, 1899. This bill makes them all subject to twenty-five per cent of the Dingley tariff.

The people of Porto Rico, partly as the result of our disturbance of their affairs, are starving. They have scarcely anything with which to buy food, if the food was there. In the exercise of our enlightened philanthropy, and from a desire to play the part of the " good Samaritan,"our first act is to increase the cost to them of the necessaries of life by a tariff, and to that extent place it beyond their power to sustain life. An allopathic dose of that brand of philanthropy would tend to depopulate the island.

Let me illustrate this for just a moment. Let us see where we are. Let us understand what we have got to meet in the coming campaign. The tariff upon coarse lumber coming from any foreign country into any part of the United States, and into Porto Rico—because that is enough a part of the United States to have the tariff apply—is two dollars a thousand. What does this bill do? Our lumbermen have the protection of two dollars a thousand, as against the Canadian lumbermen, and I see a man sitting in this hall who lives within a mile of the territory over which floats the Cross of St. George. To discriminate against its industries the Dingley bill, the work of my distinguished and lamented predecessor, with the co-operation of the great men in this House, was passed. That gave to the lumber industry a protection of two dollars on a thousand. What does this bill do? It takes off twenty-five per cent of it and leaves it with a protection of one dollar and fifty cents on a thousand. On codfish it is precisely the same in proportion.

I only use this as an illustration. Where is the warrant in Republican history, where is the warrant in a Republican platform, for discriminating against these industries and these products that happen to be exported to Porto Rico by the amount of twenty-five per cent of the Dingley tariff, and putting no duties whatever upon other products or manufactures going to other countries or other places in this country? Where is that proposition? I submit it as a Republican proposition. I make no complaint for this reason, but it illustrates the operation of the bill.

I now take the provision in this bill in which the great fundamental proposition is involved. The amount at stake I shall not take time to discuss. I do not undertake to weigh in the scales of an apothecary the integrity of the Republic or human rights of people anywhere. If they are infringed so far as I am concerned, by so much as a hair, I will not approve or adopt the proposition.

This provision does what? It imposes a tariff of one quarter of the Dingley tariff upon the products of Porto Rico coming into the United States, and upon what products? Upon sugar and upon tobacco. There is none upon coffee.

The value of the coffee produced before this awful cyclone struck this devoted island was $4,200,000 a year. The value of the sugar was $2,700,000 a year. The value of the tobacco was $300,000 a year. This imposes a tax for the revenue of Porto Rico upon two industries, sugar and tobacco, and leaves coffee entirely free, and coffee represents as much as both of them—yes, more than both of them put together. And so far as this tax is concerned, conceived in the " good Samaritan " habit, in the " good Samaritan " theory, of the gentleman from Connecticut [Mr. Russell], out of great philanthropy and benevolence—this philanthropy that takes out of a man's pocket with the right hand, and shifts it over to the left hand, and carries it back to his left-hand pocket, less expense of collection—magnificent philanthropy and benevolence, without a copper's expense to the magnificent people who exercise the philanthropy and benevolence!— upon whom does it rest? It rests solely upon the producers of sugar and tobacco.

Of course there are other industries, but these are the principal ones. It leaves the producers of sugar and tobacco paying all that tax, the coffee planters and all other property and business paying none of it. That is the practical proposition. Why is this suggested here now? What is its purpose? What is its object? It is said that it is not to protect any American industry; it is said that it does not bear grievously upon Porto Rico; but what else is said? It is said that we are here and now—and that is the great objection which I have to this bill—it is said that we are, here and now, as the representatives of the Republican party, to announce to the world our policy in connection with Porto Rico and the Philippine Archipelago.

And what is that policy? That policy is to protect the in-

dustries of the United States, against the industries of Porto
Rico and the Philippine Archipelago. That means what?
That we are going to develop those territories? That we are
going to give them an opportunity to blossom like the rose?
It means this, and you may as well meet it here as meet it
hereafter: It means that when they can raise sugar in Porto
Rico, that does not interfere with us, they can raise it and
send it here.

It means that when they raise it, so that it does interfere
with us, we will put our foot upon their necks, with a tariff,
and stop it from coming here in competition with our sugar.

It means that anywhere and everywhere, in Porto Rico
or the Philippine Archipelago, any industry or any occupation, however much it may be developed under the flag, with
our energy, and our enterprise, and our industry, the moment
it comes into competition with anything raised or manufactured in the Republic, meaning the forty-five States, according to the new theory of sublimated selfishness, just that
moment the Republic will put its hand upon it and keep it
down, so that it will not compete. How much will you develop Porto Rico and the Philippine Archipelago on that
policy?

I say here frankly, I say here coolly, and I am not excited
about this, that I do not believe that proposition will appeal
to the good sense, the fair mind, honest judgment, of the
people who have been in the habit of voting loyally the Republican ticket. I care nothing about the other side. So
far as we are concerned, I do not believe it will appeal to
them. That is the proposition—that Porto Rico and the
Philippine Archipelago are an orange for us to squeeze. The
twelve millions subject people in these islands are simply,
under this proposition, " hewers of wood and drawers of

water " for seventy-five millions free people. How much American capital will go into Porto Rico or into the Philippine Archipelago, if this proposition is to be sustained, when they know that any development they may make there is subject to the repressing hand of an American Congress? They are our own people in more senses than one, according to the theory of those who propose this bill—peculiarly our own, because they are a good deal more our own, if they have no constitutional rights, than they would be if they came in as a part of this body politic, with the political rights of American citizens, so that they could protect their own interests.

This is from the standpoint of policy and fair dealing.

The breach of good faith is another reason why I am opposed to this measure.

In 1898 the army of the United States, in a war declared in the interest of humanity, and upon the proposition that the old flag would carry with it liberty and freedom and equal opportunity and all the blessings of a Christian civilization, went where? It went to the island of Porto Rico, and Major-General Miles held the standard. I will read to the House, the proclamation with which General Miles signalized his advent upon Porto Rican soil. It is dated Ponce, Porto Rico, July 28, 1898.

In it he said, among other things, referring to the soldiers of the Union:

" They come bearing the banner of freedom, inspired by a noble purpose, to seek the enemies of our country and yours, and to destroy or capture all who are in armed resistance. They bring you the fostering arm of a nation of free people, whose greatest power is in its justice and humanity to all those living within its folds."

This is not the conversation of any Secretary of War itinerating over this magnificent island. He said further:

" We have not come to make war upon the people of a country that for centuries has been oppressed, but, on the contrary, to bring you protection, not only to yourselves but to your property, to promote your prosperity "—

And now mark the language—

—" and to bestow upon you the immunities and blessings of the liberal institutions of our government."

Now, if the gentlemen of the Ways and Means Committee, instead of spending so much time in trying to ascertain that the United States meant the United States, and that a State meant a State, and that forty-five States constitute the United States, and that the United States, meaning forty-five States, is described by the boundary line of the forty-five States— if they had taken their dictionaries and looked just for a moment at Webster, for his definition of immunity, they would have ascertained what the promise was that General Miles made to this devoted people. What does " immunity " mean?

" Freedom or exemption from any charge "—

—and it did not take me a day to hunt this up—

" Freedom or exemption from any charge, duty, obligation, office, tax, imposition, penalty, or service."

Was there any tax, in the nature of a tariff, in any part of the Republic, between the States and the Territories, when General Miles made that promise to these people? The word " immunity " in his proclamation could have referred to nothing by any decent construction of the English language except what? Immunity from charges, taxes, and service. The same immunity that the citizens of the United States en-

joyed, and in no State or Territory was there then, nor will
there ever be, any duty or tax upon exports and imports between States or Territories, or States and Territories.   That
is one of " the immunities and blessings of the liberal institutions of our government." Relying upon this proclamation these people did what?

They prostrated themselves before him; they covered him
with wreaths and garlands of flowers; they kissed the flag that
was carried there under that promise, and the delegates from
Porto Rico stand here, asking the Republican party to make
good the promise made by General Miles for the Republic,
when they eagerly delivered " The Ever-Faithful Isle " into
his all-conquering hands.   Miles, the magnificent representative of our institutions, the typical American citizen, who won
his way by sheer force of merit, ability, and valor, from the
position of a common soldier, step by step, to the position of
leader of the Armies of the Republic.

I never will vote to violate the promise he made or to repudiate the pledge.   The Republican party can not afford,
in this or any other campaign, to violate that sacred promise.
It is written in the blood of our heroes that fought at El
Caney, San Juan, and Santiago.   It was made in the presence
of all Christendom, and it is sealed by the God of battles.   The
Republic can not violate that promise made to this weak and
helpless people without sullying its honor and tarnishing its
fame.   It is not written in the history of the Republican party
that at any time, or anywhere, from the hour of its birth
agony, when it sprang into existence, full panoplied as the
unconquerable champion of liberty and freedom, under the
valiant leadership of the great Pathfinder, it ever violated
its plighted faith, or swerved from the path of rectitude and
honor. . . .

It is suggested by the gentleman from Kansas [Mr. Long], and well suggested, in a speech which it was not my pleasure to hear, but which undoubtedly has increased his reputation and demonstrates his ability, that the treaty contains a provision that Spain can have the same tariff with these possessions that we give to them, and if we give the open door to Porto Rico we give the open door to Spain. We do it unless— what? Unless we violate the agreement we made with Spain; and it is entirely competent, if the Republic sees fit to do so, to violate that agreement.

But here stand two agreements—one made with Spain, and one made with the prostrate, helpless, long-suffering, starving Porto Rico. Which shall be violated? If I had my choice, and were I compelled to determine between them, I would violate our faith with a power which, until we brushed it off the earth as a military and naval power during the last two years, had some ability to protect and defend itself. I would not go before the civilized world upon the proposition that we would break faith with the downtrodden and the oppressed.

I would go further than that. I would not break faith with either. I stand behind the eminent gentlemen who negotiated that treaty. I believe they acted in the interest of the Republic, and as faithful representatives of the American people. We cannot repudiate the promise made by General Miles on the shores of Porto Rico. I believe the Republic can afford to keep all of its promises, no matter what the consequences be. It should not violate or repudiate either.

I read now a speech made by General Henry to the alcalde and citizens of Porto Rico at the close of hostilities and the celebration of peace in Porto Rico:

" Alcalde and Citizens: To-day the flag of the United States floats as an emblem of undisputed authority over the island of Porto Rico, giving promise of protection to life, of liberty, prosperity, and the right to worship God in accordance with the dictates of conscience. The forty-five States represented by the stars emblazoned on the blue field of that flag unite in vouchsafing to you prosperity and protection as citizens of the American Union. . . . I congratulate you all on beginning your public life under new auspices, free from governmental oppression, and with liberty to advance your own country's interests by your united efforts."

Now they are learning that " protection as citizens of the American Union " was " a delusion and a snare ; " that they are not " citizens of the American Union," and it was never intended that they should be ; that the " protection " referred to was the protection of the citizens of the United States, in " the American Union," against the people of Porto Rico. This is reading between the lines with a vengeance. The alcalde, in his innocence and simplicity, replied, in part:

. . . " Porto Rico has not accepted American domination on account of force. She has suffered for many years the evils of error, neglect, and persecution, but she had men who studied the question of government, and who saw in America her redemption, and a guaranty of life, liberty, and justice. There we came willingly and freely, hoping, hand and hand with the greatest of all republics, to advance in civilization and progress, and to become part of the Republic, to which we pledge our faith forever."

I can not dwell longer upon this painful proposition. I must call your attention to what Secretary Elihu Root, the great lawyer, the honest man, the representative Republican, upon these facts, said. He says:

" But the highest considerations of justice and good faith demand that we should not disappoint the confident expectation of sharing in our prosperity with which the people of

Porto Rico so gladly transferred their allegiance to the United States, and that we should treat the interests of this people as our own, and I wish most strongly to urge that the customs duties between Porto Rico and the United States be removed."

Here you have the solemn promise made by General Miles when he conquered these islands, the promise relied upon by them, its construction by Mr. Root, Secretary of War, and the statement of that eminent Republican, that true patriot, William McKinley, when he said it is our " plain duty " to give these people free trade; and yet it is proposed that we shall act contrary to the advice of Davis, contrary to the advice of the delegates, contrary to the advice of Root, contrary to the advice of the President of the United States, in violation of our faith, and that by gentlemen who undertake to know more here than the men know there, about their condition and what ought in justice to be done.

There are two sides to this as a political proposition. I do not want to defend upon the stump—I hope there will be no occasion to do so—I do not want to defend upon the stump the proposition that the Republican party with its eyes open, with its attention, called to the fact, persisted in violating the good faith of the Republic. Why, gentlemen here say that we are about to inaugurate a policy of colonial government. I want to ask the gentlemen in this House if they desire to signalize their entry upon a colonial government, in their very first act, by a breach of good faith. Do you remember the history of proud Spain? What is it? What is it that has characterized Spain ever since the sixteenth century, ever since Pizarro rode ruthless and roughshod over Mexico, and the Duke of Alva filled the Netherlands with carnage, blood, butcheries, and indescribable horrors, in his infamous attempt to crush out the very beginning of civil and religious liberty? What is it that has characterized her and made her contemptible before every honorable nation upon the earth? It is her duplicity and her breaches of good faith.

Will the Republican party, in the teeth of the declaration of the Secretary of War and the President of the United States, signalize its embarkation upon that policy with its first act a breach of good faith? That policy upon the part of Spain, has made her for all time a "hissing and a by-word" and a reproach to all Christian peoples. I stand here, if I stand alone, as a member of the Republican party, the party that I love, the party that has done so much for the liberty and welfare and prosperity and development of the Republic, to enter my solemn protest against such an act.

Even under the guise of " good Samaritanism," even under the guise of " philanthropy " or any guise or subterfuge of any sort, I can not and will not agree to it. I leave that for my friends to discuss and reflect upon. It is hardly worth while for a man who sits in the House, and happens to hear coming from persons, unduly and unnecessarily alarmed, a demand for this legislation, to shut his eyes and think that these things do not exist because he does not then see them. They are here; they will be with us; they will be like the Old Man of the Sea; they will cling to our backs throughout the next campaign and, I fear, through many others.

Porto Rico kneels to-day, weak, helpless, starving, with her hands held toward us in supplication. She pleads for the fulfilment of this promise. Her prayers may fall upon deaf ears that will not hear in this House, but there is one tribunal to which I fully believe they may confidently appeal—the enlightened, unselfish, Christian conscience of a great and free people.

PROF. H. DRUMMOND

ENRY DRUMMOND, a distinguished Scotch theologian, evangelist, and biologist, was born at Stirling, Scotland, Aug. 17, 1851, and died at Tunbridge Wells, March 11, 1897. He was educated at Edinburgh University and at Tübingen, Germany, and in 1877 became professor of natural science at the Free Church College, Glasgow. He visited the United States early in his career on a geological exposition to the Yellowstone Park and the Rocky Mountains, afterwards paying exploratory visits to Central Africa, Japan, Australia, and elsewhere, and wrote several fascinating books relating his experiences. He also lectured with great success in the United States. The main object of his teaching was to reconcile evangelical Christianity with the doctrine of evolution. His "Natural Law in the Spiritual World," published in 1883, had a phenomenal sale on both sides of the Atlantic, and his lecture on "The Greatest Thing in the World" secured his fame as a great religious teacher. Among his other works are "Tropical Africa" (1888) and "The Ascent of Man" (1894). His life has been written by Prof. Geo. Adam Smith.

ADDRESS ON THE GREATEST THING IN THE WORLD

EVERY one has asked himself the great question of antiquity as of the modern world: what is the *summum bonum*—the supreme good? You have life before you. Once only you can live it. What is the noblest object of desire, the supreme gift to covet?

We have been accustomed to be told that the greatest thing in the religious world is Faith. That great word has been the key-note for centuries of the popular religion; and we have easily learned to look upon it as the greatest thing in the world. Well, we are wrong. If we have been told that, we may miss the mark. I have taken you, in the chapter which I have just read, to Christianity at its source; and there we have seen, " The greatest of these is love."

It is not an oversight. Paul was speaking of faith just a moment before. He says, " If I have all faith, so that I can remove mountains, and have not love, I am nothing." So far from forgetting he deliberately contrasts them, " Now abideth Faith, Hope, Love," and without a moment's hesitation the decision falls, " The greatest of these is Love."

And it is not prejudice. A man is apt to recommend to others his own strong point—Love was not Paul's strong point. The observing student can detect a beautiful tenderness growing and ripening all through his character as Paul gets old; but the hand that wrote, " The greatest of these is love," when we meet it first, is stained with blood.

Nor is this letter to the Corinthians peculiar in singling out love as the *summum bonum*. The masterpieces of Christianity are agreed about it. Peter says, " Above all things have fervent love among yourselves." *Above all things*. And John goes further, " God is love." And you remember the profound remark which Paul makes elsewhere, " Love is the fulfilling of the law." Did you ever think what he meant by that? In those days men were working their passage to Heaven by keeping the Ten Commandments, and the hundred and ten other commandments which they had manufactured out of them.

Christ said, I will show you a more simple way. If you do one thing, you will do these hundred and ten things, without ever thinking about them. If you love, you will unconsciously fulfil the whole law.

And you can readily see for yourselves how that must be so. Take any of the commandments. " Thou shalt have no other gods before me." If a man love God, you will not require to tell him that. Love is the fulfilling of that law. " Take not his name in vain." Would he ever dream of taking his name in vain if he loved him? " Remember the Sabbath day to keep it holy." Would he not be too glad to have one day in seven to dedicate more exclusively to the object of his affection?

Love would fulfil all these laws regarding God. And so, if he loved Man, you would never think of telling him to honor his father and mother. He could not do anything else. It would be preposterous to tell him not to kill. You could only insult him if you suggested that he should not steal— how could he steal from those he loved? It would be super- fluous to beg him not to bear false witness against his neigh- bor. If he loved him it would be the last thing he would do. And you would never dream of urging him not to covet what his neighbors had. He would rather they possessed it than himself. In this way " Love is the fulfilling of the law." It is the rule for fulfilling all rules, the new command- ment for keeping all the old commandments, Christ's one secret of the Christian life.

Now Paul had learned that; and in this noble eulogy he has given us the most wonderful and original account extant of the *summum bonum*. We may divide it into three parts. In the beginning of the short chapter, we have Love con- trasted; in the heart of it, we have Love analyzed, toward the end, we have Love defended as the supreme gift.

Paul begins by contrasting Love with other things that men in those days though much of. I shall not attempt to go over those things in detail. Their inferiority is already obvious.

He contrasts it with eloquence. And what a noble gift it is, the power of playing upon the souls and wills of men, and rousing them to lofty purposes and holy deeds. Paul says, " If I speak with the tongues of men and of angels, and have not love, I am become as sounding brass, or a tinkling cymbal." And we all know why. We have all felt the brazenness of words without emotion, the hollowness, the unaccountable unpersuasiveness, of eloquence behind which lies no Love.

He contrasts it with prophecy. He contrasts it with mysteries. He contrasts it with faith. He contrasts it with charity. Why is Love greater than faith? Because the end is greater than the means. And why is it greater than charity? Because the whole is greater than the part. Love is greater than faith, because the end is greater than the means. What is the use of having faith? It is to connect the soul with God. And what is the object of connecting man with God? That he may become like God. But God is Love. Hence Faith, the means, is in order to Love, the end. Love, therefore, obviously is greater than faith. It is greater than charity, again, because the whole is greater than a part. Charity is only a little bit of Love, one of the innumerable avenues of Love, and there may even be, and there is, a great deal of charity without Love.

It is a very easy thing to toss a copper to a beggar on the street; it is generally an easier thing than not to do it. Yet Love is just as often in the withholding. We purchase relief from the sympathetic feelings roused by the spectacle of misery, at the copper's cost. It is too cheap—too cheap for us, and often too dear for the beggar. If we really loved him we would either do more for him, or less.

Then Paul contrasts it with sacrifice and martyrdom. And I beg the little band of would-be missionaries—and I have the honor to call some of you by this name for the first time—to remember that though you give your bodies to be burned, and have not Love, it profits nothing—nothing! You can take nothing greater to the heathen world than the impress and reflection of the Love of God upon your own character. That is the universal language.

It will take you years to speak in Chinese, or in the dialects of India. From the day you land, the language of Love, understood by all, will be pouring forth its unconscious eloquence. It is the man who is the missionary, it is not his words. His character is his message. In the heart of Africa, among the great Lakes, I have come across black men and women who remembered the only white man they ever saw before—David Livingstone; and as you cross his footsteps in that dark continent, men's faces light up as they speak of the kind Doctor who passed there years ago. They could not understand him; but they felt the Love that beat in his heart. Take into your new sphere of labor, where you also mean to lay down your life, that simple charm, and your lifework must succeed. You can take nothing greater, you need take nothing less. It is not worth while going if you take anything less. You may take every accomplishment; you may be braced for every sacrifice; but if you give your body to be burned, and have not Love, it will profit you and the cause of Christ nothing.

After contrasting Love with these things, Paul, in three verses, very short, gives us an amazing analysis of what this supreme thing is. I ask you to look at it. It is a compound thing, he tells us. It is like light. As you have seen a man of science take a beam of light and pass it through a crystal prism, as you have seen it come out on the other side of the prism broken up into its component colors—red, and blue, and yellow, and violet, and orange, and all the colors of the rainbow—so Paul passes this thing, Love, through the magnificent prism of his inspired intellect, and it comes out on the other side broken up into its elements.

And in these few words we have what one might call the
Spectrum of Love, the analysis of Love. Will you observe
what its elements are? Will you notice that they have common names; that they are virtues which we hear about every
day, that they are things which can be practised by every
man in every place in life; and how, by a multitude of small
things and ordinary virtues, the supreme thing, the *summum
bonum*, is made up?

The Spectrum of Love has nine ingredients:

Patience . . .	" Love suffereth long."
Kindness . . .	" And is kind."
Generosity . . .	" Love envieth not."
Humility . . .	" Love vaunteth not itself, is not puffed up."
Courtesy . . .	" Doth not behave itself unseemly."
Unselfishness . .	" Seeketh not her own."
Good Temper . .	" Is not easily provoked."
Guilelessness . .	" Thinketh no evil."
Sincerity . . .	" Rejoiceth not in iniquity, but rejoiceth in the truth."

Patience; kindness; generosity; humility; courtesy; unselfishness; good temper; guilelessness; sincerity—these
make up the supreme gift, the stature of the perfect man.
You will observe that all are in relation to men, in relation
to life, in relation to the known to-day and the near to-morrow, and not to the unknown eternity. We hear much of
love to God; Christ spoke much of love to man. We make
a great deal of peace with heaven; Christ made much of
peace on earth. Religion is not a strange or added thing,
but the inspiration of the secular life, the breathing of an
eternal spirit through this temporal world. The supreme
thing, in short, is not a thing at all, but the giving of a further
finish to the multitudinous words and acts which make up the
sum of every common day.

There is no time to do more than make a passing note
upon each of these ingredients. Love is *Patience*. This is

the normal attitude of Love; Love passive, Love waiting to begin; not in a hurry; calm; ready to do its work when the summons comes, but meantime wearing the ornament of a meek and quiet spirit. Love suffers long; beareth all things; believeth all things; hopeth all things. For Love understands, and therefore waits.

Kindness. Love active. Have you ever noticed how much of Christ's life was spent in doing kind things—in *merely* doing kind things? Run over it with that in view, and you will find that he spent a great proportion of his time simply in making people happy, in doing good turns to people. There is only one thing greater than happiness in the world, and that is holiness; and it is not in our keeping; but what God *has* put in our power is the happiness of those about us, and that is largely to be secured by our being kind to them.

" The greatest thing," says some one, " a man can do for his Heavenly Father is to be kind to some of His other children."

I wonder why it is that we are not all kinder than we are? How much the world needs it. How easily it is done. How instantaneously it acts. How infallibly it is remembered. How superabundantly it pays itself back—for there is no debtor in the world so honorable, so superbly honorable, as Love. " Love never faileth." Love is success, Love is happiness, Love is life. " Love, I say," with Browning, " is energy of Life."

> " For life, with all it yields of joy or woe
> And hope and fear,
> Is just our chance o' the prize of learning love,—
> How love might be, hath been indeed, and is."

Where Love is, God is. He that dwelleth in Love dwelleth in God. God is Love. Therefore *love*. Without distinction, without calculation, without procrastination, love. Lavish it upon the poor, where it is very easy; especially upon the rich, who often need it most; most of all upon our equals, where it is very difficult, and for whom perhaps we each do least of all. There is a difference between trying to please and giving pleasure.

Give pleasure. Lose no chance of giving pleasure. For that is the ceaseless and anonymous triumph of a truly loving spirit. "I shall pass through this world but once. Any good thing therefore that I can do, or any kindness that I can show to any human being, let me do it now. Let me not defer it or neglect it, for I shall not pass this way again."

Generosity. "Love envieth not." This is love in competition with others. Whenever you attempt a good work you will find other men doing the same kind of work, and probably doing it better. Envy them not. Envy is a feeling of ill will to those who are in the same line as ourselves, a spirit of covetousness and detraction. How little Christian work even is a protection against un-Christian feeling. That most despicable of all the unworthy moods which cloud a Christian's soul assuredly waits for us on the threshold of every work, unless we are fortified with this grace of magnanimity. Only one thing truly need the Christian envy, the large, rich, generous soul which "envieth not."

And then, after having learned all that, you have to learn this further thing, *Humility*—to put a seal upon your lips and forget what you have done. After you have been kind, after Love has stolen forth into the world and done its beautiful work, go back into the shade again and say nothing about it. Love hides even from itself. Love waives even self-satisfaction. "Love vaunteth not itself, is not puffed up."

The fifth ingredient is a somewhat strange one to find in this *summum bonum: Courtesy.* This is Love in society,

Love in relation to etiquette. " Love doth not behave itself unseemly." Politeness has been defined as love in trifles. Courtesy is said to be love in little things. And the one secret of politeness is to love. Love cannot behave itself unseemly. You can put the most untutored persons into the highest society, and if they have a reservoir of Love in their heart, they will not behave themselves unseemly. They simply cannot do it.

Carlyle said of Robert Burns that there was no truer gentleman in Europe than the ploughman poet. It was because he loved everything—the mouse, and the daisy, and all the things, great and small, that God had made. So with this simple passport he could mingle with any society, and enter courts and palaces from his little cottage on the banks of the Ayr. You know the meaning of the word " gentleman." It means a gentle man—a man who does things gently with love. And that is the whole art and mystery of it. The gentle man cannot in the nature of things do an ungentle, an ungentlemanly thing. The ungentle soul, the inconsiderate, unsympathetic nature cannot do anything else. " Love doth not behave itself unseemly."

Unselfishness. " Love seeketh not her own." Observe: Seeketh not even that which is her own. In Britain the Englishman is devoted, and rightly, to his rights. But there come times when a man may exercise even the higher right of giving up his rights. Yet Paul does not summon us to give up our rights. Love strikes much deeper. It would have us not seek them at all, ignore them, eliminate the personal element altogether from our calculations.

It is not hard to give up our rights. They are often external. The difficult thing is to give up ourselves. The more difficult thing still is not to seek things for ourselves at all.

After we have sought them, bought them, won them, deserved them, we have taken the cream off them for ourselves already. Little cross then perhaps to give them up. But not to seek them, to look every man not on his own things, but on the things of others—*id opus est.* " Seekest thou great things for thyself?" said the prophet; " *seek them not.*" Why? Because there is no greatness in *things.* Things cannot be great. The only greatness is unselfish love. Even self-denial in itself is nothing, is almost a mistake. Only a great purpose or a mightier love can justify the waste. It is more difficult, I have said, not to seek our own at all, than, having sought it, to give it up. I must take that back. It is only true of a partly selfish heart. Nothing is a hardship to Love, and nothing is hard.

I believe that Christ's yoke is easy. Christ's " yoke " is just his way of taking life. And I believe it is an easier way than any other. I believe it is a happier way than any other. The most obvious lesson in Christ's teaching is that there is no happiness in having and getting anything, but only in giving. I repeat, there is no happiness in having or in getting, but only in giving. And half the world is on the wrong scent in the pursuit of happiness. They think it consists in having and getting, and in being served by others. It consists in giving, and in serving others. He that would be great among you, said Christ, let him serve. He that would be happy, let him remember that there is but one way—it is more blessed, it is more happy, to give than to receive.

The next ingredient is a very remarkable one: *Good Temper.* " Love is not easily provoked." Nothing could be more striking than to find this here. We are inclined to look upon bad temper as a very harmless weakness. We speak

of it as a mere infirmity of nature, a family failing, a matter
of temperament, not a thing to take into very serious account in estimating a man's character. And yet here, right
in the heart of this analysis of love, it finds a place; and the
Bible again and again returns to condemn it as one of the
most destructive elements in human nature.

The peculiarity of ill temper is that it is the vice of the
virtuous. It is often the one blot on an otherwise noble character. You know men who are all but perfect, and women
who would be entirely perfect, but for an easily ruffled, quick-
tempered, or " touchy " disposition.

This compatability of ill temper with high moral character
is one of the strangest and saddest problems of ethics. The
truth is there are two great classes of sins—sins of the Body,
and sins of the Disposition. The Prodigal Son may be taken
as a type of the first, the Elder Brother of the second. Now
society has no doubt whatever as to which of these is the
worse. Its brand falls, without a challenge, upon the
Prodigal.

But are we right? We have no balance to weigh one another's sins, and coarser and finer are but human words; but
faults in the higher nature may be less venial than those in
the lower, and to the eye of Him who is Love, a sin against
Love may seem a hundred times more base. No form of vice,
not worldliness, not greed of gold, not drunkenness itself,
does more to un-Christianize society than evil temper.

For embittering life, for breaking up communities, for
destroying the most sacred relationships, for devastating
homes, for withering up men and women, for taking the
bloom off childhood, in short, for sheer gratuitous misery-
producing power, this influence stands alone.

Look at the Elder Brother, moral, hard-working, patient,

dutiful—let him get all credit for his virtues—look at this man, this baby, sulking outside his own father's door. "He was angry," we read, "and would not go in." Look at the effect upon the father, upon the servants, upon the happiness of the guests. Judge of the effect upon the Prodigal—and how many prodigals are kept out of the Kingdom of God by the unlovely character of those who profess to be inside? Analyze, as a study in Temper, the thunder-cloud itself as it gathers upon the Elder Brother's brow. What is it made of?

Jealously, anger, pride, uncharity, cruelty, self-righteousness, touchiness, doggedness, sullenness—these are the ingredients of this dark and loveless soul. In varying proportions, also, these are the ingredients of all ill temper. Judge if such sins of the disposition are not worse to live in, and for others to live with, than sins of the body. Did Christ indeed not answer the question Himself when he said, "I say unto you, that the publicans and the harlots go into the Kingdom of Heaven before you." There is really no place in Heaven for a disposition like this. A man with such a mood could only make Heaven miserable for all the people in it. Except, therefore, such a man be born again, he cannot, he simply cannot, enter the Kingdom of Heaven. For it is perfectly certain—and you will not misunderstand me— that to enter Heaven a man must take it with him.

You will see then why Temper is significant. It is not in what it is alone, but in what it reveals. This is why I take the liberty now of speaking of it with such unusual plainness. It is a test for love, a symptom, a revelation of an unloving nature at bottom. It is the intermittent fever which bespeaks unintermittent disease within; the occasional bubble escaping to the surface which betrays some rottenness underneath; a sample of the most hidden products of the soul dropped involuntarily when off one's guard; in a word, the lightning form of a hundred hideous and un-Christian sins. For a want of patience, a want of kindness, a want of generosity, a want of courtesy, a want of unselfishness, are all instantaneously symbolized in one flash of Temper.

Hence it is not enough to deal with the Temper. We must go to the source, and change the inmost nature, and the angry humors will die away of themselves. Souls are made sweet not by taking the acid fluids out, but by putting something in—a great Love, a new Spirit, the Spirit of Christ. Christ, the Spirit of Christ, interpenetrating ours, sweetens, purifies, transforms all. This only can eradicate what is wrong, work a chemical change, renovate and regenerate, and rehabilitate the inner man. Will-power does not change men. Time does not change men. Christ does.

Therefore, "Let that mind be in you which was also in Christ Jesus." Some of us have not much time to lose. Remember, once more, that this is a matter of life or death. I cannot help speaking urgently, for myself, for yourselves. "Whoso shall offend one of these little ones, which believe in me, it were better for him that a millstone were hanged about his neck, and that he were drowned in the depth of the sea." That is to say, it is the deliberate verdict of the Lord Jesus that it is better not to live than not to love. It is better not to live than not to love.

Guilelessness and *Sincerity* may be dismissed almost with a word. Guilelessness is the grace for suspicious people. And the possession of it is the great secret of personal influence. You will find, if you think for a moment, that the people who influence you are people who believe in you. In an atmosphere of suspicion men shrivel up; but in that atmos-

phere they expand, and find encouragement and educative
fellowship.   It is a wonderful thing that here and there in
this hard, uncharitable world there should still be left a few
rare souls who think no evil.   This is the great unworldliness.
Love " thinketh no evil," imputes no motive, sees the bright
side, puts the best construction on every action.   What a delightful state of mind to live in!   What a stimulus and benediction even to meet with it for a day!   To be trusted is to
be saved.   And if we try to influence or elevate others, we
shall soon see that success is in proportion to their belief of
our belief in them.   For the respect of another is the first
restoration of the self-respect a man has lost; our ideal of
what he is becomes to him the hope and pattern of what he
may become.

" Love rejoiceth not in iniquity, but rejoiceth in the
truth."   I have called this Sincerity from the words rendered
in the Authorized Version by " rejoiceth in the truth."   And,
certainly, were this the real translation, nothing could be
more just.   For he who loves will love Truth not less than
men.   He will rejoice in the Truth—rejoice not in what he
has been taught to believe; not in this Church's doctrine or
in that; not in this ism or in that ism; but " in the Truth."
He will accept only what is real; he will strive to get at facts;
he will search for Truth with a humble and unbiased mind,
and cherish whatever he finds at any sacrifice.   But the more
literal translation of the Revised Version calls for just such
a sacrifice for truth's sake here.

For what Paul really meant is, as we there read, " Rejoiceth not in unrighteousness, but rejoiceth with the truth,"
a quality which probably no one English word—and certainly
not Sincerity—adequately defines.   It includes, perhaps
more strictly, the self-restraint which refuses to make capital

out of others' faults; the charity which delights not in expos-
ing the weakness of others, but " covereth all things;" the
sincerity of purpose which endeavors to see things as they
are, and rejoices to find them better than suspicion feared or
calumny denounced.

So much for the analysis of Love. Now the business of
our lives is to have these things fitted into our characters.
That is the supreme work to which we need not address ourselves in this world, to learn Love. Is life not full of opportunities for learning Love? Every man and woman every
day has a thousand of them. The world is not a playground;
it is a schoolroom. Life is not a holiday, but an education.
And the one eternal lesson for us all is how better we can
love.

What makes a man a good cricketer? Practice. What
makes a man a good artist, a good sculptor, a good musician?
Practice. What makes a man a good linguist, a good stenog-
rapher? Practice. What makes a man a good man?
Practice. Nothing else.

There is nothing capricious about religion. We do not
get the soul in different ways, under different laws, from
those in which we get the body and the mind. If a man
does not exercise his arm he develops no biceps muscle; and
if a man does not exercise his soul, he acquires no muscle
in his soul, no strength of character, no vigor of moral fibre,
nor beauty of spiritual growth. Love is not a thing of enthusiastic emotion. It is a rich, strong, manly, vigorous
expression of the whole round Christian character—the
Christlike nature in its fullest development. And the con-
stituents of this great character are only to be built up by
ceaseless practice.

What was Christ doing in the carpenter's shop? Practising. Though perfect, we read that he learned obedience, and grew in wisdom and in favor with God. Do not quarrel, therefore, with your lot in life. Do not complain of its never-ceasing cares, its petty environment, the vexations you have to stand, the small and sordid souls you have to live and work with. Above all, do not resent temptation; do not be perplexed because it seems to thicken round you more and more, and ceases neither for effort nor for agony nor prayer. That is your practice. That is the practice which God appoints you; and it is having its work in making you patient, and humble, and generous, and unselfish, and kind, and courteous. Do not grudge the hand that is molding the still too shapeless image within you. It is growing more beautiful, though you see it not, and every touch of temptation may add to its perfection. Therefore keep in the midst of life. Do not isolate yourself. Be among men, and among things, and among troubles, and difficulties, and obstacles. You remember Goethe's words: *Es bildet ein Talent sich in der Stille, Doch ein Character in dem Strom der Welt:* "Talent develops itself in solitude; character in the stream of life." Talent develops itself in solitude—the talent of prayer, of faith, of meditation, of seeing the unseen; Character grows in the stream of the world's life. That chiefly is where men are to learn love.

How? Now, how? To make it easier, I have named a few of the elements of love. But these are only elements. Love itself can never be defined. Light is a something more than the sum of its ingredients—a glowing, dazzling, tremulous ether. And love is something more than all its elements—a palpitating, quivering, sensitive, living thing. By snythesis of all the colors, men can make whiteness, they cannot make light. By synthesis of all the virtues, men can make virtue, they cannot make love. How then are we to have this transcendent living whole conveyed into our souls? We brace our wills to secure it. We try to copy those who have it. We lay down rules about it. We watch. We pray. But these things alone will not bring Love into our nature. Love is an effect. And only as we fulfil the right conditions can we have the effect produced. Shall I tell you what the cause is?

If you turn to the Revised Version of the First Epistle of John you will find these words: "We love because he first loved us." "We love," not "We love him." That is the way the old version has it, and it is quite wrong. "We love—because he first loved us." Look at that word "because." It is the cause of which I have spoken. "Because he first loved us," the effect follows that we love, we love him, we love all men.

We cannot help it. Because he loved us, we love, we love everybody. Our heart is slowly changed. Contemplate the love of Christ, and you will love. Stand before that mirror, reflect Christ's character, and you will be changed into the same image from tenderness to tenderness. There is no other way. You cannot love to order. You can only look at the lovely object, and fall in love with it, and grow into likeness to it. And so look at this Perfect Character, this Perfect Life. Look at the great Sacrifice as he laid down himself, all through life, and upon the Cross of Calvary; and you must love him. And loving him, you must become like him.

Love begets love. It is a process of induction. Put a piece of iron in the presence of an electrified body, and that piece of iron for a time becomes electrified. It is changed into a temporary magnet in the mere presence of a permanent magnet, and as long as you leave the two side by side they are both magnets alike.

Remain side by side with him who loved us, and gave himself for us, and you too will become a permanent magnet, a permanently attractive force; and like him you will draw all men unto you, like him you will be drawn unto all men. That is the inevitable effect of Love. Any man who fulfils that cause must have that effect produced in him.

Try to give up the idea that religion comes to us by chance, or by mystery, or by caprice. It comes to us by natural law, or by supernatural law, for all law is Divine. Edward Irving went to see a dying boy once, and when he entered the room he just put his hand on the sufferer's head, and said, " My boy, God loves you," and went away. And the boy started from his bed, and called out to the people in the house, " God loves me! God loves me! "

It changed that boy. The sense that God loved him overpowered him, melted him down, and began the creating of a new heart in him. And that is how the love of God melts down the unlovely heart in man, and begets in him the new creature, who is patient and humble and gentle and unselfish. And there is no other way to get it. There is no mystery about it. We love others, we love everybody, we love our enemies, because he first loved us. Now I have a closing sentence or two to add about Paul's reason for singling out love as the supreme possession. It is a very remarkable reason. In a single word it is this: it lasts.

" Love," urges Paul, " never faileth." Then he begins again one of his marvellous lists of the great things of the day, and exposes them one by one. He runs over the things that men thought were going to last, and shows that they are all fleeting, temporary, passing away.

" Whether there be prophecies, they shall fail." It was
the mother's ambition for her boy in those days that he should
become a prophet. For hundreds of years God had never
spoken by means of any prophet, and at that time the prophet
was greater than the King. Men waited wistfully for another
messenger to come, and hung upon his lips when he appeared
as upon the very voice of God. Paul says, " Whether there
be prophecies, they shall fail." This Book is full of prophecies. One by one they have " failed "; that is, having been
fulfilled their work is finished; they have nothing more to do
now in the world except to feed a devout man's faith.

Then Paul talks about tongues. That was another thing
that was greatly coveted. " Whether there be tongues, they
shall cease." As we all know, many, many centuries have
passed since tongues have been known in this world. They
have ceased. Take it in any sense you like. Take it, for
illustration merely, as languages in general—a sense which
was not in Paul's mind at all, and which though it cannot
give us the specific lesson will point the general truth.

Consider the words in which these chapters were written—
Greek. It has gone. Take the Latin—the other great
tongue of those days. It ceased long ago. Look at the
Indian language. It is ceasing. The language of Wales,
of Ireland, of the Scottish Highlands is dying before our
eyes The most popular book in the English tongue at the
present time, except the Bible, is one of Dickens's works, his
" Pickwick Papers." It is largely written in the language of London street-life; and experts assure us that in
fifty years it will be unintelligible to the average English
reader.

Then Paul goes farther, and with even greater boldness
adds, " Whether there be knowledge, it shall vanish away."

The wisdom of the ancients, where is it? It is wholly gone. A schoolboy to-day knows more than Sir Isaac Newton knew. His knowledge has vanished away. You put yesterday's newspaper in the fire. Its knowledge has vanished away. You buy the old editions of the great encyclopædias for a few pence. Their knowledge has vanished away.

Look how the coach has been superseded by the use of steam. Look how electricity has superseded that, and swept a hundred almost new inventions into oblivion. One of the greatest living authorities, Sir William Thompson, said the other day, "The steam-engine is passing away."

"Whether there be knowledge, it shall vanish away." At every workshop you will see, in the back yard, a heap of old iron, a few wheels, a few levers, a few cranks, broken and eaten with rust. Twenty years ago that was the pride of the city. Men flocked in from the country to see the great invention; now it is superseded, its day is done.

And all the boasted science and philosophy of this day will soon be old. But yesterday, in the University of Edinburgh, the greatest figure in the faculty was Sir James Simpson, the discoverer of chloroform. The other day his successor and nephew, Professor Simpson, was asked by the librarian of the University to go to the library and pick out the books on his subject that were no longer needed. And his reply to the librarian was this: "Take every text-book that is more than ten years old, and put it down in the cellar." Sir James Simpson was a great authority only a few years ago: men came from all parts of the earth to consult him; and almost the whole teaching of that time is consigned by the science of to-day to oblivion. And in every branch of science it is the same. "Now we know in part. We see through a glass darkly."

Can you tell me anything that is going to last? Many things Paul did not condescend to name. He did not mention money, fortune, fame; but he picked out the great things of his time, the things the best men thought had something in them, and brushed them peremptorily aside. Paul had no charge against these things in themselves. All he said about them was that they would not last.

They were great things, but not supreme things. There were things beyond them. What we are stretches past what we do, beyond what we possess. Many things that men denounce as sins are not sins; but they are temporary. And that is a favorite argument of the New Testament. John says of the world, not that it is wrong, but simply that it "passeth away." There is a great deal in the world that is delightful and beautiful; there is a great deal in it that is great and engrossing; but it will not last. All that is in the world, the lust of the eye, the lust of the flesh, and the pride of life, are but for a little while. Love not the world therefore. Nothing that it contains is worth the life and consecration of an immortal soul. The immortal soul must give itself to something that is immortal. And the only immortal things are these: "Now abideth faith, hope, love, but the greatest of these is love."

Some think the time may come when two of these three things will also pass away—faith into sight, hope into fruition. Paul does not say so. We know but little now about the conditions of the life that is to come.

But what is certain is that Love must last. God, the Eternal God, is Love. Covet therefore that everlasting gift, that one thing which it is certain is going to stand, that one coinage which will be current in the Universe when all the other coinages of all the nations of the world shall be useless and unhonored. You will give yourselves to many things, give yourselves first to Love. Hold things in their proportion. Hold things in their proportion. Let at least the first great object of our lives be to achieve the character defended in these words, the character—and it is the character of Christ—which is built round Love.

I have said this thing is eternal. Did you ever notice how continually John associates love and faith with eternal life? I was not told when I was a boy that "God so loved the world that he gave his only begotten Son, that whosoever believeth in him should have everlasting life." What I was told, I remember, was, that God so loved the world that, if I trusted in him, I was to have a thing called peace, or I was to have rest, or I was to have joy, or I was to have safety. But I had to find out for myself that whosoever trusteth in him—that is, whosoever loveth him, for trust is only the avenue to Love—hath everlasting life. The gospel offers a man life.

Never offer men a thimbleful of Gospel. Do not offer them merely joy, or merely peace, or merely rest, or merely safety; tell them how Christ came to give men a more abundant life than they have, a life abundant in love, and therefore abundant in salvation for themselves, and large in enterprise for the alleviation and redemption of the world. Then only can the Gospel take hold of the whole of a man, body, soul, and spirit, and give to each part of his nature its exercise and reward. Many of the current Gospels are addressed only to a part of man's nature. They offer peace, not life; faith, not Love; justification, not regeneration. And men slip back again from such religion because it has never really held them. Their nature was not all in it. It offered no deeper and gladder life-current than the life that was lived before. Surely it stands to reason that only a fuller love can compete with the love of the world.

To love abundantly is to live abundantly, and to love forever is to live forever. Hence, eternal life is inextricably bound up with love. We want to live forever for the same reason that we want to live to-morrow. Why do you want to live to-morrow? It is because there is some one who loves you, and whom you want to see to-morrow, and be with, and love back. There is no other reason why we should live on than that we love and are beloved. It is when a man has no one to love him that he commits suicide. So long as he has friends, those who love him and whom he loves, he will live; because to live is to love. Be it but the love of a dog, it will keep him in life; but let that go and he has no contact with life, no reason to live. He dies by his own hand.

Eternal life also is to know God, and God is love. This is Christ's own definition. Ponder it. " This is life eternal, that they might know thee the only true God, and Jesus Christ whom thou has sent."

Love must be eternal. It is what God is. On the last analysis, then, love is life. Love never faileth, and life never faileth, so long as there is love. That is the philosophy of what Paul is showing us; the reason why in the nature of things Love should be the supreme thing—because it is going to last; because in the nature of things it is an Eternal Life. It is a thing that we are living now, not that we get when we die; that we shall have a poor chance of getting when we die unless we are living now. No worse fate can befall a man in this world than to live and grow old alone, unloving, and unloved. To be lost is to live in an unregenerate condition, loveless and unloved; and to be saved is to love; and he that dwelleth in love dwelleth already in God.   For God is love.

Now I have all but finished.   How many of you will join me in reading this chapter once a week for the next three months?   A man did that once and it changed his whole life. Will you do it?   It is for the greatest thing in the world. You might begin by reading it every day, especially the verses which describe the perfect character.   " Love suffer- eth long, and is kind; love envieth not; love vaunteth not itself."

Get these ingredients into your life.   Then everything that you do is eternal.   It is worth doing.   It is worth giving time to.   No man can become a saint in his sleep; and to fulfil the condition required demands a certain amount of prayer and meditation and time, just as improvement in any direction, bodily or mental, requires preparation and care.

Address yourselves to that one thing; at any cost have this transcendent character exchanged for yours.   You will find as you look back upon your life that the moments that stand out, the moments when you have really lived, are the moments when you have done things in a spirit of love.   As memory scans the past, above and beyond all the transitory pleasures of life, there leap forward those supreme hours when you have been enabled to do unnoticed kindnesses to those round about you, things too trifling to speak about, but which you feel have entered into your eternal life.

I have seen almost all the beautiful things God has made; I have enjoyed almost every pleasure that he has planned for man; and yet as I look back I see standing out above all the life that has gone four or five short experiences when the love of God reflected itself in some poor imitation, some small act of love of mine, and these seem to be the things which alone of all one's life abide. Everything else in all our lives is transitory. Every other good is visionary. But the acts of love which no man knows about, or can ever know about—they never fail.

In the Book of Matthew, where the Judgment Day is depicted for us in the imagery of One seated upon a throne and dividing the sheep from the goats, the test of a man then is not, "How have I believed?" but "How have I loved?"

The test of religion, the final test of religion, is not religiousness, but Love. I say the final test of religion at that great Day is not religiousness, but Love; not what I have done, not what I have believed, not what I have achieved, but how I have discharged the common charities of life. Sins of commission in that awful indictment are not even referred to. By what we have not done, by sins of omission, we are judged.

It could not be otherwise. For the withholding of love is the negation of the spirit of Christ, the proof that we never knew him, that for us he lived in vain. It means that he suggested nothing in all our thoughts, that he inspired nothing in all our lives, that we were not once near enough to him to be seized with the spell of his compassion for the world. It means that—

> " I lived for myself, I thought for myself,
> For myself, and none beside—
> Just as if Jesus had never lived,
> As if he had never died."

It is the Son of Man before whom the nations of the world shall be gathered. It is in the presence of *Humanity* that we shall be charged. And the spectacle itself, the mere sight of it, will silently judge each one. Those will be there whom we have met and helped; or there, the unpitied multitude whom we neglected or despised.

No other Witness need be summoned. No other charge than lovelessness shall be preferred. Be not deceived. The words which all of us shall one Day hear sound not of theology but of life, not of churches and saints but of the hungry and the poor, not of creeds and doctrines but of shelter and clothing, not of Bibles and prayer-books but of cups of cold water in the name of Christ.

Thank God the Christianity of to-day is coming nearer the world's need. Live to help that on. Thank God men know better, by a hairsbreadth, what religion is, what God is, who Christ is, where Christ is. Who is Christ? He who fed the hungry, clothed the naked, visited the sick. And where is Christ? Where?—whoso shall receive a little child in My name receiveth Me. And who are Christ's? Every one that loveth is born of God.

HERBERT H. ASQUITH

IGHT HON. HERBERT HENRY ASQUITH, P.C., M.P., K.C., English Liberal statesman and lawyer, was born at Morley, Yorkshire, Sept. 12, 1852. He was educated at the city of London School and Balliol College, Oxford. He was called to the Bar at Lincoln's Inn, London, in 1876, appointed Queen's Counsel in 1890, and elected member of Parliament for East Fife in 1886, and again in 1892. Together with the Lord Chief-justice (then Sir Charles Russell) he was engaged on behalf of the late Irish leader, Charles Parnell, during the Parnell Commission. In August, 1892, he was mover of the amendment to the Queen's Speech, which led to the division fatal to Lord Salisbury's government. When Mr. Gladstone formed his ministry, he was appointed Home Secretary, was sworn of the Privy Council, and placed on the Ecclesiastical Commission. During the labor disputes of 1893, Mr. Asquith took a consistent attitude which commanded the approval of Parliament, and in 1894 he acted as arbitrator in the London cab strike. In February, 1893, he was nominated for the lord rectorship of Glasgow. As a speaker, he has shown high gifts of oratory, somewhat qualified by an academic manner. He belongs to the Imperial wing of the Liberal party.

ISSUES—TRUE AND FALSE

SPEECH DELIVERED AT LADYBANK, ENGLAND, SEPTEMBER 15, 1900

I COME before you this afternoon in the novel and somewhat embarassing position of a man who is under sentence of death, but who has not yet been acquainted with the date of the execution; but if all we hear, or half of what we hear, is true, desperate efforts are at this moment being made by a large number of those who were responsible for bringing the present Parliament into life to hurry it prematurely out of existence. I cannot tell you, for I have no information, whether these endeavours are likely to be successful, but I am happy to think, whether they succeed or fail, that we can view the result in East Fife with considerable equanimity.

Fife, I have more than once in days gone by had occasion to remind you, has an unbroken Liberal tradition, and whether the election comes next week or next spring, or this time next year, I believe we are still as prepared as ever to speak with our enemy within the gate. If I may adopt for a moment the military dialect, which comes so natural to one's lips in these days, I should say that there is not a town or a village in this county in which the Liberal party has not its pom-poms in readiness, and unless I am mistaken there are not a few places at this moment apparently slumbering in quietness—in apathy—in which the moment when hostilities are declared Long Toms of the latest pattern will be unmasked. We have in days gone by, you and I, encountered and defeated opposition more formidable, as far as I can judge, than any which menaces us at the present moment. In the great general stampede of 1895 you stood firm, and inflicted upon a confident enemy a blow from which he seems only now to have partially recovered, and while I am certain that you will omit, when the hour strikes, no precaution, and will strain every nerve, I cannot bring myself for a moment to doubt that East Fife will maintain its historical record as an impregnable fortress of Liberalism.

That the Tory party throughout the country are eager, are anxious, for an immediate dissolution is beyond dispute. It is true that the register is exhausted; it includes numbers who have no title, and excludes numbers who have the best title, to record a vote. But the majority of the Government in both Houses of Parliament is still unimpaired, and to hold a general election under such conditions is without any precedent in our history, and it has been prophetically denounced by the oracle of latter-day Toryism, the late Lord Beaconsfield himself. But all these considerations count for nothing, and are swallowed up in absorbing apprehension of what may happen if an appeal to the country is delayed for twelve months, or even six months. The election is to be hustled on. Why? In order that the issue may be artificially narrowed. The patriotic fervour which has animated the whole nation is to be exploited, if possible, in the interests of a particular party. Finance, domestic legislation, social reform, the unfulfilled pledges of 1895, the subventions by which during these five years the prosperity of our national resources has been frittered away to particular interests and classes, even the conduct and management of the war itself, all these gloomy and inconvenient topics are to be huddled out of sight.

The fear of the future is clothing from top to bottom the Tory party. From the Under-Secretary of State for Foreign Affairs down to the humblest member of the rank and file of the supporters of the strongest Government of modern times there has gone up during the past few weeks a pleasing chorus of appeal to the silent figure at the polls. "In Heaven's name let us get it over before all the gas is out of the balloon." Is there any other hypothesis which explains the fact? It is certainly not the case that our opponents have become converted to the doctrine of shorter Parliaments. We are still under a seven years' law, reduced by constitutional practice to six years. There are many of us —I, myself, am one of them—who are strongly of opinion that there ought to be a further curtailment of the normal duration of the life of the House of Commons. But what is the argument which weighs with us in support of that view? It is that you may assure that the representative body at any time should be an accurate reflection, and therefore a more faithful organ of the opinions and sentiments of those which it professes to represent. We can hardly imagine a method better calculated to defeat the object than to hold an election upon a reduced register, from which is shut out practically every man in the country whose qualifition is not at least two years old.

Before I proceed to examine in a little more detail the pretences which are put forth in support of this appeal let me ask you this question—What is the purpose or function of a general election? This—is it not?—that the people may determine upon what lines, in what spirit, and by what men their affairs shall be conducted, it may be, for the next six years. Never in the history of mankind have responsibilities so heavy and interests so complex been entrusted to the stewardship and to the judgment of the democracy. Our empire, if you include in it the territories for which we are indirectly responsible, covers some thirteen millions of square miles, and contains a population largely exceeding four hundred millions of human beings. We have at home some forty millions of people, vast numbers of whom are living and working under conditions which are a disgrace to humanity—slaves of intemperance, victims of overcrowding, enjoying in many cases of freedom in the real sense nothing but the empty name. Our industrial supremacy was never more seriously menaced; there is not a market in the world in which we are not finding every day we have to face the increasing severity of competition. Our administrative system, in some departments at any rate, under the strain of recent events has exhibited rents and creakings and leakages which are seen of all thinking men. It is time it should be properly and effectively overhauled. We have added steadily year by year to our territorial burdens, and we are adding this year to our National Debt. We have to face this growing array of problems, the difficulties at home and abroad, and the constantly diminishing share of the goodwill of the rest of the human race. I ask you—I ask my fellow-countrymen—are we to be told that the nation, solemnly invoked to pronounce its judgment upon this world-wide theme of interests and duties, is practically to confine its function to the small corner which we call South Africa, and to think of nothing, to listen to nothing, to vote about nothing but the war? That is not the way in which I read the Constitution, and whenever the dissolution takes place, be it soon or late, there are those of us, at any rate, who will do our best to bring home to the electorate the length and breadth of the issues upon which they will be called upon to make up their minds.

You will not suppose from what I have said that I am going now or hereafter to shirk the question of the war. Indeed, one of my chief purposes in addressing you this evening is to deal with that topic, and to endeavour to discuss, as temperately and candidly as I can, what, if any, are the issues which at the stage we have now reached the war presents. I don't think I can do better than take as my text the electioneering letter that has been published this week from the pen of Mr. Chamberlain. The genesis of that curious document is not obscure; it is written to support the candidature of Mr. Frederick Lambton, who is standing as the Unionist candidate for one of the divisions of Durham. Now, it so happens that up to now no incident in connection with the coming election has done more to disconcert those whom I may call the khaki wirepullers than the appearance as a Liberal candidate of Captain Hedworth Lambton, the gallant defender of Ladysmith, and one of the notable figures of the war. Captain Lambton is not only a Liberal, but

a fighting Liberal, and as at Ladysmith, so now, he keeps
his batteries in good working order. It was only a week
or two ago that a well-directed shell from one of them severely wounded the Under Secretary for Foreign Affairs,
who has since judiciously retired out of range. Well, this
kind of thing is peculiarly annoying to Mr. Chamberlain,
who cannot understand how anyone can presume to call himself a friend of the Empire, to be proud of its great traditions and alive to its still greater responsibilities, and yet
decline to prostrate himself before this strident and vul-
garized Imperialism which of late has been the fashion of
the hour. Hence it is, at least we may so conjecture, that
Mr. Frederick Lambton is the recipient of this letter, which
for boldness of statement and innuendo I think deserves
a high place among compositions of its class. What does
Mr. Chamberlain tell his correspondent? He says that the
majority of the Liberal party are opposed to the war and to
a satisfactory settlement, that it was his predecessors in office
that allowed the question to drift, and that there is every
reason to fear that if they were now to be returned to power
they would be ready to throw away, in regard to that settlement the position so hardly gained by the sacrifices of
the war.

Let me for a few moments examine those statements in
detail. And, first of all, what is the meaning of the first
of them—that the majority of the Liberal party are opposed
to war? As regards the causes of the war there have, of
course, been wide differences of opinion. I am one of those
who think, and I have never disguised my views, as you
know, that the ultimate responsibility for the war does not
rest upon the shoulders of the Government or the people
in this country. The holding of the opinion, may I add,

does not imply any approval of or sympathy with the manner and methods of what is called the new diplomacy. The real fault of our diplomacy in this particular matter, as it has always seemed to me, is not so much that it was unsuccessful in averting the war as that, we having, as I believe we had, a good case, it was so handled and so presented to the world that a very large proportion of the civilized opinion of mankind believed, and still believes, we had a very bad case indeed.

But that does not affect, nor, I think, ought to affect my judgment. The war was not of our seeking, but was forced upon us against our will. There are distinguished men, some of them of our own party, who have always taken a different view, and who have held that the war was provoked, or at any rate could have been prevented, by this country. But those who hold that view, and hold it conscientiously, should have held it throughout. There is not, I undertake to say, one in a thousand who, after the war was declared, and British territory invaded did not approve of the prosecution of the war and the voting of all the supplies necessary for the purpose. All classes in this country, whatever may have been their views—all classes in this country, without distinction of party, have shared with one heart in the anxieties and in the trials of the struggle. All have contributed freely both from public and private sources, all have shown themselves ready to offer the greatest of all sacrifices—the lives of those whom they love best. I say, then, the question whether the war could or could not have been obviated is one upon which historians and moralists will probably differ to the end of time, but there is no body of responsible politicians in this country but will hold it is the first duty of the country to bring the war to a successful and satisfactory issue.

Mr. Chamberlain's next suggestion or insinuation, which-
ever it is to be called, that his predecessor allowed affairs in
South Africa to drift deserves, I think, only two or three
sentences of passing comment.   Mr. Chamberlain knows, or
ought to know, that for a long time the Outlanders in the
Transvaal deprecated any intervention on the part of the
home Government, and it was only when their term of office
was drawing to a close that Lord Loch was instructed to
make representations on their behalf.   The arming of the
South African Republic began to a serious extent in 1895,
when the present Government came into power, and continued with a great and increasing activity for four years,
until the Transvaal had become, as we know to our own
cost, an armed camp of the most formidable kind.   Now,
it does not lie in the mouth of the statesman who allowed
all this to go on without remonstrance or check and made
no endeavour whatsoever to provide for the protection of
two British colonies against the risk of invasion—I say it
does not lie in the mouth of a statesman with that record
to reproach his predecessors or any one else with having
pursued a policy of drift.   Mr. Chamberlain, I think, was
singularly inspired when out of the whole dictionary he selected that word as a missile to throw at us, for it is that
word "drift" that is written in the largest possible capitals
at the top of every page of our dealings with South Africa
from 1895 to 1899.

Mr. Chamberlain, in his anxiety to discredit the Opposition and to make party capital if he can out of the national
emergency, goes on to declare that a majority of the Liberal
Party are opposed to a satisfactory settlement; that the Liberal Party, if it were returned to power, would throw away
the results of the war.   What and where is the evidence of

that allegation? Everyone who looks at the matter dispassionately must agree that the state of things at present is too fluid and chaotic, and any information too imperfect and fragmentary, to make the presentation of a cut and dried scheme for the future of South Africa within the range of statesmanship. I speak not my own mind only, but the opinion of the majority of those with whom I am politically associated, when I say that it is clear that the two communities or territories recently annexed must be, and will be, permanently incorporated with the British Empire.

It is quite true, as I believe, that when last year we were seeking to obtain from President Kruger adequate guarantees for the civil and political freedom of our countrymen in the Transvaal, it formed no part of the policy of any responsible statesman to put an end to the existing status of the two Republics. That was not our object at all. We were prepared to guarantee the independence of both if President Kruger on his side would concede reforms which public opinion in this country declared to be both expedient and necessary. I have seen quoted a phrase of my own, used, I think, at Dundee nearly a year ago, as though I had declared that under no conditions or circumstances could annexation be defensible. Anyone who reads the context of what I said will see that I was protesting, as I should protest with equal emphasis now, against annexation in any such sense or shape as to involve the subordination of Boer to Briton, that negation of the doctrine of equality, the substitution of the artificial ascendancy of one race for the artificial ascendancy of another. I repeatedly in speech declared that we ought not to prejudge the form as distinct from the principle of the settlement.

At the same time, I do not hesitate to say that it has not

been without reluctance that I arrived at the conclusion that only by annexation can what are the central, the capital objects of a wise South African policy be attained. Like most liberals, and I suppose a considerable number even of our opponents, I regret, except in a case of clear proof, the necessity of the extinction of small States with a history and a patriotism of their own, and the enlargements of the areas and the burdens of British responsibilities. But no lover of freedom need shed any tears for the disappearance of the South African Republic—an unhappy specimen of one of the worst kinds of political imposture, a caricature or mockery of liberty under a democratic form. The case of the Orange Free State stands on a different footing. It was, on the whole, a well-governed community, with whom we had no cause of quarrel whatever, and whose integrity and independence we were prepared scrupulously to respect, provided only it would maintain neutrality in the war. Whether under the pressure of supposed treaty obligations or under the impulse of a chivalrous sympathy with their kinsmen, or from other and more mixed motives, the Free State, unhappily, became joint aggressors with the South African Republic. They invaded our colonies, they contemplated annexing our territories, and they showed themselves as great enemies as the Boers themselves. We, therefore, are as free in their case as in the case of the Transvaal to take such steps as seems best in the general interests of South Africa. The war has taught us many things which we did not know before. It has revealed to us the existence of dangers which under less favourable conditions—for instance had our hands been entangled in some complication elsewhere— might have cost us South Africa. The possible recurrence of these dangers it is our duty to prevent. A little reflection, I think will show that any measures actually effected for this purpose would require as much interference with the sovereignty or independence in any real sense of these two Republics as their incorporation in the British Empire.

I will go further and I will say this: A little group of protected or vassal States, with their privileges and obligations defined, or sought to be defined, by written conventions, possessing neither the reality of independence nor the full status of partners in the Empire, is, in my judgment, of all possible attempts to solve the South African problem, the one which would be attended with a maximum of friction and a minimum of possible permanence. For these and many other reasons, with which time will not permit me to deal fully to-night, I have come to the conclusion that the annexations recently made are irrevocable, and that no Government, to whatever party in the State it might belong, could or would undo what has been done, and, so far as I know, that is the opinion of the vast majority of the Liberal party. Mr. Chamberlain mentions in his letter Sir Henry Campbell-Bannerman, our leader in the House of Commons. As far back as last Whitsuntide, Sir Henry Campbell-Bannerman, I think at Glasgow, expressed substantially the same conviction which I have just laid before you. So far, then, as the settlement has yet proceeded—the incorporation of the two Republics in the Empire—there is no shadow of foundation for Mr. Chamberlain's statement that the majority of the Liberal party is opposed to a satisfactory settlement.

The annexation of the conquered territory is of course the first step. It is far easier to tear down a bad state of matters than to build up a good state of matters to take its place; but as to the difficult future which lies before us, two main aims of our policy have been clearly proclaimed by statements from both sides of politics, and do not, as far as I know, form the subject matter of controversy. Let me recapitulate them in a few sentences. In the first place, as I have said, we must guard against the renewal of the dangers and struggles which we hope are now coming to an end. In the next place, as soon as the exigencies of order will allow, we must set to work to lay the foundations of that system of equal civil and political rights which has been the avowed purpose of our action. Lastly, in the years that are to come it will be our imperative duty to promote by every means in our power the mitigation and gradual extinction of racial animosities, so that in South Africa, as in Canada and elsewhere, the British flag may be alike when it waves over the conquered territories and over our old colonies, the symbol of that which is the life-giving and life-preserving principle of our empire—the union and blending of local patriotism with Imperial loyalty. In working out that task, if we are to succeed, it can only be by removing South Africa from the contentious field of politics here at home, and for my part I deprecate as the worst disservice that could at this moment be done to the Empire, from whatever quarter it may proceed, the creating of fictitious differences for party benefit.

But while neither the origin of the conflict nor the character of the statesmen are matters for the present moment, there are a number of questions arising out of the conduct of the war the answer to which must to a large extent govern our decision on the policy and foresight of the Government, and which also are of vital importance to the efficiency of our army as a fighting and administrative machine and to the maintenance of our Empire in the future. To take two or three illustrations, I may mention the character and quality of our guns, the constitution and management of the transport and the medical services, the training both of our officers and men, and, above all, the adequacy of our home defences when we are engaged in a distant war. As regards all these matters there is grave, widespread, and well-justified disquietude. I observe that Mr. Brodrick the other day selected—I observed it with a good deal of amusement—as one of the main reasons of what is called the khaki resolution that the Government wanted a mandate from the country to reform the War Office. It was Mr. Brodrick who succeeded in turning out the late Government on a question of army administration. During the first three years of the present Government he himself occupied a distinguished and responsible post at the War Office. They had their mandate, but apparently they were so dissatisfied with the use they had made of it that they are now calling to the country to give them another. Why, some of the most serious problems connected with the condition of the army and the conduct of the war are at this moment a subject of actual or promised inquiry—an additional illustration, if it is neded, of the absurdity and insincerity of this clamour for immediate dissolution. Two things, I submit, are abundantly clear—the first, that the time has come for an overhauling of our army system, both on its civil and military side, in the same large spirit in which a similar task was taken up by Lord Cardwell thirty years ago; and the second is that the task will not be accomplished unless you put at the head of the War Office a man who knows his own mind and can get his own way. Whether the best means of accomplishing these desirable results is to give a fresh mandate to the gentlemen who ask for it on the strength of five years of failure—that is a matter for the electors to determine.

I have devoted the main part of my observations to questions connected with the war, because it is necessary, first, to clear the ground of false issues in order that the real issues which the country will have to decide may be seen in their true proportion and perspective. The real question, as I said at the outset, is this: In what spirit and by what methods do you desire your Government to be conducted? Are you satisfied with the record of the last five years? Does it inspire you with pride in the past or with confidence for the future? What of the national finances? Six years ago Sir William Harcourt remodelled the death duties. He was denounced by the whole Tory party for striking a death blow at the accumulation of capital and the prosperity of the country. His censors have been living on those death duties ever since, and they have provided out of them a magnificent annual endowment for some of those friendly interests which are their most useful allies. They raided the sinking fund in a time of unexampled prosperity in order to avoid the unpopularity of imposing fresh taxation. It is in the same spirit that they are now dealing with the expenses of the war. Is the country, I ask you, so dead to the great traditions of Peel and of Gladstone that it is going to condone this pusillanimous finance?

Look at the field of social reform. Has there ever been a Government which, with an irresistible majority for five years in both Houses of Parliament, promised so much and accomplished so little? Think of the promises which were placarded over every wall in 1895. Old-age pensions. Well, that was not a promise, by the way; it was only a proposal. Nevertheless it was good enough to catch votes. What has become of it? Relegated first to one Committee and then to another to try to devise a scheme, until years had elapsed, and there was no money left in the Exchequer. Compensation for accidents—promised to all, and given, even if you take the latest supplement into account, to perhaps little more than half of the working population of the country. The problem of overcrowding, one of the greatest and most urgent which could confront them, met by two tinkering measures which are a mockery to statesmanship. Temperance, declared six years ago by a leading member of the present Government to be the most urgent of all social questions, and not advanced by one single proposal. I might add indefinitely to the list. What has been done for secondary and technical education, our deficiencies in which are threatening our industrial supremacy? What has been done for a fairer and better adjustment of local taxation? What attempt has been made to grasp and grapple with the problems that are connected with ownership and occupation of land? Can we wonder that this catalogue of pledges shirked and reforms attempted—can we wonder at the feverish anxiety to hold an election while the Union Jack is still waving, and criticism, as it is fondly hoped, can be met and drowned in the strains of "Rule Britannia" and "Soldiers of the Queen?"

The last word of counsel I will venture to offer to my fellow-Liberals here and elsewhere is this; it is contained in one single word, "Concentration." Eschew side issues, self interests, personal rivalries. If we fight and work in that spirit, whether the election comes soon or late, and whether fortune smiles or frowns, we shall have done what in us lies to maintain the traditions of a great party, and to open for our country in the dawning century a nobler and more fruitful chapter of its history.

CECIL RHODES

IGHT HON. CECIL RHODES, P. C., an eminent English statesman and financier, and South African railway and mining magnate, was born at Bishop Stortford, England, July 7, 1853, where his father was vicar of the parish. He was educated at Bishop Stortford grammar school, where he manifested a love for athletics and was a successful scholar, winning several prizes and a senior classical scholarship. Instead of going up to Cambridge, as he had intended, he went, in 1870, to Natal, where his brother Herbert was a cotton planter. In 1871, he set out to the diamond fields and settled at Colesberg, Kopje, now known as Kimberley. In 1873, he returned to England and matriculated at Oriel College, Oxford, but, being threatened with lung disease, he returned to South Africa. Here, the dry, rainless air of the veldt gradually reëstablished his health, and he entered with characteristic energy into the labors of diamond-digging, and later on in railway projects. Thus beginning with a share in a single small mine, he succeeded, by the application of remarkable sagacity, concentration, and perseverance, in building up a large fortune. At first he planned only the amalgamation of the diamond mines into one vast monopoly. Afterward he lent all the force of his capital and energies to building up an extension of the British Empire in South Africa.

In 1884, he became treasurer-general of the Cape Colony, deputy commissioner of Bechuana Land (now Rhodesia), and director of the British South Africa Company, which he has done much since to develop. In 1890, he was Premier of Cape Colony and Commissioner of Crown Lands; and in 1894, Minister of Native Affairs. He has also been member for Barkly West in the legislative assembly, Cape Colony, but resigned in consequence of the Jameson raid. In alliance with the Dutch Afrikander party at the Cape, he took part in the Metabele War. When the present Boer War broke out, in 1899, Mr. Rhodes shut himself up in the great diamond-mining town of Kimberley, having previously equipped, at his own expense, a town guard of 400 men. Mr. Rhodes was a man of vast energy and a capable and practical man of affairs. He died at Capetown, South Africa, March 26, 1902.

ON THE CRISIS IN SOUTH AFRICA

DELIVERED JULY 20, 1899

I THANK you for the address you have given me. I have also to thank Mr. Louw for greeting me here. I specially refer to Mr. Louw because our difficulties are very great in South Africa at the present time, and Mr. Louw

CECIL RHODES

belongs to that portion of his race who have not bowed down to the terrorism that exists with a large section of their party.

I am sorry to say that I have extreme opponents, while there are also moderate men who in their hearts support the true policy of Imperialism; but there are others, like Mr. Louw, who, in spite of coercion and everything that may be brought to bear upon them, have stood all obloquy from a section of their party in order to support what they thought the right thing in the interests of South Africa. We have not only all the inhabitants of the English race on our side, but almost the whole of the colored community as well, although it happens at present that a large section of another race in this country are strongly opposed to our thoughts and ideas. It is for us to thank those of that race who, after considering the question very carefully, have approved of everything which they think right for the good of South Africa.

With reference to the special work as to which you have greeted me, I would point out that there has been a great change in the opinions of our people at home.

When I first commenced the idea of expansion in Africa I found myself with few supporters out here. People at home also, whatever party they belonged to, if they did not show any opposition, were absolutely without enthusiasm. Now all that has changed. I need not go into details of the change, but I would remark that, whatever might have been the rights of the question of confining our great country to the British Isles, and perhaps a few dependencies that were then possessed, the policy of the world was to shut her out.

I can tell you a good story on this point. Mr. Gladstone once talked to me upon this very question of expansion, and said to me:

"Mr. Rhodes, we have enough; our obligations are too great; but, apart from the question of increasing our obligations in every part of the world, what advantage do you see to the English race in the acquisition of territory was it that every Power in the world, including our kinsmen the Americans, as soon as they took new territory, placed hostile tariffs against British goods."

I said we must remember Great Britain is a very small island, not nearly the size of France, and she has not that wonderful wine industry, nor has she a continent like the Americans. Great Britain's position depends on her trade, and if we do not take and open up the dependencies of the world which are at present devoted to barbarism, we shall be shut out from the world's trade. For this reason.

The question of tariffs is not with our opponents a question of revenue; they simply wish to put on such tariffs as will absolutely exclude Great Britain from the trade of their dependencies.

I remember so well that Mr. Gladstone replied, with his bright intelligence, that he could not believe that; and said that other countries might go temporarily wrong, but surely in the end the principles of free trade would prevail.

I said in answer: "Mr. Gladstone, I should like to think so. In logic you are all right, but in practice you will be all wrong. You will find that as each new country is taken up, the possessing Power will put a prohibitive tariff against you. Now England depends upon her working up raw goods, turning them into the manufactured articles, and distributing them to the world, and if the markets of the world are shut against us, where shall we be?"

Mr. Gladstone said he would quite agree with me if he really believed that, for, if in every new country, taken by ancther Power, hostile tariffs were put against us, it was a poor lookout; but he [Mr. Gladstone] believed in the success of free-trade principles.

It is needless for me to tell you that free-trade principles have not prevailed; on the contrary it has been the policy of every Power that had acquired a new dependency to introduce these hostile tariffs.

Take, for example, the case of Madagascar. When France took that island there were certain treaties in connection with it which allowed equality of trade. That was allowed on the basis of the island being a protectorate; but as soon as France annexed it the French tariff was dead against us. Her Majesty's Prime Minster continuously remonstrated without avail, and rightly so from the French point of view.

The French said, " We have been at all the trouble and expense of taking this island, and we want the advantage of possessing it. It is all very well for you English people to talk about equality of trade, but that equality means that we shall not be in it at all. We find that you English are always admirably logical on any point that is in your favor. Practically we could not compete with you. We have spent millions in taking this island, and we mean to have its trade."

As I have said before, it is an admirable thing for one cricketing eleven to say to another eleven, " We will play with you on equal terms," when that one knows that it will be absolutely victorious.

The opponents, however, require eighteen, and even demand twenty-four, and sometimes will not play at all. And so with the French. They say, " It is an admirable case, but if we place you on an equality with us in Madagascar we shall have no trade at all. We did not take that island and spend those millions for amusement. We took that island to expand our trade, and the only way we can do that is by putting hostile tariffs against you."

You may ask what I mean by that argument—what I am leading to. Well, I think that English public opinion has changed, owing to the thought of the workmen.

The workmen find that although the Americans are exceedingly fond of them, and are just now exchanging the most brotherly sentiments with them, yet they are shutting out their goods. The workmen also find that Russia, France, and even Germany locally are doing the same, and the workmen see that if they do not look out they will have no places in the world to trade with at all. And so the workmen have become Imperialist, and the Liberal party are following.

Now, when we commenced that policy of taking over the North—and you must not give me the sole credit of it—the thought that guided one in one's ideas was that the world was limited, and that the country to which we all belong should have as much of it as it could possibly get. This was a consideration which affected not only the people at home, but the people here, including not only English, but Dutch.

If we are a great people it is because we are an amalgamation of races. I have found that the strongest point urged by the opponents of territorial expansion is that they say:

" You are always talking about the annexation of territories, but what do you do? We helped Canada through all her wars, and gave her self-government, and the first thing they do is to place huge tariffs against us and shut out our goods. Australia has done the same, and every colony to which we give self-government does everything in its power to follow suit."

Now, practically, apart from the sentiment of a great Empire, the British are a commercial people, and yet these colonies, having gained all the advantages of self-government, shut out British goods, and made bad clothes and bad boots at the expense of the general community.

Having thought over this matter a great deal, we have now, in the constitution of a new country—namely, Rhodesia— the best reply to the Little Englanders, for that constitution contains a clause that in a territory representing 800,000 square miles of the world's surface the duties on British goods shall not exceed the present Cape tariff. We have a fairly high tariff, but it is for revenue, not for the protection of industries. Having adopted that principle, it is the constitution of the country, and I see no possibility of its being changed. It is a sacred thing, and that is the return to England for the blood and treasure that she may spend on the protection and security of the new country.

From the colonists' point of view we have a fair tariff, if there were an opportunity of development. We have a fair stimulant in the present tariff, and we will not have a tariff so high as to give the people bad articles simply for the promotion of local industry. If you follow that thought, and secure federation, that will be the basis of the tariff system in Africa.

With such a system we could make the best reply to the mother country, saying: "We do not talk of sentiment to you; we have done a practical thing; we have asked nothing from you in return, but have placed on record in our constitution an upper limit for your goods, which will give you practically the sole trade of our territories."

I had a great battle over how the clause should be worded. The late Ministry wished me to put it that the duty on imported goods should not exceed the present Cape tariff, but I said, " No, I will have it ' British '—not ' imported.' "

The politics of the next hundred years are going to be tariffs and nothing else. We are not going to war for the amusement of royal families as in the past, but we mean practical business. The next war may be not with guns and rifles, say with America, but America will have to be told that they must change their tariff or Great Britain will put a tariff against them.

The United States would not hold out for twenty-four hours, but would say it was perfectly good business, and would meet us on the tariff basis. With regard to South Africa, the present difficulties are only temporary, but supposing we had put into the Rhodesian constitution only the word " imported," and the mother country had adopted our policy for the sake of free trade in the world, that constitution would bar it here because the word " imported " covers the world, but the present constitution of Rhodesia—which is the Cinderella of the Cape—contains the word " British."

The time will come, although probably most of us will be gone, when her Majesty's government will say to the world, " We will give you free trade and admit your raw products, but you must admit our manufactures, and until you do so we will not give you equal privileges."

I think that the best reply possible to the Little Englander when he uses the phrase " *Cui bono* "—" To what advantage ? " I reply the advantage of the trade of Rhodesia. Great Britain will have a perpetual market for her goods until the constitution of Rhodesia is changed, and you must remember there is one thing which human beings never change, and that is the sacred constitution on which their country is founded. It was the sacredness of the constitution of Washington which brought about the American war and which appealed so powerfully to the American citizens. I feel sure that when federation in South Africa is arrived at this idea of an upper limit for British goods will remain in the constitution of the federated States, and will be their return to the mother country for the blood and treasure she has spent in their behalf.

I will now relate to you a rather amusing incident. If I have had one persistent opponent in connection with my thoughts of expansion, it is Sir William Harcourt. Just when I was getting my fresh capital, Sir William went out of his way to make one of those ponderous speeches which are only equaled by the size of his frame, describing the scheme of a Cape Town-to-Cairo railway as a wild-cat scheme. Well, you know that the line up to Bulawayo is already paying interest upon construction, and also that we have raised from three to four millions, which will take it to Tanganyika; and without running the risk of being accused of repetition I may add there are very good grounds for supposing that we shall see Lord Kitchener shortly steaming steadily away from Khartoum to Uganda.

But, oh, the ironies of fate! Sir William Harcourt had to retire compulsorily from the representation of Derby, being beaten by Mr. Drage, who, I understand, is the chairman of the South African Committee, and who assured me that he defeated Sir William upon the Imperial question, the question that England meant to solemnly recognize her obligations to retain her colonies, thus encouraging the doctrine of honest expansion.

Then Sir William Harcourt had to retire to the delights of Wales. After a happy rest within the precincts of Rome, he returned the other day, not to attack the Budget, as a

gentleman said, but to visit his constituents, and now came
the irony of the situation. After a delightful speech he
visited the ironworks of his principal supporters, a large
number of the voters of his division, and was exceedingly
pleased with what he saw. But there was one horrid writing
on the wall. They were making rails for the line to Cairo.
They had an order for about fifty miles, and had lately got
an order for another fifty, and he met the wild-cat scheme
everywhere. The wages of the workmen, the profits of the
owners, the industry that was shown him, all of it was production for this wild-cat scheme. I think that story is an
amusing one, and it contains a lesson.

I would almost be happy to go and stand for that constit-
uency. I notice that all those gentlemen, with the exception of Mr. Morley, are now declaring that they are not
Little Englanders, but people must judge them by their past
speeches and not their present or future utterances, because
they are only waiting and hoping for a reverse to return
to the point. They hoped it might come in China, or in
Fashoda, but I do not think they really expect it in the
Transvaal.

That notion is too ridiculous. I always think that President Kruger must be very proud of himself. I should feel
alarmed if I heard that the Tsar was going to Pekin, or that
the French were moving in Newfoundland or the Niger territories, or were quarrelling over the Fashoda settlement.
But when I am told the President of the Transvaal is caus-
ing trouble I cannot really think about it. It is too ridiculous. If you were to tell me that the native chief in Samoa
was going to cause trouble to her Majesty's government, then
I would discuss the proposition that the Transvaal was a
danger to the British Empire.

If you asked me to discuss the position, I would like to take a Boer child and give him a picture of the present Transvaal government, and I feel sure that the child would say to his father, " Father, that doesn't exist in this country. You are not telling me the truth. That might have happened six hundred years ago, but it is impossible now."

And that is the judgment of the world. I will repeat something which has struck those in high places more than anything. Consider the small output of the new country of Rhodesia, which has had everything against it, but has every confidence in its administration, and the fact that I have obtained nine millions of money. With the greatest production of gold in the world, a most beautiful climate, a most energetic people producing seventeen millions per annum, my neighboring friend could not get two millions of money. The whole of the world's money is not in London. There were Berlin and Paris to apply to also; but the financial people felt that the Transvaal system of administration was so bad that they would not even part with two millions, no matter what terms were offered.

Well, we hope it will change. Of course it is going to change. Her Majesty's government are determined to have a redress of the Uitlanders' grievances. The President is doing the usual thing, he is playing up to the Raad. I wish to be quite clear on what I state. I have talked to no Ministers on the subject, and I do not wish it to be inferred that I have spoken to the Cabinet. But I have talked to people in London during the last three months, and I can say that her Majesty's government are determined to have a redress of the Uitlanders' grievances.

The matter throws my recollection back to the Drifts

question, when the Drifts were closed against our trade, and
you know that if such a thing were allowed the trade of the
Colony would be cut off. You know the story, and I would
say this, that there was no one stronger in the Cabinet than
the present Prime Minister. The Cape government, having
demanded intervention, were asked were they prepared to
give a passage for troops and pay half the expenses of the
undertaking, the argument being that it was the affair of
the Cape and not of Great Britain.

After considerable discussion the Cabinet decided unanimously that they were prepared to pay half the expense of
introducing British troops, to use violence if necessary. I
felt that Mr. Kruger would then give in, and so he did, and
I am equally sure that the President is going to give her
Majesty the terms which her Majesty now demands.

Some of you may remember the trouble in years past with
Bechuanaland, when Kruger desired to cut off the Colony and to have the centre for himself. Well, with the help
of your present member [Mr. F. R. Thompson], who threw
his ability and determination into the work, the British
authorities were successful. I remember one morning, after
one of those horrid night journeys in a Cape cart, I arrived
at the camp of the head of the Boer commando on the Hartz
River. There I was told there was a good deal of " blood-
and-thunder " talk, and I was asked by the commandant.

" Who are you ? "

I replied, " My name is Cecil Rhodes," and the leader re-
torted, " Oh, you're the Administrator," and thereafter there
were some more threats and the statement " bloed zal
vloeien "—blood will flow.

I said to him, " Don't talk nonsense; I'm very hungry;
come and give me some breakfast."

I stopped there a week, and on my departure there was a little function; I became the godfather of the Boer commandant's grandchild. The same sort of thing is going to happen just now.

Before I leave the subject I will say that there is not the slightest chance of war, but her Majesty's government are going to get the terms which are demanded as being fair and right to the Uitlanders. I will leave that question now, because, as I have said, it is only a temporary trouble in Africa.

But there is a much more serious question. You have been congratulating me upon my work in the North, and have supported me most admirably during my time of trouble, when I had to suffer for certain conduct of my own. I have steadily gone on with the work in the North on the basis of equal rights for every class of citizen, and have been trying to obtain as much money for development as I can secure. I have been most fortunate in that, but still I have to look at the future.

You will recognize the enormous changes here, and the prosperity of the country, especially in this place, because the railways of Africa have been made like the palm of my hand, and we propose to continue that policy of extension. But you have to remember that there are ports on the East and West, and that the only certain security for keeping the position in the South is a union of the States of South Africa.

I was a little alarmed when some measures were submitted to the new Council in Rhodesia, at the feeling shown about that fact that Cape products were being treated on a different footing. It was demanded that rates should be imposed against the Cape, just the same as against other countries. I know, without desiring in the least to threaten, that there is a tendency in the North, as there always is with new States, to be independent.

And I may say, in this connection, that in the Transvaal there is no love for Jan Hofmeyr; they will use him, but they do not care about him. You have never got one sixpence from the Transvaal. You have indulged in a good deal of sentiment, but got nothing in return. Well, the whole solution for the Cape is a simple one. We are getting far into the interior of Africa, but there is a time coming in the ordinary course of nature for my disappearance, and you must not let this North drift away from you. On the North depends the Transvaal, because it is surrounded. You need not think about this temporary difficulty in the Transvaal; but I believe that with the great community which has arisen in that State, amounting to about 80,000; knowing the extent of the deep-levels and the distance to which the gold-belts stretch, I may say there will be half a million of people there in course of time.

If we are to realize our dream of a South African Union (I can speak frankly now, because the question of the value of the North is settled, and if some of you really believed that it would only produce whip-sticks, we know now that it is rich in gold), one has to consider that the time has arrived for you to work for a solution.

I know Natal is ready for it, and I think the people in the North would consider it; although, when they had a large output, goodness knew what they would do, people got so uplifted. As to the Transvaal, I believe the new population, if they had their rights, would work for union in Africa. There is a practical point in it. They know that whatever Rhodesia possesses it will possess the whole labor factor; that north and south of the Zambesi we have native laborers in millions, and labor is the question.   We have thus an asset for bargaining with.

I am aware that in thinking out this question of Union a charge will be made in relation to the flag question in the neighboring States.   To that I reply, Go and read Mr. Bryce's book on South Africa, and you will find it shown that there have been federations in Europe with different flags.   We can federate without bringing up that awful question of the flag.   One knows in the end what flag will fly.

What does that confederation mean?   It means a great future for your children.   It means a distribution of thought in your families, between mining, commercial, and political work—all those classes of work which are given to human beings to accomplish.   It means that in a great area of territory which compares very favorably with any other portion of the world, you have gold, diamonds, copper, coal, wine, sheep, everything almost you can think of; and you only want a united people for the proper development of that huge extent of country.

How is that idea to be brought about?   Are the majority of the people south of the Zambesi in favor of it?   Most distinctly they are.

I wonder if any one has gone into figures.   I would not make the charge for one moment that the Dutch are against you.   I do not believe that.   There is a bold section, like my friend, Mr. Louw, and a few others.   These have spoken out their thoughts and have suffered for it.   But even if I were to take it that the whole of the Dutch race was against us, let us count up the States of Africa and their population, taking it on a basis of males.

We have already 12,000 with us in Matabeleland.   It is only a commencement of the mining industry, and it is a simple arithmetical question. If we have 12,000 with a few mines, when we have, say, 200 mines, we know how many more supporters we shall have for federation. It is fair to state that in the neighboring State, the Transvaal, the new population represents 80,000, who are deprived of their franchise rights, although most interesting little lads are made burghers; and those Transvaal students, when they come to Stellenbosch, are enabled to vote as British subjects, while at the same time they are burghers of the Transvaal. I may say that the new population are the Progressives of the Transvaal, and I distinctly claim that a large section of the Dutch are also supporters of reform. That gives you 92,000 on your side. Then in Natal, a plucky little colony—there are 40,000 white inhabitants, of which number you are entitled to claim at least 10,000 as Progressives. Coming to the old Cape Colony, we can deal with absolute statistics. The number of voters is 108,000, but a certain number do not vote. After a careful examination of the lists, however, you will find that the Bond received 33,000, while the Progressives received 46,000 votes. That is a fair representation, but I will allow the Dutch one half. If, therefore, you add 54,000 in the Cape to the 102,000 already estimated in the North, Natal, and the Transvaal, you arrive at the number of Progressives who would probably support union, namely, about 150,000, making allowance for those who do not vote, exclusive of the Free State. It is safe to say that there is an enormous majority in South Africa absolutely in favor of federation.

Then why does not federation come about in the usual way? Why are not delegates from Natal, the Cape Colony, the Transvaal, and Rhodesia called together to agree to a federal constitution, which, as you know, means that the big questions would be left for settlement to the federal government, full liberty being given to the local governments to dispose of all local questions?

Rhodesia is just coming on the scene, but without trespassing on the position of the High Commissioner I have noticed that the 80,000 in the Transvaal are described in a despatch as helots, who were Spartan slaves. These 80,000 are slaves, to use a John Bull term, and they are our fellow countrymen, and friends from other countries. They cannot vote at all. I repeat that plucky little Natal, with her great ideas of expansion and a mind large in proportion to her size, would fall in with federation. The elections in the Cape have shown that if there was fair representation this colony also would join in a South African Union.

As the oldest State, and the parent of all, its duty is to take the lead. It can be maintained without dispute, even from our most extreme opponents, that if the Progressives had proper representation they would have a majority of members. By an accident they are three or four behind; in one case, that of Aliwal North, Tengo Jabavu's brother making the difference.

What, then, is it that stops federation? Both sides of the House are quite clear on the black question. I have had some doubts about the Bond, but was delighted when Mr. Vander Walt said that one thing he was hoping for was to see Jabavu sitting side by side with him in the House. The pure natives in Tembuland voted with the Bond, although the Progressives had declared their programme of equality of rights for every civilized man south of the Zambesi.

By that we mean that any men, provided they can write their names, place of residence, and occupation, and that they are workers or possessed of some property, quite irrespective of color, would be entitled to these rights. But the Bond has gone one better still. They are hungering for Tengo Jabavu in the House, and the Bond gained its present position in the House by the support of the pure native voters.

As for the colored people, I owe them a deep debt of obligation for the work they have done for me in Rhodesia. It was they who, with their corps, stormed the fastnesses of Matabeleland. They did so not once, but repeatedly, and I regard them as one of the great sources of prosperity in this country.

Changing from the Matoppos to my fruit farms, I have ascertained from Californians, with whom I have discussed the question of labor, that they have nothing in California to equal the colored man as a laborer. That is my contribution to the position of the colored men in this country, and I am thankful to take the opportunity of making such a statement. I will add that I do not make that remark to get the colored voters, because the Progressives have them already.

I will also say openly that where Dutch people have a position and a stake in this country, I have noticed in each district I have visited, while they fairly remonstrated with me in connection with my conduct in the raid, yet broadly, on the point of equality of rights in South Africa, they were with me.

They simply said they would no longer be under the domination of the Bond. I have been under the domination of the Bond myself, and other Ministries will also be under that domination until we carry out that thought of equality. Well, it may be asked, with such a thought, with such an idea, and with such a majority, why it is not carried out? Well, there is one thing that stops the whole question, and that is that the old population has got it into their heads that equality of rights and union means the loss of their political position, and that the—well, I will not say ignorant, but simple, farmer in the country is imbued with the Bond view that to have the Progressives in power means that the old population would become a kind of serfs—helots, as I just now used the word in another connection.

My reply is: How can that be where, under the British constitution, there are equal rights for all, and he who wins is the best man, of whatever race he may be? Take the great city of Cape Town, which chose Mr. Wiener, a German, for years to represent it. There was no thought of race. They never left him, but he left them when his Progressive ideas were changed into those of the Bond. It was not a question of race. It was because he left that equality principle that he lost his seat. Probably Mr. Wiener thought that the other party would be successful. Well, temporarily yes, but not permanently. The question is whether we could not educate these people to the true state of affairs.

Well, first we must get them to abandon that stupid idea that because somebody came to this country a hundred years ago, his children are in a special position. It is the prevalence of that idea that has disturbed everything. Besides, if you take the case of the Transvaal, the people there who have that idea have only been in the country some fifty years, and surely in that time, not quite a lifetime, they cannot fairly claim special privileges. Still they do, and speak of " ons volk " and " ons land." Well, I take " ons land " to be our land, and I say I am a partner in that, although I am told I am not a partner and that I am here on sufferance. Well, it will be your duty to change that position. It should also be remembered that this was not the thought of the old people who took this country. It is the thought of some men who have made an oligarchy, and who have prevailed upon their own simple people to think that. It is they who delay this thought of equality, and I will tell you why.

It is because two or three men in Pretoria, and one or two in Cape Town, govern the whole country, and they need never appear. I have been told that a gentleman who was before the Mikado in Japan maintained his position by never being seen. I think the system of the Bond party is to govern through an individual who was never heard, at any rate, in their House, where he should have been.

And this government by the unseen must pass away as many other things must pass away. You are here and your party, and you are in a position to do that, but still you are willing that all should have equal rights, and you welcome even your most extreme opponents of the Bond to share in the development of South Africa. You must hold out for equal rights, and let the best men come to the front independent of race or the accident of birth. Although I was born at home, it does not stop me from being faithful to this country, and I am doing the best I can for the country which I have adopted as my dwelling-place. Through the whole of our difficulties there is just this one thought that comes out perfectly clear.

We must fight for equal rights, and the practical result will be the federal union of South Africa. With regard to myself, you must not think I am neglecting my duties because you do not see me in the House. I am doing my best, and I carry with me everywhere that thought for the union of South Africa, and I hope that when you have realized that thought it will not be too late.

I have tried hard to secure from the Colony privileges in the North. Now the people there are looking to the ports on the East and the West Coast, and I greatly fear that before this country wakes up to the situation that great inheritance may have passed away from you in the South, and that is what you must work to prevent.

The Present Ministry, if they could only see it, have an enormous chance before them. I know that I myself, owing to various reasons, am not particularly pleasing to the Bond party, but I see no reason why others should not take up my work, and that is the union of South Africa. I do not care a jot who wears the peacock's feathers so long as the work is done. Let us get to the practical result—union. Natal is ready, Rhodesia is ready, and even the Republics could federate, as Professor Bryce has pointed out, without loss of dignity so far as the flag is concerned. That is the position I wish to be able to carry out, and that is what must come.

BOOKER T. WASHINGTON

OOKER TALIAFERRO WASHINGTON, M.'A., a distinguished American educator, principal of the Tuskegee Normal and Industrial Institute, was born a slave near Hale's Ford, Va., about the year 1856. After the close of the Civil War he removed with his parents to Maldon, W. Va., where he was able to obtain a little schooling while working for his own living. He subsequently went to Hampton Institute, where he worked his way through the course in three years and spent two years more in the Institute as a teacher. In 1881, he became the head of an institution at Tuskegee, Ala., since incorporated as the Tuskegee Normal and Industrial Institute, of which he is still (1902) the president. From small beginnings the school has grown to large proportions, mainly through his efforts, he having delivered many addresses in the northern States setting forth the needs of this institution for the training of the negro. He has also made a number of notable public speeches and contributed to the periodicals on educational themes. In June, 1896, Harvard University conferred upon him the honorary degree of Master of Arts. This was the first time in American history that such a distinction was ever conferred upon a colored man. Mr. Washington's book, "The Future of the American Negro," appeared in 1899, and his Autobiography in 1901, the latter of which has been translated into several foreign languages. He is an able and interesting speaker on racial and educational subjects.

THE RACE PROBLEM

[Address delivered at the opening of the Cotton States and International Exposition, at Atlanta, Ga., September 18, 1895.]

MR. PRESIDENT AND GENTLEMEN OF THE BOARD OF DIRECTORS AND CITIZENS,— One third of the population of the South is of the negro race. No enterprise seeking the material, civil, or moral welfare of this section can disregard this element of our population and reach the highest success. I but convey to you, Mr. President and Directors, the sentiment of the masses of my race when I say that in no way have the value and manhood of the American negro been more fittingly and generously recognized than by the managers of this magnificent Exposition at every stage of its progress. It is a recognition that will do more to cement the friendship of the two races than any occurrence since the dawn of our freedom.

(312)

HENRY WOODFEN GRADY.

Not only this, but the opportunity here afforded will awaken among us a new era of industrial progress. Ignorant and inexperienced, it is not strange that in the first years of our new life we began at the top instead of at the bottom; that a seat in Congress or the State legislature was more sought than real estate or industrial skill; that the political convention or stump speaking had more attractions than starting a dairy farm or truck garden.

A ship lost at sea for many days suddenly sighted a friendly vessel. From the mast of the unfortunate vessel was seen a signal: " Water, water; we die of thirst! "

The answer from the friendly vessel at once came back: " Cast down your bucket where you are." A second time the signal, " Water, water; send us water! " ran up from the distressed vessel, and was answered: " Cast down your bucket where you are." And a third and fourth signal for water was answered: " Cast down your bucket where you are."

The captain of the distressed vessel, at last heeding the injunction, cast down his bucket, and it came up full of fresh, sparkling water from the mouth of the Amazon River. To those of my race who depend on bettering their condition in a foreign land, or who underestimate the importance of cultivating friendly relations with the Southern white man, who is their next-door neighbor, I would say: " Cast down your bucket where you are "—cast it down in making friends in every manly way of the people of all races by whom we are surrounded.

Cast it down in agriculture, mechanics, in commerce, in domestic service, and in the professions. And in this connection it is well to bear in mind that whatever other sins the South may be called to bear, when it comes to business, pure and simple, it is in the South that the negro is given a man's chance in the commercial world, and in nothing is this Exposition more eloquent than in emphasizing this chance.

Our greatest danger is that in the great leap from slavery to freedom we may overlook the fact that the masses of us are to live by the productions of our hands, and fail to keep in mind that we shall prosper in proportion as we learn to dignify and glorify common labor and put brains and skill into the common occupations of life; shall prosper in proportion as we learn to draw the line between the superficial and the substantial, the ornamental gewgaws of life and the useful. No race can prosper till it learns that there is as much dignity in tilling a field as in writing a poem. It is at the bottom of life we must begin, and not at the top. Nor should we permit our grievances to overshadow our opportunities.

To those of the white race who look to the incoming of those of foreign birth and strange tongue and habits for the prosperity of the South, were I permitted I would repeat what I say to my own race, " Cast down your bucket where you are."

Cast it down among the eight million negroes whose habits you know, whose fidelity and love you have tested in days when to have proved treacherous meant the ruin of your firesides. Cast down your bucket among these people who have, without strikes and labor wars, tilled your fields, cleared your forests, builded your railroads and cities, and brought forth treasures from the bowels of the earth, and helped make possible this magnificent representation of the progress of the South.

Casting down you bucket among my people, helping and

encouraging them as you are doing on these grounds, and to education of head, hand, and heart, you will find that they will buy your surplus land, make blossom the waste places in your fields, and run your factories.

While doing this, you can be sure in the future, as in the past, that you and your families will be surrounded by the most patient, faithful, law-abiding, and unresentful people that the world has seen.

As we have proved our loyalty to you in the past, in nursing your children, watching by the sick bed of your mothers and fathers, and often following them with tear-dimmed eyes to their graves, so in the future, in our humble way, we shall stand by you with a devotion that no foreigner can approach, ready to lay down our lives, if need be, in defense of yours, interlacing our industrial, commercial, civil, and religious life with yours in a way that shall make the interests of both races one. In all things that are purely social we can be as separate as the fingers, yet one as the hand in all things essential to mutual progress.

There is no defense or security for any of us except in the highest intelligence and development of all. If anywhere there are efforts tending to curtail the fullest growth of the negro, let these efforts be turned into stimulating, encouraging, and making him the most useful and intelligent citizen. Effort or means so invested will pay a thousand per cent interest. These efforts will be twice blessed—" blessing him that gives and him that takes."

There is no escape through law of man or God from the inevitable:

> " The laws of changeless justice bind
> Oppressor with oppressed;
> And close as sin and suffering joined
> We march to fate abreast."

Nearly sixteen millions of hands will aid you in pulling the load upward, or they will pull against you the load downward. We shall constitute one third and more of the ignorance and crime of the South, or one third its intelligence and progress; we shall contribute one third to the business and industrial prosperity of the South, or we shall prove a veritable body of death, stagnating, depressing, retarding every effort to advance the body politic.

Gentlemen of the Exposition, as we present to you our humble effort at an exhibition of our progress, you must not expect overmuch. Starting thirty years ago with ownership here and there in a few quilts and pumpkins and chickens, remember the path that has led from these to the inventions and production of agricultural implements, buggies, steam engines, newspapers, books, statuary, carving, paintings, the management of drug stores and banks, has not been trodden without contact with thorns and thistles. While we take pride in what we exhibit as a result of our independent efforts, we do not for a moment forget that our part in this exhibition would fall far short of your expectations but for the constant help that has come to our educational life, not only from the Southern States, but especially from Northern philanthropists, who have made their gifts a constant stream of blessing and encouragement.

The wisest among my race understand that the agitation of questions of social equality is the extremest folly, and that progress in the enjoyment of all the privileges that will come to us must be the result of severe and constant struggle rather than of artificial forcing. No race that has anything to contribute to the markets of the world is long in any degree ostracized. It is important and right that all privileges of the law be ours, but it is vastly more important that we be prepared for the exercise of these privileges. The opportunity to earn a dollar in a factory just now is worth infinitely more than the opportunity to spend a dollar in an opera house.

In conclusion, may I repeat that nothing in thirty years has given us more hope and encouragement, and drawn us so near to you of the white race, as this opportunity offered by the Exposition; and here bending, as it were, over the altar that represents the results of the struggles of your race and mine, both starting practically empty-handed three decades ago, I pledge that in your effort to work out the great and intricate problem which God has laid at the doors of the South you shall have at all times the patient, sympathetic help of my race; only let this be constantly in mind that, while from representations in these buildings of the product of field, of forest, of mine, of factory, letters, and art, much good will come, yet far above and beyond material benefits will be that higher good, that let us pray God will come, in a blotting out of sectional differences and racial animosities and suspicions, in a determination to administer absolute justice, in a willing obedience among all classes to the mandates of law. This, this, coupled with our material prosperity, will bring into our beloved South a new heaven and a new earth.

SPEECH AT HARVARD UNIVERSITY

[Delivered at the alumni dinner, June 24, 1896, after receiving the honorary degree of Master of Arts.]

M R. PRESIDENT AND GENTLEMEN,—It would in some measure relieve my embarrassment if I could, even in a slight degree, feel myself worthy of the great honor which you do me to-day. Why you have called me from the Black Belt of the South, from among my humble people, to share in the honors of this occasion, is not for me to explain; and yet it may not be inappropriate for me to suggest that it seems to me that one of the most vital questions that touch our American life is how to bring the strong, wealthy, and learned into helpful touch with the poorest, most ignorant, and humble, and at the same time make the one appreciate the vitalizing, strengthening influence of the other. How shall we make the mansions on yon Beacon Street feel and see the need of the spirits in the lowliest cabin in Alabama cotton fields or Louisiana sugar bottoms? This problem Harvard University is solving, not by bringing itself down, but by bringing the masses up.

If, through me, an humble representative, seven millions of my people in the South might be permitted to send a message to Harvard—Harvard that offered up on death's altar, young Shaw, and Russell, and Lowell, and scores of others, that we might have a free and united country, that message would be, " Tell them that the sacrifice was not in vain. Tell them that by the way of the shop, the field, the skilled hand, habits of thrift and economy, by way of industrial school and college, we are coming.

" We are crawling up, working up, yea, bursting up. Often through oppression, unjust discrimination, and prejudice, but through them all we are coming up, and with proper habits, intelligence, and property, there is no power on earth that can permanently stay our progress."

If my life in the past has meant anything in the lifting up of my people and the bringing about of better relations between your race and mine, I assure you from this day it will mean doubly more. In the economy of God there is but one standard by which an individual can succeed—there is but one for a race. This country demands that every race measure itself by the American standard. By it a race must rise or fall, succeed or fail, and in the last analysis mere sentiment counts for little. During the next half century and more, my race must continue passing through the severe American crucible. We are to be tested in our patience, our forbearance, our perseverance, our power to endure wrong, to withstand temptations, to economize, to acquire and use skill; our ability to compete, to succeed in commerce, to disregard the superficial for the real, the appearance for the substance, to be great and yet small, learned and yet simple, high and yet the servant of all. This, this is the passport to all that is best in the life of our Republic, and the negro must possess it or be debarred.

While we are thus being tested, I beg of you to remember that wherever our life touches yours we help or hinder. Wherever your life touches ours you make us stronger or weaker. No member of your race in any part of our country can harm the meanest member of mine, without the proudest and bluest blood in Massachusetts being degraded. When

Mississippi commits crime, New England commits crime, and
in so much lowers the standard of your civilization.   There
is no escape—man drags man down, or man lifts man up.

In working out our destiny, while the main burden and
centre of activity must be with us, we shall need in a large
measure, in the years that are to come, as we have in the past,
the help, the encouragement, the guidance that the strong
can give the weak.   Thus helped, we of both races in the
South soon shall throw off the shackles of racial and sectional
prejudice and rise as Harvard University has risen, and as we
all should rise, above the clouds of ignorance, narrowness, and
selfishness, into that atmosphere, that pure sunshine, where
it will be our highest ambition to serve Man, our brother,
regardless of race or previous condition.

ADDRESS AT THE UNVEILING OF THE ROBERT GOULD SHAW MONUMENT

DELIVERED IN BOSTON, MASSACHUSETTS, MAY 31, 1897

MR. CHAIRMAN AND FELLOW CITIZENS,—In
this presence and on this sacred and memorable day,
in the deeds and death of our hero we recall the old,
old story, ever old, yet ever new, that when it was the will of
the Father to lift humanity out of wretchedness and bondage
the precious task was delegated to him who among ten thousand was altogether lovely and was willing to make himself
of no reputation that he might save and lift up others.

If that heart could throb, and if those lips could speak,
what would be the sentiment and words that Robert Gould

Shaw would have us feel and speak at this hour? He would
not have us dwell long on the mistakes, the injustice, the
criticisms of the days—

> " Of storm and cloud, of doubt and fears,
> Across the eternal sky must lower,
> Before the glorious noon appears."

He would have us bind up with his own undying fame and
memory, and retain by the side of his monument, the name
of John A. Andrew, who with prophetic vision and strong
arm helped make the existence of the Fifty-fourth Regiment
possible, and that of George L. Stearns, who, with hidden
generosity and a great, sweet heart, helped to turn the darkest hour into day and in so doing so freely gave service, fortune, and life itself to the cause which this day commemo-
rates.

Nor would he have us forget those brother officers, living
and dead, who, by their baptism in blood and fire, in defence
of union and freedom, gave us an example of the highest and
purest patriotism.

To you who fought so valiantly in the ranks, the scarred
and shattered remnant of the Fifty-fourth Regiment, who
with empty sleeve and wanting leg have honored this occasion
with your presence, to you, your commander is not dead.
Though Boston erected no monument and history recorded no
story, in you and the loyal race which you represent Robert
Gould Shaw would have a monument which time could not
wear away.

But an occasion like this is too great, too sacred for mere
individual eulogy. The individual is the instrument, national
virtue the end. That which was three hundred years being
woven into the warp and woof of our democratic institutions
could not be effaced by a single battle as magnificent as was

that battle; that which for three centuries had bound master and slave, yea, North and South, to a body of death, could not be blotted out by four years of war, could not be atoned for by shot and sword nor by blood and tears.

No many days ago, in the heart of the South, in a large gathering of the people of my race, there were heard from many lips praises and thanksgiving to God for his goodness in setting them free from physical slavery. In the midst of that assembly a Southern white man arose, with gray hair and trembling hands, the former owner of many slaves, and from his quivering lips there came the words: " My friends, you forgot in your rejoicing that in setting you free God was also good to me and my race in setting us free."

But there is a higher and deeper sense in which both races must be free than that represented by the bill of sale. The black man who cannot let love and sympathy go out to the white man is but half free. The white man who could close the shop or factory against a black man seeking an opportunity to earn an honest living is but half free. The white man who retards his own development by oppressing a black man is but half free.

The full measure of the fruit of Fort Wagner and all that this monument stands for will not be realized until every man covered by a black skin shall, by patience and natural effort, grow to that height in industry, property, intelligence, and moral responsibility where no man in all our land will be tempted to degrade himself by withholding from this black brother any opportunity which he himself would possess. Until that time comes this monument will stand for effort, not victory complete. What these heroic souls of the 54th Regiment began we must complete. It must be completed not in malice, not narrowness, nor artificial progress, nor in efforts at mere temporary political gain, nor in abuse of another section or race.

Standing as I do to-day in the home of Garrison and Phillips and Sumner, my heart goes out to those who wore the grey as well as to those clothed in blue, to those who returned defeated to destitute homes, to face blasted hopes and a shattered political and industrial system.

To them there can be no prouder reward for defeat than by a supreme effort to place the negro on that footing where he will add material, intellectual, and civil strength to every department of state. This work must be completed in public school, industrial school, and college. The most of all it must be completed in the effort of the negro himself, in his effort to withstand temptation, to economize, to exercise thrift, to disregard the superficial for the real—the shadow for the substance, to be great and yet small, in his effort to be patient in the laying of a firm foundation, to so grow in skill and knowledge that he shall place his services in demand by reason of his intrinsic and superior worth. This, this is the key that unlocks every door of opportunity, and all others fail. In this battle of peace the rich and poor, the black and white, may have a part.

What lesson has this occasion for the future? What of hope, what of encouragement, what of caution? " Watchman tell us of the night, what the signs of promise are."

If, through me, an humble representative of nearly ten millions of my people might be permitted to send a message of gratitude to Massachusetts, to the committee whose untiring energy has made this memorial possible, to the family who gave their only boy that we might have life more abundantly, that message would be:

" Tell them that the sacrifice was not in vain, that up from the depths of ignorance and poverty we are coming, and if we come through oppression out of the struggle we are gaining strength.

" By way of the school, the well-cultivated field, the skilled hand, the Christian home, we are coming up: that we propose to take our place upon the high and undisputed ground of usefulness, generosity, and honesty, and that we propose to invite all who will to step up and occupy this position with us.

" Tell them that we are learning that standing-ground for a race, as for an individual, must be laid in intelligence, industry, thrift, and property, not as an end, but as a means to the highest privileges: That we are learning that neither the conqueror's bullet nor fiat of law could make an ignorant voter an intelligent voter, could make a dependent man an independent man, could give one citizen respect for another, a bank account, a foot of land, or an enlightened fireside. Tell them that, as grateful as we are to artist and patriotism for placing the figures of Shaw and his comrades in physical form of beauty and magnificence, after all, the real monument, the greater monument, is being slowly but safely builded among the lowly in the South, in the struggles and sacrifices of a race to justify all that has been done and suffered for it."

One of the wishes that lay nearest to Colonel Shaw's heart was that his black troops might be permitted to fight by the side of white soldiers   Have we not lived to see that wish realized, and will it not be more so in the future? Not at Wagner, not with rifle and bayonet, but on the field of peace, in the battle of industry, in the struggle for good government, in the lifting up of the lowest to the fullest opportunities.   In this we shall fight by the side of white men North and South.

And if this be true, as under God's guidance it will, that old flag, that emblem of progress and security which brave Sergeant Carny never permitted to fall upon the ground, will still be borne aloft by Southern soldier and Northern soldier, and in a more potent and higher sense we shall all realize that—

> " The slave's chain and the master's alike are broken,
> The one curse of the races held both in tether.
> They are rising, all are rising,
> The black and the white together."

THE NEGRO'S LOYALTY TO THE STARS AND STRIPES

DELIVERED AT THE THANKSGIVING PEACE JUBILEE EXERCISES,
CHICAGO, OCTOBER 16, 1898

MR. CHAIRMAN, LADIES, AND GENTLEMEN,— On an important occasion in the life of the Master, when it fell to him to pronounce judgment on two courses of action, these memorable words fell from his lips: " And Mary hath chosen the better part." This was the supreme test in the case of an individual. It is the highest test in the case of a race or nation. Let us apply this test to the American negro.

In the life of our republic, when he has had the opportunity to choose, has it been the better or worse part? When, in the childhood of this nation, the negro was asked to submit to slavery or choose death and extinction, as did the aborigines, he chose the better part, that which perpetuated the race.

When, in 1776, the negro was asked to decide between British oppression and American independence, we find him choosing the better part, and Crispus Attucks, a negro, was the first to shed his blood on State Street, Boston, that the white American might enjoy liberty forever, though his race remained in slavery.

When, in 1814, at New Orleans, the test of patriotism came again, we find the negro choosing the better part, and General Andrew Jackson himself testifying that no heart was more loyal and no arm more strong and useful in defence of righteousness.

When the long and memorable struggle came between union and separation, when he knew that victory on the one hand meant freedom, and defeat on the other his continued enslavement, with a full knowledge of the portentous meaning of it all, when the suggestion and the temptation came to burn the home and massacre wife and children during the absence of the master in battle, and thus ensure his liberty, we find him choosing the better part, and for four long years protecting and supporting the helpless, defenceless ones entrusted to his care.

When, in 1863, the cause of the Union seemed to quiver in the balance, and there was doubt and distrust, the negro was asked to come to the rescue in arms, and the valor displayed at Fort Wagner and Port Hudson and Fort Pillow testify most eloquently again that the negro chose the better part.

When, a few months ago, the safety and honor of the republic were threatened by a foreign foe, when the wail and anguish of the oppressed from a distant isle reached his ears, we find the negro forgetting his own wrongs, forgetting the laws and customs that discriminate against him in his own country, and again we find our black citizen choosing the better part. And if you would know how he deported himself in the field at Santiago, apply for answer to Shafter and Roosevelt and Wheeler. Let them tell how the negro faced death and laid down his life in defence of honor and human-

.ty, and when you have gotten the full story of the heroic conduct of the negro in the Spanish-American war—heard it from the lips of Northern soldiers and Southern soldiers, from ex-abolitionists and ex-masters, then decide within yourselves whether a race that is thus willing to die for its country should not be given the highest opportunity to live for its country.

In the midst of all the complaints of suffering in the camp and field, suffering from fever and hunger, where is the official or citizen that has heard a word of complaint from the lips of a black soldier? The only request that has come from the negro soldier has been that he might be permitted to replace the white soldier when heat and malaria began to decimate the ranks of the white regiment, and to occupy at the same time the post of greatest danger.

This country has been most fortunate in her victories. She has twice measured arms with England and has won. She has met the spirit of rebellion within her borders and was victorious. She has met the proud Spaniard, and he lies prostrate at her feet. All this is well; it is magnificent. But there remains one other victory for Americans to win—a victory as far-reaching and important as any that has occupied our army and navy. We have succeeded in every conflict except the effort to conquer ourselves in the blotting out of racial prejudices.

We can celebrate the era of peace in no more effectual way than by a firm resolve on the part of Northern men and Southern men, black men and white men, that the trenches which we together dug around Santiago shall be the eternal burial-place of all that which separates us in our business and civil relations. Let us be as generous in peace as we have been brave in battle. Until we thus conquer ourselves, I make no empty statement when I say that we shall have, especially in the Southern part of our country, a cancer gnawing at the heart of the republic that shall one day prove as dangerous as an attack from an army without or within.

In this presence and on this auspicious occasion I want to present the deep gratitude of nearly ten millions of my people to our wise, patient, and brave Chief Executive for the generous manner in which my race has been recognized during this conflict,—a recognition that has done more to blot out sectional and racial lines than any event since the dawn of our freedom.

I know how vain and impotent is all abstract talk on this subject.   In your efforts to " rise on stepping-stones of your dead selves," we of the black race shall not leave you unaided. We shall make the task easier for you by acquiring property, habits of thrift, economy, intelligence, and character, by each making himself of individual worth in his own community. We shall aid you in this as we did a few days ago at El Caney and Santiago, when we helped you to hasten the peace we here celebrate.   You know us; you are not afraid of us. When the crucial test comes, you are not ashamed of us.   We have never betrayed or deceived you.   You know that as it has been, so it will be.   Whether in war or in peace, whether in slavery or in freedom, we have always been loyal to the Stars and Stripes.

Wm. BOURKE COCKRAN

ILLIAM BOURKE COCKRAN, Irish-American lawyer and orator, was born in County Sligo, Ireland, Feb. 28, 1854, and educated in his native island and in France. He came to the United States in 1871, and, after engaging in teaching for a few years, studied law and was admitted to the Bar in 1876. He established himself in New York city, and in 1881, while delegate to the State Democratic Convention at Syracuse, made his reputation as a political orator. In 1884, he was the spokesman of Tammany Hall at the National Democratic Convention. After filling one term in Congress as a Democratic Representative, 1887–1888, he declined reëlection in the latter year, but was, however, reëlected by a large majority in 1890, and in the fifty-second Congress introduced and secured the passage of a bill to encourage American shipping. In 1892, he spoke again in behalf of Tammany Hall, in the Democratic National Convention of that year, and was again returned to Congress in the autumn. While in Congress during its next session he advocated the repeal of the purchasing clause of the Sherman Silver Law and opposed the Carlisle Currency Bill. In 1896, he espoused the cause of sound money and the single gold standard, delivering a number of forcible and stirring speeches during the campaign of that season, and by his position, regarding the currency, directly opposed Tammany Hall and the mass of the Democratic party. He has recently been identified with the anti-imperialist movement, and in March, 1900, delivered an able and eloquent address at a meeting of the anti-imperialist league in Faneuil Hall, Boston.

REPLY TO WILLIAM J. BRYAN

FROM SPEECH DELIVERED AT THE MADISON SQUARE GARDEN NEW YORK, AUGUST 18, 1896

I WILL venture to say here now that if the face of Providence should be averted from this land and such a calamity as Mr. Bryan's election were permitted to overtake it, the man who would suffer most by that event would be the false prophet, who, having torn down the temple of credit and of industry, would himself be torn to pieces by a people whose prosperity he had ruined.

But let us follow Mr. Bryan's argument a little. Let us see what he means to do, according to the light which he himself has kindled for us.

We see that he can't enrich one man without impoverishing another. Government never can be generous and just, at the same time, because if it be generous to one it must be oppressive to another. Mr. Bryan does not pretend that by any power given him from heaven he can find anything of value on the surface of this earth that is without an owner, and therefore he can't honestly bestow it upon a favorite. But his financial scheme contemplates an increase in the price of certain commodities. (Cry of " Except gold.") I don't think that anything Mr. Bryan can do with reference to gold will ever affect it.

But, my friends, we are coming now pretty close to the woodpile behind which the traditional African is concealed; we are approaching the very crux of this discussion. Mr. Bryan proposes to increase the price of commodities. If he means anything, he means that, although I am not sure that he means anything. Now, if everything in the world or in this country, including labor, be increased in value to-morrow in like proportion, not one of us would be affected in any degree. If that were the whole of Mr. Bryan's scheme, he would never have received a Populist nomination to give him importance in the eyes of the community. If that were all that the Chicago platform meant, he would not be supporting it, and I would not be taking the trouble to oppose it. If everything in the world were increased ten per cent. in value, why we should pay ten per cent. more for what we should buy, and get ten per cent. more for what we should sell, and we would all be in the same place which we occupy now.

It is fair to assume that such a lame and impotent conclusion is not the object which this revolutionary movement contemplates.

What, then, is the object of those whom Mr. Bryan leads? It is to increase the price of commodities and allow labor to shift for itself. If the price of commodities be increased and the price of labor left stationary, it must be plain to the most limited intelligence that a reduction in the rate of wages is accomplished. If, instead of a dollar which is equal to one hundred cents, with the purchasing power of one hundred cents anywhere in the world, the laborer is to be paid in dollars worth fifty cents each, he can only buy half as much with a day's wages as he can buy now, and the rate of his wages would be diminished one-half. If the value of this Populist scheme is to be tested for himself by any laboring man in this country, let him ask Mr. Bryan and his Populist friends the simple, common, everyday question, " In your scheme of beneficence where do I come in? " Mr. Bryan himself has a glimmering idea of where the laborer will come in, or, rather, of where he will be left out.

There is one paragraph in his speech of acceptance, which, whether it was the result of an unconscious stumbling into candor, or whether it was a contribution to truth exacted by logic in the stress of discussion, I am unable to say. But it sheds a flood of light upon the whole purpose underlying this Populist agitation.

" Wage earners," Mr. Bryan says, " know that while a gold standard raises the purchasing power of the dollar, it also makes it more difficult to obtain possession of the dollar; they know that employment is less permanent, loss of work more probable and re-employment less certain."

This clearly is a statement that a cheaper dollar would give the laborer steadier employment and a better chance to get re-employment after he had been discharged. Now, if that means anything to a sane man, it means that if the laborer is willing to have his wages reduced he will get more work.

This statement is not original with Mr. Bryan. There never was an employer of labor who meant to make a cut in wages that did not say the same thing. I have never yet heard of anybody who attempted to cut down the rate of wages, and who told his men that he did it because he liked to do it. On the contrary, such an employer would tell his men: "If you do not submit to such a cut in wages, I cannot employ you more than half the time," and Mr. Bryan says exactly the same thing when he proposes that the laboring masses of this community accept their wage in a dollar of reduced purchasing power, so that employment will become more certain and the chance of re-employment more frequent. If it were true that a reduction in the rate of wages would increase the chances of employment, I would not blame Mr. Bryan for telling the truth, because, however unpalatable the truth may be, I believe that any man who assumes to address his fellow citizens should never shrink from stating the whole truth, no matter what may be the consequences to himself.

But, as a matter of fact, a diminution in the rate of wages does not indicate an increase but a decrease in the field of employment. If this audience has done me the honor to follow me while I explained the principle on which wages were fixed, it must be clear that the more abundant the product, the higher the wages. You cannot have high wages unless there is an extensive production in every department of industry, and that is why I claim that the rate of wages is the one infallible test of a country's condition. An abundant production of commodities is obviously impossible unless labor be widely employed, and an active demand for labor necessarily involves a high rate of wages. High wages, then, is the necessary fruit of abundant production, and abundance necessarily means prosperity. Mr. Bryan, on the other hand, would have you believe that prosperity is advanced by cheapening the rate of wages. But a fall in the rate of wages always comes from a restricted production, because a reduction in the volume of products necessarily causes a narrower demand for labor. When, after the panic of 1873, the price of labor fell to ninety cents, it was harder to obtain employment than when the rate of wages was two dollars a day.

The difference between the Populist who seeks to cut down the rate of wages and the Democrat who seeks to maintain it is, that the Democrat believes that high wages and prosperity are inseparable and interdependent, while the Populist thinks lower wages would diminish the cost of agricultural production, and he thinks he can carry this election by tempting the farmer to make war upon his own workingmen.

Well, but the Populist tells us, and Mr. Bryan leads the van in saying, that the creditor is a public enemy who should be deprived of the rights which he now enjoys under the laws of this country. Mr. Bryan says there will be two kinds of metallic money in existence when his system of coinage shall have been established, and if there be a difference of value between them he argues that the debtor should have the option as to the metal in which he should pay his debt; that is to say, he should be permitted by the law to commit an act of dishonesty. In order that you should understand just how a change in the standard of value would enable men to cheat each other you must consider the function which money plays in measuring debts.

If I had paid ten dollars for ten yards of cloth, to be delivered to me next week, and in the interim the government
should pass a law declaring that hereafter the yard measure
should consist of eighteen inches and that all existing contracts should be settled by the new standard of measure, I
would be cheated out of half the cloth for which I had paid.
If, on the other hand, I owed a cloth merchant ten dollars
for ten yards which he had delivered to me, and before the
date at which my debt became payable the government
should change the standard of value and cut down the unit
of coinage one-half, then I would settle that debt with the
equivalent of five dollars as they now exist, and the cloth
merchant would have been cheated out of the half of his
just due.   That is just what the Populist programme proposes to do, and the important question that arises to the
workman in this country is, who are the creditors and who
are the debtors in this land?

Now, the Populist loves to say that the creditor is a person who oppresses the Western farmer.   He invariably
paints him as loud of dress, gaudy of ornament, coarse of
features, with a cruel expression on his face, vicious in
morals and hateful in appearance.   He always declares that
the money lender and the creditor are synonymous expressions, but as a matter of fact the creditors of this country
are not the bankers; they are not the so-called capitalists;
they are the laborers, and if the creditor is to be cheated
by the reduction in the value of the dollar it is at the expense of labor that change must be made.   During a discussion in the House of Representatives I advanced the
proposition that a banker, in the nature of things, was not a
creditor but a debtor, when I was interrupted by Mr. Bryan,
who put to me a question which contains exactly the same

statement concerning banks as that which he made here in his speech a week ago. I will read it to you:

" I would like to ask the gentleman," he says, " whether it is not true that every solvent bank has for every dollar that it owes, either somebody's note or the money in the vault and its own capital besides? "

Now, my answer to that I can give here. " The loans and reserves of a solvent bank, taken together, must exceed its liabilities; the excess represents its capital and profit; but as between their debts and their credits, all banks are debtors," which, my friends, will be apparent to you in a moment, if you will consider that a bank cannot loan all its deposits at interest, but must keep twenty-five per cent. of them in reserve. The very business of banking is the business of being in debt. It is the business of dealing with other people's money, and of course the money that a bank deals with is the money which it owes to its depositors.

But the laborer is always a creditor for at least one day's work. When any man can show me a laborer who has been paid in advance for a day's work, I will acknowledge the existence of a laborer who is a debtor. But every laborer that I have known in my experience, every laborer of whom I have ever heard in my examination of the conditions of men, must, by the very law of his being, be a creditor for at least one day's work, and he is generally a creditor for a week's, or two weeks' work. Every great industrial enterprise has for its chief creditors its own laborers. The heaviest account in every department of industry, whatever it may be, is always the wage account.

The influence which maintains in active operation the whole scheme of civilization is the confidence men have in

each other—confidence in their honesty, confidence in their
integrity, confidence in their industry, confidence in their
success.   It has been said that if we adopt a silver coinage,
we still would have the same soil, the same mines, the same
natural resources.   And it is true, but the same rivers
which flow past our cities, turning the wheels of industry as
they pass, flowed in the same channels four hundred years
ago; the same mountains were piled full of mineral treasures; the same atmosphere enwrapped this continent; the
same soil covered the fields; the same sun shone in the
heavens; yet no sound then broke the silence of desolation
except the savage pursuing the pathway of war through
sombre forests, and the rivers bore no sign of life except
the Indian in his canoe, bent on bloodshed and destruction.
The Indian could not avail himself of the bounties of nature,
because he was a savage incapable of joining in that general
industrial co-operation by which men aid each other in taking from the bosom of the earth the property which makes
life bearable; the protection of which leads to the establishment of war, and makes civilization possible.   Anything which attacks that basis of human confidence is a crime
against civilization and a blow against the foundations of
social order.

Now, the underlying trouble with all Populists is that
they have a fundamental misconception of the principles
on which civilized society is constructed.   All through Mr.
Bryan's speech, all through Mr. Tillman's utterances in
the Convention, we find the argument proceeds upon the
theory that the interests of men are irreconcilably hostile to
each other; that the condition of life is one of contest, cruel,
ceaseless, merciless.   At Chicago, Mr. Bryan declared:

" When you come before us and tell us that we shall disturb your business interests, we reply that you have disturbed our business interests. We have petitioned, and our petitions have been scorned. We have entreated, and our entreaties have been disregarded. We have begged, and they have mocked, and our calamity came. We beg no longer; we entreat no more; we petition no more. We defy them ! "

(A voice, " He was right.")

He was, my friend, he was quite right. When a man is bereft of all sense, he has an irresistible tendency to defy those who possess any. In a convention of extremists the most extreme will always be selected for a leader. Your own prospects are not bad.

I merely desire to call the attention of this gathering to the character of the speech which won for Mr. Bryan the nomination that makes him conspicuous; to the underlying spirit which pervades it, and then to ask the workingman of this country, to ask the citizens of this Nation, if the government should be trusted to the hands of men whose conception of civilized society is one of warfare and of strife?

We believe the very essence of civilization is mutual interest, mutual forbearance, mutual co-operation. We believe the world has made great strides in the pathway of progress since the time when men's hands were at one another's throats. We believe to-day that civilized men wherever they may be, at whatever tasks they may labor, are working together for a common purpose beneficial to all; and we believe that this attempt to arbitrarily reduce wages in this country, which means an attempt to attack the prosperity of all, will be resisted not by a class, but by the whole Nation. What labor has gained, that it shall keep.

The rate of wages that is paid to it to-day is the lowest rate
the intelligent laborers of this country will ever willingly
accept. We look forward to a further and a further increase in the prosperity of workingmen, not merely by an
increase in the rate of wages, but by a further increase in
the purchasing power of wages. Men who tell us that the
farmer suffers because the prices of farm products have
fallen while the cost of labor has risen, forget that the
efficiency of labor has increased and the cost of production
has been reduced through the aid of machinery, even
though the wages of the individual laborer may have risen.

While wages remain at their present rate I hope there
will be a further and continued decrease in the cost of living.
There is no way in which I can be admitted to a share of
God's bounty except through a fall in the necessaries of life.
While we preserve in existence that system of mutual co-
operation which is but another name for civilized society,
all men must share in all the favors which Providence
showers upon the earth. The dweller in the tenement-
house, stooping over a bench at which he toils through all
the hours of the day, who never sees a field of waving corn,
who never inhales the breezes which sweep, over meadows
laden with the perfume of grasses and flowers, is yet made
a participator in the benefits which flow from the growing
fertility of the soil, the purifying influence of the atmosphere, the ripening rays of the sun, when the necessaries of
life are cheapened to him by an abundant harvest.

It is from his share in this bounty that the Populist wants
to exclude the American workingman by increasing the
prices of bread and meat without any corresponding increase in the rate of wages. To him we say, in the name of
humanity, in the name of progress, in the name of civiliza-

tion, " You shall neither place a crown of thorns upon the brow of labor nor lay a scourge upon his back. You shall not rob him of any one advantage which he has gained by long years of steady progress in the skill with which he exercises his craft and by efficient organization among those who work with him at the same bench. You shall not obscure the golden prospect of a further improvement in his condition by a further cheapening in the cost of living, as well as by a further appreciation of the dollar in which his wages are paid." The man who raises his hand against the progress of the workingman raises his hand against prosperity. He seeks to restrict the volume of production. He seeks to degrade the condition of the man who in his own improvement is accomplishing an improvement in the condition of all mankind.

This wild attempt to divide the industrious people of this country into classes hostile to each other will fail. I do not regret this campaign. I am glad this issue has arisen. The time has come when the citizens of this country will show their capacity for self-government so that no man will again venture to challenge it. By defeating with crushing majorities the forces of disorder, they will prove that the men who have led the world in the pathway of progress will always be the vigilant guardians of liberty and order. They will not be seduced from honor by appeals to their cupidity or swerved from duty by threats of injury. They will forever jealously guard and trim the lamp of Freedom. They will ever relentlessly extinguish under their heels the red torch of Populist destruction.

When this tide of agitation shall have receded, when this Populist assault upon common honesty and upon industry shall have been repelled, the foundations of this republic

will remain undisturbed; this government will stand; still
sheltering a people indissolubly wedded to freedom and law,
sternly forbidding any distinction of burden or of privilege; conserving property, maintaining morality; resting
forever upon the broad basis of American patriotism, American virtue, and American intelligence.

PRESIDENT ROOSEVELT

IS EXCELLENCY, THEODORE ROOSEVELT, distinguished American statesman, soldier, author, President of the United States, was born at New
York, Oct. 27, 1858, and in 1880 graduated at Harvard University.
After a year of foreign travel he sat in the New York Assembly as a
Republican member, 1882–84, in which period he introduced and secured the passage
of the first State civil service bill. In 1886, he was an unsuccessful independent
candidate for the office of mayor of New York, and in 1889 was appointed by President Harrison a member of the United States Civil Service Commission, holding
office till 1895. In the latter year he became president of the board of police com-
missioners of New York, and during his two years' occupancy of that position he
introduced several greatly needed and drastic reforms. He resigned in 1897, to accept
the post of assistant secretary of the navy, but at the outbreak of the Spanish-
American War, in 1898, he resigned this position also, and, having raised a volunteer cavalry regiment, known as the "Rough Riders," he entered the army as
lieutenant-colonel, being shortly after commissioned colonel. With his regiment he
took active part in the attack on Santiago de Cuba. At the close of 1898, he was
elected Governor of New York, and in 1900 was elected Vice-president of the United
States; on the assassination of President McKinley he became President, Sept. 14,
1901. His published works embrace: "The Naval War of 1812" (1882); "Hunting
Trips of a Ranchman" (1883); "Life of Thomas Hart Benton" (1886); "Life of
Gouverneur Morris" (1888); "Ranch Life and the Hunting Trail" (1888); "Hunt-
ing] Trips on the Prairie" (1890); "The Winning of the West" (1889–95); "Essays
on Practical Politics" (1892); "The Wilderness Hunter" (1893); "American Political
Ideals" (1898); "The Rough Riders" (1899); "Oliver Cromwell" (1900); and a
"History of New York City" (1901). President Roosevelt is a man of great force
of character, of strong convictions, fearless courage, and indomitable will.

ON NATIONAL QUESTIONS

SPEECH DELIVERED AT CHICAGO, APRIL 10, 1899

IN speaking to you, men of the greatest city of the West,
men of the State which gave to the country Lincoln
and Grant, men who pre-eminently and distinctly
embody all that is most American in the American character,
I wish to preach, not the doctrine of ignoble ease, but the doctrine of the strenuous life, the life of toil and effort, of labor
and strife; to preach that highest form of success which comes,

(341)

not to the man who desires mere easy peace, but to the man who does not shrink from danger, from hardship, or from bitter toil, and who out of these wins the splendid ultimate triumph.

A life of ignoble ease, a life of that peace which springs merely from lack either of desire or of power to strive after great things, is as little worthy of a nation as of an individual. I ask only that what every self-respecting American demands from himself and from his sons shall be demanded of the American nation as a whole. Who among you would teach your boys that ease, that peace is to be the first consideration in their eyes—to be the ultimate goal after which they strive?

You men of Chicago have made this city great, you men of Illinois have done your share, and more than your share, in making America great, because you neither preach nor practice such a doctrine. You work yourselves, and you bring up your sons to work. If you are rich and are worth your salt, you will teach your sons that though they may have leisure it is not to be spent in idleness; for wisely used leisure merely means that those who possess it, being free from the necessity of working for their livelihood, are all the more bound to carry on some kind of non-remunerative work in science, in letters, in art, in exploration, in historical research—work of the type we most need in this country, the successful carrying out of which reflects most honor upon the nation.

We do not admire the man of timid peace. We admire the man who embodies victorious efforts, the man who never wrongs his neighbor, who is prompt to help a friend, but who has those virile qualities necessary to win in the stern strife of actual life. It is hard to fail, but it is worse never to have tried to succeed. In this life we get nothing save by effort.

Freedom from effort in the present merely means that

there has been stored up effort in the past. A man can be freed from the necessity of work only by the fact that he or his fathers before him have worked to good purpose. If the freedom thus purchased is used aright, and the man still does actual work, though of a different kind, whether as a writer or a general, whether in the field of politics or in the field of exploration and adventure, he shows he deserves his good fortune.

But if he treats this period of freedom from the need of actual labor as a period not of preparation, but of mere enjoyment, even though perhaps not of vicious enjoyment, he shows that he is simply a cumberer on the earth's surface; and he surely unfits himself to hold his own with his fellows, if the need to do so should again arise. A mere life of ease is not in the end a very satisfactory life, and, above all, it is a life which ultimately unfits those who follow it for serious work in the world.

As it is with the individual, so it is with the nation. It is a base untruth to say that happy is the nation that has no history. Thrice happy is the nation that has a glorious history. Far better is it to dare mighty things, to win glorious triumphs, even though checkered by failure, than to take rank with those poor spirits who neither enjoy much nor suffer much, because they live in the gray twilight that knows neither victory nor defeat. If in 1861 the men who loved the Union had believed that peace was at the end of all things, and war and strife the worst of all things, and had acted up to their belief, we would have saved hundreds of thousands of lives; we would have saved hundreds of millions of dollars. Moreover, besides saving all the blood and treasure we then lavished we would have prevented the heartbreak of many women, the dissolution of many homes, and we would have spared the country those months of gloom and shame, when it seemed as if our armies marched only to defeat.

We could have avoided all this suffering simply by shrinking from strife. And if we had thus avoided it, we would have shown that we were weaklings, and that we were unfit to stand among the great nations of the earth. Thank God, for the iron in the blood of our fathers, the men who upheld the wisdom of Lincoln and bore sword or rifle in the armies of Grant.

Let us, the children of the men who proved themselves equal to the mighty days—let us, the children of the men who carried the great Civil War to a triumphant conclusion, praise the God of our fathers that the ignoble counsels of peace were rejected; that the suffering and loss, the blackness of sorrow and despair, were unflinchingly faced, and the years of strife endured, for in the end the slave was freed, the Union restored, and the mighty American Republic placed once more as a helmeted queen among nations.

We of this generation do not have to face a task such as that our fathers faced, but we have our tasks, and woe to us if we fail to perform them! We cannot, if we could, play the part of China, and be content to rot by inches in ignoble ease within our borders, taking no interest in what goes on beyond them; sunk in a scrambling commercialism, heedless of the higher life, the life of aspiration, of toil and risk; busying ourselves only with the wants of our bodies for the day, until suddenly we find beyond a shadow of question what China has already found, that in this world the nation that has trained itself to a career of unwarlike and isolated ease is bound in the end to go down before other nations which have not lost the manly and adventurous qualities. If we are to be a really great people, we must strive in good faith to play a great part in the world. We cannot avoid meeting great issues. All that we can determine for ourselves is, whether we shall meet them well or ill. Last year we could not help being brought face to face with the problem of war with Spain. All we could decide was whether we should shrink like cowards from the contest or enter into it as beseemed a brave and high-spirited people, and, once in, whether failure or success should crown our banners.

No country can long endure if its foundations are not laid deep in the material prosperity which comes from thrift, from business energy and enterprise, from hard, unsparing effort in the fields of industrial activity, but neither was any nation ever yet truly great if it relied upon material prosperity alone. All honor must be paid to the architects of our material prosperity; to the great captains of industry who have built our factories and our railroads; to the strong men who toil for wealth with brain or hand, for great is the debt of the nation to these and their kind. But our debt is yet greater to the men whose highest type is to be found in a statesman like Lincoln, a soldier like Grant. They showed by their lives that they recognized the law of work, the law of strife; they toiled to win a competence for themselves and those dependent upon them, but they recognized that there were yet other and even loftier duties—duties to the nation and duties to the race.

We cannot sit huddled within our borders and avow ourselves merely an assemblage of well-to-do hucksters, who care nothing for what happens beyond. Such a policy would defeat even its own end; for as the nations grow to have ever wider and wider interests, and are brought into closer and closer contact, if we are to hold our own in the struggle for naval and commercial supremacy, we must build up our power without our own borders. We must build the Isthmian canal, and we must grasp the points of vantage which will enable us to have our say in deciding the destiny of the oceans of the East and West.

So much for the commercial side. From the standpoint of international honor, the argument is even stronger. The guns that thundered off Manila and Santiago left us echoes of glory, but they also left us a legacy of duty. If we drove out a mediæval tyranny only to make room for savage anarchy, we had better not have begun the task at all. It is worse than idle to say that we have no duty to perform and can leave to their fates the islands we have conquered. Such a course would be the course of infamy. It would be followed at once by utter chaos in the wretched islands themselves. Some stronger, manlier Power would have to step in and do the work, and we would have shown ourselves weaklings, unable to carry to successful completion the labors that great and high-spirited nations are eager to undertake.

The work must be done. We cannot escape our responsibility; and if we are worth our salt, we shall be glad of the chance to do the work—glad of the chance to show ourselves equal to one of the great tasks set to modern civilization. But let us not deceive ourselves as to the importance of the task. Let us not be misled by vainglory into underestimating the strain it will put on our powers. Above all, let us, as we value our own self-respect, face the responsibilities with proper seriousness, courage, and high resolve. We must demand the highest order of integrity and ability in our public men who are to grapple with these new problems. We must hold to a rigid accountability those public servants who show unfaithfulness to the interests of the nation or inability to rise to the high level of the new demands upon our strength and our resources. Of course, we must remember not to judge any public servant by any one act, and especially should we beware of attacking the men who are merely the occasions and not the causes of disaster.

Let me illustrate what I mean by the army and the navy. If twenty years ago we had gone to war, we should have found the navy as absolutely unprepared as the army.

In the early '80's the attention of the nation became directed to our naval needs. Congress most wisely made a series of appropriations to build up a new navy, and under a succession of able and patriotic Secretaries, of both political parties, the navy was gradually built up, until its material became equal to its splendid personnel, with the result that last summer it leaped to its proper place as one of the most brilliant and formidable fighting navies in the entire world.

We rightly pay all honor to the men controlling the navy at the time, honor to Secretary Long and Admiral Dewey, to the captains who handled the ships in action, to the daring lieutenants who braved death in the smaller craft, and to the heads of bureaus at Washington, who saw that the ships were so commanded, so armed, so equipped, so well engined as to ensure the best results. But let us also keep ever in mind that all of this would not have availed if it had not been for the wisdom of the men who during the preceding fifteen years had built up the navy.

Keep in mind the Secretaries of the Navy during these years; keep in mind the Senators and Congressmen who by their votes gave the money necessary to build and armor the ships, to construct the great guns and to train the crews; remember also those who actually did build the ships, the armor, and the guns, and remember the admirals and captains who handled battle-ship, cruiser, and torpedo-boat on the high seas, alone and in squadrons, developing the seamanship, the gunnery and the power of acting together, which their successors utilized so gloriously at Manila and off Santiago.

And, gentlemen, remember the converse, too. Remember that justice has two sides. Be just to those who built up the navy, and for the sake of the future of the country keep in mind those who opposed its building up. Read " The Congressional Record."

Find out the Senators and Congressmen who opposed the grants for building the new ships, who opposed the purchase of armor, without which the ships were worthless; who opposed any adequate maintenance for the Navy Department, and strove to cut down the number of men necessary to man our fleets. The men who did these things were one and all working to bring disaster on the country.

They have no share in the glory of Manila, in the honor of Santiago. They have no cause to feel proud of the valor of our sea captains, of the renown of our flag. Their motives may or may not have been good, but their acts were heavily fraught with evil. They did ill for the national honor, and we won in spite of their sinister opposition.

Now, apply all this to our public men of to-day. Our army has never been built up as it should be built up. I shall not discuss with an audience like this the puerile suggestion that a nation of 70,000,000 of freemen is in danger of losing its liberties from the existence of an army of 100,000 men, three fourths of whom will be employed in certain foreign islands, in certain coast fortresses, and on Indian reservations. No man of good sense and stout heart can take such a proposition seriously. If we are such weaklings as the proposition implies, then we are unworthy of freedom in any event. To no body of men in the United States is the country so much indebted as to the splendid officers and enlisted men of the regular army and navy; there is no body from which the country has less to fear, and none of which it should be prouder, none of which it should be more anxious to upbuild.

Our army needs complete reorganization—not merely enlarging—and the reorganization can only come as the result of legislation. A proper general staff should be established, and the positions of ordnance, commissary, and quartermaster officers should be filled by detail from the line. Above all, the army must be given the chance to exercise in large bodies.

Never again should we see, as we saw in the Spanish war, major-generals in command of divisions who had never before commanded three companies together in the field.

Yet, incredible to relate, the recent Congress has showed a queer inability to learn some of the lessons of the war. There were large bodies of men in both branches who opposed the declaration of war, who opposed the ratification of peace, who opposed the upbuilding of the army, and who even opposed the purchase of armor at reasonable price for the battle-ships and cruisers, thereby putting an absolute stop to the building of any new fighting ships for the navy.

If, during the years to come, any disaster should befall our arms, afloat or ashore, and thereby any shame come to the United States, remember that the blame will lie upon the men whose names appear upon the roll-calls of Congress on the wrong side of these great questions. On them will lie the burden of any loss of our soldiers and sailors, of any dishonor to the flag; and upon you and the people of this country will lie the blame if you do not repudiate in no unmistakable way what these men have done.

The blame will not rest upon the untrained commander of untried troops; upon the civil officers of a department the organization of which has been left utterly inadequate; or upon the admiral with an insufficient number of ships; but upon the public men who have so lamentably failed in forethought as to refuse to remedy these evils long in advance, and upon the nation that stands behind those public men.

So at the present hour no small share of the responsibility for the bloodshed in the Philippines, the blood of our brothers and the blood of their wild and ignorant foes, lies at the thresholds of those who so long delayed the adoption of the treaty of peace, and of those who by their worse than foolish words deliberately invited a savage people to plunge into a war fraught with sure disaster for them; a war, too, in which our brave men who follow the flag must pay with their blood for the silly, mock-humanitarianism of the prattlers who sit at home in peace.

The army and the navy are the sword and the shield which this nation must carry if she is to do her duty among the nations of the earth—if she is not to stand merely as the China of the Western hemisphere. Our proper conduct toward the tropic islands we have wrested from Spain is merely the form which our duty has taken at the moment. Of course, we are bound to handle the affairs of our own household well. We must see that there is civic honesty, civic cleanliness, civic good sense in our home administration of city, state, and nation. We must strive for honesty in office, for honesty toward the creditors of the nation and of the individual. But because we set our own household in order, we are not thereby excused from doing our duty to the State.

In the West Indies and the Philippines alike we are confronted by most difficult problems. It is cowardly to shrink from solving them in the proper way; for solved they must be, if not by us, then by some stronger and more manful race; if we are too weak, too selfish, or too foolish to solve them, some bolder and abler people must undertake the solution. Personally I am far too firm a believer in the greatness of my country and the power of my countrymen to admit for one moment that we shall ever be driven to the ignoble alternatives.

The problems are different for the different islands. Porto Rico is not large enough to stand alone. We must govern it wisely and well, primarily in the interest of its own people. Cuba is, in my judgment, entitled ultimately to settle for itself whether it shall be an independent State or an integral portion of the mightiest of Republics. But until order and stable liberty are secured, we must remain in the island to ensure them; and infinite tact, judgment, moderation, and courage must be shown by our military and civil representatives in keeping the island pacified, in relentlessly stamping out brigandage, in protecting all alike, and yet in showing proper recognition to the men who fought for Cuban liberty.

The Philippines offer a yet graver problem. Their population includes half-caste and native Christians, warlike Moslems and wild Pagans. Many of their people are utterly unfit for self-government and show no signs of becoming fit. Others may in time become fit, but at present can only take part in self-government under a wise supervision at once firm and beneficent. We have driven Spanish tyranny from the islands. If we now let it be replaced by savage anarchy, our work has been for harm and not for good.

I have scant·patience with those who fear to undertake the task of governing the Philippines, and who openly avow that they do fear to undertake it, or that they shrink from it because of the expense and trouble; but I have even scantier patience with those who make a pretence of humanitarianism to hide and cover their timidity, and who cant about "liberty" and the "consent of the governed" in order to excuse themselves for their unwillingness to play the part of men. Their doctrines, if carried out, would make it incumbent upon us to leave the Apaches of Arizona to work out their own salvation and to decline to interfere in a single Indian reservation. Their doctrines condemn your forefathers and mine for ever having settled in these United States.

England's rule in India and Egypt has been of great benefit to England, for it has trained up generations of men accustomed to look at the larger and loftier side of public life. It has been of even greater benefit to India and Egypt. And finally and most of all, it has advanced the cause of civilization. So, if we do our duty aright in the Philippines, we will add to that national renown which is the highest and finest part of national life; will greatly benefit the people of the Philippine Islands, and above all, we will play our part well in the great work of uplifting mankind.

But to do this work, keep ever in mind that we must show in a very high degree the qualities of courage, of honesty, and of good judgment. Resistance must be stamped out. The first and all-important work to be done is to establish the supremacy of our flag. We must put down armed resistance before we can accomplish anything else, and there should be no parleying, no faltering in dealing with our foe. As for those in our own country who encourage the foe, we can afford contemptuously to disregard them; but it must be remembered that their utterances are saved from being treasonable merely from the fact that they are despicable.

When once we have put down armed resistance, when once our rule is acknowledged, then an even more difficult task will begin; for then we must see to it that the islands are administered with absolute honesty and with good judgment. If we let the public service of the islands be turned into the prey of the spoils politician, we shall have begun to tread the path which Spain trod to her own destruction. We must send out there only good and able men, chosen for their fitness and not because of their partisan service, and these men must not only administer impartially justice to the natives and serve their own government with honesty and fidelity, but must show the utmost tact and firmness, remembering that with such people as those with whom we are to deal, weakness is the greatest of crimes, and that next to weakness comes lack of consideration for their principles and prejudices.

I preach to you, then, my countrymen, that our country calls not for the life of ease, but for the life of strenuous endeavor. The twentieth century looms before us big with the fate of many nations. If we stand idly by, if we seek merely swollen, slothful ease and ignoble peace, if we shrink from the hard contests where men must win at hazard of their lives, and at the risk of all they hold dear, then the bolder and stronger peoples will pass us by and will win for themselves the domination of the world.

Let us therefore boldly face the life of strife, resolute to do our duty well and manfully; resolute to uphold righteousness by deed and by word, resolute to be both honest and brave, to serve high ideals, yet to use practical methods.

Above all, let us shrink from no strife, moral or physical, within or without the nation, provided we are certain that the strife is justified; for it is only through strife, through hard and dangerous endeavor, that we shall ultimately win the goal of true national greatness.

SPEECH SECONDING THE NOMINATION OF McKINLEY

DELIVERED AT PHILADELPHIA, JUNE 21, 1900

MR. CHAIRMAN,—I rise to second the nomination of William McKinley, the President who has had to meet and solve problems more numerous and more important than any other President since the days of mighty Abraham Lincoln; the President under whose administration this country has attained a higher pitch of prosperity at home and honor abroad than ever before in its history. Four years ago the Republican party nominated William McKinley as its standard bearer in a political conflict of graver moment to the nation than any that had taken place since the close of the Civil War saw us once more a reunited country. The Republican party nominated him, but before the campaign was many days old he had become the candidate not only of all Republicans but of all Americans who were both far sighted enough to see where the true interests of the country lay and clear minded enough to be keenly sensitive to the taint of dishonor. President McKinley was triumphantly elected on certain distinct pledges, and those pledges have been made more than good. We were then in a condition of industrial paralysis. The capitalist was plunged in ruin and disaster; the wage-worker was on the edge of actual want;

the success of our opponents would have meant not only immense aggravation of the actual physical distress, but also a stain on the nation's honor so deep that more than one generation would have to pass before it would be effectually wiped out. We promised that if President McKinley were elected not only should the national honor be kept unstained at home and abroad, but that the mill and the workshop should open, the farmer have a market for his goods, the merchant for his wares, and that the wage-workers should prosper as never before.

We did not promise the impossible; we did not say that, by good legislation and good administration, there would come prosperity to all men. But we did say that each man should have a better chance to win prosperity than he had ever yet had. In the long run the thrift, industry, energy, and capacity of the individual must always remain the chief factors in his success. By unwise or dishonest legislation or administration on the part of the national authorities all these qualities in the individual can be nullified, but wise legislation and upright administration will give them free scope. And it was this free scope that we promised should be given.

Well, we kept our word. The opportunity has been given, and it has been seized by American energy, thrift, and business enterprise. As a result we have prospered as never before, and we are now prospering to a degree that would have seemed incredible four years ago, when the cloud of menace to our industrial wellbeing hung black above the land.

So it has been in foreign affairs. Four years ago the nation was uneasy because right at our doors an American island lay writhing in awful agony under the curse of worse than mediæval tyranny and misrule. We had our Armenia at our very doors, for the situation in Cuba had grown intolerable, and such that this nation could no longer refrain from interference and retain its own self-respect. President McKinley turned to this duty as he had turned to others. He sought by every effort possible to provide for Spain's withdrawal from the island which she was impotent longer to do aught than oppress. Then, when pacific means had failed and there remained the only alternative, we waged the most righteous and brilliantly successful foreign war that any country has waged during the lifetime of the present generation. It was not a great war, simply because it was won too quickly, but it was momentous indeed in its effects. It left us, as all great feats must leave those who perform them, an inheritance both of honor and of responsibility, and under the lead of President McKinley the nation has taken up the task of securing orderly liberty and the reign of justice and law in the islands from which we drove the tyranny of Spain, with the same serious realization of duty and sincere purpose to perform it that have marked the national attitude in dealing with the economic and financial difficulties that face us at home.

This is what the nation has done in the three years that have elapsed since we made McKinley President, and all this is what he typifies and stands for. We here nominate him again, and in November next we shall elect him again, because it has been given to him to personify the cause of honor abroad and prosperity at home; of wise legislation and straightforward administration. We all know the old adage about swapping horses while crossing a stream, and the still older adage about letting well enough alone. To change from President McKinley now would not be merely to swap horses, it would be to jump off the horse that had carried us

across and wade back into the torrent; and to put him for
four years more into the White House means not merely to
let well enough alone, but to insist that when we are thriving
as never before we shall not be plunged back into the abyss
of shame and panic and disaster.

We have done so well that our opponents actually use this
very fact as an appeal for turning us out. We have put the
tariff on a foundation so secure, we have passed such wise
laws on finance that they actually appeal to the patriotic,
honest men who deserted them at the last election to help
them now because, forsooth, we have done so well that nobody need fear their capacity to undo our work. I am not
exaggerating. This is literally the argument that is now
addressed to the Gold Democrats as a reason why they need
no longer stand by the Republican party. To all such who
may be inclined to listen to these arguments I would address
an emphatic word of warning.

Remember that, admirable though our legislation has been
during the last three years, it has been rendered possible and
effective only because there was good administration to back
it. Wise laws are invaluable, but, after all, they are not as
necessary as wise and honest administration of the laws. The
best law ever made, if administered by those who are
hostile to it and who mean to break it down, cannot be wholly
effective, and may be wholly ineffective. We have at last
put our financial legislation on a sound basis, but no possible
financial legislation can save us from fearful and disastrous
panic if we trust our finances to the management of any man
who would be acceptable to the leaders and guides of the
Democracy in its present spirit. No Secretary of the
Treasury who would be acceptable to or who could without
loss of self-respect serve under the Populistic Democracy

could avoid plunging this country back into financial chaos.
Until our opponents have explicitly and absolutely repudiated the principles which in 1896 they professed and the
leaders who embody these principles, their success means the
undoing of the country. Nor have they any longer even
the excuse of being honest in their folly. They have raved,
they have foamed at the mouth, in denunciation of trusts, and
now, in my own State, their foremost party leaders, including
the man before whom the others bow with bared head and
trembling knee, have been discovered in a trust which really
is of infamous and perhaps of criminal character; a trust in
which these apostles of Democracy, these prophets of the
new dispensation, have sought to wring fortunes from the
dire need of their poorer brethren.

I rise to second the nomination of William McKinley because with him as leader this country has trod the path of
national greatness and prosperity with the strides of a giant,
and because, under him, we can and will once more and
finally overthrow those whose success would mean for the
nation material disaster and moral disgrace. Exactly as we
have remedied the evils which in the past we undertook to
remedy, so now, when we say that a wrong shall be righted
it most assuredly will be righted.

We have nearly succeeded in bringing peace and order
to the Philippines. We have sent thither and to the other
islands toward whose inhabitants we now stand as trustees
in the cause of good government men like Wood, Taft, and
Allen, whose very names are synonyms of integrity and
guarantees of efficiency. Appointees like these, chosen on
grounds of merit and fitness alone, are evidence of the spirit
and methods in and by which this nation must approach its
new and serious duties. Contrast this with what would be

the fate of the islands under the spoils system so brazenly advocated by our opponents in their last national platform.

The war still goes on because the allies in this country of the bloody insurrectionary oligarchy have taught their foolish dupes abroad to believe that if the rebellion is kept alive until next November Democratic success at the polls here will be followed by the abandonment of the islands— that means their abandonment to savages who would scramble for what we desert until some powerful civilized nation stepped in to do what we would have shown ourselves unfit to perform. Our success in November means peace in the islands. The success of our political opponents means an indefinite prolongation of misery and bloodshed.

We of this Convention now renominate the man whose name is a guarantee against such disaster. When we place William McKinley as our candidate before the people we place the Republican party on record as standing for the performance which squares with promise, as standing for the redemption in administration and legislation of the pledges made in the platform and on the stump, as standing for the upbuilding of the national honor and interest abroad and the continuance at home of the prosperity which it has already brought to the farm and the workshop.

We stand on the threshold of a new century, a century big with the fate of the great nations of the earth. It rests with us now to decide whether in the opening years of that century we shall march forward to fresh triumphs, or whether at the outset we shall deliberately cripple ourselves for the contest.

Is America a weakling, to shrink from the world work that must be done by the world Powers?

No. The young giant of the West stands on a continent,

and clasps the crest of an ocean in either hand. Our nation, glorious in youth and strength, looks into the future with fearless and eager eyes and rejoices as a strong man to run a race. We do not stand in craven mood, asking to be spared the task, cringing as we gaze on the contest.

No, we challenge the proud privilege of doing the work that Providence allots us, and we face the coming years high of heart and resolute of faith that to our people is given the right to win such honor and renown as has never yet been granted to the peoples of mankind.

A NATION OF PIONEERS

LAST ADDRESS DELIVERED IN HIS CAPACITY AS VICE-PRESIDENT, AT STATE FAIR AT MINNEAPOLIS, SEPTEMBER 2, 1901

IN his admirable series of studies of twentieth century problems Dr. Lyman Abbott has pointed out that we are a nation of pioneers; that the first colonists to our shores were pioneers, and that pioneers selected out from among the descendants of these early pioneers, mingled with others selected afresh from the old world, pushed westward into the wilderness and laid the foundations for new commonwealths. They were men of hope and expectation, of enterprise and energy; for the men of dull content or more dull despair had no part in the great movement into and across the new world. Our country has been populated by pioneers; and, therefore, it has in it more energy, more enterprise, more expansive power than any other in the wide world.

You whom I am now addressing stand for the most part but one generation removed from these pioneers. You are typical Americans, for you have done the great, the characteristic, the typical work of our American life. In making homes and carving out careers for yourselves and your children, you have built up this state; throughout our history the success of the homemaker has been but another name for the upbuilding of the nation. The men who, with axe in the forest and pick in the mountains and plow on the prairies, pushed to completion the dominion of our people over the American wilderness have given the definite shape to our nation. They have shown the qualities of daring, endurance and far-sightedness, of eager desire for victory and stubborn refusal to accept defeat, which go to make up the essential manliness of the American character. Above all they have recognized in practical form the fundamental law of success in American life — the law of worthy work, the law of high, resolute endeavor.

We have but little room among our people for the timid, the irresolute and the idle; and it is no less true that there is scant room in the world at large for the nation with mighty thews that dares not to be great.

Surely in speaking to the sons of men who actually did the rough and hard, and infinitely glorious work of making the great northwest what it now is, I need hardly insist upon the righteousness of this doctrine. In your own vigorous lives you show by every act how scant is your patience with those who do not see in the life of effort the life supremely worth living. Sometimes we hear those who do not work spoken of with envy. Surely the willfully idle need arouse in the breast of a healthy man no emotion stronger that that of contempt — at the outside no emotion stronger than angry contempt. The feeling of envy would have in it an admission of inferiority on our part, to which the men who know not the sterner joys of life are not entitled.

Poverty is a bitter thing, but it is not as bitter as the existence of restless vacuity and physical, moral and intellectual flabbiness to which those doom themselves who elect to spend all their years in that vainest of all pursuits, the pursuit of mere pleasure as a sufficient end in itself.

The willfully idle man, like the willfully barren woman, has no place in a sane, healthy and vigorous community. Moreover, the gross and hideous selfishness for which it stands defeats even its own miserable aims.

Exactly as infinitely the happiest woman is she who has borne and brought up many healthy children, so infinitely the happiest man is he who has toiled hard and successfully in his life work. The work may be done in a thousand different ways; with the brain or the hands, in the study, the field or the workshop; if it is honest work, honestly done and well worth doing, that is all we have a right to ask. Every father and mother here, if they are wise, will bring up their children not to shirk difficulties, but to meet and overcome them; not to strive after a life of ignoble ease, but to strive to do their duty, first to themselves and their families, and then to the whole state; and this duty must inevitably take the shape of work in some form or other. You, the sons of pioneers, if you are true to your ancestry, must make your lives as worthy as they made theirs. They sought for true success, and, therefore, they did not seek ease. They knew that success comes only to those who lead the life of endeavor.

It seems to me that the simple acceptance of this fundamental fact of American life, this acknowledgment that the law of work is the fundamental law of our being, will help us to start aright in facing not a few of the problems that confront us from without and from within. As regards internal affairs, it should teach us the prime need of remembering that after all has been said and done, the chief factor in any man's success or failure must be his own character; that is, the sum of his common sense, his courage, his virile energy and capacity. Nothing can take the place of this individual factor.

I do not for a moment mean that much cannot be done to supplement it. Besides each one of us working individually, all of us have got to work together. We cannot possibly do our best work as a nation unless all of us know how to act in combination as well as how to act each individually for himself. The acting in combination can take many forms; but, of course, its most effective form must be when it comes in the shape of law; that is, of action by the community as a whole through the law-making body.

But it is not possible ever to insure prosperity merely by law. Something for good can be done by law, and bad laws can do an infinity of mischief; but, after all, the best law can only prevent wrong and injustice and give to the thrifty, the far-seeing and the hard-working a chance to exercise to the best advantage their special and peculiar abilities. No hard and fast rule can be laid down as to where our legislation shall stop in interfering between man and man, between interest and interest.

All that can be said is that it is highly undesirable on the one hand to weaken individual initiative, and, on the other hand, that, in a constantly increasing number of cases, we shall find it necessary in the future to shackle cunning as in the past we have shackled force.

It is not only highly desirable, but necessary, that there

should be legislation which shall carefully shield the interests of wageworkers, and which shall discriminate in favor of the honest and humane employer by removing the disadvantage under which he stands when compared with unscrupulous competitors who have no conscience, and will do right only under fear of punishment. Nor can legislation stop only with what are termed labor questions. The vast individual and corporate fortunes, the vast combinations of capital, which have marked the development of our industrial system, create new conditions and necessitate a change from the old attitude of the state and nation toward property. It is probably true that the large majority of the fortunes that now exist in this country have been amassed, not by injuring our people, but as an incident to the conferring of great benefits upon the community; and this, no matter what may have been the conscious purpose of those amassing them. There is but the scantiest justification for most of the outcry against the men of wealth as such; and it ought to be unnecessary to state that any appeal which directly or indirectly leads to suspicion and hatred among ourselves, which tends to limit opportunity, and, therefore, to shut the door of success against poor men of talent, and, finally, which entails the possibility of lawlessness and violence, is an attack upon the fundamental properties of American citizenship.

Our interests are at bottom common; in the long run we go up or go down together. Yet more and more it is evident that the state, and, if necessary, the nation has got to possess the right of supervision and control as regards the great corporations which are its creatures; particularly as regards the great business combinations which derive a portion of their importance from the existence of some monopolistic tendency. The right should be exercised with caution and self-restraint; but it should exist, so that it may be invoked if the need arises.

So much for our duties, each to himself and each to his neighbor, within the limits of our own country. But our country, as it strides forward with ever-increasing rapidity to a foremost place among the world powers, must necessarily find, more and more, that it has world duties also.

There are excellent people who believe that we can shirk these duties and yet retain our self-respect; but these good people are in error. Other good people seek to deter us from treading the path of hard but lofty duty by bidding us remember that all nations that have achieved greatness, that have expanded and played their part as world powers, have in the end passed away. So they have; so have all others. The weak and the stationary have vanished as surely as, and more rapidly than, those whose citizens felt within them the lift that impels generous souls to great and noble effort.

This is another way of stating the universal law of death, which is itself part of the universal law of life. The man who works, the man who does great deeds, in the end dies as surely as the veriest idler who cumbers the earth's surface; but he leaves behind him the great fact that he has done his work well. So it is with nations. While the nation that has dared to be great, that has had the will and the power to change the destiny of the ages, in the end must die. Yet no less surely the nation that has played the part of the weakling must also die; and, whereas, the nation that has done nothing leaves nothing behind it, the nation that has done a great work really continues, though in changed form, forevermore. The Roman has passed away, exactly as all nations of antiquity which did not expand when he expanded have passed away; but their very memory has vanished, while he himself is still a living force throughout the wide world in our entire civilization of today, and will so continue through countless generations, through untold ages.

It is because we believe with all our heart and soul in the greatness of this country, because we feel the thrill of hardy life in our veins, and are confident that to us is given the privilege of playing a leading part in the century that has just opened, that we hail with eager delight the opportunity to do whatever task Providence may allot us. We admit with all sincerity that our first duty is within our own household; that we must not merely talk, but act, in favor of cleanliness and decency and righteousness, in all political, social and civic matters. No prosperity and no glory can save a nation that is rotten at heart. We must ever keep the core of our national being sound, and see to it that not only our citizens in private life; but above all, our statesmen in public life, practice the old commonplace virtues which from time immemorial have lain at the root of all true national well-being. Yet while this is our first duty, it is not our whole duty. Exactly as each man, while doing first his duty to his wife and the children within his home, must yet, if he hopes to amount to much, strive mightily in the world outside his home; so our nation, while first of all seeing to its own domestic well-being, must not shrink from playing its part among the great nations without.

Our duty may take many forms in the future as it has taken many forms in the past. Nor is it possible to lay down a hard and fast rule for all cases. We must ever face the fact of our shifting national needs, of the always-changing opportunities that present themselves. But we may be certain of one thing; whether we wish it or not, we cannot avoid hereafter having duties to do in the face of other nations. All that we can do is to settle whether we shall perform these duties well or ill.

Right here let me make as vigorous a plea as I know how in favor of saying nothing that we do not mean, and of acting without hesitation up to whatever we say. A good many of you are probably acquainted with the old proverb: " Speak softly and carry a big stick — you will go far." If a man continually blusters, if he lacks civility, a big stick will not save him from trouble; and neither will speaking softly avail, if back of the softness there does not lie strength, power. In private life there are few beings more obnoxious than the man who is always loudly boasting, and if the boaster is not prepared to back up his words, his position becomes absolutely contemptible. So it is with the nation. It is both foolish and undignified to indulge in undue self-glorification, and above all, in loose-tongued denunciation of other peoples. Whenever on any point we come in contact with a foreign power, I hope that we shall always strive to speak courteously and respectfully of that foreign power.

Let us make it evident that we intend to do justice. Then let us make it equally evident that we will not tolerate injustice being done us in return.

Let us further make it evident that we use no words which we are not prepared to back up with deeds, and that while our speech is always moderate, we are ready and willing to make it good. Such an attitude will be the surest possible guarantee of that self-respecting peace, the attainment of which is and must ever be the prime aim of a self-governing people.

This is the attitude we should take as regards the Monroe doctrine. There is not the least need of blustering about it. Still less should it be used as a pretext for our own aggrandizement at the expense of any other American state. But, most emphatically, we must make it evident that we intend on this point ever to maintain the old American position. Indeed, it is hard to understand how any man can take any other position now that we are all looking forward to the building of the Isthmian canal. The Monroe doctrine is not international law, but there is no necessity that it should be. All that is needful is that it should continue to be a cardinal feature of American policy on this continent; and the Spanish-American states should, in their own interests, champion it as strongly as we do. We do not by this doctrine intend to sanction any policy of agression by one American commonwealth at the expense of any other, nor any policy of commercial discrimination against any foreign power whatsoever. Commercially, as far as this doctrine is concerned, all we wish is a fair field and no favor; but if we are wise we shall strenuously insist that under no pretext whatsoever shall there be any territorial aggrandizement on American soil by any European power, and this, no matter what form the territorial aggrandizement may take.

We most earnestly hope and believe that the chance of our having any hostile military complication with any foreign power is very small. But that there will come a strain, a jar, here and there, from commercial and agricultural — that is, from industrial — competition, is almost inevitable. Here again we have got to remember that our first duty is to our own people; and yet that we can best get justice by doing justice. We must continue the policy that has been so brilliantly successful in the past, and so shape our economic system as to give every advantage to the skill, energy and intelligence of our farmers, merchants, manufacturers and wageworkers; and yet we must also remember, in dealing with other nations that benefits must be given when benefits are sought. It is not possible to dogmatize as to the exact way of attaining this end; for the exact conditions cannot be foretold. In the long run one of our prime needs is stability and continuity of economic policy; and yet, through treaty or by direct legislation, it may at least in certain cases become advantageous to supplement our present policy by a system of reciprocal benefit and obligation.

Throughout a large part of our national career our history has been one of expansion, the expansion being of different kinds at different times. This explanation is not a matter of regret, but of pride. It is vain to tell a people as masterful as ours that the spirit of enterprise is not safe.

The true American has never feared to run risks when the prize to be won was of sufficient value. No nation capable of self-government and of developing by its own efforts a sane and orderly civilization, no matter how small it may be, has anything to fear from us.

Our dealings with Cuba illustrate this, and should be forever a subject of just national pride. We speak in no spirit of arrogance when we state as a simple historic fact that never in recent years has any great nation acted with such disinterestedness as we have shown in Cuba. We freed the island from the Spanish yoke. We then earnestly did our best to help the Cubans in the establishment of free education, of law and order, of material prosperity, of the cleanliness necessary to sanitary well-being in their great cities. We did all this at great expense of treasure, at some expense of life; and now we are establishing them in a free and independent commonwealth, and have asked in return nothing whatever save that at no time shall their independence be prostituted to the advantage of some foreign rival of ours, or so as to menace our well-being. To have failed to ask this would have amounted to national stultification on our part.

In the Philippines we have brought peace, and we are at this moment giving them such freedom and self-government as they could never under any conceivable conditions have obtained had we turned them loose to sink into a welter of blood and confusion, or to become the prey of some strong tyranny without or within. The bare recital of the facts is sufficient to show that we did our duty; and what prouder title to honor can a nation have than to have done its duty? We have done our duty to ourselves, and we have done the higher duty of promoting the civilization of mankind. The first essential of civilization is law. Anarchy is simply the hand-maiden and forerunner of tyranny and despotism. Law and order enforced by justice and by strength lie at the foundation of civilization. Law must be based upon justice, else it cannot stand, and it must be enforced with resolute firmness, because weakness in enforcing it means in the end that there is no justice and no law, nothing but the rule of disorderly and unscrupulous strength. Without the habit of orderly obedience to the law, without the stern enforcement of the laws at the expense of those who defiantly resist them, there can be no possible progress, moral or ma-

terial, in civilization. There can be no weakening of the
law-abiding spirit at home if we are permanently to succeed; and just as little can we afford to show weakness
abroad. Lawlessness and anarchy were put down in the
Philippines as a prerequisite to inducing the reign of justice.

Barbarism has and can have no place in a civilized world.
It is our duty toward the people living in barbarism to see
that they are freed from their chains, and we can only free
them by destroying barbarism itself. The missionary, the
merchant and the soldier may each have to play a part in
this destruction, and in the consequent uplifting of the
people. Exactly as it is the duty of a civilized power
scrupulously to respect the rights of all weaker civilized
powers and gladly to help those who are struggling towards
civilization, so it is its duty to put down savagery and
barbarism. As in such a work human instruments must be
used, and as human instruments are imperfect, this means
that at times there will be injustice; that at times merchant,
or soldier, or even missionary may do wrong. Let us instantly condemn and rectify such wrong when it occurs,
and if possible punish the wrongdoer. But, shame, thrice
shame to us, if we are so foolish as to make such occasional
wrongdoing an excuse for failing to perform a great and
righteous task. Not only in our own land, but throughout
the world, throughout all history, the advance of civilization
has been of incalculable benefit to mankind, and those
through whom it has advanced deserve the highest honor.
All honor to the missionary, all honor to the soldier, all
honor to the merchant who now in our day have done so
much to bring light into the world's dark places.

Let me insist again, for fear of possible misconstruction,
upon the fact that our duty is twofold, and that we must

raise others while we are benefiting ourselves. In bringing order to the Philippines, our soldiers added a new page to the honor-roll of American history, and they incalculably benefited the islanders themselves. Under the wise administration of Governor Taft the islands now enjoy a peace and liberty of which they have hitherto never even dreamed. But this peace and liberty under the law must be supplemented by material, by industrial development. Every encouragement should be given to their commercial development, to the introduction of American industries and products; not merely because this will be a good thing for our people, but infinitely more because it will be of incalculable benefit to the people of the Philippines.

We shall make mistakes; and if we let these mistakes frighten us from work, we shall show ourselves weaklings. Half a century ago Minnesota and the two Dakotas were Indian hunting grounds. We committed plenty of blunders, and now and then worse than blunders, in our dealings with the Indians. But who does not admit at the present day that we were right in wresting from barbarism and adding to civilization the territory out of which we have made these beautiful states? And now we are civilizing the Indian and putting him on a level to which he could never have attained under the old conditions.

In the Philippines let us remember that the spirit and not the mere form of government is the essential matter. The Tagalogs have a hundredfold the freedom under us that they would have if we had abandoned the lands.

We are not trying to subjugate a people; we are trying to develop them, and make them a law-abiding, industrious and educated people, and we hope, ultimately, a self-governing people. In short, in the work we have done, we are but carrying out the true principles of our democracy. We work in a spirit of self-respect for ourselves and of goodwill toward others; in a spirit of love for and of infinite faith in mankind. We do not blindly refuse to face the evils that exist; or the shortcomings inherent in humanity; but across blundering and shirking, across selfishness and meanness of motive, across short-sightedness and cowardice, we gaze steadfastly toward the far horizon of golden triumph.

If you will study our past history as a nation you will see we have made many blunders and have been guilty of many shortcomings, and yet that we have always in the end come out victorious because we have refused to be daunted by blunders and defeats — have recognized them, but have persevered in spite of them. So it must be in the future. We gird up our loins as a nation, with the stern purpose to play our part manfully in winning the ultimate triumph, and, therefore, we turn scornfully aside from the paths of mere ease and idleness, and with unfaltering steps tread the rough road of endeavor, smiting down the wrong and battling for the right as Greatheart smote and battled in Bunyan's immortal story.

JONATHAN P. DOLLIVER

ONATHAN PRENTISS DOLLIVER, American Republican congressman and lawyer, was born near Kingwood Preston Co., Va., Feb. 6, 1858. In 1875, he graduated from the West Virginia University and was admitted to the Bar in 1878. He was elected to the fifty-first Congress as a Republican representative from the tenth congressional district of Iowa, and was also a member of the House in the 52d, 53d, 54th, and 56th Congresses. In July, 1900, he was appointed to succeed the late Hon. J. H. Gear, in the United States Senate, and took his seat in that body Dec. 3, 1900. His home is at Fort Dodge, Ia.

ON PORTO RICO AND THE PHILIPPINES

SPEECH DELIVERED IN THE HOUSE OF REPRESENTATIVES, FEBRUARY 27, 1900

THIS bill, which is a temporary measure—and I will advise the House will be so declared in an amendment to be offered by the committee—aims simply to provide a revenue for the island of Puerto Rico. Yet it has been magnified by this debate in a strange way to include the whole problem of our government of the possessions that have come to us under the treaty of Paris as a result of the war with Spain.

The President of the United States in his annual message recommended that Congress should abolish all customs tariffs between Puerto Rico and the United States, and should admit their products to our markets without duty. The argument upon which the President's recommendation was based, was drawn mainly, I may say entirely, from a consideration of the position in which the people of Puerto Rico have been placed by our disturbance of their connection

(374)

with Spain and by the unfortunate experience of flood and storm through which nearly the whole of the island has recently passed. It was evidently the purpose of the President, and the only purpose which he had, to do something to give that people a chance to rebuild its fallen fortunes and to begin anew its commercial and industrial life. Now, notwithstanding the abuse that has been heaped upon this bill on this floor and in the public press, I undertake to say that it does in substance exactly what the President had in mind to do.

At the same time it keeps account of the fact that whatever form of government is finally established in the island of Puerto Rico will, from the beginning, stand in exigent need of money to pay its expenses and to provide for the education and material development of the community. . . .

We have been accused of a conspiracy to rob and to levy tribute upon a helpless and unfortunate people. We have been charged with "treating Puerto Rico as an orange to be squeezed," and the intimation has been thrown out to the public that this Government proposes to appropriate the juice, when in point of fact we are simply fixing a nominal rate of duties for the sole purpose of guaranteeing a working revenue for the necessary uses of the Puerto Rican government for the time being, until it has prepared and put in operation a fiscal system of its own.

It will be seen, therefore, that the committee has done in substance exactly what the President recommended should be done. We have given to these people the least burdensome method of taxation that can be devised.

The open door of Asia, through which the enlightened community of American business, North and South, looks forward to broaden with the centuries—that is the larger question that is on trial here. We are in the Philippine Islands under circumstances known and read of all men. Our going there was not an act of statesmanship; it was not an act of partisan policy. It was an act of war, a step in the strategy of a military campaign, a fruit of victory presented to the American people by our great Admiral in Asia when his day's work in the harbor at Manila was done. . . . . . .

Nobody blames us for putting an end to the sovereignty of Spain, and even Mr. Bryan has been careful not to demand the withdrawal of our army, leaving the islands to their fate; yet he appears to reject the only two propositions in connection with the subject that, according to my friend from Missouri (Mr. De Armond), have any sense in them, namely: That we shall stay there as in duty bound by the treaty, and administer their affairs; or that we shall leave them, notwithstanding the treaty, and let them work out their own salvation.

The proposition which Mr. Bryan makes concedes that without us the islands would become a prey to those nations which are accustomed to protect the interests of their people in the out-of-the-way places of the world. He therefore asks us to first recognize the government of an insurgent tribe, representing only a small minority of the population of the islands, to commit the sovereignty which we acquired from Spain and which we hold in trust for several millions of people, embracing over sixty tribes, to the dictatorship of the military chieftains of a single one, and then stand off at our own expense with our Army and Navy, responsible for all that follows, but without a vestige of authority to direct the course of affairs. I undertake to say that in the whole history of the world no such blatant stupidity has ever masqueraded for wisdom, even in the leadership of a forlorn political hope.

It may be set down for sure that, whatever else happens, this clumsy and unmanageable thing will not happen. If we go, we will take our baggage with us, leaving the police duties of civilization, after our ignominious default of our treaty obligations, to be performed by the nations interested. If we stay, we will stay in our own right, exercising the functions of our own Government, deriving our authority from the treaty which defines our responsibility.

My own conviction, strengthened by months of solicitous inquiry and confirmed in the unanimous report of the official board whose report has just been laid before Congress is that we can not leave the Philippine Islands without surrendering the national character, without disowning the sacrifices we have made, without turning our backs on the mission of the Republic among the nations of the world. Our Navy is there, still glorious in the renown of its great sailors; our Army is there, patient and uncomplaining amid the hardships of a strange land; our flag is there, with no stain upon it except the blood of the brave men who have died in its defense.

No American army ever volunteered for a service more arduous; none ever had a better right to look to their countrymen at home for encouragement and sympathy; none ever earned a higher title to the love of a generous people. In camp and garrison, on the march and in the field, in the tangle of swamps and over the passes of untraveled mountains they have borne the flag of the American Republic— that flag which never yet stood and never can stand for anything except the liberty of men.

That little army of volunteers stayed in the service nearly a year after the term of their enlistment had expired. When the returning regiments came back they were welcomed with all the signs of public honor in every city and village from San Francisco to their homes, and the President of the United States did not think it below the dignity of his office to leave this capital and go out to meet the men who had served the nation, take each one of them by the hand, and speak to him in words of appreciation and gratitude.

With gracious sympathy he consoled the sorrow of those whose loved ones had fallen in battle or died in the hospitals of disease, and in the presence of the living he comforted broken hearts with this sentiment, native to the feelings of kindly and patriotic men everywhere, "They died on the altar of their country." A few days later the Omaha World-Herald, Mr. Bryan's personal organ in Nebraska, printing the Associated Press cable containing General Otis's official list of the dead and wounded (I have a copy of the paper before me), set over it, in jest and mimicry of the President's gentle words, this infamous headline: "Still dying on 'the altar,'" and then follows the pathetic roll of our poor boys fallen in a land of strangers in the discharge of a soldier's duty.

I have been accused of calling men traitors, though I never did. I give every man the same right to his views that I claim for myself. I have been accused of calling men copperheads, though I never did. I recognize every man's right to his own opinions. But if I had done so in a case like this, I would apologize to the old rebels of the South and the old copperheads of the North, for I declare here that political degradation never before fell so low as to turn into jest and ridicule the death reports of the army either North or South.

A few days ago in this city, in a stately ceremonial, his comrades carried to Arlington the bravest of the brave. It was he who, at the time when the printing presses of America were busy with deeds of valor furnished in manuscript by gentlemen who performed them, standing before the multitude at Macon, could only say, "I am not an orator; I am a soldier. I am not a hero; I am a Regular."

What right have people living under the shelter of our laws to embitter the service of a man like that as he rides under unfriendly skies, careless even of his life, at the head of an American command? Is it not a shame that this old soldier, who for forty years had obeyed the orders of this Government, receiving hardly enough to support his family and educate his children, with no ambition except to do his duty, should in his last great campaign hear messages from home so filled with banter and criticism and reproach that his heart sank within him, and in his agony of spirit, seeing the shadow upon him, he wrote the words I am about to read?

I wish to God that this whole Philippine situation could be known by every one in America as I know it. If the real history, inspiration, and conditions of this insurrection, and the influences, local and external, that now encourage the enemy, as well as the actual possibilities of these islands and peoples and their relations to this great East could be understood at home, we would hear no more talk of unjust "shooting of government" into the Filipinos or of hauling down our flag in the Philippines.

If the so-called anti-imperialists would honestly ascertain the truth on the ground, and not in distant America, they, whom I believe to be honest men misinformed, would be convinced of the error of their statements and conclusions and of the unfortunate effect of their publications here. If I am shot by a Filipino bullet, it might as well come from one of my own men, because I know from observation confirmed by captured prisoners that the continuance of the fighting is chiefly due to reports that are sent out from America.

Standing by the grave of Henry W. Lawton, I appeal to the patriotic millions of my countrymen without regard to politics to put an end to the pestilent fire in the rear which for nearly two years has followed our Army in the Philippines, filling the hearts of our own soldiers with despair and the hearts of their enemy with comfort and good cheer.

It will require no extraordinary wisdom on our part to give to the Philippine Islands a freer government than Thomas Jefferson gave to Louisiana, or James Monroe, by means of the dictatorship of bluff old Andrew Jackson, gave to the Floridas. And if we manage to keep as close to the Constitution of the United States as the men kept who saw it made and helped to put it in operation, we may expect to live through the storm of pedantic criticism which now fills the air of both Houses of Congress.

My friend from Texas (Mr. Bailey), with the Dred Scott decision before him, finds no power in Congress to acquire territory, except for the purpose of making new States out of it. But again and again Chief Justice Marshall declared that the power to make war and the power to make treaties, each of them, includes the power to acquire and govern territory.

These powers are of the essence of political sovereignty. Can absurdity go any further than to claim that in entering into a war the Government is required to stop in the field, and inquire into the fitness of territory to be used as raw material for States? It is at liberty to exercise the rights that belong to a war-making power. Besides all this, it is evident to anyone who carefully peruses the debates incident to the Louisiana treaty that there was more doubt about the right of the Government to make States out of that territory than there was about the right of Mr. Jefferson to acquire it, even after he himself had sought in vain for constitutional authority to do so.

Fortunately for mankind, he was not a constitutional lawyer; but he had an intuitive foresight which enabled him to feel and know the inner springs of the national development. . . .

Every year since I have been a member of this House I have gone at least once to the library of the State Department to look upon the original draft of the Declaration in the handwriting of Thomas Jefferson, with its erasures and interlineations. By its side, also in Mr. Jefferson's handwriting, is the rude drawing of the monument which he desired to be erected to his memory, together with the inscription which he wished to have carved upon it. He asked to be remembered, first of all, as the author of the Declaration of Independence, a title surely to an immortality which belongs to only a few of the great names of history.

I yield to no man in my reverence for that handwriting, and the only favor I have to ask of those gentlemen who are now using that document to waylay the progress of civil liberty in the earth is to concede to the author of the Declaration of Independence at least the same right to interpret it and apply its meaning in practical affairs which they arrogate to themselves; for no sooner had Mr. Jefferson established the Territorial government of Louisiana than this exact question arose.

The consent of the inhabitants was neither sought nor obtained; and even before the President had entered upon the task of administering their local government, memorials began to pour in upon both Houses of Congress protesting against the despotism which had been established. There were Frenchmen and Spaniards, frontiersmen, and Indian tribes, and in the shadow of every settlement and garrison there crouched a figure which in years to come was to play a bloody part in the tragedy of the national affliction—the abject and pitiable figure of the negro slave.

The petitioners quoted the Declaration of Independence in the face of the man who wrote it, and, strange to say, one of their grievances was that the act of Congress had cut them off from the blessings of the slave trade. Their complaints, while without effect on the policy of the Government, did not fail to excite the sympathy of men who concealed their malice against the Administration in their noisy declamations on the subject of human liberty. . . .

The experience of the last two years has given the American people a national ideal from which it is not possible to fall away—an ideal shaped in the ministry of the Son of Man, in obedience to which every human life becomes a sacrament of help and mercy, and every true national life stands willing to pour itself out in the service of mankind.

The great nations of the world are the nations that bear the heavy burdens of the world—these are the great nations upon whose shoulders are laid the heavy responsibilities and the appointed duties of these passing centuries. Every man knows with what motive the American people broke the peace of the world, and the time is coming when every man shall know with what motive we have taken up these burdens which are not our own. I do not believe that the American Republic will be allowed to fail in the midst of its duties, honestly and manfully trying to perform them.

In the masterpieces of prose fiction you remember that on the day of Waterloo the Supreme Equity which is in the heavens, enters a decree that in the nineteenth century there is no longer room for Napoleon the Great; that the time has come to make an end of his affairs. That is the gleam of a lofty imagination, but there is in the heart of the American people the steady light of a faith more sublime even than that, a faith in the greatness of our country, a faith in the future of humanity, a faith in the divine guidance which has watched over the national life from its infancy unto this hour.

It is not hard to see the dangers that beset us; it is not hard to point out the cares that are upon us; it is not hard to fill the future with the creations of doubt and uncertainty and fear; but none of these things can move us if in the midst of all dangers and all burdens and all doubts and fears we recognize the hand of God, stretched forth from the stars, touching the American Republic upon the shoulder and giving it a high commission to stand in the arena of the world's great affairs, living no longer to itself alone, but in willing submission to the divine appointment, ready at last to become the faithful servant even of the lowliest and most helpless of His children.

We have heard it said that the days of the Republic are numbered. Such a speech belongs to the blackness of the darkness of a past generation. The old Union army made it possible for us and our children to live in an atmosphere no longer overshadowed by that awful dread. Whatever may be in store for us, whatever political party may rise or fall, this Government shall live to scatter the riches of human liberty to races yet uncivilized and to nations yet unborn.

I believe in the United States of America; I back the old Republic of our fathers against the world; nor since Abraham Lincoln fell in the midst of duties far more arduous than ours has there been upon the helm of our affairs a steadier, wiser, kindlier, braver hand than the hand of William McKinley, president of the United States.

FERNAND LABORI

ERNAND LABORI, great French advocate and author, editor-in-chief of "le Grande Revue," was born at Rheims, France, April 18, 1860, and after receiving a liberal education was admitted to practice at the Paris Bar. For some years he remained unknown outside the ranks of his profession. His opportunity came when Émile Zola published an address to President Faure, accusing certain officials and army officers of conspiring to convict Captain Alfred Dreyfus of selling military secrets to Germany. This action led to Zola's arrest for libel. At the subsequent trial of the great novelist, he was defended so ably by Labori that, when the latter emerged from the court room, he had become one of the most celebrated lawyers in France. At the second trial of Captain Dreyfus, before the court-martial held at Rennes in August, 1899, Labori was employed to defend the accused, and on the 14th of the month was shot at on his way to the court room and severely wounded. In spite of the wound, his able counsel appeared before the court-martial after a brief absence, and conducted the case to its close.

THE CONSPIRACY AGAINST DREYFUS

REFLECT what the word of a minister of war must mean to military judges, whatever their good faith. The superior pledges his word, and they take it. But what an abyss of iniquity! If, again, such things were to occur amid the storms of war, it would be a different thing. What, then, matters one man's life, or a little more or less of justice? But these things took place in a state of peace when the country was perfectly secure. Or, again, if our army were an army of mercenaries, soldiers only, accepting the responsibilities of the military trade, which in that case is only a trade, perhaps then I would bow. But this is a matter of the national army; a matter that concerns all the young men of the nation, who are liable to have to appear before a military tribunal; a matter that concerns your sons, gentlemen. . . .

Your sons, innocent or guilty, are liable to be summoned before a military tribunal. You see that we introduce no venom into the debate. You see that the rights of the nation, the liberty of all, civilization itself is at stake; and if the country, when it shall know the truth and its full significance, does not revolt in indignation, I shall be unable to understand it.

That, gentlemen, is why it is necessary that those who understand and measure the gravity of this' affair should take the floor; why it is necessary that all men of good-will, all true liberals, those who believe in the innocence of Dreyfus and those who do not, those who know and those who do not know, should unite in a sort of sacred phalanx to protest in the name of eternal morality; and that is what M. Zola has done.

In spite of closed doors, gentlemen, and by the great mass of Frenchmen who could not know at what price the verdict had been secured, Dreyfus might have been forgotten. But there was a little fireside in mourning where memory remained, and with memory hope. This fireside was that of the Dreyfus family, in regard to which so many calumnies have been spread; and, since this court refused to hear M. Lalance, let me read you what he has just said and published in the newspapers. I read from "Le Journal des Débats":

"The Dreyfus family consists of four brothers—Jacques, Léon, Mathieu, and Alfred. They are closely united—one soul in four bodies. In 1872 Alsatians were called upon to choose their nationality. Those who desired to remain Frenchmen had to make a declaration and leave the country. The three younger so chose, and left. The oldest, Jacques, who was past the age of military service, and who, moreover, had served during the war in the Legion of Alsace-Lorraine, did not so choose, and was declared a German. He sacrificed himself in order to be able, without fear of expulsion, to manage the important manufacturing establishment which constituted the family estate. But he promised himself that, if he had any sons, they should all be Frenchmen. The German law, in fact, permits a father to take out a permit of emigration for a son who has reached the age of seventeen. This son loses his German nationality, and cannot re-enter the country until he is forty-five years old. Jacques Dreyfus had six sons. In 1894 the two elder were preparing for the Polytechnic School and Saint Cyr. After the trial they had to go away; their career was broken. Two other brothers were in the Belfort School. They were driven out. What was the father to do, knowing that his young brother had been unjustly and illegally condemned? Was he to change his name, as other Dreyfuses have done? Should he abandon his projects, and resolve to have his sons serve in the German army for a year, that they might then re-enter the paternal house, and live in a city where the family was respected, and where everybody pitied and esteemed it? Had he done that, no one would have thrown a stone at him. In 1895 and 1896 his third and fourth sons reached the age of seventeen. He said to them: 'My children, you are now to leave your father's house, never more to come back to it. Go to that country where your name is cursed and despised. It is your duty. Go.' And finally, in 1897, the father left his house, his business, and all his friends, and went to establish himself at Belfort, the city of which they wanted to make a fortress. He demanded French naturalization for himself and his two younger sons."

There you have a document to oppose to the floods of calumny and falsehood. In this family there were two

members whose convictions could not be shaken, M. Mathieu Dreyfus and Mme. Dreyfus, whose fidelity is perhaps the most striking evidence of the innocence of her
husband, for she, indeed, must know the truth. Mme.
Dreyfus had lived beside this man; she knew his daily
life; she saw his attitude throughout the trial; she knew
the absence of proof; she knew what you yourselves know
now, gentlemen. And she had seen the perseverance and
firmness of her husband in ascending this Calvary; his
courage at the moment of degradation; his attitude, always
the same, even up to the present moment. . . . I think
it is indispensable that you should hear this cry, always the
same, as strong as ever, in spite of the prolongation of the
torture. I read you a letter from the Iles du Salut, dated
September 4, 1897:

DEAR LUCIE—I have just received the July mail. You
tell me again that you are certain of complete light. This
certainly is in my soul. It is inspired by the rights that
every man has to ask it, when he wants but one thing—the
truth. As long as I shall have the strength to live in a
situation as inhuman as it is undeserved, I shall write you
to animate you with my indomitable will. Moreover, the
late letters that I have written you are my moral testament,
so to speak. In these I spoke to you first of our affection;
I confessed also my physical and mental deterioration; but
I pointed out to you no less energetically your duty. The
grandeur of soul that we have all shown should make us
neither weak nor vainglorious. On the contrary, it should
ally itself to a determination to go on to the end, until all
France shall know the truth and the whole truth. To be
sure, sometimes the wound bleeds too freely, and the heart
revolts. Sometimes, exhausted as I am, I sink under the
heavy blows, and then I am but a poor human creature in
agony and suffering. But my unconquered soul rises again,

vibrating with grief, energy, and implacable will, in view of that which to us is the most precious thing in the world, our honor and that of our children. And I straighten up once more to utter to all the thrilling appeal of a man who asks only justice in order to kindle in you all the ardent fire that animates my soul, and that will be extinguished only with my life.

I live only on my fever, proud when I have passed through a long day of twenty-four hours. As for you, you have not to consider what they say or what they think. It is for you to do your duty inflexibly, and to insist no less inflexibly on your right, the right of justice and truth. If in this horrible affair there are other interests than ours, which we have never failed to recognize, there are also the imprescriptible rights of justice and truth. There is the duty of all to put an end to a situation so atrocious, so undeserved. Then I can wish for us both and for all only that this frightful, horrible, and unmerited martyrdom may come to an end. . . .

Now I read to you what M. de Cassagnac wrote on September 14, 1896:

"Our *confrère,* 'Le Jour,' pretends, not to prove the innocence of Dreyfus, but to show that his guilt is not demonstrated. This is already too much. Not that we reproach our *confrère* for pursuing such a demonstration, but that this demonstration is impossible. Like most of our fellow-citizens, we believe Dreyfus guilty, but, like our *confrère,* we are not sure of it. And, like our *confrère* also, we have the courage to say so, since we cannot be suspected of being favorable to the Jews, whom we combat here as persistently as we combat the Freemasons. The real question is: Can there be any doubt as to the guilt of Dreyfus? Now, thanks to the stupidity and the cowardice of the government of the Republic, this question, far from being closed, remains perpetually open. Why? Because the government did not dare to conduct the trial in the open, so that public opinion might be settled. . . .

"Yes, traitors are abominable beings, who should be pitilessly shot like wild beasts; but, for the very reason that the punishment incurred is the more frightful and the more deserved, and carries with it no pity, it should not have been possible for the cowardice of the government with reference to Germany to have left us in a horrible doubt which authorizes us to ask ourselves sometimes if really there is not on Devil's Island a human being undergoing in innocence a superhuman torture. Such doubt is a frightful thing, and it will continue, because publicity of trial furnishes the only basis for a revision. Now there is no revision. There is no appeal from a sentence wrapped in artificial and deliberate darkness."

That is what M. de Cassagnac said, and, when he wrote it, he did not know what you have learned during the last fortnight. You see, then, the source of the campaign to which Colonel Picquart alluded in one of his letters to General Gonse. It is not the article in "L'Eclair," for those letters appeared before September 15. It is these articles that I have just read you, the Dreyfusian campaign, there you have it. The article in "L'Eclair," in which the name of Dreyfus was falsely written in full, was simply an infamy resorted to to stop that campaign.

. . . .

For a moment, gentlemen, it was the intention of the War Department to let the light shine. But, when the interpellation was announced, it failed in courage. That is the truth. And so, when M. Castelin asked for information concerning the pretended escape of the traitor and the campaign that was beginning, General Billot ascended the tribune and pronounced for the first time these words, which were the beginning of the events which you are now witnessing:

"Gentlemen, the question submitted to the Chamber by the honorable M. Castelin is serious. It concerns the justice of the country and the security of the State. This sad affair two years ago was the subject of a verdict brought about by one of my predecessors in the War Department. Justice was then done. The examination, the trial, and the verdict took place in conformity with the rules of military procedure. The council of war, regularly constituted, deliberated regularly, and, in full knowledge of the cause, rendered a unanimous verdict. The council of revision unanimously rejected the appeal. The thing, then, is judged, and it is allowable for no one to question it. Since the conviction, all precautions have been taken to prevent any attempt at escape. But the higher reasons which in 1894 necessitated a closing of the doors have lost nothing of their gravity. So the government appeals to the patriotism of the Chamber for the avoidance of a discussion which may prevent many embarrassments, and, at any rate, for a closing of the discussion as soon as possible."

Well, gentlemen, note this reply of General Billot. It is the heart of the question, and it is here that begins the fault, or, if you prefer, the error, of the government. It is easy to accuse law-abiding citizens of inciting odious campaigns in their country; but, if we go back to the sources, it is easy to see where the responsibility lies, and here I have put my finger upon it. We are told confidently of the wrong done by the defenders of the traitor in not demanding either a revision or a nullification of the verdict of 1894. Nullification? Why, it is the business of the Minister of Justice to demand that. Listen to Article 441 of the Code of Criminal Examination, applicable in military matters:

"When, upon the exhibition of a formal order given to him by the Minister of Justice, the prosecuting attorney before the Court of Appeals shall denounce in the criminal branch of that court judicial acts, decrees, or verdicts contrary to the law, these acts, decrees, or verdicts may be annulled, and the police officials or the judge prosecuted, if there is occasion, in the manner provided in Chapter III. of Title 4 of the present book."

Well, the secret document, gentlemen, was known in September, 1896. The article in "L'Eclair" appeared September 15; the Castelin interpellation was heard on November 16; a petition from Mme. Dreyfus was laid before the Chamber, and is still unanswered, as is also a letter from M. Demange to the President of the Chamber on the same subject. Now, what was the government's duty when this question first arose? Unquestionably to deny the secret document from the tribune, if it had not been communicated; and, if it had been, to declare that the procedure was in contempt of all law and should lead to the nullification of the verdict. That is what a free government would have done.

Now I wish to say a word of the difficulty of procuring the documents mentioned in the bordereau, upon which so much stress has been laid in order to exculpate Major Esterhazy. I will not dwell on the Madagascar note, which was of February, 1894, and not of August, as has been said, and which consequently was not the important note of which General Gonse spoke. I wish to emphasize only one point, because it is the only one which, in the absence of the questions that I was not permitted to ask, has not been made perfectly clear by the confrontations of the witnesses, and which yet has a considerable significance. General de Pel-

lieux spoke to you of the piece one hundred and twenty and
its hydraulic check.   I believe it is the first item mentioned
in the bordereau.   This check, said General Gonse, is important.   I asked him at what date it figured in the military
regulations, and at what date the official regulation had been
known to the army.   General Gonse answered that he was
unable to give information on that point.   Well, gentlemen,
the truth is this.   The official regulations concerning siege
pieces were put on sale at the house of Berger-Lebrault &
Co., military booksellers, and they bear the date—do not
smile, gentlemen, remembering that the bordereau was written in 1894—they bear the date 1889.   On page twenty-one
you will find mention of the hydraulic check.   "The purpose of the hydraulic check [it says] is to limit the recoil of
the piece."   In 1895 a new check was adopted for the piece
one hundred and twenty, and this new check, as appears
from the official regulations bearing date of 1895, is not
known as a hydraulic check, but as the hydro-pneumatic
check.   Either the author of the bordereau, speculating on
the innocence of foreigners, sent them in 1894 a note on the
hydraulic check of the piece one hundred and twenty, which
had been a public matter since 1889, and then really it is not
worth while to say that Major Esterhazy could not have procured it; or else he sent them in 1894 a note on the hydro-
pneumatic check, and then—there is no doubt about it—he
could not have been an artilleryman.

You have been spoken to also concerning the *troupes de
couverture*.   Well, there are cards on sale in the most official
manner, which appear annually, and which show in the
clearest way the distribution of the troops of the entire
French army for the current year.   I do not know at all
what the author of the bordereau sent, and General Gonse

knows no better than I do.   When he sends a document
like the firing manual, he is very careful to say that it is
a document difficult to procure, and he says it in a French
that seems a little singular to one who remembers the
French that Dreyfus writes in his letters.   But, when he
gives notes, he says nothing.   So I infer that these notes
are without interest and without importance.

Furthermore, the impossibilities were no less great for
Dreyfus.   For instance, it is impossible that a staff officer
should speak of the firing manual in the way in which it is
spoken of in the *bordereau*.   They say the writer must have
been an artilleryman.   Well, that is not my opinion, for all
the officers will tell you that there is not one of them who
would refuse to lend his manual to an officer of infantry,
especially if the request were made by a superior officer.
General Mercier himself in an interview has declared that
the documents have not the importance that is attributed to
them; and it is true that they have not, for a firing manual
that is new in April or in August is no longer new in November or December.   The foreign military *attachés* see these
things at the grand manœuvres, and get all the information
that they want. . . .

I desire to place myself, gentlemen, exclusively on the
ground chosen by the Minister of War, and on that ground
we find that in 1894, the charge against Dreyfus being about
to fall to the ground for want of proof, a man who was not
a dictator, but simply an ephemeral cabinet minister in a
democracy where the law alone is sovereign, dared to take
it upon himself to judge one of his officers and hand him
over to a court-martial, not for trial, but for a veritable
execution.   We find that, since then, nothing has been left
undone in order to cover up this illegality.   .   .   .

CURTIS GUILD, Jr

URTIS GUILD, JR., an American editor and politician, was born at Boston, Mass., Feb. 2, 1860, and graduated at Harvard University in 1881. Besides acting as assistant to his father, editor of the Boston "Commercial Bulletin," he contributed occasional articles to the "North American Review" and other magazines and periodicals. In political questions he took an active part as a public speaker on the Republican side, and in 1896 was delegate-at-large from Massachusetts to the National Republican Convention. He was brigadier-general in the State militia at the outbreak of the Spanish War, and was on Gen. Fitzhugh Lee's staff in Cuba. Later on, he was offered a colonial appointment by the late President McKinley, but declined it.

SUPREMACY AND ITS CONDITIONS

MR. MAYOR, FELLOW CITIZENS,— The Commonwealth of Massachusetts is devoted by the legend beneath her shield to peace and to law and order. We meet to commemorate both a war and a breach of the peace.

Carried beyond restraint by the attempt of a personally virtuous king to re-establish in both England and America the royal prerogative lost by the elder Charles, a mob of men and boys on a moonlight night in the early spring of 1770 assaulted a solitary British sentinel pacing his beat on King Street in the town of Boston. Goaded beyond endurance by shouts of "Lobsters," "Bloody-backs," and more lethal missiles, the sentinel and the nine comrades who rallied to his support fired one volley, and one volley only, on the swarming crowd.

At the trial which followed, John Adams and Josiah Quincy joined in the defence of the soldiers before a Boston

judge and jury.   All the accused were acquitted of murder.
Two only were convicted, and punished with what in those
days was a light penalty for manslaughter.   The circumstances viewed in themselves are not especially remarkable.
Similar brawls occur in Berlin, in London, in Albany, in
Chicago, without altering the course of history.   Yet for
over one hundred years, commencing with the oration of
James Lovell on March 5, 1771, this deadly street fight, in
what was then the largest town in America, has been com-
memorated by an annual address on American history, delivered under the auspices of the authorities, first of the
town, then of the city of Boston.

In the Boston town meeting, on March 5, 1783, after the
delivery of the annual oration on the Boston Massacre, it
was moved that instead of its anniversary, the Fifth of
March, that " The Anniversary of the Fourth Day of July,
1776, . . . shall be constantly celebrated by the delivery of
a public oration . . . in which the orator shall consider the
feelings, manners, and principles which led to this great national event, as well as the important and happy effects,
whether general or domestic, which have already, and will
forever continue to flow from this auspicious epoch."

The first Fourth of July oration delivered in accordance
with this motion, which was later adopted, was pronounced
by Dr. John Warren, July 4, 1783.   The honor of serving
as the first orator of the nineteenth century was given to
Charles, the gifted son of Robert Treat Paine, so soon afterward cut off in the very flower of promise.   It is no small
privilege to be permitted to stand in the first year of the
twentieth century here in Faneuil Hall, where my kinsman
stood a hundred years ago, and if I fail to carry out the noble
purpose of the ancient custom may I at least say, as he wrote

to the Boston selectmen of his day, " I trust my imperfect performance will find an apology in the purity of my intentions."

Sismondi, in his introduction to his great history of the Italian Republics, sets forth at the outset that—

" One of the most important conclusions to be drawn from the study of history is that government is the most effective cause of a people's character . . . that government preserves or annihilates in those submitted to it those qualities which originally are the common heritage of man."

If this be but another way of denying that mere race or natural surroundings are the moving cause of a nation's progress, what community has more reason to join in grateful memory of its inheritance than the city of Boston, than the Commonwealth of Massachusetts ? The Boston Massacre may have been but a street mob, but with the removal of British soldiers from King street to Castle William there was removed also the principle that an English king had the right to quarter troops in an American city without the consent of its inhabitants. Not without reason was Massachusetts singled out from all the colonies for especial punishment. New York broke her agreement in regard to importations from the mother country, Rhode Island and New Hampshire broke theirs. Delaware and New York did not vote on the question of National Independence. South Carolina and Pennsylvania voted against it. Massachusetts stood first, as Virginia most certainly stood second, in enduring determination that neither bribes, concessions, nor privileges should secure from her citizens consent to be taxed by the voice of any government but one of their own choosing.

That the colonies ever did unite is extraordinary. Up to the Revolution it had never been possible, even when

threatened by annihilation by Indians and French, to secure
united action from the various colonies for the common good.
Boston and Massachusetts declined to contribute one shilling
or one soldier to preserve the settlers in other colonies from
the tomahawk of Pontiac.   Colonies that did not feel themselves the pressure of the Molasses Act or the Boston Port
Bill were similarly slow to come to the rescue of Massachusetts.

Yet somehow, thanks to the steady education of public
opinion, neither by making taxed goods cheaper than un-
taxed, nor by conferring the government patronage of the
Stamp Act on Americans alone, nor even by force of arms,
was a British parliament or a British king able to collect
money in Massachusetts by any means that did not include
the consent of those who contributed, or to prevent the union
of the thirteen colonies.

It is the judgment of the English historian, Lecky, as to
the colonies—and there are many who will agree with him—
that—

" The movement which at last arrayed them in a united
front against England was not a blind, instinctive patriotism
or community of sentiment like that which animates old
countries.   It was the deliberate calculation of intelligent
men, who perceived that by such union alone could they
obtain the objects of their desire."

Among such Americans Bostonians have a noble place.
It was Benjamin Franklin who urged, in the Albany Plan,
the union of all the colonies for the common defence.   It
was James Otis who, springing to leadership with his denunciation of the blanket warrants that left no warehouse,
no home sacred from the just or unjust search of the custom-
house officer, steadily pleaded year after year for permanent

principle rather than present advantage. It was John Hancock who not only risked fortune, but faced the felon's rope, that he might preside in turn over conference, convention, and Congress.

Finally, the very author of resistance, the "Father of the Revolution," the busy patriot whose brain framed the conception of committees of correspondence for Massachusetts, which were to expand into committees of correspondence for the colonies and finally into the Continental Congress; the statesman whose advice in the debate over the Declaration of Independence was, "I should advise persisting in our struggle for liberty though it were revealed from heaven that nine hundred and ninety-nine were to perish and one out of a thousand were to survive and retain his liberty"; the American who sought no rank for himself but the first rank for his country was Samuel Adams of Boston.

The future of the United States, the results that have since flown from the "auspicious epoch" of American Independence, were foreseen, and by some even before independence itself was a fact. Forty years before the first gathering of American statesmen in Philadelphia the Marquis d'Argenson, foreign minister of Louis XV, described not only the United States of a hundred years ago but the United States of to-day. George Washington, too, viewing almost with inspired eye the stress and trials yet to come, urged upon his fellow countrymen in his will some plan "which would have a tendency to spread systematic ideas through all parts of this rising empire, thereby to do away with local attachments and State prejudices, as far as the nature of things would or indeed ought to admit, from our National Councils."

The inspiring principles of the epoch laid the axe to the root of the upas tree of feudalism in France. They inspired, as George III foresaw they would inspire, the Reform Bill in England. They led Kossuth in his struggle for an independent Hungary, and cheered the dark hours of Garibaldi with hopes of a united Italy.

The words in which those principles have been expressed have been found too, alas, in the mouth of every demagogue who has since sought to establish a dictatorship or an oligarchy on the ruins of law and order, from Maximilien Robespierre in France to Juan Gualberto Gomez in Cuba.

With the opening of the new century we have entered upon the inheritance promised us over one hundred and fifty years ago by the minister of the most absolute despot of his time, but in the spirit, let us hope, of the first republican of modern times. The dream of the great minister of Louis *le Bienaimé* has been more than realized, and with a speed that in the light of history may well stimulate, if not apprehension, at least caution among such Americans as are eager not so much for brilliant achievement as for enduring success. Not with the ordered march of a great star, but with the headlong rush of a comet, have we risen not merely to the ranks of the great Powers but to that dominant position that can be challenged alone by a coalition of the nations.

Not until five hundred years after the date set for the foundation of Rome did the Roman republic rise as a world power upon the ruins of Carthage. The first German emperor was not crowned till eight hundred years had rolled by after the victory of Arminius checked the advance of Rome beyond the Rhine. Not till six hundred years after Sempach did England, Cromwell's England, sit at the board of the masters in the councils of Europe, and half a thousand years drenched unhappy Italy with tears and blood before

Giuseppe Garibaldi succeeded where Cola di Rienzi had failed.

We have crushed the work of six centuries into one. England sought to oppress us. We obtained our freedom. France seized our merchantmen. We became a naval power. The Barbary States demanded blackmail, and piracy vanished from the Mediterranean in the smoke of Decatur's guns. England sought to press our seamen. We seized from her the freedom of the seas. Mexico tried to subject Texas. She lost California. A State made independent of England in spite of its own vote fired upon the emblem of the Union at Sumter, and from the ashes of the old federation of South Carolina and her sister States there rose up at Appomattox a united nation. Spain forgot that the American people, slow to anger, will never endure the murder of those who serve beneath our colors, and to the Spanish islands of the sea have gone the free American election, the free American public school, the fruit, the seed of modern civilization.

The aged fingers of the dying century seize the stylus to record as the last startling deed of the world's most startling hundred years, the partition of the great Empire of the East among the great Powers of the West. The stylus falls. The Powers have paused. Diplomacy no longer masks destruction. A new century grasps the tablets, and above the guiding hand that writes there bends a new face, child's no longer, calm with the serene strength that seeks for peace but fears not war—the United States of America.

The United States that Washington left was an undeveloped federation of jealous, almost of incongruous States. The United States that Lincoln left was a nation fused in the crucible of war, but with resources undeveloped and with few responsibilities beyond its own borders. The United

States of McKinley is one of the Powers of earth with the destiny of nations in its grasp, and with a responsibility not to itself alone but to the Greater Power that has made it great.

Barely a century ago Franklin was seeking the alliance of France to aid us against a single European nation. Now Europe seeks the coalition of a continent against the supreme influence of the United States. Five years ago Massachusetts manufacturers were asking protection against European goods in the United States. To-day, the Vienna Chamber of Commerce asks that the sale of Massachusetts shoes be prohibited in Austria.

Russia has passed the United States as a producer of petroleum but we surpass all other nations in the production of cotton, of corn, of wheat, of copper, of iron, of coal. No nation surpasses us now as a manufacturer of iron or copper or leather, and we are passing England as a manufacturer of wool and cotton and France as a manufacturer of silk.

The little nation of farmers and fishermen, so barren of industries that they fought their first pitched battle with British guns and French powder, has become the greatest industrial, the greatest commercial, but, alas, not yet the greatest maritime nation in the world. For the first time in this first year of the twentieth century it is possible to say that no other nation excels or equals the United States in exports. The exports of American manufactured products alone are more than the entire exports of Austria-Hungary, Belgium, Italy, or Russia.

The nations of the East who sold cotton textiles to the fathers have become the customers of the sons. American shoes tramp the " back blocks " of Australia, American bicycles spin across the sun-baked plains of South Africa, Ameri-

can reaping machines rattle across the pampas of South
America, American rails traverse the steppes of Asia, American trolley cars whiz beneath the shadows of the Parthenon,
American hardware fills the markets of Germany, American
bridges span the swamps of Burmah, American-built cruisers
fly the blue saltire of Russia in the very face of the Tsar's
window, American telephones convey the bargains, the hopes,
the aspirations of humanity to the uttermost ends of the
earth.

The first President of the Republic in his second message
to Congress congratulated our well-nigh creditless nation
that a loan of three million florins had been secured in Holland. Europe now floats her securities in the Western Republic which, in spite of a pension list enormously exceeding
the cost of the war establishments of Europe, has a national
debt smaller than that of any great Power and a per
capita debt smaller than that of any nation in the world except Mexico, Japan, and India.

In the last generation, the last thirty years of the nineteenth century, the Latin-American nations have increased
their indebtedness fifty per cent, the continental nations of
Europe one hundred per cent, those of Asia two hundred
per cent, the British colonies, except India, four hundred per
cent. Two great nations only reduced their indebtedness in
that period. The United Kingdom reduced its national debt
twenty-five per cent. The United States reduced its national
debt fifty per cent.

Not without reason does American credit head the list.
Not without reason does London wait upon New York. Not
without reason can we claim, at last, by the test of finance as
well as by that of industry and commerce, the leadership of
the world.

Alexander, sighing for more worlds to conquer, had his antithesis in the blessed Michael, sometime Seigneur de Montaigne, who, in his essay on vanity, quotes with approval the lines of a worthy gossip:

" Ayme l'estat tel que tu le vois estre.
S'il est royal ayme la royauté,
S'il est de peu, ou bien communauté
Ayme l'aussi, car Dieu t'y a facit naistre." [1]

Unhappily the world will not stand still. We cannot return to the isolated little nation that our fathers left us or to the political conditions of our infancy, and much as we may love the exact governmental setting and usage to which we were born we must either develop or die.

We may cordially agree with Macaulay that " mere extent of empire is not necessarily an advantage." We may even say of the alien peoples whom the new century has placed upon the lap of the United States, as Macaulay said of the people of India, " It were far better that these people were well governed and independent of us than ill governed and subject to us."

Yet with India in his day, as with the Philippines, as with Porto Rico in ours, that alternative is not possible. India loosed from English leading-strings, would have lapsed again into the perpetual condition of pestilence, warfare, unrelieved famine, infant sacrifice, and private murder that existed before the English came. Porto Rico, without the restraining hand of an American governor, would have already bankrupted its credit to pay the private debts of its coffee planters. Cuba would have followed Lacret into a slough of corruption with

---

[1] " Love the state such as thou seest it.
If it is royal love royalty,
If it is of small account or well inhabited
Still love it for God made it your birthplace."

his plans for a Cuban navy of sixty vessels and a huge staff of highly salaried admirals. Luzon ere this would have been well on the way to the present condition of Hayti with Aguinaldo in the rôle of Dessalines.

Recognizing the dangers, recognizing the perils, recognizing the risks and the burdens that would follow, the greatest of English essayists in the great speech from which I have quoted, predicted upon the floor of the House of Commons that England would not shirk her duty in India.

We shall not shirk our duty in the Philippines.

We are asked to abandon them because the task of lifting them up from ignorance and slavery does not pay. We are asked to follow the easy path of leaving them to their own devices. That course was once adopted in the West Indies in regard to a people nominally as Christian as the Tagalogs, and to the awful horrors of outrage and massacre of all whites, regardless of age or sex, there has succeeded a century's carnival of robbery, lust, and murder.

Leaders with a superficial education, a superficial acceptance of the Christian religion, but untrained in restraint or self-government and suddenly left to themselves, have brought the richest district of the Antilles back to the conditions of the jungle. Martial law, oligarchy, republic, empire, kingdom, and dictatorship have succeeded each other in a whirling round of delirium until almost within sight of the coast of Florida there exists to-day not merely the pathless wilderness, but the snake worship and cannibal sacrifices of West Africa.

Our withdrawal from the Philippines would not mean the establishing of a second United States. It would be criminal to permit the existence of a second Hayti.

The lions in our path are many. The supreme court has

disposed of one. We have the constitutional power to govern Porto Rico or the Philippines as we have for years governed Alaska.

We have not been particularly successful in handling the Indian race within our borders. The Indian has passed through a process not so much of assimilation as of deglutition. We have as yet failed in our attempt to establish equal social and political rights for the negro, and we have frankly run away from the Chinaman as a domestic problem.

To say that a problem is difficult, however, is not to say it is impossible. We have failed to induce most Indians and Eskimoes to become other than wild men. We have not failed in governing Alaska. We have failed to set the negro by the side of the white man, but we have raised him immeasurably above the level of the slave.

American rule in the tropics has not meant their translation to the seventh heaven, but at least it has meant that the world for the first time is free from yellow fever. It has meant law and order. It has meant, too, the only measure of self-government those lands have ever known.

Two years ago we inherited two island dominions and entered temporarily upon the occupation of another. Neither Cuba, Porto Rico, nor the Philippines were completely civilized. A band of organzed bandits roamed in Porto Rico, Cuba had never known what it was to be free of roving guerillas, and every traveller's letter on the Philippines expressly stated that the Spaniards were masters only of the towns, and not of the lawless savages of the interior.

Corruption masqueraded as government, the great mass of the people were hopelessly ignorant, yellow fever and leprosy grinned from century-old deposits of filth, and the grossest immorality was the commonplace of life. To such conditions has the United States applied not experience, but good will and common sense. Six years after Yorktown we managed to organize a United States. It is but three years since Santiago. They have not been without results.

The population of the American colonies was well educated, accustomed to local self-government, and, if not rich, at least in comfortable circumstances. A Swedish traveller in the British colonies in America, in the middle of the eighteenth century, notes with surprise that he has journeyed twelve hundred miles without meeting a beggar.

The population of our new possessions is almost wholly illiterate, and in large part to be compared not to the men who planned the American Revolution, but to the slaves of the South, to whom July 4th brought no message of freedom, and to the "Indians not taxed" of the West, who were expressly excluded from the rights of citizenship in Washington's Constitution as they are to-day in ours.

Yet we in this latter day have extended, and, with God's help, propose still further to extend even to such as our fathers excluded from freedom, a steadily increasing measure of those blessings for which our fathers fought, but which they themselves denied even to men of the race of Crispus Attucks and Peter Salem.

Porto Rico has an organized government, accepted with enthusiasm by a vast majority of her voters in the first election ever held on the island. Cuba is forming her own government in an island already freed from ignorance, filth, pestilence, and famine.

Local self-government has been set up in the Philippines and law and order established in districts where for centuries the bolo kept what the bolo won. The roving robber has for the first time in three hundred years been stamped out in the Spanish West Indies, and if he has not yet disappeared from the Philippines it may at least be said that American law and order has been extended further than ever did that of Spain.

The United States has gained in exports to these islands, it is true, but they have gained also in exports to the United States. Their sales to us to-day annually out-value our sales to them, and by millions of dollars. The islands have commercially infinitely more to gain from us than we have to gain from them by a union of our interests.

In all these islands peculation has been followed by punishment, education has gone to the ignorant, hospitals have risen for the diseased, sanitation has cleansed the pestilence, honesty has put to flight corruption, and justice has supplanted bribery.

The population of the world is increasing, and it is as absurd to contend that great fertile sections of the habitable globe should remain savage or revert to savagery as it is to bewail the fact that in another century the lion and the giraffe will be extinct. The history of our dealings with the Indians is not altogether a pleasant history, but who will claim that the world as a whole would be better off to-day if the white man had been permanently excluded from the great food raising districts which the Indian wrested from Skraeling or Mound Builder?

It is unquestionably better for the world that the French flag flies in Algiers. The Dutch have been brilliantly successful in handling tropical colonies with a population seven times that of the mother country. The thriving colonies of England girdle the earth and, with few exceptions, for the benefit of the world as well as of England.

Is it manly for a nation that boasts its dominance over

Europe to shrink from the task of Europeans? If Japan can succeed in Formosa, shall the United States fail in Luzon?

Whether it please us or not the task is ours. Whether it please us or not the peace of the world is partly in our keeping.

The leadership of the United States may well lift up the heart, its awful responsibility may well bend the knee.

Not Tagalogs in arms, not the navies of Europe, but the recklessness, the greed, the treachery of her own sons may yet send this great nation staggering to its ruin.

The conquest to which we have to set our faces is the conquest not of weaker races but the conquest of ourselves. It needs no Cassandra to prophesy a downfall as swift as our upbuilding if the idols of hypocrisy, of patronage, of commercialism reek longer with the smoke of sacrifice in our market-places. The economy that starves a consular to glut a congress district, the system that too often entrusts our commerce, our honor in foreign lands, to men untrained in languages or law, save the language of the lobby and the law of compensation, the commercialism that has made the profits of the counting-room blot out the duties of the caucus: these are the avenging furies that yet may whip us to destruction.

The expansion of our territories abroad accords but ill with the contraction of the merit system at home. With cheerful inconsistency we exhibit our goods to the South American nations in an international exposition, while to compete with the well paid experts who manage the business of Europe in Latin America we send untrained men with salaries too low to secure good service but too high for such as is given.

It will be well indeed if this new and mighty task that has

been put upon our shoulders forces us to establish our civil service, forces us to establish our consular service upon a sounder basis than mere political favoritism, and forces the United States to pay its public servants salaries commensurate with the labors imposed upon them, that the best blood and brains of the United States may not be drawn from public service by the greater rewards of private life.

Allen, Wood, Taft, three men that will forever be associated with high desert in American public life, have every one been forced to make a sacrifice before which this rich and prosperous country should hang its head in shame. The governor of British Guiana, with a population of 300,000, receives a salary of $24,000 a year. The governor of Porto Rico, with a population of 1,000,000, receives a salary of $8,000 a year.

European nations make the diplomatic, the civil, the colonial service attractive with a secure tenure of office dependent only on good behavior, and offer pensions for a life spent in the public service. Holland governs Java in peace, order, and prosperity, with a viceroy wielding absolute power and residents representing him by the side of the native rajahs, France admits colonial representatives to her legislative chamber in Paris, England varies her system from practical independence to benevolent despotism, according to race and conditions. The systems of the nations differ, but the men active in each are subjected to rigid examinations, are promoted from grade to grade, are not subject to the whirling winds of party politics.

The clerk in a French consulate becomes subconsul at a small port in China, consul at Boston, chargé d'affaires at Washington. The district magistrate on a British rock in the West Indies becomes colonial secretary of Bermuda, colonial secretary of Gilbraltar, colonial secretary of Guiana, governor of Guiana, and ends his career with the accolade of knighthood on his shoulders and the order of St. Michael and St. George on his breast.

I quote actual and not extraordinary cases in the diplomatic service of France, in the colonial service of Great Britain.

The educated youth of France, of Germany, of Holland, most of all of England, sees in the foreign, the diplomatic service, enormous possibilities for a permanent career in life with promotion for merit and an old age secure from want. There is not an empire in Europe in which the highest diplomatic rank is necessarily barred to the poor in purse. The only nation in the world whose niggardly salaries fail to meet the ordinary and necessary expenses of an ambassador, the only nation that simply cannot be represented by a poor man at the great courts of Europe, is the United States of America.

It is a terrible code that teaches that money making is the chief end of man and that success in the acquisition of wealth is to be the first condition of high public office. It is well to call a warning when above the cry from pulpit and platform, " Is it right? " there comes with increasing frequency the murmur of the exchanges, " Will it pay? "

The opportunities for money-making under our flag are so vast that those who avail themselves of them are too prone to forget that flag and opportunities alike exist only because some Americans remember that above the privileges of American wealth are the duties of American citizenship.

One hundred years ago the young Boston orator, born in the same year as the Republic, warned his hearers in this hall of the perils of commercialism. I can conceive to-day

no more hideous betrayal of the first principles of American
manhood than the advice to young men publicly given by the
president of the gigantic steel corporation that is controlling
the industry of the world.

It is a melancholy comment on our civilization that the
poor boy who has risen under its institutions to the head of
the world's greatest industrial organization has, in the hour
of his success, no better word to his fellows than a cynical
hint to eschew the higher education and to leave the school
for the work-bench, if possible, in childhood.

" Education is useless," he cries, " unless it can be coined."
Literature, music, art, history, and philosophy have never a
word for him.   There is no money in them.   The lofty impulse which thrusts the reformer into public life, the soldier
into battle, that in losing all he may help his country, finds
no echo in this latest product of American civilization, to
whom Brutus is a fool and Iago a prophet.

Twice in history has supreme power been given to a nation
that has made a god of riches, once to Carthage, once to Spain.
The great merchant princes of Carthage were ready that
Hannibal and his mercenaries should fight their battles.
They, too, deified the education of the counting-house.   They,
too, hired from abroad their poets and soldiers and musicians
and artists and lived but that they might accumulate the
means of hiring—and the dust of the desert is their monument and the record of their destruction their only title to
a page in history.

The discovery of a new continent opened a Golconda to
Spain.   Neither torture nor slavery was forbidden to the
adventurer who sought to fill his purse; the rack and the
stake awaited the student who dared to fill his mind.   Yet
the very riches of her galleons taught Spain's sea foes how

to fight her, and at the bottom of her Pandora box, emptied alike of goods and glory, she found at last not hope, but the mere memory of pride.

We pride ourselves, and with reason, that we have faced these new problems not as partisans but as Americans. We rejoice that a policy that prefers natives to Americans and that has made a commencement of a sound civil service system has so far controlled affairs in our new possessions. We rejoice that in China the United States means Rockhill and Chaffee, that in the Philippines it means Taft and McArthur, that in Porto Rico it means Charles Allen, and in Cuba Leonard Wood.

It is not enough that this President has trusted the task to such men; no American that loves his country can rest content till the civil service, the consular service, the diplomatic corps of the United States is set upon so stable a foundation that no President can appoint any but such men. It is not enough that a good President may set a Bliss in a Havana custom-house. The day must come when no bad system can set a Neely in a Havana post-office. The duties of a great Power demand the instant abolition of an eighteenth-century system in which influence can force bad appointments, or, what is infinitely more common, secure even under the civil service law the promotion of those least fit to rise.

Commercialism and partisan patronage have been enormously increased by the very same forces that have made us great. We must destroy them, or they will destroy us.

It is not true, however, that to be patriotic a nation must necessarily be poor, nor that with riches there invariably must come degeneracy.

Rome was already rich when law and civilization spread

over the world with her legions. Freedom first arose after her sleep in the Middle Ages not among the poor peasants in the fields, but among the rich burghers in the towns. They were men of substance who stood up for freedom in Italy, in Flanders, in the Hanseatic League. The most desperate and triumphant resistance to civil and religious slavery in the whole history of the world was made by the thriving merchants and handicraftsmen of the Netherlands, and the last stand for feudal despotism and the divine right of kings was made by the barefooted scythemen of Brittany and the raggad swordsmen of the Scottish clans.

It is well to know our strength, it is better to know our weakness, it is best, knowing both, to make our weakness strong.

Nations, like men, become great not by difficulties avoided but by difficulties overcome, and the spell that overcomes them is neither riches nor poverty, but sacrifice.

There is not a mighty viaduct, not a great cathedral, not a line of rails traced across the stretches of veldt or steppe or praire that has not Moloch-like demanded the tribute of human life.

The spread of civilization demands no less. That the many may rejoice the few must suffer. There will be, as there have been, demands from some for the sacrifice of wealth, comfort, ambition, livelihood, of human life itself.

The Egyptian died, but he left the pyramids behind him. The Phœnician died, but he left to the world the alphabet and navigation. The Greek died, but poetry and philosophy blossomed where he had striven. The Roman died, but the Barbarian who slew him could not shake that mighty fabric of law that was to be the basis of social order. The Swede and the German died, but in the murky smoke of thirty years of battle there was kindled the pure white fire of religious liberty. The Frenchman died, but beneath his heroic corpse lay the dead feudal system, never to rise again. The Englishman has died, but the wastes of Australia and Manitoba yield food to the hungry of Europe, the monsters of the Ganges no longer feed on helpless children, the girl widow no longer dies in torment on the funeral pyre, and the haunts of the Thug, the Dacoit, and the tiger have become the highways of commerce and the field of the husbandman's increase.

The torch of civilization is in our hands. Do we fear the sparks and smoke, or shall we bear on the message? Difficulty? Yes. Danger? Yes. Death? Perhaps. It needs not that the American republic should become an imperial Rome, but at the worst it were better to die as Rome than to live as Capua.

Not with eyes cast down to the shadows at their feet did our fathers meet their trials. Let us set, like them, our faces toward the morning.

Not after the trials of the Civil War alone, but after every trial, may we lift our hearts with Lowell in hope as in thanksgiving:

> " Oh Beautiful! my Country! ours once more!
> Smoothing thy gold of war-dishevelled hair
> O'er such sweet brows as never other wore,
>   And letting thy set lips,
>   Freed from wrath's pale eclipse,
> The rosy edges of their smile lay bare.
> What words divine of lover or of poet
> Can tell our love and make thee know it,
> Among the nations bright beyond compare?
>   What were our lives without thee?
>   What all our lives to save thee?
>   We reck not what we gave thee,
>   We will not dare to doubt thee,
> But ask whatever else and we will dare."

WILLIAM J. BRYAN

WILLIAM J. BRYAN

WILLIAM JENNINGS BRYAN, American Democratic politician and lawyer, was born at Salem, Ill., March 19, 1860. He received his education at Illinois College, Jacksonville, and in law at Chicago. He then removed to Lincoln, Neb., and represented a district of the State of Nebraska in Congress for a time, but made little impression on the public mind until he appeared as a delegate in the National Convention of the Democratic party, held at Chicago in 1896, where he delivered the oration in favor of the free coinage of silver at the ratio of 16 to 1, known as "The Cross of Gold" speech, and which obtained for him the nomination to the Presidency. He secured from the people a larger number of votes than had ever been previously cast for any candidate, whether Democratic or Republican; nevertheless, he obtained only 176 electoral votes, against 271 obtained by the late William McKinley. After having served during the war with Spain, as colonel of a Nebraska regiment of volunteers, he was renominated for the Presidency in 1900 by the Democratic National Convention, held at Kansas City, Mo., but was again unsuccessful.

THE "CROSS OF GOLD

Mr. Chairman and Gentlemen of the Convention:

I WOULD be presumptuous, indeed, to present myself against the distinguished gentlemen to whom you have listened if this were a mere measuring of abilities; but this is not a contest between persons. The humblest citizen in all the land, when clad in the armor of a righteous cause, is stronger than all the hosts of error. I come to speak to you in defence of a cause as holy as the cause of liberty— the cause of humanity.

When this debate is concluded, a motion will be made to lay upon the table the resolution offered in commendation of the Administration, and also the resolution offered in condemnation of the Administration. We object to bringing this question down to the level of persons. The individual is but an atom; he is born, he acts, he dies; but principles are eternal; and this has been a contest over a principle.

Never before in the history of this country has there been witnessed such a contest as that through which we have just passed. Never before in the history of American politics has a great issue been fought out as this issue has been, by the voters of a great party. On the fourth of March, 1895, a few Democrats, most of them members of Congress, issued an address to the Democrats of the nation, asserting that the money question was the paramount issue of the hour; declaring that a majority of the Democratic party had the right to control the action of the party on this paramount issue; and concluding with the request that the believers in the free coinage of silver in the Democratic party should organize, take charge of, and control the policy of the Democratic party. Three months later, at Memphis, an organization was perfected, and the silver Democrats went forth openly and courageously proclaiming their belief, and declaring that, if successful, they would crystallize into a platform the declaration which they had made. Then began the conflict. With a zeal approaching the zeal which inspired the Crusaders who followed Peter the Hermit, our silver Democrats went forth from victory unto victory until they are now assembled, not to discuss, not to debate, but to enter up the judgment already rendered by the plain people of this country. In this contest brother has been arrayed against brother, father against son. The warmest ties of love, acquaintance, and association have been disregarded; old leaders have been cast aside when they have refused to give expression to the sentiments of those whom they would lead, and new leaders have sprung up to give direction to this cause of truth. Thus has the contest been waged, and we have assembled here under as binding and solemn instructions as were ever imposed upon representatives of the people.

We do not come as individuals. As individuals we might have been glad to compliment the gentleman from New York (Senator Hill), but we know that the people for whom we speak would never be willing to put him in a position where he could thwart the will of the Democratic party. I say it was not a question of persons; it was a question of principle, and it is not with gladness, my friends, that we find ourselves brought into conflict with those who are now arrayed on the other side.

The gentleman who preceded me (ex-Governor Russell) spoke of the State of Massachusetts; let me assure him that not one present in all this Convention entertains the least hostility to the people of the State of Massachusetts, but we stand here representing people who are the equals, before the law, of the greatest citizens in the State of Massachusetts. When you (turning to the gold delegates) come before us and tell us that we are about to disturb your business interests, we reply that you have disturbed our business interests by your course.

We say to you that you have made the definition of a business man too limited in its application. The man who is employed for wages is as much a business man as his employer; the attorney in a country town is as much a business man as the corporation counsel in a great metropolis; the merchant at the cross-roads store is as much a business man as the merchant of New York; the farmer who goes forth in the morning and toils all day, who begins in spring and toils all summer, and who by the application of brain and muscle to the natural resources of the country creates wealth, is as much a business man as the man who goes upon the Board of Trade and bets upon the price of grain; the miners who go down a thousand feet into the earth, or climb two thousand feet upon the cliffs, and bring forth from their hiding places the precious metals to be poured into the channels of trade are as much business men as the few financial magnates who, in a back room, corner the money of the world. We come to speak of this broader class of business men.

Ah, my friends, we say not one word against those who live upon the Atlantic Coast, but the hardy pioneers who have braved all the dangers of the wilderness, who have made the desert to blossom as the rose—the pioneers away out there (pointing to the West), who rear their children near to Nature's heart, where they can mingle their voices with the voices of the birds—out there where they have erected schoolhouses for the education of their young, churches where they praise their creator, and cemeteries where rest the ashes of their dead—these people, we say, are as deserving of the consideration of our party as any people in this country. It is for these that we speak. We do not come as aggressors. Our war is not a war of conquest; we are fighting in the defence of our homes, our famiiles, and posterity. We have petitioned, and our petitions have been scorned; we have entreated, and our entreaties have been disregarded; we have begged, and they have mocked when our calamity came. We beg no longer; we entreat no more; we petition no more. We defy them!

The gentleman from Wisconsin has said that he fears a Robespierre. My friends, in this land of the free you need not fear that a tyrant will spring up from among the people. What we need is an Andrew Jackson to stand, as Jackson stood, against the encroachments of organized wealth.

They tell us that this platform was made to catch votes. We reply to them that changing conditions make new issues; that the principles upon which Democracy rests are as everlasting as the hills, but that they must be applied to new conditions as they arise. Conditions have arisen, and we are here to meet those conditions. They tell us that the income tax ought not to be brought in here; that it is a new idea. They criticise us for our criticism of the Supreme Court of the United States. My friends, we have not criticised; we have simply called attention to what you already know. If you want criticisms, read the dissenting opinions of the court. There you will find criticisms. They say that we passed an unconstitutional law; we deny it. The income tax law was not unconstitutional when it was passed; it was not unconstitutional when it went before the Supreme Court for the first time; it did not become unconstitutional until one of the udges changed his mind, and we cannot be expected to know when a judge will change his mind. The income tax is just. It simply intends to put the burdens of government justly upon the backs of the people. I am in favor of an income tax. When I find a man who is not willing to bear his share of the burdens of the government which protects him, I find a man who is unworthy to enjoy the blessings of a government like ours.

They say that we are opposing national bank currency; it is true. If you will read what Thomas Benton said, you will find he said that, in searching history, he could find but one parallel to Andrew Jackson; that was Cicero, who

destroyed the conspiracy of Catiline and saved Rome.
Benton said that Cicero only did for Rome what Jackson
did for us when he destroyed the bank conspiracy and
saved America. We say in our platform that we believe
that the right to coin and issue money is a function of
government. We believe it. We believe that it is a part
of sovereignty, and can no more with safety be delegated
to private individuals than we could afford to delegate to
private individuals the power to make penal statutes or
levy taxes. Mr. Jefferson, who was once regarded as good
Democratic authority, seems to have differed in opinion
from the gentleman who has addressed us on the part of
the minority. Those who are opposed to this proposition
tell us that the issue of paper money is a function of the
bank, and that the government ought to go out of the
banking business. I stand with Jefferson rather than with
them, and tell them, as he did, that the issue of money is a
function of government, and that the banks ought to go
out of the governing business.

They complain about the plank which declares against
life tenure in office. They have tried to strain it to mean
that which it does not mean. What we oppose by that
plank is the life tenure which is being built up in Washington, and which excludes from participation in official
benefits the humbler members of society.

Let me call your attention to two or three important
things. The gentleman from New York says that he will
propose an amendment to the platform providing that the
proposed change in our monetary system shall not affect
contracts already made. Let me remind you that there is
no intention of affecting those contracts which, according
to present laws, are made payable in gold; but if he means

to say that we cannot change our monetary system without protecting those who have loaned money before the change was made, I desire to ask him where, in law or in morals, he can find justification for not protecting the debtors when the act of 1873 was passed, if he now insists that we must protect the creditors.

He says he will also propose an amendment which will provide for the suspension of free coinage if we fail to maintain a parity within a year. We reply that when we advocate a policy which we believe will be successful, we are not compelled to raise a doubt as to our own sincerity by suggesting what we shall do if we fail. I ask him, if he would apply his logic to us, why he does not apply it to himself. He says he wants this country to try to secure an international agreement. Why does he not tell us what he is going to do if he fails to secure an international agreement? There is more reason for him to do that than there is for us to provide against the failure to maintain the parity. Our opponents have tried for twenty years to secure an international agreement, and those are waiting for it most patiently who do not want it at all.

And now, my friends, let me come to the paramount issue. If they ask us why it is that we say more on the money question than we say upon the tariff question, I reply that, if protection has slain its thousands, the gold standard has slain its tens of thousands. If they ask us why we do not embody in our platform all the things that we believe in, we reply that when we have restored the money of the Constitution all other necessary reforms will be possible; but that until this is done there is no other reform that can be accomplished.

Why is it that within three months such a change has

come over the country? Three months ago when it was confidently asserted that those who believe in the gold standard would frame our platform and nominate our candidates, even the advocates of the gold standard did not think that we could elect a President. And they had good reason for their doubt, because there is scarcely a State here to-day asking for the gold standard which is not in the absolute control of the Republican party. But note the change. Mr. McKinley was nominated at St. Louis upon a platform which declared for the maintenance of the gold standard until it can be changed into bimetallism by international agreement. Mr. McKinley was the most popular man among the Republicans, and three months ago everybody in the Republican party prophesied his election. How is it to-day? Why, the man who was once pleased to think that he looked like Napoleon—that man shudders to-day when he remembers that he was nominated on the anniversary of the battle of Waterloo. Not only that, but as he listens he can hear with ever-increasing distinctness the sound of the waves as they beat upon the lonely shores of St. Helena.

Why this change? Ah, my friends, is not the reason for the change evident to any one who will look at the matter? No private character, however pure, no personal popularity, however great, can protect from the avenging wrath of an indignant people a man who will declare that he is in favor of fastening the gold standard upon this country, or who is willing to surrender the right of self-government and place the legislative control of our affairs in the hands of foreign potentates and powers.

We go forth confident that we shall win. Why? Because upon the paramount issue of this campaign there is

not a spot of ground upon which the enemy will dare to
challenge battle. If they tell us that the gold standard is
a good thing, we shall point to their platform and tell them
that their platform pledges the party to get rid of the gold
standard and substitute bimetallism. If the gold standard
is a good thing, why try to get rid of it? I call your attention to the fact that some of the very people who are in this
Convention to-day and who tell us that we ought to declare
in favor of international bimetallism—thereby declaring that
the gold standard is wrong and that the principle of bimetallism is better—these very people four months ago were open
and avowed advocates of the gold standard, and were then
telling us that we could not legislate two metals together,
even with the aid of all the world. If the gold standard is
a good thing, we ought to declare in favor of its retention
and not in favor of abandoning it; and if the gold standard
is a bad thing why should we wait until other nations are
willing to help us to let go? Here is the line of battle,
and we care not upon which issue they force the fight; we
are prepared to meet them on either issue or on both. If
they tell us that the gold standard is the standard of civilization, we reply to them that this, the most enlightened of
all the nations of the earth, has never declared for a gold
standard and that both the great parties this year are declaring against it. If the gold standard is the standard of
civilization, why, my friends, should we not have it? If
they come to meet us on that issue we can present the history of our nation. More than that; we can tell them that
they will search the pages of history in vain to find a single
instance where the common people of any land have ever
declared themselves in favor of the gold standard. They
can find where the holders of fixed investments have

declared for a gold standard, but not where the masses have. Mr. Carlisle said in 1878 that this was a struggle between "the idle holders of idle capital" and "the struggling masses, who produce the wealth and pay the taxes of the country"; and, my friends, the question we are to decide is: Upon which side will the Democratic party fight; upon the side of "the idle holders of idle capital" or upon the side of "the struggling masses"? That is the question which the party must answer first, and then it must be answered by each individual hereafter. The sympathies of the Democratic party, as shown by the platform, are on the side of the struggling masses who have ever been the foundation of the Democratic party. There are two ideas of government. There are those who believe that, if you will only legislate to make the well-to-do prosperous, their prosperity will leak through on those below. The Democratic idea, however, has been that if you legislate to make the masses prosperous, their prosperity will find its way up through every class which rests upon them.

You come to us and tell us that the great cities are in favor of the gold standard; we reply that the great cities rest upon our broad and fertile prairies. Burn down your cities and leave our farms, and your cities will spring up again as if by magic; but destroy our farms and the grass will grow in the streets of every city in the country.

My friends, we declare that this nation is able to legislate for its own people on every question, without waiting for the aid or consent of any other nation on earth; and upon that issue we expect to carry every State in the Union. I shall not slander the inhabitants of the fair State of Massachusetts nor the inhabitants of the State of New York by saying that, when they are confronted with the proposition, they will declare that this nation is not able to attend to its own business. It is the issue of 1776 over again. Our ancestors, when but three millions in number, had the courage to declare their political independence of every other nation; shall we, their descendants, when we have grown to seventy millions, declare that we are less independent than our forefathers?

No, my friends, that will never be the verdict of our people. Therefore, we care not upon what lines the battle is fought. If they say bimetallism is good, but that we cannot have it until other nations help us, we reply that, instead of having a gold standard because England has, we will restore bimetallism, and then let England have bimetallism because the United States has it. If they dare to come out in the open field and defend the gold standard as a good thing, we will fight them to the uttermost. Having behind us the producing masses of this nation and the world, supported by the commercial interests, the laboring interests and the toilers everywhere, we will answer their demand for a gold standard by saying to them: You shall not press down upon the brow of labor this crown of thorns, you shall not crucify mankind upon a cross of gold.

ALBERT J. BEVERIDGE

LBERT JEREMIAH BEVERIDGE, an American Congressman, was born in Highland Co., O., Oct. 6, 1862. Soon after his birth, his parents removed to Indiana, where his early life was one of privation and hard labor. His youth was spent in farm work, and at fourteen he was a laborer on railway construction, and a teamster the year after. He secured time for study in the winter months, however, and obtained an education at De Pauw University. He then became a law clerk at Indianapolis, Ind., and in 1884 entered political life by delivering speeches in behalf of Blaine in the campaign of that year. He opened the State political campaign in 1892, and general attention was drawn to him by his speeches in 1895-96. In 1899, he was elected to the United States Senate as a Republican. In the same year, he visited the Philippine Islands, and on Jan. 9, 1900, addressed the Senate on that topic. He is known as a strong party man, and is said to have made more speeches in Indiana, and devoted more time to his party, than any one else in his State.

THE MARCH OF THE FLAG

SPEECH DELIVERED AT INDIANAPOLIS, IND., SEPT. 16, 1898

FELLOW CITIZENS,—It is a noble land that God has given us; a land that can feed and clothe the world; a land whose coast lines would enclose half the countries of Europe; a land set like a sentinel between the two imperial oceans of the globe, a greater England with a nobler destiny. It is a mighty people that he has planted on this soil; a people sprung from the most masterful blood of history; a people perpetually revitalized by the virile, man-producing workingfolk of all the earth; a people imperial by virtue of their power, by right of their institutions, by authority of their heaven-directed purposes—the propagandists and not the misers of liberty. It is a glorious history our God has bestowed upon his chosen people; a history whose keynote was struck by Liberty Bell; a history heroic with faith in our mission and our future; a history of statesmen who flung the boundaries of the Republic out into unexplored lands and savage wildernesses; a history of soldiers who carried the flag across the blazing deserts and through the ranks of hostile mountains, even to the gates of sunset; a history of a multiplying people who overran a continent in half a century; a history of prophets who saw the consequences of evils inherited from the past and of martyrs who died to save us from them; a history divinely logical, in the process of whose tremendous reasoning we find ourselves to-day.

Therefore, in this campaign, the question is larger than a party question. It is an American question. It is a world question. Shall the American people continue their resistless march toward the commercial supremacy of the world? Shall free institutions broaden their blessed reign as the children of liberty wax in strength, until the empire of our principles is established over the hearts of all mankind?

Have we no mission to perform, no duty to discharge to our fellow-man? Has the Almighty Father endowed us with gifts beyond our deserts and marked us as the people of his peculiar favor, merely to rot in our own selfishness, as men and nations must, who take cowardice for their companion and self for their Deity—as China has, as India has, as Egypt has?

Shall we be as the man who had one talent and hid it, or as he who had ten talents and used them until they grew to riches? And shall we reap the reward that waits on our discharge of our high duty as the sovereign power of earth; shall we occupy new markets for what our farmers raise, new markets for what our factories make, new markets for what our merchants sell—aye, and, please God, new markets for what our ships shall carry?

Shall we avail ourselves of new sources of supply of what we do not raise or make, so that what are luxuries to-day will be necessities to-morrow? Shall our commerce be encouraged until, with Oceanica, the Orient, and the world, American trade shall be the imperial trade of the entire globe?

Shall we conduct the mightiest commerce of history with the best money known to man, or shall we use the pauper money of Mexico, of China, and of the Chicago platform?...

What are the great facts of this administration? Not a failure of revenue; not a perpetual battle between the executive and legislative departments of government; not a rescue from dishonor by European syndicates at the price of tens of millions in cash and national humiliation unspeakable. These have not marked the past two years—the past two years, which have blossomed into four splendid months of glory!

But a war has marked it, the most holy ever waged by one nation against another—a war for civilization, a war for a permanent peace, a war which, under God, although we knew it not, swung open to the Republic the portals of the commerce of the world. And the first question you must answer with your vote is, whether you indorse that war? We are told that all citizens and every platform indorses the war, and I admit, with the joy of patriotism that this is true. But that is only among ourselves—and we are of and to ourselves no longer. This election takes place on the stage of the world, with all earth's nations for our auditors. If

the administration is defeated at the polls, will England believe that we accept the results of the war?

Will Germany, that sleepless searcher for new markets
for her factories and fields, and therefore the effective med-
dler in all international complications—will Germany be
discouraged from interfering with our settlement of the war,
if the administration is defeated at the polls?

Will Russia, that weaver of the webs of commerce into
which province after province and people after people falls,
regard us as a steadfast people if the administration is defeated at the polls?

The world is observing us to-day. Not a Foreign Office
in Europe that is not studying the American republic and
watching the American elections of 1898 as it never watched
an American election before. Are the American people the
chameleon of the nations? "If so, we can easily handle
them," say the diplomats of the world.

Which result, say you, will have the best effect for us
upon the great Powers who watch us with the jealousy
strength always inspires—a defeat, at the hand of the American people, of the administration which has conducted our
foreign war to a world-embracing success, and which has
in hand the most important foreign problems since the Revolution; or, such an endorsement of the administration by
the American people as will swell to a national acclaim?

No matter what your views on the Dingley or the Wilson
laws; no matter whether you favor Mexican money or the
standard of this republic, we must deal from this day on with
nations greedy of every market we are to invade; nations
with statesmen trained in craft, nations with ships and guns
and money and men. Will they sift out the motive for your
vote, or will they consider the large result of the endorse-

ment or rebuke of the administration? The world still rubs
its eyes from its awakening to the resistless power and sure
destiny of this republic. Which outcome of this election
will be best for America's future—which will most health-
fully impress every people of the globe with the steadfastness
of character and tenacity of purpose of the American people—the triumph of the government at the polls, or the success of the Opposition?

I repeat, it is more than a party question. It is an American question. It is an issue in which history sleeps. It is
a situation which will influence the destiny of the republic. . . .

And yet have we peace? Does not the cloud of war linger
on the horizon? If it does not—if only the tremendous problems of peace now under solution remain, ought not the administration be supported in its fateful work by the endorsement of the American people? Think of England abandoning its ministry at the moment it was securing the fruits of
a successful war! Think of Germany rebuking Bismarck
at the moment he was dictating peace to France! What
would America say of them if they should do such a deed
of mingled insanity, perfidy, and folly? What would the
world say of America, if, in the very midst of peace negotiations upon which the nations are looking with jealousy, fear,
and hatred, the American people should rebuke the administration in charge of those peace negotiations and place a hostile House and Senate in Washington? God forbid! When
a people show such inconstancy, such childish fickleness as
that, their career as a power among nations is a memory.

But, if possible war lurks in the future, what then? Shall
we forsake our leaders at the close of a campaign of glory
and on the eve of new campaigns for which it has prepared?

Yet, that is what the success of the Opposition to the government means. What is that old saying about the idiocy of him who changed horses while crossing a stream? It would be like discharging a workman because he was efficient and true. It would be like court-martialing Grant and discharging his heroes in dishonor because they took Vicksburg.

Ah! the heroes of Vicksburg and Peach Tree Creek, Atlanta, Mission Ridge, the Wilderness, and all those fields of glory, of suffering, and of death!

Soldiers of 1861! A generation has passed and you have reared a race of heroes worthy of your blood—heroes of El Caney, San Juan, and Cavité, of Santiago and Manila—ay! and 200,000 more as brave as they, who waited in camp with the agony of impatience the call of battle, ready to count the hellish hardship of the trenches the very sweets of fate, if they could only fight for the flag.

For every tented field was full of Hobsons, of Roosevelts, of Wheelers, and their men; full of the kind of soldiers that in regiments of rags, starving, with bare feet in the snows of winter, made Val'ey Forge immortal; full of the same kind of boys that endured the hideous hardships of the Civil War, drank from filthy roadside pools as they marched through swamps of death, ate food alive with weevils, and even corn picked from the horses' camp, slept in the blankets of the blast with sheets of sleet for covering, breakfasted with danger and dined with death, and came back—those who did come back—with a laugh and a shout and a song of joy, true American soldiers, pride of their country, and envy of the world.

For that is the kind of boys the soldiers of 1898 are, notwithstanding the slanders of politicians and the infamy of a leprous press that try to make the world believe our soldiers

are suckling babes and womanish weaklings, and our government, in war, a corrupt machine, fattening off the suffering
of our armies. In the name of the sturdy soldiery of
America I denounce the hissing lies of politicians out of an
issue, who are trying to disgrace American manhood in the
eyes of the nations.

In the name of patriotism, I arraign these maligners of
the soldierhood of our nation before the bar of the present
and the past. I call to the witness stand that Bayard of our
armies, General Joe Wheeler. I call that Hotspur of the
South, Fitzhugh Lee. I call the 200,000 men, themselves,
who went to war for the business of war.

And I put all these against the vandals of politics who are
blackening their fame as soldiers and as men. I call history
to the witness stand. In the Mexican war the loss from
every cause was twenty-five per cent, and this is on incom-
plete returns; in the present war the loss from every cause
is only three per cent. In the Mexican war the sick lay
naked on the ground with only blankets over them and were
buried with only a blanket around them. Of the volunteer
force 5,423 were discharged for disability, and 3,229 died
from disease. When Scott marched to Mexico, only 96 men
were left out of one regiment of 1,000. The average of a
Mississippi company was reduced from 90 to 30 men. From
Vera Cruz to Mexico a line of sick and dying marked his
line of march.

General Taylor publicly declared that, in his army, five
men died from sickness for every man killed in battle. Scott
demanded surgeons. The government refused to give them.
The three-months men lost nearly nine per cent; the six-
months men lost fourteen per cent; the twelve-months men
twenty-nine per cent; the men enlisted for the war lost

thirty-seven per cent; 31,914 soldiers enlisted for the war, and 11,914 of these were lost, of whom 7,369 are unaccounted for.

In the war for the Union—no, there is no need of figures there. Go to the field of Gettysburg and ask. Go ask that old veteran how fever's fetid breath breathed on them and disease rotted their blood. And in the present war, thank God, the loss and suffering is less than in any war in all the history of the world!

And if any needless suffering there has been, if any deaths from criminal neglect, if any hard condition not a usual incident of sudden war by a peaceful people has been permitted, William McKinley will see that the responsible ones are punished. Although our loss was less than the world ever knew before; although the condition of our troops was better than in any conflict of our history, McKinley the Just, has appointed, from both parties, a commission of the most eminent men in the nation to lay the facts before him.

Let the investigation go on, and when the report is made the people of America will know how black as midnight is the sin of those who, for the purpose of politics, have shamed the hardihood of the American soldiers before the world, attempted to demoralize our army in the face of the enemy, and libeled the government at Washington to delighted and envious nations.

And think of what was done! Two hundred and fifty thousand men suddenly called to arms; men unused to the life of camps; men fresh from the soft comforts of the best homes of the richest people on earth. Those men, equipped, transported to camps convenient for instant call to battle; waiting there the command which any moment might have brought; supplies purchased in every quarter of the land and carried hundreds, even thousands of miles; uniforms procured, arms purchased, ammunition bought, citizens drilled into the finest soldiers on the globe; a war fought in the deadliest climate in the world, beneath a sun whose rays mean madness, and in Spanish surroundings—festering with fever—and yet the least suffering and the lowest loss ever known in all the chronicles of war.

What would have been the result if those who would have plunged us into war before we could have prepared at all, could have had their way? What would have happened if these warriors of peace, who denounced the President as a traitor when he would not send the flower of our youth against Havana, with its steaming swamps of fever, its splendid outworks and its 150,000 desperate defenders—what would have happened if they could have had their way?

The mind shrinks and sickens at the thought. Those regiments, which we greeted the other day with our cheers of pride, would not have marched back again. All over this weeping land the tender song, " We shall meet but we shall miss him; there will be one vacant chair," would have risen once again from desolated homes. And the men who would have done this are the men who are assailing the government at Washington to-day and blaspheming the reputation of the American soldier.

But the wrath of the people will pursue them. The scorpion whips of the furies will be as a caress to the deep damnation of those who seek a political issue in defaming the manhood of the republic. God bless the soldiers of 1898, children of the heroes of 1861, descendants of the heroes of 1776! In the halls of history they will stand side by side with those elder sons of glory, and the Opposition to the government at Washington shall not deny them.

No! they shall not be robbed of the honor due them, nor shall the republic be robbed of what they won for their country. For William McKinley is continuing the policy that Jefferson began, Monroe continued, Seward advanced, Grant promoted, Harrison championed, and the growth of the republic has demanded. Hawaii is ours; Porto Rico is to be ours; at the prayer of the people Cuba will finally be ours; in the islands of the East, even to the gates of Asia, coaling-stations are to be ours; at the very least the flag of a liberal government is to float over the Philippines, and I pray God it may be the banner that Taylor unfurled in Texas and Fremont carried to the coast—the Stars and Stripes of glory.

And the burning question of this campaign is, whether the American people will accept the gifts of events; whether they will rise as lifts their soaring destiny; whether they will proceed upon the lines of national development surveyed by the statesmen of our past; or whether, for the first time, the American people doubt their mission, question fate, prove apostate to the spirit of their race, and halt the ceaseless march of free institutions.

The Opposition tells us that we ought not to govern a people without their consent. I answer, The rule of liberty that all just government derives its authority from the consent of the governed, applies only to those who are capable of self-government. I answer, We govern the Indians without their consent, we govern our territories without their consent, we govern our children without their consent. I answer, How do you assume that our government would be without their consent? Would not the people of the Philippines prefer the just, humane, civilizing government of this republic to the savage, bloody rule of pillage and extortion from which we have rescued them?

Do not the blazing fires of joy and the ringing bells of gladness in Porto Rico prove the welcome of our flag?

And, regardless of this formula of words made only for enlightened, self-governing peoples, do we owe no duty to the world? Shall we turn these peoples back to the reeking hands from which we have taken them? Shall we abandon them to their fate, with the wolves of conquest all about them —with Germany, Russia, France, even Japan, hungering for them? Shall we save them from those nations, to give them a self-rule of tragedy? It would be like giving a razor to a babe and telling it to shave itself. It would be like giving a typewriter to an Eskimo and telling him to publish one of the great dailies of the world. This proposition of the Opposition makes the Declaration of Independence preposterous, like the reading of Job's lamentations would be at a wedding or an Altgeld speech on the Fourth of July.

They ask us how we will govern these new possessions. I answer: Out of local conditions and the necessities of the case methods of government will grow. If England can govern foreign lands, so can America. If Germany can govern foreign lands, so can America. If they can supervise protectorates, so can America. Why is it more difficult to administer Hawaii than New Mexico or California? Both had a savage and an alien population; both were more remote from the seat of government when they came under our dominion than Hawaii is to-day.

Will you say by your vote that American ability to govern has decayed; that a century's experience in self-rule has failed of a result? Will you affirm by your vote that you are an infidel to American vigor and power and practical sense? Or, that we are of the ruling race of the world; that ours is the blood of government; ours the heart of dominion;

ours the brain and genius of administration? Will you remember that we do but what our fathers did—we but pitch the tents of liberty further westward, further southward—we only continue the march of the flag.

The march of the flag!

In 1789 the flag of the republic waved over 4,000,000 souls in thirteen states, and their savage territory which stretched to the Mississippi, to Canada, to the Floridas. The timid minds of that day said that no new territory was needed, and, for the hour, they were right. But Jefferson, through whose intellect the centuries marched; Jefferson, whose blood was Saxon but whose schooling was French, and therefore whose deeds negatived his words; Jefferson, who dreamed of Cuba as a state of the Union; Jefferson, the first imperialist of the republic—Jefferson acquired that imperial territory which swept from the Mississippi to the mountains, from Texas to the British possessions, and the march of the flag began!

The infidels to the gospel of liberty raved, but the flag swept on! The title to that noble land out of which Oregon, Washington, Idaho, and Montana have been carved was uncertain; Jefferson, strict constructionist of constitutional power though he was, obeyed the Anglo-Saxon impulse within him, whose watchword then and whose watchword throughout the world to-day is, " Forward," another empire was added to the republic, and the march of the flag went on!

Those who deny the power of free institutions to expand urged every argument, and more, that we hear, to-day; but the people's judgment approved the command of their blood, and the march of the flag went on!

A screen of land from New Orleans to Florida shut us

from the gulf, and over this and the Everglade Peninsula
waved the saffron flag of Spain; Andrew Jackson seized both,
the American people stood at his back, and, under Monroe,
the Floridas came under the dominion of the republic, and
the march of the flag went on!

The Cassandras prophesied every prophecy of despair we
hear, to-day, but the march of the flag went on! Then
Texas responded to the bugle calls of liberty, and the march
of the flag went on! And, at last, we waged war with
Mexico, and the flag swept over the Southwest, over peer-
less California, past the Gate of Gold, to Oregon on the
north, and from ocean to ocean its folds of glory blazed.

And, now, obeying the same voice that Jefferson heard
and obeyed, that Jackson heard and obeyed, that Monroe
heard and obeyed, that Seward heard and obeyed, that
Ulysses S. Grant heard and obeyed, that Benjamin Harrison
heard and obeyed, William McKinley plants the flag over
the islands of the seas, outposts of commerce, citadels of
national security, and the march of the flag goes on! Bryan,
Bailey, Bland, and Blackburn command it to stand still, but
the march of the flag goes on! And the question you will
answer at the polls is, whether you stand with this quartet
of disbelief in the American people, or whether you are
marching onward with the flag.

Distance and oceans are no arguments. The fact that all
the territory our fathers bought and seized is contiguous,
is no argument. In 1819 Florida was further from New
York than Porto Rico is from Chicago to-day; Texas, further from Washington in 1845 than Hawaii is from Boston
in 1898; California, more inaccessible in 1847 than the
Philippines are now. Gibraltar is further from London than
Havana is from Washington; Melbourne is further from

Liverpool than Manila is from San Francisco. The ocean does not separate us from lands of our duty and desire— the oceans join us, a river never to be dredged, a canal never to be repaired.

Steam joins us; electricity joins us—the very elements are in league with our destiny. Cuba not contiguous! Porto Rico not contiguous! Hawaii and the Philippines not contiguous! Our navy will make them contiguous. Dewey and Sampson and Schley have made them contiguous, and American speed, American guns, American heart and brain and nerve will keep them contiguous forever.

But the Opposition is right—there is a difference. We did not need the western Mississippi Valley when we acquired it, nor Florida, nor Texas, nor California, nor the royal provinces of the far Northwest. We had no emigrants to people this imperial wilderness, no money to develop it, even no highways to cover it. No trade awaited us in its savage fastnesses. Our productions were not greater than our trade. There was not one reason for the land-lust of our statesmen from Jefferson to Grant, other than the prophet and the Saxon within them.

But, to-day, we are raising more than we can consume. To-day, we are making more than we can use. To-day, our industrial society is congested; there are more workers than there is work; there is more capital than there is investment. We do not need more money—we need more circulation, more employment. Therefore we must find new markets for our produce, new occupation for our capital, new work for our labor. And so, while we did not need the territory taken during the past century at the time it was acquired, we do need what we have taken in 1898, and we need it now.

Think of the thousands of Americans who will pour into

Hawaii and Porto Rico when the republic's laws cover those islands with justice and safety! Think of the tens of thousands of Americans who will invade mine and field and forest in the Philippines when a liberal government, protected and controlled by this republic, if not the government of the republic itself, shall establish order and equity there! Think of the hundreds of thousands of Americans who will build a soap-and-water, common-school civilization of energy and industry in Cuba, when a government of law replaces the double reign of anarchy and tyranny!—think of the prosperous millions that Empress of Islands will support when, obedient to the law of political gravitation, her people ask for the highest honor liberty can bestow, the sacred Order of the Stars and Stripes, the citizenship of the Great Republic!

What does all this mean for every one of us? It means opportunity for all the glorious young manhood of the republic—the most virile, ambitious, impatient, militant manhood the world has ever seen. It means that the resources and the commerce of these immensely rich dominions will be increased as much as American energy is greater than Spanish sloth; for Americans henceforth will monopolize those resources and that commerce.

In Cuba, alone, there are 15,000,000 acres of forest unacquainted with the axe. There are exhaustless mines of iron. There are priceless deposits of manganese, millions of dollars of which we must buy to-day from the Black Sea districts. There are millions of acres yet unexplored.

The resources of Porto Rico have only been trifled with. The riches of the Philippines have hardly been touched by the finger-tips of modern methods. And they produce what we cannot, and they consume what we produce—the very predestination of reciprocity—a reciprocity " not made with hands, eternal in the heavens." They sell hemp, silk, sugar, cocoanuts, coffee, fruits of the tropics, timber of price like mahogany; they buy flour, clothing, tools, implements, machinery, and all that we can raise and make. And William McKinley intends that their trade shall be ours.

Do you indorse that policy with your vote? It means creative investment for every dollar of idle capital in the land—an opportunity for the rich man to do something with his money besides hoarding it or lending it. It means occupation for every workingman in the country at wages which the development of new resources, the launching of new enterprises, the monopoly of new markets always brings.

Cuba is as large as Pennsylvania, and is the richest spot on all the globe. Hawaii is as large as New Jersey; Porto Rico half as large as Hawaii; the Philippines larger than all New England, New York, New Jersey, and Delaware. All these are larger than the British Isles, larger than France, larger than Germany, larger than Japan. The trade of these islands, developed as we will develop it by developing their resources, monopolized as we will monopolize it, will set every reaper in this republic singing, every spindle whirling, every furnace spouting the flames of industry.

I ask each one of you this personal question: Do you believe that these resources will be better developed and that commerce best secured; do you believe that all these priceless advantages will be better availed of for the benefit of this republic by Bryan, Bailey, Bland, and Blackburn and the Opposition; or, by William McKinley and a House and Senate that will help and not hinder him?

Which do you think will get the most good for you and the American people out of the opportunities which Provi-

dence has given us—the Government at Washington or the
Opposition in Nebraska, Texas, Kentucky, and Missouri?

Which side will you belong to—those who pull forward
in the traces of national prosperity and destiny, or those who
pull back in those traces, balk at every step of advancement,
and bray at every mile-post of progress?

If any man tells you that trade depends on cheapness and
not on government influence, ask him why England does not
abandon South Africa, Egypt, India. Why does France
seize South China, Germany the vast region whose port is
Kiouchou? Consider the commerce of the Spanish islands.
In 1897 we bought of the Philippines $4,383,740, and we
sold them only $94,597. Great Britain, that national ex-
pert in trade, did little better, for, in 1896, she bought
$6,223,426 and sold only $2,063,598. But Spain—Spain,
the paralytic of commerce—Spain bought only $4,818,344
and sold $4,973,589! Fellow citizens, from this day on that
proportion of trade, increased and multiplied, must belong
to the American republic. I repeat, increased and multiplied, for with American brains and energy, with American
methods and American government, does any one here, to-
night, doubt that American exports will exceed Spain's imports twenty times over? Does any one of you doubt that
$100,000,000 of food and clothing and tools and implements
and machinery will ultimately be shipped every year from
the United States to that archipelago of tremendous possibilities? And will anyone of you refuse to welcome that
golden trade with your vote?

What lesson does Cuba teach? Cuba can raise no ce-
reals—no wheat, no corn, no oats, no barley, and no rye.
What we make and raise Cuba consumes, and what she makes
and raises we consume; and this order of commerce, is fixed

forever by the unalterable decrees of nature. And she is at our doors, too—only an ocean river between us.

Yet, in 1896, we bought $40,017,703 of her products, and we sold her only $7,193,173 of our products; while Spain bought only $4,257,360 and sold her $26,145,800—and that proportion existed before the insurrection. Fellow citizens, from this day on, that order must be reversed and increased. Cuba's present population is only about 1,000,000; her proper population is about 10,000,000. Tens of millions of acres of her soil are yet untouched by enterprise. If Spain sells Cuba $21,000,000 in 1891, and $26,000,000 in 1896, America will sell Cuba $200,000,000 in 1906. In 1896 we bought of Porto Rico $2,296,653, and sold her only $1,985,-888, and yet Spain bought only $5,423,760 and sold her $7,328,880. William McKinley proposes that those figures shall be increased and reversed, and the question is, whether you will indorse him in that resolution of prosperity. The practical question, for each one of us, is, whether we had better leave the development of all this tremendous commerce to the administration which liberated these island continents and now has the settlement of their government under way; or, risk the future in the hands of those who oppose the government at Washington and the commercial supremacy of the republic.

How will all this help each one of us. Our trade with Porto Rico and Hawaii will be as free as between the States of the Union, while every other nation on earth must pay our tariff before they can compete with us. Until Cuba and the Philippines shall ask for annexation, our trade with them will, at the very least, be like the preferential trade of Canada with England—a trade which gives the republic the preference over the rest of the world—a trade which applies the principle of protection to colonial commerce, the principle which all the world employs, to-day; the principle which England uses whenever she fears for a market and which she has put into practice against us in Canada. That, and the excellence of our goods and products; that, and the convenience of traffic; that, and the kinship of interests and destiny, will give the monopoly of these markets to the American people.

And then—then, the factories and mills and shops will call again to their hearts of fire the workingmen of the republic, to receive once more the wages and eat once more the bread of prosperous times; then the farmer will find at his door, once more, the golden home market of those who work in factory and mill, and who want flour and meat and butter and eggs and garments of wool, and who have once more the money to pay for it all.

It means new employment and better wages for every laboring man in the Union. It means higher prices for every bushel of wheat and corn, for every pound of butter and meat, for every item that the farmers of this republic produce. It means active, vigorous, constructive investment of every dollar of moldy and miserly capital in the land.

It means all this, to-morrow, and all this forever, because it means not only the trade of the prize provinces, but the beginning of the commercial empire of the republic. And, amid these great events, will you march forward with the endless column of prosperity, or, sit with Bryan, Bailey, Bland, and Blackburn on the rotten and crumbling rail-fence of dead issues and hoot at the procession as it passes by?

I said the commercial empire of the republic. That is the greatest fact of the future. And that is why these islands involve considerations larger than their own commerce. The commercial supremacy of the republic means that this nation is to be the sovereign factor in the peace of the world.

For the conflicts of the future are to be conflicts of trade—struggles for markets—commercial wars for existence. And the golden rule of peace is impregnability of position and invincibility of preparation. So, we see England, the greatest strategist of history, plant her flag and her cannon on Gibraltar, at Quebec, the Bermudas, Vancouver, everywhere, until, from every point of vantage, her royal banner flashes in the sun. So Hawaii furnishes us a naval base in the heart of the Pacific; the Ladrones another, a voyage farther into the region of sunset and commerce; Manila, another, at the gates of Asia—Asia, to the trade of whose hundreds of millions American merchants, American manufacturers, American farmers, have as good a right as those of Germany or France or Russia or England; Asia, whose commerce with England alone, amounts to billions of dollars every year; Asia, to whom Germany looks to take the surplus of her factories and foundries and mills; Asia, whose doors shall not be shut against American trade. Within two decades the bulk of Oriental commerce will be ours,—the richest commerce in the world. In the light of that golden future, our chain of new-won stations rise like ocean sentinels from the night of waters,—Porto Rico, a nobler Gibraltar; the Isthmian canal, a greater Suez; Hawaii, the Ladrones, the Philippines, commanding the Pacific!

Ah! as our commerce spreads, the flag of liberty will circle the globe, and the highways of the ocean—carrying trade of all mankind, be guarded by the guns of the republic. And, as their thunders salute the flag, benighted peoples will know that the voice of Liberty is speaking, at last, for them; that civilization is dawning, at last, for them—Liberty and

Civilization, those children of Christ's gospel, who follow and never precede, the preparing march of commerce!

It is the tide of God's great purposes made manifest in the instincts of our race, whose present phase is our personal profit, but whose far-off end is the redemption of the world and the Christianization of mankind. And he who throws himself before that current is like him who, with puny arm, tries to turn the gulf stream from its course, or stay, by idle incantations, the blessed processes of the sun.

Shall this future of the race be left with those who, under God, began this career of sacred duty and immortal glory; or, shall we risk it to those who would scuttle the ship of progress and build a dam in the current of destiny's large designs. . . .

And now, on the threshold of our career as the first Power of earth, is the time to permanently adjust our system of finance. The American people have the most tremendous tasks of history to perform. They have the mightiest commerce of the world to conduct. They cannot halt their imperial progress of wealth and power and glory and Christian civilization to unsettle their money system every time some ardent imagination sees a vision and dreams a dream. Think of Great Britain becoming the commercial monarch of the world with her financial system periodically assailed! Think of Holland or Germany or France bearing their burdens, and, yet, sending their flag to every sea, with their money at the mercy of politicians out of an issue.

Let us settle the whole financial question on principles so sound that a revolution cannot shake their firm foundations. And then, like men and not like children, let us on to our tasks—on to our mission and on to our destiny. We are speeding up the shining rails of an immortal history; yonder, in the rear, is the nightmare swamp of free silver. Why go back to it, like the victim of opium to his deadly pipe?

Why not accept the gifts of nature and events—events, which have made the oceans our servants, the trade winds our allies, and the stars in their courses our champions?

Nature, which has thrown the wealth of Klondike, the new found gold of the Philippines, the unsuspected and exhaustless mines of Colorado and the Cape into the crucible of financial agitation, and thus dissolved the last excuse for war upon the golden standard of civilization,—the excuse that the gold supply is insufficient and is failing.

Now, when new rivers of gold are pouring through the fields of business, the foundations of all silver-standard arguments are swept away. Why mumble the meaningless phrases of a tale that is told, when the golden future is before us, the world calls us, its wealth awaits us, and God's command is upon us?

Why stand in the fatal stupor of financial fallacies muttering old sophistries that time has exploded, when opportunity beckons you all over the world—in Cuba, Hawaii, the Philippines, on the waters of commerce, in every market of Occident and Orient, and in your factories and stores and fields, here in our own beloved country, holy America, land of God's promise and home of God's providence?

There are so many real things to be done—canals to be dug, railways to be laid, forests to be felled, cities to be builded, unviolated fields to be tilled, priceless markets to be won, ships to be launched, peoples to be saved, civilization to be proclaimed and the flag of liberty flung to the eager air of every sea. Is this an hour to waste upon triflers with nature's laws? Is this a season to give our destiny over to word-mongers and prosperity-wreckers? Is this a day to think of office-seekers, to be cajoled by the politician's smile, or seduced by the hand-shake of hypocrisy? No! No! my fellow citizens!

It is an hour to remember your duty to the home. It is a moment to realize the opportunities fate has opened to this favored people and to you. It is a time to bethink you of the conquering march of the flag. It is a time to bethink you of your nation and its sovereignty of the seas. It is a time to remember that the God of our fathers is our God and that the gifts and the duties he gave to them, enriched and multiplied, he renews to us, their children.

And so it is an hour for us to stand by the government at Washington, now confronting the enemy in diplomacy, as our loyal hearts on land and sea stood to their guns and stood by the flag when they faced the enemy in war. It is a time to strengthen and sustain that devoted man, servant of the people and of the Most High God, who, patiently, silently, safely is guiding the republic out into the ocean of world interests and possibilities infinite. It is a time to cheer the beloved President of God's chosen people, till the whole world is vocal with American loyalty to the American government.

Fellow Americans, we are God's chosen people. Yonder at Bunker Hill and Yorktown his providence was above us. At New Orleans and on ensanguined seas his hand sustained us. Abraham Lincoln was his minister and his was the Altar of Freedom, the boys in blue set on a hundred battlefields. His power directed Dewey in the East and delivered the Spanish fleet into our hands on the eve of Liberty's natal day, as he delivered the elder Armada into the hands of our English sires two centuries ago. His great purposes are revealed in the progress of the flag, which surpasses the intentions of Congresses and Cabinets, and leads us like a holier pillar of cloud by day and pillar of fire by night into situations unforeseen by finite wisdom, and duties unexpected by the unprophetic heart of selfishness. The American people cannot use a dishonest medium of exchange; it is ours to set the world its example of right and honor. We cannot fly from our world duties; it is ours to execute the purpose of a fate that has driven us to be greater than our small intentions. We cannot retreat from any soil where Providence has unfurled our banner; it is ours to save that soil for Liberty and Civilization. For Liberty and Civilization and God's promise fulfilled, the flag must henceforth be the symbol and the sign to all mankind—the flag!—

> " Flag of the free heart's hope and home,
>   By angel hands to valor given,
> Thy stars have lit the welkin dome,
>   And all their hues were born in heaven!
> Forever wave that standard sheet,
>   Where breathes the foe but falls before us,
> With freedom's soil beneath our feet
>   And freedom's banner streaming o'er us! "

FOR THE GREATER REPUBLIC, NOT FOR IMPERIALISM

ADDRESS DELIVERED AT THE UNION LEAGUE OF PHILADELPHIA, FEBRUARY 15, 1899

GENTLEMEN OF THE UNION LEAGUE,—The Republic never retreats. Why should it retreat? The Republic is the highest form of civilization, and civilization must advance. The Republic's young men are the most virile and unwasted of the world, and they pant for enterprise worthy of their power. The Republic's preparation has been the self-discipline of a century, and that preparedness has found its task. The Republic's opportunity is as noble as its strength, and that opportunity is here. The

Republic's duty is as sacred as its opportunity is real, and Americans never desert their duty.

The Republic could not retreat if it would; whatever its destiny, it must proceed. For the American Republic is a part of the movement of a race,—the most masterful race of history,—and race movements are not to be stayed by the hand of man. They are mighty answers to Divine commands. Their leaders are not only statesmen of peoples— they are prophets of God. The inherent tendencies of a race are its highest law. They precede and survive all statutes, all constitutions. The first question real statesmanship asks is: What are the abiding characteristics of my people? From that basis all reasoning may be natural and true. From any other basis all reasoning must be artificial and false.

The sovereign tendencies of our race are organization and government. We govern so well that we govern ourselves. We organize by instinct. Under the flag of England our race builds an empire out of the ends of earth. In Australia it is to-day erecting a nation out of fragments. In America it wove out of segregated settlements that complex and wonderful organization called the American Republic. Everywhere it builds. Everywhere it governs. Everywhere it administers order and law. Everywhere it is the spirit of regulated liberty. Everywhere it obeys that Voice not to be denied which bids us strive and rest not, makes of us our brothers' keeper, and appoints us steward under God of the civilization of the world.

Organization means growth. Government means administration. When Washington pleaded with the States to organize into a consolidated people, he was the advocate of perpetual growth. When Abraham Lincoln argued for the indivisibility of the Republic, he became the prophet of the Greater Republic. And when they did both, they were but the interpreters of the tendencies of the race. That is what made them Washington and Lincoln. Had they been separatists and contractionists they would not have been Washington and Lincoln—they would have been Davis and Calhoun. They are the great Americans because they were the supreme constructors and conservers of organized government among the American people, and to-day William McKinley, as divinely guided as they, is carrying to its conclusion the tremendous syllogism of which the works of Washington and Lincoln are the premises.

God did not make the American people the mightiest human force of all time simply to feed and die. He did not give our race the brain of organization and heart of domination to no purpose and no end. No; he has given us a task equal to our talents. He has appointed for us a destiny equal to our endowments. He has made us the lords of civilization that we may administer civilization. Such administration is needed in Cuba. Such administration is needed in the Philippines. And Cuba and the Philippines are in our hands.

If it be said that, at home, tasks as large as our strength await us,—that politics are to be purified, want relieved, municipal government perfected, the relations of capital and labor better adjusted,—I answer: Has England's discharge of her duty to the world corrupted her politics? Are not her cities, like Birmingham, the municipal models upon which we build our reforms? Is her labor problem more perplexed than ours? Considering the newness of our country, is it as bad as ours? And is not the like true of Holland—even of Germany?

And what of England? England's immortal glory is not
Agincourt or Waterloo. It is not her merchandise or commerce. It is Australia, New Zealand, and Africa reclaimed.
It is India redeemed. It is Egypt, mummy of the nations,
touched into modern life. England's imperishable renown
is in English science throttling the plague in Calcutta, English law administering order in Bombay, English energy
planting an industrial civilization from Cairo to the Cape,
and English discipline creating soldiers, men, and finally
citizens, perhaps, even out of the fellaheen of the dead land
of the Pharaohs. And yet the liberties of Englishmen were
never so secure as now. And that which is England's undying fame has also been her infinite profit, so sure is duty
golden in the end.

And what of America? With the twentieth century the
real task and true life of the Republic begins. And we are
prepared. We have learned restraint from a hundred years
of self-control. We are instructed by the experience of
others. We are advised and inspired by present example.
And our work awaits us.

The dominant notes in American history have thus far
been self-government and internal improvement. But these
were not ends only; they were means also. They were modes
of preparation. The dominant notes in American life heretofore have been self-government and internal development.
The dominant notes in American life henceforth will be not
only self-government and internal development, but also
administration and world improvement. It is the arduous
but splendid mission of our race. It is ours to govern in the
name of civilized liberty. It is ours to administer order and
law in the name of human progress. It is ours to chasten,
that we may be kind. It is ours to cleanse, that we may

save. It is ours to build, that free institutions may finally enter and abide. It is ours to bear the torch of Christianity where midnight has reigned a thousand years. It is ours to reinforce that thin red line which constitutes the outposts of civilization all around the world.

If it be said that this is vague talk of an indefinite future, we answer that it is the specific program of the present hour. Civil government is to be perfected in Porto Rico. The future of Cuba is to be worked out by the wisdom of events. Ultimately, annexation is as certain as the island's existence. Even if Cubans are capable of self-government, every interest points to union. We and they may blunder forward and timidly try the devices of doubt; but in the end Jefferson's desire will be fulfilled and Cuba will be a part of the great Republic. And, whatever befalls, definite and immediate work awaits us. Harbors are to be dredged, sanitation established, highways built, railroads constructed, postal service organized, common schools opened—all by or under the government of the American Republic.

The Philippines are ours forever. Let faint hearts anoint their fears with the thought that some day American administration and American duty there may end. But they never will end. England's occupation of Egypt was to be temporary; but events, which are the commands of God, are making it permanent. And now God has given us this Pacific empire for civilized administration. The first office of administration is order. Order must be established throughout the archipelago. The spoiled child, Aguinaldo, may not stay the march of civilization. Rebellion against the authority of the flag must be crushed without delay, for hesitation encourages revolt; and without anger, for the turbulent children know not what they do. And then civil-

ization must be organized, administered, and maintained.
Law and justice must rule where savagery, tyranny, and
caprice have rioted. The people must be taught the art of
orderly and continuous industry. A hundred wildernesses
are to be subdued. Unpenetrated regions must be explored.
Unviolated valleys must be tilled. Unmastered forests must
be felled. Unriven mountains must be torn asunder, and
their riches of iron and gold and ores of price must be delivered to the world. We are to do in the Philippines what
Holland does in Java, or England in New Zealand or the
Cape, or else work out new methods and new results of our
own nobler than any the world has seen. All this is not
indefinite; it is the very specification of duty.

The frail of faith declare that these peoples are not fitted
for citizenship. It is not proposed to make them citizens.
Those who see disaster in every forward step of the Republic
prophesy that Philippine labor will overrun our country and
starve our workingmen. But the Javanese have not so overrun Holland; New Zealand's Malays, Australia's bushmen,
Africa's Kaffirs, Zulus, and Hottentots, and India's millions
of surplus labor have not so overrun England. Whips of
scorpions could not lash the Filipinos to this land of fervid
enterprise, sleepless industry, and rigid order.

Those who measure duty by dollars cry out at the expense. When did America ever count the cost of righteousness? And, besides, this Republic must have a mighty navy
in any event. And new markets secured, new enterprises
opened, new resources in timber, mines, and products of the
tropics acquired, and the vitalization of all our industries
which will follow will pay back a thousandfold all the Government spends in discharging the highest duty to which the
Republic can be called.

Those who mutter words and call it wisdom deny the constitutional power of the Republic to govern Porto Rico, Cuba, the Philippines; for if we have the power in Porto Rico, we have the power in the Philippines. The Constitution is not interpreted by degrees of latitude or longitude. It is a hoary objection. There have always been those who have proclaimed the unconstitutionality of progress. The first to deny the power of the Republic's government were those who opposed the adoption of the Constitution itself, and they and their successors have denied its vitality and intelligence to this day. They denied the Republic's government the power to create a national bank; to make internal improvements; to issue greenbacks; to make gold the standard of vallue; to preserve property and life in States where treasonable Governors refused to call for aid.

Let them read Hamilton, and understand the meaning of implied powers. Let them read Marshall, and learn that the Constitution is the people's ordinance of national life, capable of growth as great as the people's growth. Let them learn the golden rule of constitutional interpretation. The Constitution was made for the American people; not the American people for the Constitution. Let them study the history, purposes, and instincts of our race, and then read again the Constitution, which is but an expression of the development of that race. Power to govern territory acquired! What else does the Constitution mean when it says, " Congress shall have power to dispose of and make all needful rules and regulations respecting the territory or other property of the United States ? "

But aside from these express words of the American Constitution, the Republic has power to govern in the Pacific, the Caribbean, or in any other portion of the globe where

Providence commands. Aside from the example of Alaska, all our territories, and the experience of a century, the Republic has the power to administer civilization wherever interest and duty call. It is the power which inheres in and is a part of the Government itself. And the Constitution does not deny the Government this inherent power residing in the very nature of all government. Who, then, can deny it? Those who do, write a new Constitution of their own, and interpret that. Those who do, dispute history. Those who do, are alien to the instincts of our race.

All protests against the Greater Republic are tolerable except this constitutional objection. But they who resist the Republic's career in the name of the Constitution are not to be endured. They are jugglers of words. Their counsel is the wisdom of verbiage. They deal not with realities, neither give heed to vital things. The most magnificent fact in history is the mighty movement and mission of our race, and the most splendid phase of that world-redeeming movement is the entrance of the American people as the greatest force in all the earth to do their part in administering civilization among mankind, and they are not to be halted by a ruck of words called constitutional arguments. Pretenders to legal learning have always denounced all virile interpretations of the Constitution. The so-called constitutional lawyers in Marshall's day said that he did not understand the Constitution, because he looked, not at its syllables, but surveyed the whole instrument, and beheld in its profound meaning and infinite scope the sublime human processes of which it is an expression. The Constitution is not a prohibition of our progress. It is not an interdict to our destiny. It is not a treatise on geography. Let the flag advance; the word " retreat " is not in the Constitution. Let the Republic govern as conditions demand; the Constitution does not benumb its brain nor palsy its hand.

The Declaration of Independence applies only to peoples capable of self-government. Otherwise, how dared we administer the affairs of the Indians? How dare we continue to govern them to-day? Precedent does not impair natural and inalienable rights. And how is the world to be prepared for self-government? Savagery can not prepare itself. Barbarism must be assisted toward the light. Assuming that these people can be made capable of self-government, shall we have no part in this sacred and glorious cause?

And if self-government is not possible for them, shall we leave them to themselves? Shall tribal wars scourge them, disease waste them, savagery brutalize them more and more? Shall their fields lie fallow, their forests rot, their mines remain sealed, and all the purposes and possibilities of nature be nullified? If not, who shall govern them rather than the kindest and most merciful of the world's great race of administrators, the people of the American Republic? Who lifted from us the judgment which makes men of our blood our brothers' keepers?

We do not deny them liberty The administration of orderly government is not denial of liberty. The administration of equal justice is not denial of liberty. Teaching the habits of industry is not denial of liberty. Development of the wealth of the land is not denial of liberty. If they are, then civilization itself is denial of liberty. Denial of liberty to whom? There are 12,000,000 of people in the Philippines, divided into thirty tribes. Aguinaldo is of the Tagal tribe of 2,000,000 souls, and he has an intermittent authority over less than 50,000 of these.

To deliver these islands to him and his crew would be to

establish an autocracy of barbarism. It would be to license spoliation. It would be to plant the republic of piracy, for such a government could not prevent that crime in piracy's natural home. It would be to make war certain among the powers of earth, who would dispute with arms each other's possession of a Pacific empire from which that ocean can be ruled. The blood already shed is but a drop to that which would flow if America should desert its post in the Pacific. And the blood already spilled was poured out upon the altar of the world's regeneration. Manila is as noble as Omdurman, and both are holier than Jericho.

Retreat from the Philippines on any pretext would be the master cowardice of history. It would be the betrayal of a trust as sacred as humanity. It would be a crime against Christian civilization, and would mark the beginning of the decadence of our race. And so, thank God, the Republic never retreats.

The fervent moral resolve throughout the Republic is not "a fever of expansion." It is a tremendous awakening of the people, like that of Elizabethan England. It is no fever, but the hot blood of the most magnificent young manhood of all time; a manhood begotten while yet the splendid moral passion of the war for national life filled the thought of all the land with ideals worth dying for, and charged its very atmosphere with noble purposes and a courage which dared put destiny to the touch—a manhood which contains a million Roosevelts, Woods, Hobsons, and Duboces, who grieve that they, too, may not so conspicuously serve their country, civilization, and mankind.

Indeed, these heroes are great because they are typical. American manhood to-day contains the master administrators of the world, and they go forth for the healing of the nations. They go forth in the cause of civilization. They go forth for the betterment of man; they go forth, and the word on their lips is Christ and his peace—not conquest and its pillage. They go forth to prepare the peoples, through decades, and may be centuries, of patient effort, for the great gift of American institutions. They go forth, not for imperialism, but for the Greater Republic.

Imperialism is not the word for our vast work. Imperialism, as used by the opposers of national greatness, means oppression, and we oppress not. Imperialism, as used by the opposers of national destiny, means monarchy, and the days of monarchy are spent. Imperialism, as used by the opposers of national progress, is a word to frighten the faint of heart, and so is powerless with the fearless American people.

Who honestly believes that the liberties of 80,000,000 Americans will be destroyed because the Republic administers civilization in the Philippines? Who honestly believes that free institutions are stricken unto death because the Republic, under God, takes its place as the first power of the world? Who honestly believes that we plunge to our doom when we march forward in a path of duty prepared by a higher wisdom than our own? Those who so believe have lost their faith in the immortality of liberty. Those who so believe deny the vitality of the American people. Those who so believe are infidels to the providence of God. Those who so believe have lost the reckoning of events, and think it sunset when it is, in truth, only the breaking of another day—the day of the Greater Republic, dawning as dawns the twentieth century.

The Republic never retreats. Its flag is the only flag that has never known defeat. Where the flag leads we follow, for we know that the hand that bears it onward is the unseen hand of God. We follow the flag and independence is ours. We follow the flag and nationality is ours. We follow the flag and oceans are ruled. We follow the flag and, in Occident and Orient, tyranny falls and barbarism is subdued. We follow the flag at Trenton and Valley Forge; at Saratoga and upon the crimson seas; at Buena Vista and Chapultepec; at Gettysburg and Missionary Ridge; at Santiago and Manila; and everywhere and always it means larger liberty, nobler opportunity, and greater human happiness, for everywhere and always it means the blessings of the Greater Republic. And so God leads, we follow the flag, and the Republic never retreats.

E. HOWARD GRIGGS

DWARD HOWARD GRIGGS, educationist and lecturer, was born in Minnesota in 1868, his boyhood being spent in Madison, Ind., where he was educated in the public schools. At an early age he was employed in a wholesale business house in Indianapolis, where he remained for five years. During this period he continued his education and prepared himself to enter the University of Indiana, from which he graduated in 1889. His further work at this University as instructor in English, and later as professor in literature, proved admirable training for his career as a lecturer. In 1891, he extended his field of work by accepting the assistant-professorship in ethics at the Leland Stanford, Jr., University. While occupying this post he spent two years in travel and study in England, Germany, and Italy. When he resigned from the university, in 1899, he was head of the department of ethics and education. From his university days in Indiana, Professor Griggs has had a growing power as a lecturer. He possesses an unusual gift of eloquence and a magnetic power which insures for him, wherever he is heard, a large and appreciative audience. Covering a wide range of subjects, he has been instrumental in stimulating his students to higher and nobler activities, both in intellectual and spiritual life. Since 1899, Professor Griggs has devoted himself mainly to independent public teaching in the large cities of the East. He is staff lecturer to the American Society for the Extension of University Teaching, and also lecturer to the Brooklyn Institute of Arts and Sciences.

THE NEW SOCIAL IDEAL[1]

THE modern world stands on the brink of the unknown. It is impossible to foresee adequately the developments of even a few decades, and changes of momentous importance are occurring in every direction. This must be true to some extent of all epochs, for each is modern to the men of it. They see the past completed in the present; but it is with difficulty that they can detect even a few of the organic filaments which are weaving the world of to-morrow. But in a singular way this is true of our own time. A new human ideal is taking possession of the world,

---

[1] By permission. Copyright, 1899, by Edward Howard Griggs.

the consequences of which will be limitless in significance. All past epochs of civilization found their justification in the few men who came to the surface and had some share in the ends of life. It was never dreamed that all men might have some part in these ends, and should have every opportunity to seek them. Ancient democracies were not democratic in the modern sense. They were oligarchies, where within the ruling class some measure of democratic relations prevailed. But this class stood on the backs of the mass of the people. Even Aristotle, humane and far-seeing as he was, assumed frankly that civilization must always rest upon slavery. Throughout the middle ages similar conditions prevailed. The vocations respected for themselves were, as in the ancient world, war and political life, with the addition of the priestly career. The fundamental activities of society, agricultural, commercial, industrial, were carried on by slaves, or men but little removed from the condition of serfs.

In the art of the ancient and mediæval world it is religion, the traditions of the ruling class, or war and chivalry that furnish the subject, never common humanity. In the literature of Europe in all centuries preceding the renaissance, there is but an occasional glimpse into the life of the people. Hesiod gives their despairing wail, and Langland an echo of their misery and their stubborn endurance, but these are isolated exceptions. Homer presents a rare Thersites only to make him an object of ridicule; and Dante sublimely and arrogantly ignores the existence of the untutored mass, whose destiny was not sufficiently interesting to him to find treatment in either hell or heaven.

But the era of humanity has arisen. Art is transformed in every department. The sailor at the pumps on a sinking vessel, the fisher's wife moaning alone in the gray dawn, the physician beside the bed of the child whose agonized parents stand beseechingly in the background—these furnish worthy subjects for modern painting. I remember the impression of this thought which was made upon me by the modern gallery in the Academy at Florence. Weeks had been spent visiting the churches, monasteries, and galleries, studying the exquisite remains of renaissance painting; and on the last day of our stay in Florence, chiefly from curiosity, we found our way into the collection of pictures by modern Italian artists. The result was unexpectedly startling. There were very few worthy paintings among these; but those which did stand out possessed a meaning that is not found in the paintings of the renaissance. One represented the dying Raphael. At his feet knelt the woman he loved, tears streaming from her eyes; at his side sat the old cardinal, perplexed and grave, anxious if possible to sooth the painter's last moments. There was nothing unusual in the scene; it was but the common human tragedy; yet such a subject is not found in all the paintings of the renaissance.

Another canvas represented the painter Fra Lippo Lippi making love to the nun who served as his model. In the woman's face was depicted the awakened struggle between the life to which she had consecreated herself, the old ideal she had cherished, and the world of new desires surging up into consciousness; not even Leonardo, of the painters before the nineteenth century, could have grasped and fixed that conflict.

The third and most powerful picture represented a group of wandering musicians lost in the snow, with the pitiless winter night coming on. The instruments of their craft were huddled on the ground. The man was half-kneeling, with hands raised to his head in an attitude of abject despair. In terror his little lad clung to him, while rigid and still on the ground lay a girlish woman figure just frozen to death. All about were the pathless snow fields with the ominous depth of the forest behind. It is only a common tragedy; yet only a modern artist could have wrung our heart-strings with that human appeal.

And art is learning to transfigure the humblest life with the divine significance that dwells at the heart of humanity, and is greater than the awe of a traditional religion or the splendor of an old mythology. Literature is flooded with the surging sea of common life; its old limits are swamped, and it is at once distorted and ennobled by the impulsion of new forces. The novel of real life, often sordid and bare, at times majestic and transfigured, replaces the romance of heroes and the epic of kings.

The struggle is but the birth-throes of a new ideal, an ideal of common humanity. It is not enough for us that here and there a rare saint or hero attains, it is not enough that the work of civilization is accomplished in a few individuals. To stand upon the backs of a dumb multitude, or furnish our own shoulders for the feet of arrogant heroes, are conceptions equally repulsive and unendurable to us. We demand life for ourselves, and we demand it for every human being. Our entire society is being transformed by the desire to give every man and woman, together with ourselves, all opportunity and help in striving for life, happiness, culture, intelligence, helpfulness—all ends of life that are worth seeking.

There is something thrilling in the unquestioning faith and enthusiasm with which the world is turning toward this ideal. A breath fresh and strong, like that which blows through the sagas of the Norseland, and gives their endless attractiveness to its Thors and Odins, is felt in the new impetus of modern life. It is perhaps because we are unconscious of the implications of our ideal that we can champion it so unquestioningly. No moral effort of history, not even the Christianization of Europe, or the conversion of Asia to Buddhism, involved the difficulties and perils which are in the path of this supreme attempt of modern life. As children, if young enough, will try any task, so we with the enthusiasm of youth challenge the universe with our supreme ideal. And it is well that it is so, for a full consciousness of the significance and the difficulty of the task we have set before us might paralyze our effort and unnerve our hands. To carry every man and woman, not as dependents, but through the free and co-operative activity of each with all, on toward all the ends of life that are worth seeking, is inconceivably and appallingly difficult.

Yet some measure of intelligent appreciation of the magnitude and meaning of our undertaking is necessary to successful action. An understanding of the immense difference between modern civilization and those epochs which have preceded it, is indispensible to even a partial achievement of our aim.

In America the new ideal is more frankly taken as the object of civilization than anywhere else in the world, yet it is as well throughout Europe the creative force modifying all expressions of life. England stands to-day on the threshold of a new epoch. Her imperialism has pushed Anglo-Saxon speech and institutions all over the globe, and developed a pride of race and nation unequaled since Rome. But within herself is the ferment of a new life—if not the dissolution of the empire, at least the reorganization of all her institutions and activities. The English character is conservative and tenacious of old forms; yet even it is incapable of resisting the forces of the new life. Since 1870 England has seen the most astounding developments in the education of her people. Before that time there was practically no distinctively state education in England; since then board schools have been established all over the land, and successive Parliaments have given increased grants for popular education. The result is the creation of a great democracy, growing increasingly discontented under the admirable oligarchic rule which satisfied its predecessors. Parallel with the educational movement has been the growth of ethical and industrial socialism, and the permeation over wider areas of the popular life of the new human ideal.

Germany is suffering from the natural reaction against the splendid patriotism of the seventies. National unity being accomplished, the evils of imperialism become evident, and the deadly sameness of institutions reacting toward mediævalism chills the enthusiasm which local patriotism and the competition between small, rival states produced. But the spirit of social democracy, hard and materialistic as it is in some aspects, steadily gains ground in Germany, and tends to supplant the cold arrogance of ritualistic religion and the pessimism that accompanies selfish industrialism with some measure of enthusiasm for humanity.

The trail of the serpent of cynical unbelief is over a part of French literature, Paris contains much that is degenerate, the alternate artificial effervescence and pale sombreness of decadence is present in much French art; and the result of thirty years' devotion to militarism by an impulsive people shows sadly in the insanity that supposes an " honor of the army," or of the people, can exist which is not based upon justice and truth. Yet the higher meaning of the French revolution is not forgotten; and under the hard military bureaucracy, and in spite of the extravagant reactions of anarchy, the new humanity slumbers in France and will waken one day,—here and there are echoes of its dreams. In the splendid protest of the " intellectuals " against the pitiless dominance of the mob, France has proved that her culture is not all decadence, and that she will have her place in the world of to-morrow.

Spain is sunk under the corruption of her institutions; Italy starves beneath her unwarranted military equipment; Austria is torn by race dissensions; and Russia pushes her hard imperialism remorselessly onward. But in Tolstoi and Ada Negri, in Dostoievsky and Sienkiewicz, in Carducci and in the songs of the Bohemian peasants are there not prophecies for to-morrow?

The end of a century does mean a change in human affairs, only because men so regard it; and everywhere are prophecies that the twentieth century will differ profoundly from the nineteenth. The proposal for a peace congress, with universal disarmament as its aim, made by the one absolute despot in Europe, is no accident of selfish diplomacy. Politically nationalistic, Europe is industrially cosmopolitan. Each nation is bound intimately with others through the exchange of industrial and artistic products. Russia attempted at one time to isolate herself from the rest of Europe, and develop without foreign capital and stimulus, and she has learned from sad experience how disastrous is such an attempt. It is not the Triple Alliance or the Franco-Russian understanding which holds Europe together, but mutual industrial dependence. The pressure of common interests is a tremendous support to the new dream of the spirit in the work of civilization.

The difficulty in carrying out the new ideal is vastly in-creased by the complication of modern life. This is true even of the most superficial aspects of our civilization. The mechanical invention and discovery which furnishes the theme for every cheap eulogy of our epoch, changes in all aspects the conditions of our problem. The possibility which earlier periods possessed of working out a solution for a small fragment of humanity, isolated from the rest of man-kind, has utterly passed away. In the merest mechanical fashion the world has been closely unified, and the surface unity finds a deeper corollary in the spiritual life. The en-tire change in international principles and relations since the eighteenth century, and the dawn of an era of greater peace, accentuate the acuteness of the industrial problem.

The movement from the country to the city, which is steadily going on all over the world, is a cause and a result of the increasing tension in the struggle for existence. Vast masses of human beings are heaped together in great cities. In one aspect such a collection of humanity as is London, seems to be an immense vortex, in which innumerable lives are ceaselessly drawn down. Up and down the great thoroughfares surges the endless stream of men and women, each seeming to be merely a member of some vast organism, yet being an individual, with his own circle of life, and his own hopes and fears—like the vortex rings in the ether which some physicists have supposed to be the ultimate con-stituents of matter. The smoke from a thousand factories and a million chimneys hangs like a sombre pall over the im-mense monster. Day and night the ceaseless hum of the city goes on. It is not the roll of the myriad omnibuses on the thoroughfares; it is not the harsh rattle of the underground trains; it is not the murmur of the million voices, harshly or

tenderly speaking, madly or mockingly laughing; it is not
the roar of the machinery, or the echo of the innumerable
feet. Deeper than any of these, inspiring at once terror, pity,
and love, it is the sound formed of many tones, containing
the strident notes of evil laughter and the faint echo of
tender sighs, with an undertone of endless and measureless
yearning, and a wild note of joy and love:—it is the sound
of humanity which the Earth Spirit at the humming loom
of Time, forever is weaving, as the revealing yet concealing
garment of God.

In the day it is dominated by the noise of the nearer
vehicles, in the night, in the hours just past the madder rush
of the midnight, it sinks into the deep sombre hum, and then
is almost still. Thrilling or menacing, it is a fit symbol of
the exigency of the crisis that civilization must meet to-day.
Were the tension less constant, did it rise and fall fitfully like
the winds or the sea, it would seem less ominous. But this
pressure always intense, this sound that sinks only to become more sombre—there is no mistaking the significance of
this.

Such changes as the creation of great cities and the trans-
formation of industrial relations illustrate the vast increase
in the intellectual problem of civilization. Man changes
very slowly in biological structure, so slowly that it is difficult to discover any increase in actual brain power if we compare a man of to-day with a Greek in the age of Pericles.
That is, in two thousand years there is not sufficient biological
advance to be appreciable. Yet the accumulation of the
material of civilization has been doubled more than once
within a century. The progress of civilization consists
chiefly in the accumulation of the material of life, and in
the earlier and better initiation of the individual, through

education, into the experience of the race, that he may take and use his inheritance from the past. The inherited equipment consists of material wealth, mechanical inventions and plants, vast organized institutions, cities and means of communications, libraries, museums,—in fact all the apparatus of civilization. The objective progress we are able to see in history lies almost entirely in the increase in this apparatus, and in the skill to use it effectively.

Unused tools are always a burden; and unless the inherited equipment of culture is a help to us, it will distinctly hamper our lives. Thoreau, in his half whimsical fashion, gives expression to the thought in Walden:

"I see young men, my townsmen, whose misfortune it is to have inherited farms, houses, barns, cattle, and farming tools; for these are more easily acquired than got rid of. Better if they had been born in the open pasture and suckled by a wolf, that they might have seen with clearer eyes what field they were called to labor in. . . . How many a poor immortal soul have I met well nigh crushed and smothered under its load, creeping down the road of life, pushing before it a barn seventy-five feet by forty, its Augean stables never cleansed, and one hundred acres of land, tillage, mowing, pasture, and wood-lot! The portionless who struggle with no such unnecessary inherited encumbrances, find it labor enough to subdue and cultivate a few cubic feet of flesh."

The idea is not all a jest:

> "Was du ererbt von deinen Vätern hast,
> Erwirb es, um es zu besitzen,"

we are told in Faust; and the history of the sons of wealthy men is a sufficient illustration of the truth. To command and use the opportunities of civilization which we have inherited from the past we must win them anew.

Thus the problem of education becomes increasingly more

difficult. To be educated as well as the men of some past epoch is to be insufficiently trained for the needs of to-day. Better a return to barbarism than to be burdened with a vast institutional, material, and intellectual equipment of civilization which we are unable to master and use. The question is, whether the biological basis of human existence is a sufficient oundation for the vast superstructure of life, whether the orain is capable of grappling with the increasingly difficult problem of existence. The failure of a small farmer in England is connected with the opening up of vast wheat raising tracts in Argentine Republic. The wages of a factory girl in a small town in Massachusetts are connected with the advance of Russia in northern China. The relations are becoming too intricate, the factors too highly complicated. The effort of legislation to deal with the problem is a kind of pitiful empirical tinkering not unlike the attempt to build a dam across a quickening torrent. Industrial distress is lightly attributed to the predominance of a political party, or the accidents of particular legislation; but the causes are as far-reaching as the intricate relations of modern life. It is obviously impossible to legislate ourselves into permanent prosperity, when the causes of distress are much deeper than any legislation. The condition of modern civilization is only too much like that of Florence as Dante describes her:

> " How oft, within the time of thy remembrance,
>   Laws, moneys, offices and usages
>   Hast thou remodeled, and renewed thy members?
> And if thou mind thee well, and see the light,
>   Thou shalt behold thyself like a sick woman,
>   Who cannot find repose upon her down,
> But by her tossing wardeth off her pain."

As our ideal and problem are unprecedented, so must be the answer. Old battle-cries fail to meet new issues. The radicalism of yesterday is the conservatism of to-day, and the heresy of to-day is the orthodoxy of to-morrow. To imagine that a solution which met a past difficulty must be adequate to the new issue is to obscure the gravity of the problem. A particular principle of financial or industrial legislation, once championed as the standard of liberty, may become a mere shibboleth, superstitious reverence for which hinders progress.

The battle-cry of yesterday in the most advanced nations of the world was political democracy. The institutions which have been fought out along the line of progress hitherto have been in that sphere, and the significance of the movement is yet unexhausted. But it is evident that the realization in any measure of the ideal that dominates the modern spirit cannot be achieved through political reforms alone. The storm centre in the movement of the new democracy is increasingly in the sphere of social relations, and in the struggle toward greater industrial freedom. Is not, therefore, the insistence upon particular measures of political democracy as the cure for all our ills, a distinct injury, through obscuring the nature of the problem, and blinding us to the progress of events? There was a time when the extension of political suffrage was the movement of freedom. To-day we must recognize that political enfranchisement may co-exist with social and industrial slavery. To suppose that the extension of the ballot will cure all our diseases is to be lulled into a false sense of security, as if one should go to sleep over the crater of a live volcano. There was a time when the right of free speech was the cry of progress; to-day it may be used as a shibboleth to permit the lawless use of power by irresponsible and criminal newspapers. To expect a single series of political movements to meet all the evils of society is to place oneself beside the ignorant prey of the quack, who trusts a single nostrum to cure all diseases. Increasing industrial freedom must follow the attainment of political freedom. The distribution of the measureless production that results from modern methods and machinery, the bringing together of land and labor, tools and workmen, the relation of the different factors in production and distribution, must not be left to chance and the blind action of natural causes. When a great country stagnates with " overproduction," while people freeze and starve in the cities, something is wrong; and the wrong is one that the human will and intellect can remedy, if it but consecrate itself to the task.

It is sad to see how rare is a truly cosmopolitan and human view of the problem. The spirit of competition, which has its place in the struggle of life, is in danger of becoming a virulent disease which blinds us to the unity of the spiritual world. The effort of one nation to aggrandize itself at the expense of others may give a superficial prosperity, but is opposed to the deeper interests of its life. The modern industrial problems are universal over the human world, and they are to be solved by one people, only when they are answered to some extent for all. Were it possible to build a Chinese wall around one nation, and isolate it industrially from the rest, the result would be, not only a cowardly abdication of the leadership each owes the others, but an invitation to the dwarfing egotism and stagnation of China—as though a great nation were to take the veil of monastic isolation.

When we study the ancient Greek world we think with contempt of the narrowness of its patriotism. Each city sought to advance itself at the expense of its neighbors.

Patriotic as far as his city was concerned, the Greek was unconscious of a larger unity of life. Only one man ever discovered the idea of a Greek nation; and Pericles inevitably failed because he could lead only a few friends to understand his meaning. Greece went down because of the narrow selfishness of her cities. We realize that the true interest of any city cannot be obtained by blindly struggling for itself against all others; we have attained the national idea. But quite generally we fail to see that what was true of the relations of cities in ancient Greece is true of the relations of nations to-day. The patriotism that would advance one nation at the expense of others is only another form of selfishness, sure to meet the punishment its blindness deserves. Only a cosmopolitanism as broad as humanity is capable of realizing the modern ideal.

The industrial questions rest back upon something still more fundamental—the problem of social relations. While the modern ideal leads toward greater social integration, many new conditions of activity accentuate the difficulties in the path of its attainment. Modern industrial methods increase temporarily social segregation. Rich and poor, cultured and ignorant, tend to become more widely separated. In any large city residence districts are defined with increasing reference to class distinctions. The districts of wealth and culture are far removed from the quarters of poverty and ignorance. The rapid growth of the suburban system, depopulating the cities of the better middle class, leaves the wretches heaped together in tenement districts in undisturbed sordidness. Even the measure of social intercourse involved in the kindly offices of charity tends to pass away, as social and personal helpfulness is more and more delegated to charity organizations; with an immense increase in economy and justice it is true, but with a great loss of vital social relationship. Even in the religious life this social segregation is too evident to require discussion.

The social problem lies behind the ferment in the modern industrial world, and there is no hope of permanently meeting the crisis in the latter sphere unless the needs in the former can be answered. The separation of classes in all phases of life is a curse to high and low alike. Tolstoi has always insisted that unjust extremes of poverty and wealth injure both rich and poor, and he is profoundly right. Nothing is more deadening to life than isolation in a highly differentiated class. In such a condition we are victims of that too great specialization which hampers the range of our adaptability, as evidenced in the plant and animal world, as well as in human sphere. No great realization of life is possible which does not spring from the heart of common humanity. When literature is cultivated by a narrow class, isolated from the broad life of the people, it is devitalized. It may present polished conceits, but it must lack the throbbing life that pulsates in all great masterpieces. When art of any kind does not embody the life and answer the need of the mass of the people it is emasculated. Life is inevitably barren without a deep and wide social contact of different classes.

At the same time there must be fearless and consecrated leadership. It is said that democracy tends toward a dead level of the average; and there is some justice in the accusation. There are two opposing principles which it seems difficult to reconcile. It is said, one must be in line with common humanity to achieve true greatness; and again, that one must fearlessly follow one's own independent conviction, unmoved by the caprices of the mob, and if one stoop to flatter it one is lost.   These principles seem to be in hopeless opposition; but the contradiction is resolved in a higher unity.

What is the mob?   It surges through the streets from the chill drawn until the midnight; ever changing, yet the same.   Grey with toil, gaudy with artificial adornments, black with lust and murder, it surges on, choking the streets and alleys, but with renewed pulsations of its vast heart sweeping them clear again.   Many-headed, yet with one masterful heart; stretching out its innumerable members in an inextricable maze of seemingly distorted actions, yet drawing them all into one unity of rest; a chameleon monster with as many hues and aspects as the day and night, yet with one voice that mingles them together in one vast, strident, menacing, sombre roar—the Mob!

Yet this Mob is Humanity.   Each member of it is Man, potentially all that the rest have expressed.   With earnest striving, with tears of pity and ringing laughter of childish joy, with a miracle of love and an eternal struggle after ideals that lift steadily toward the image of God,—the Mob is Humanity!   It can be stirred to blind passion, or wakened to love; degraded to madness, or transfigured to heroism. From it are made murderers and martyrs, slaves and saviors: the Mob is Humanity!

The difference lies in the line of appeal.   When Shakespeare appealed to the London mob he transfigured it into humanity; when the modern sensational newspaper appeals to humanity it degrades humanity into the mob.   Men will respond to what is universally human, or yield to selfish passion.   One can gain power with the mass by flattering its blind prejudice or by appealing to what is fundamental in the common heart.   " One touch of nature makes the whole world kin," whether it be the nature of the brute or of the spirit.

Thus the social unity that is necessary is one consistent with independent courage and fearless devotion to truth. There must be no catering to the whims and caprices of the mob, but an appeal to that humanity which is implicit in each individual. Indeed, one of the two principles which seemed so opposed is impossible without the other. There can be no true heroism, no independent greatness which does not spring from the heart of common humanity; and there can be no true social union which does not depend upon the highest individuality, the most independent consecration to truth.

The absence of the one quality is the measure of the decay of the other. Instead of true social union, and fearless and consecrated personality and leadership, we have too often the selfish and whimsical mob, and the flattering demagogue, the lawless and irresponsible use of power in the newspaper.

Thus the evolution of social solidarity is the necessary complement of the development of personal life. There is no true good for one that is not good for all. If I share my loaf of bread with my neighbor I have half a loaf left, but the love that prompted the division grows by the process. Every intellectual advance attained by one man is an added intellectual power to all others. The interests of the spiritual world are common, for life is possible to one only through the integration of his life with all. Intellectual realization of one's self consists in the widening of the relation of the individual to the universe. Emotional realization of life means the unity of each with all in love, through the medium of a union with other individuals. Volitional realization of one's self lies in action that expresses character, and is helpful to all.   Giordano Bruno understood it when he said: "Intelligence therefore is perfected, not in one, in another, or in many, but in all."   And Goethe, the apostle of self-culture, knew that man is man only in union with humanity, for he could say sublimely: "If now, during our own lifetime, we see that performed by others, to which we ourselves felt an earlier call, but which we had been obliged to give up, with much besides: then the beautiful feeling enters the mind, that only mankind together is the true man, and that the individual can be joyous and happy only when he has the courage to feel himself in the whole."

Individual human beings are like members of a vast orchestra engaged in the creation of the sublime music of humanity.   Each must express his own ideal through the instrument he has chosen.   But unless the tones he produces are in unison with the rest, they are not music but discordant sounds: in harmony with the creative effort of all, they are indispensable elements in the symphony of life.